HEROISM AND GENIUS

William J. Slattery

HEROISM AND GENIUS

How Catholic Priests Helped to Build—and Can
Help Rebuild—Western Civilization

IGNATIUS PRESS   SAN FRANCISCO

Cover art: Alejandro Ferrant y Fischermans, *Cisneros, Fundador del Hospital de la Caridad de Illescas*, 1892. Oil on canvas. © Fundación Hospital Ntra. Sra. de la Caridad—Memoria Benéfica de Vega.

Cardinal Francisco Ximénez de Cisneros (1436–1517), the priest who reluctantly became statesman, regent of the Spanish empire, and leading protagonist in bringing his nation into its Golden Age, founding among other institutions the Complutense University of Madrid, and defending the Native Americans. The painting by Alejandro Ferrant shows him directing the construction of the hospital La Virgen de la Caridad at Illescas, near Toledo.

Back cover photo: The author, Father William Slattery, at the Great Saint Bernard Pass in the Swiss Alps (8,100 ft).

Cover design by Davin Carlson

© 2017 by Ignatius Press, San Francisco
ISBN 978-1-62164-014-1
Library of Congress Control Number 2014911482
Printed in the United States of America ∞

Cecilia Lawrence, *Our Lady, Queen of Chivalry*.

To the
"woman
clothed with the sun,
with the moon under her feet,
and on her head a crown of twelve stars" (Rev 12:1).

To my father and mother,
Thomas and Margaret,
with deep gratitude for their self-sacrificing love
and for giving me life's greatest treasure: the Catholic Faith.

To Paul and Hélène,
"[M]ay you see your children, and your children's children, unto the third
and fourth generation: and may your seed be blessed by the God of Israel,
who reigneth for ever and ever" (Tob 9:11; Douay-Rheims).

CONTENTS

List of Illustrations   xi

Preface   xiii

Introduction   xv

Part 1: The Catholic Matrix of Western Civilization

Chapter 1: The Womb and the Embryo   3

Historians Have Spoken: The Verdict   3

Priests: Channels of Lifeblood   5

Milestones of the Catholic Struggle to Build a New Civilization,

circa A.D. *200–1300*   9

Part 2: Laying the Foundations of a New Civilization, circa A.D. 300–1000

Chapter 2: The Church Amid Dark Ages   15

Night Falls over Rome   15

Rescuing from a Burning City   17

Saga of Centuries: The Conversion of Europe   18

Shouldering Society: Bishops from the Fifth to the Seventh Centuries   21

Birth of a Remarkable Institution: The Parish   23

The Hair's Breadth   31

Chapter 3: Fathers of Western Culture: Ambrose, Augustine, Leo, and Gregory   32

Ambrose: Defender of the City   32

Augustine: Converter of Culture   35

  Man of His Century and of Every Century   35

  Intellect and Heart Forged by Priesthood   38

  Blueprints for a New Culture   42

  Blueprints for a New Sociopolitical Order   44

  Standing Upright to the End   49

Leo the Great: Rome at the Center   49

Gregory the Great and the Thrust toward the Barbarians   52

Chapter 4: Creative Minorities: The Benedictine and Irish Monks 56

Benedict and the Shaping of the Western Mind 56
Columbanus and the Irish Monks 63
    D–Days: Disembarking of Columbanus in France and of
        Columba in Scotland 63
    "Who Are These Men?" 71
    The Silent Revolution 78
        Plight of Church and Society at the Arrival of Columbanus 78
        The Engine of Renewal: The Irish Method of Confession 81
    Mission Accomplished 88
Boniface: Seed Sower of Civilization in Germany 91

Chapter 5: Alcuin and the Idealists behind the First Europe 94

The New Alliance: Papacy-Monasticism-Frankish Monarchy 94
Charlemagne: "Rough-Hewn from Gnarled Germanic Wood" 97
The Ideal behind Charlemagne's Empire 100
The Reality 102
The Idealists around Charlemagne 104
    An International Group 104
    Alcuin 106
        The Man Whom Charlemagne Called "My Mentor" 106
        Educator of an Empire's Educators 114
        Restorer of the Tools of Intellectual Culture 117
        Thrust toward Universal Education 120
After Alcuin and Charlemagne (814–1000) 125
    Relations between Church, State, and Society 125
    The Flame Kept Burning: Renaissance of Culture, Naissance
        of Christendom 129

Part 3: Distinctive Features of Western Civilization
That Budded in the Dark Ages

Chapter 6: Guardians of the Ancient Rite: The Traditional Mass and
the Culture of Christendom 139

The Ancient Rite 139
The Embodiment of Catholicism 142
From Sacrifice to Sacrificial Love 143
Embedded Deep in the Existence of Catholics 145

Chapter 7: Fathers of Chivalry: A New Type of Warrior 148

Vigil of Arms 148
Baptizing Men with Claws 153
Training Warriors to Wield and Sheathe the Sword 155
The Silhouette of the Christian Warrior Appears 157
The Knight's Vision of Christ 160

Idealist of Chivalry: Bernard of Clairvaux   162
    The Man behind the Statutes of the Templars   162
    Background to the Templars: The Crusades   166
    Foundation, Development, and Influence of the Templars   167
Chivalry's Finished Product: A King, a Hero, a Man—Louis IX   172
Ever Relevant: "The Living Symbol of Force Subjected to the Spirit"   176

Chapter 8: Clandestine Revolutionaries of Romanticism   182

Romanticism   182
A Millennium-Long Struggle on Behalf of Women   183
Birth of Chivalric Romantic Love   187
Clash: The Chivalric Romantic Ideal versus Troubadourism and Courtly Love   191
Triumph: A Sublime and Enduring Romanticism   194

Chapter 9: Men with Music, Artistry, and Drama in Their Souls   198

"Total Art on the Grandest Scale": Gothic Architecture   198
    The Man behind Gothic: Abbot Suger   202
    Before and After Gothic and Always   204
Music That Rose into the Night: Gregorian Chant   206

Chapter 10: Founders of Free-Market Economics   211

The Catholic Ideal behind Western Economic Progress   211
First Incubators of Free Enterprise Principles   219
Worldly Ascetics: The Priests Who Pioneered Modern Economics   224
    Medieval and Renaissance Economic Thinkers   224
    Sketches of Personalities   229
    Men Alive with New Ideas   231
    Installing the Engine of Free Market Economics   234
    Exile to Intellectual Siberia and Return   237

Conclusion: Standing on the Capitoline: Gazing toward Past and
Future Horizons   241

Horizons   241
In Order to Build the Future: Remember!   243

Afterword: May the Long Line Never Be Broken!   247

Selected Bibliography   249

Art Credits   255

Index   259

ILLUSTRATIONS

Migrations and Invasions of the Roman Empire, A.D. 100–500   16

Europe Becomes Christian, 400–1450   19

Renaissance Powerhouses of Western Europe: Celtic Monasteries   64

Travels and Influence of a "Father of Europe": Columbanus, 575–615   66

Celtic Torchbearers of European Renaissance, Sixth–Ninth Centuries   79

The "First Europe": Charlemagne's Empire, circa 800   95

Plan of a Medieval Monastery   221

PREFACE

One hot, muggy August afternoon, the inspiration to write *Heroism and Genius* struck me as I worked in the seventeenth-century rare books room of the library at the Casa Santa Maria, the graduate house of the Pontifical North American College, in Rome's historic center.

Thanks to Bishop Nicola de Angelis of the Diocese of Peterborough, I had come back to Rome, most unexpectedly, studying firstly for a licentiate in theology at the Lateran University, and then for a Ph.D. in philosophy at the Gregorian. As those years went by, the mind was quickened and the spirit renewed amid the ancient churches, catacombs, and cobblestoned streets of the Eternal City, where linger not only memories but mystic presence of so many saints and martyrs. How naturally a work like *Heroism and Genius* can be conceived in that setting where so many men and women creatively and heroically poured out their lifeblood for the most sublime and necessary of ideals—the honor of God through pursuit of the eternal salvation of souls! To stand in spirit among these great Christians is to penetrate not only the past but the present; they provoke you to question the status quo in society, in Church, and, most urgently, in oneself; to leave their presence is to go forth with the soul invigorated unto emulation. Moreover, the closer one gets to these heroes and creators, the better one is able to see, through them, and towering above them, the person of history's one flawless hero and one divine genius. In the most heroic and creative heart that has ever existed, that of the God-Man, one recognizes the source of the ingenuity and courage that, century after century, empowers the Church to have her phoenix hour. One's conviction that he is the One who matters deepens; and that even a glimpse of him is enough to make life sublimely beautiful while we journey in hope through often dark valleys toward the light of our eternal homeland.

That is the impulse behind this work. It is also the inspiration for the new religious order of priests that has likewise been conceived in these years: the Society of Ignatians (www.societyofignatians.com). God willing, with the Church's approval, in a diocese of the United States of America, the first group of Ignatian candidates will officially begin their formation on the Feast of Saint Ignatius of Loyola, on July 31, 2018.

I express my gratitude firstly to Bishop Nicola de Angelis, C.F.I.C., for his support over the years, enabling me to have the time for research and to put pen to paper. In a special way to Cardinal Raymond Burke, I extend my appreciation for his interest and encouragement. I am indebted to Cardinal Walter Brandmüller, president emeritus of the Pontifical Committee for Historical Sciences, for having generously critiqued the first draft.

My sister, Catherine, the first to see the completed text, and ever-willing to support her siblings, gave cherished encouragement. For the following are offered grateful prayers that God may bless them for their generous efforts, directly or indirectly, in bringing *Heroism and Genius* to birth: Mr. and Mrs. Eugene J. Zurlo, Mr. William M. Cousins Jr., Mrs. Agnes Doyle, Mr. Michael Pascucci, Mr. and Mrs. Owen Smith, Mr. and Mrs. Shawn Tilson, Mr. and Mrs. Alberto Cefis, Mr. Robert Dilenschneider, and Mr. and Mrs. Michael P. Mallardi.

My thoughts also retrace their steps with indebtedness to the selfless, gifted, and inspiring priests whom God has granted me to know from childhood, through youth and seminary, to priesthood. May we all meet again, if not in this life, in the "Land of the Trinity".

I harbor enduring gratitude to the teachers of my childhood and youth at Abbeyside National School in Dungarvan, "my home by the sea"—especially to Seán Prendergast, to Sister Philomena and the other Sisters of Mercy earlier on, and to priests and lay staff of St. Augustine's College in Abbeyside afterward, as well as to other dedicated mentors in Salamanca, Dublin, and Rome. Some of them helped shape this book by strengthening the convictions of the Faith; others through teaching Gaelic, French, Spanish, Latin, Greek, and Italian opened windows onto the vast landscapes of Catholicism, its culture, civilization, and eternal horizons.

William J. Slattery, Ph.D., S.T.L.
Feast of Our Lady of Good Counsel, 2016

Ordination of the author by Saint John Paul II,
January 3, 1991, in St. Peter's Basilica, Rome.

INTRODUCTION

Cathedral of Notre-Dame d'Amiens, France; central portal by night.

But my home, such as I have, [said Aragorn,] is in the North. For here the heirs of Valandil have ever dwelt in long line unbroken from father unto son for many generations. Our days have darkened, and we have dwindled; but ever the Sword has passed to a new keeper....

And this I will say to you, Boromir, ere I end. Lonely men are we, Rangers of the wild, hunters—but hunters ever of the servants of the Enemy; for they are found in many places, not in Mordor only.

If Gondor, Boromir, has been a stalwart tower, we have played another part. Many evil things there are that your strong walls and bright swords do not stay. You know little of the lands beyond your bounds. Peace and freedom, do you say? The North would have known them little but for us. Fear would have destroyed them. But when dark things come from the houseless hills or creep from sunless woods, they fly from us. What roads would any dare to tread, what safety would there be in quiet lands or in the homes of simple men at night, if the Dúnedain were asleep or were all gone into the grave?

And yet less thanks have we than you. Travelers scowl at us, and countrymen give us scornful names. "Strider" I am to one fat man who lives within a day's march of foes that would freeze his heart or lay his little town in ruin if he were not guarded ceaselessly. Yet we would not have it otherwise. If simple folk are free from care and fear, simple they will be, and we must be secret to keep them so. That has been the task of my kindred, while the years have lengthened and the grass has grown.

But now the world is changing once again. A new hour comes. Isildur's Bane is found. Battle is at hand. The Sword shall be reforged.

—J. R. R. Tolkien, *The Lord of the Rings*

Heroism and Genius has three parts.

Part 1 has a triple objective. Firstly, it sketches an overview of recent conclusions among historians regarding the Church's role in the forging of Western civilization. Secondly, it explains what exactly this book means when it asserts that Catholic priests were its constructors. Thirdly, it lays out the milestones in the saga from circa A.D. 200 through circa A.D. 1300.

Part 2, comprising chapters 2 through 5, describes the gradual shaping from A.D. 300 to A.D. 1000 of the embryo of medieval Christendom: the sociopolitical-cultural unity that was at the heart of Western civilization. Chapter 2 is an introduction to the Dark Ages, sketching the role of the Church against the background of the collapse of the Western Roman Empire and the massive immigration-invasion of the barbarians. Chapter 3 presents the four priests who can arguably be described as "Fathers of Western Culture"[1]—Ambrose, Augustine, Leo the Great, and Gregory the Great—in whose footsteps numerous bishops followed, shouldering society in the midst of the semianarchy that reigned especially from the fifth to the seventh centuries. Chapter 4 introduces firstly the role of Saint Benedict and the Benedictine monks who, through the genius of their monastic Rule, played a key role in forming the Western mind-set; secondly, it shows the under-the-radar importance of the interior revolution triggered by Columbanus and the Irish monks through their spreading of the Irish method of confession; and thirdly, it singles out one Benedictine, Boniface, who became the chief planter of the seeds of Western civilization in Germany. Chapter 5 deals with the role of Alcuin and his associates as architects of the sociopolitical and cultural framework of Charlemagne's empire, a tentative and faltering ninth-century precursor—"the baby figure of the giant mass of things to come"[2]—of medieval Christendom from the twelfth to the fifteenth centuries, Western civilization with its distinctively Catholic ethos.

Part 3, comprised of chapters 6 through 10, aims to show the decisive role of priests in the building of some of the landmark social, artistic, and economic institutions that mark Western civilization as both original and originating in the Catholic matrix. Chapter 6 sketches the role of the "ancient rite", the traditional form of the Mass that functioned as the chief channel of Catholicism for the creation of the culture of Christendom. Chapter 7 outlines how medieval chivalry, conceived amid cloisters, not only tamed the savagery of the barbarian warrior class but also configured the ideal of Western manhood. Chapter 8 shows how the priesthood led the way in bringing about a new and sublime idealism of womanhood, unprecedented in world history, prompting a culture of romanticism that still lingers in the air of the West. Chapter

[1] Christopher Dawson, *Religion and the Rise of Western Culture* (New York: Doubleday, 1991), p. 26.
[2] William Shakespeare, *Troilus and Cressida*, act 1, scene 3, lines 808–9.

9 presents natural offspring of Catholicism—Gothic architecture and Gregorian chant—and the hearts and minds of the men behind them, especially the "Father of Gothic", Abbot Suger. Chapter 10, "Founders of Free Enterprise Economics", sketches the Catholic worldview from which key features of the free-market system emerged, points to its first monastic incubators, and portrays some of the Renaissance priests whose genius unfolded its principles. The conclusion, "Standing on the Capitoline", briefly speculates on the meaning of these achievements for those who stand amid the ruins of Western civilization, living under a now-dominant post-Western secularized world order, but determined to play their role in building another Christian civilization worthy of humanity.

The thrust is always fourfold: firstly, to outline how certain foundational paradigms, ideals, and institutions of sociocultural life in Western civilization were derived from Catholicism; secondly, to paint miniature sketches of the priests who were largely responsible for making this happen—sketches, not portraits, because I am very conscious that these do not offer the richness of detail and color of a more finished painting (still, I hope that they will enable the reader to be fascinated enough to want to continue getting to know these individuals); thirdly, *Heroism and Genius* endeavors to highlight what made these priests "tick": their world vision, aspirations, motivations, and lifestyle. This last dimension is missing from many history books that give coverage instead to sociopolitical events that explain how, but not fully why, Western civilization was born. But "what is essential is invisible to the eye".[3] How can you possibly understand events without piercing to some degree the souls of the men involved?

The fourth driving motive seeks to point out, on the basis of yesteryear's achievements and with an eye on the immediate future, the role of Catholics, and particularly of priests, in civilization building. The hour has already struck, and we have awoken to the fact that we now live in a post-Western secularized civilization that is not only anti-Christian in its culture but indeed antihuman due to its agenda to redefine the individual person in defiance of nature. Although "Christendom is not the description of an ideal state but of an accepted ideal",[4] it *was* an ideal and still *is* an ideal, one from which we can learn in order to emulate the grandeur and avoid the errors. And now is the time to rouse our intellects, consecrate our energies, and channel our passions in the thrust toward the creation of a Christian culture that will protect all that is true, good, and beautiful for the sake of every man and woman.

Allow me to mention an unease that occurred to me one night while writing *Heroism and Genius*. I thought that since I am a priest it is only natural for you to wonder if I am not somewhat biased in these portrayals. For a while I considered using a pseudonym; this would have allowed you to judge the contents exclusively on their own merits with possibly less reticence. However, in the end I decided instead to place my trust in your open-mindedness and good judgment. If you ask me whether I was neutral while writing, the answer is definitely no. I find it hard to imagine any author being able to endure the ordeals of research, composition, and revision through long days and nights without the passion that flows from deeply

---

[3] Antoine de Saint-Exupéry, *The Little Prince* (London: Wordsworth Classics, 1995), p. 82.

[4] George MacLeod, *We Shall Rebuild* (Glasgow: Iona Community, 1942), quoted in F.J. Rae, "Entre Nous", *The Expository Times* 57, no. 3 (1945): 83.

held convictions. Nevertheless, as we all know from personal experience, passion and truth can blaze side by side; indeed they often merge. Just as a fiery love for Catholicism prevents one from covering up sordid crimes and intrigues of ecclesiastics, it also makes impossible any effort to talk unfeelingly about some of the great priests of history whose radiant grandeur, untarnished by the centuries, irresistibly attracts us still. The Catholic historian cannot empty his heart when he writes about the Church; he has the eyes of a lover, enchanted by the beauty of his bride, and they remain the eyes of a lover even when she has been dressed in rags by treacherous men; he will always chronicle as a builder who wants to learn from history how to renew the institution he loves. In any case, I think that you will glimpse in the facts, footnotes, and bibliographies the painstaking quest of the author for truth and justice.

As the ink flowed onto the paper, I began to realize that a book on Western civilization gains certain advantages by having a priest as the author. For since this civilization was born from the womb of Catholicism and midwifed by the priesthood, an insider's empathy facilitates understanding. It is, in a way, similar to an orchestra conductor's knowledge of music or an alpinist's ability to guide you through the mountains—an x factor whereby certain insights occur spontaneously due to one's role, training, and experience. This priestly empathy can be seen in the selection of topics and in the emphases given to certain realities. Consequently, this book relegates to a few paragraphs certain events that take up entire chapters in the works of other historians—for instance, the importance of the Irish monks due to their preservation of classical culture. Without denying this, it is argued that they exercised another role, one largely under the radar of most historians, one that brought about a silent, subtle, but vital revolution in the Dark Ages and that continued to affect the lives of millions in later centuries—the Irish method of confession and the popularizing of the role of the spiritual director, invisible factors of often crucial importance at the nerve centers of European cultural and political power.

Another question that may readily come to your mind as you read through these pages is why the book is subtitled *How Catholic Priests Helped to Build—and Can Help Rebuild—Western Civilization* when the importance of monks and the monastic institution seems to overshadow that of the clergy in the Dark Ages. Indeed, time and again, the history of the first millennium shows the renewal of the Church and the spread of culture occurring through the monasteries. Nevertheless, as will be explained in greater detail further on, in spite of the crucial role of monasteries in the construction of Western civilization, it is nevertheless the priesthood that spearheaded the transformation of society. However, it did so *with* and *through* monasticism. It was the symbiosis of the triple priestly mission of teaching, sanctifying, and governing, with the intensity of lifestyle, training, and prayer in the Irish and Benedictine monks, that became the most effective medium for winning over the Europe of the Dark Ages to the Catholic Faith. Without monasticism the priesthood in the Dark Ages would not have had the launching pad for its missionary thrusts throughout Europe; but without the priestly triple mission, monasteries might have remained as mere havens of Christian life, peace, and culture in an otherwise barbarian society.

While writing *Heroism and Genius* I have sought to travel in the company of authoritative historians, many of them non-Catholics, scholars like Maurice Keen, Marc Bloch, Régine Pernoud, Richard Barber, Patricia Ranft, Christopher Dawson, Oscar Watkins, Rodney Stark, Thomas Woods, Marjorie Grice-Hutchinson, Erwin

Panofsky, Sidney Painter, Harold Berman, Pierre Duhem, Henri Pirenne, Fernand Braudel, Joseph Schumpeter, and Jean Gimpel.

Some people may be surprised over some of the other names who give their opinions in these pages on events and persons in the Church's past. I suppose that, if you were to classify them, they could fit under the heading of "outsiders to Catholicism". Indeed, that's putting it rather mildly, for some of them are known for their charming anti-Catholic attitudes and for being quite adept at damning us for our not-so-glorious members. Nevertheless, the opinions of these men of wide knowledge and incisive judgment who view the Church with a mixture of intellectual sophistication, and at times plain astonishment, are insightful. They include Voltaire, Arnold J. Toynbee, the Jewish statesman and prime minister of England Benjamin Disraeli, the philosopher David Hume, the novelist Robert Louis Stevenson, and Alfred North Whitehead, a British agnostic who at one point in his life identified himself as a Christian but never crossed the Catholic threshold. Nor are they all Europeans. On the other side of the Atlantic, included are President Woodrow Wilson, Mark Twain, and the historian Francis Parkman—all illustrious American Anglo-Saxons and Protestants except for Parkman, who was agnostic; also present are Francis Fukuyama, author of *The Origins of Political Order*; and Murray Rothbard, who was Jewish and a renowned economist and libertarian political philosopher.

Even some of the Catholic historians who are sources for *Heroism and Genius* wrote, in a certain sense, as "outlanders". One of them is Christopher Dawson, who converted to Catholicism at twenty-five and retained throughout his life that freshness of view typical of a newcomer. As a historian with a global vision, he proposes, with facts readily available, the key role that religion plays in making or breaking cultures. His grasp of the root causes of the implosion of contemporary Western society led to his call for a realistic assessment of Western civilization in the Middle Ages: "The outstanding example in history of the application of faith to life: the embodiment of religion in social institutions and eternal forms, and therefore both its achievements and failures are worthy of study."[5]

Another is Henri Daniel-Rops, author of the ten-volume *History of the Church of Christ*.[6] An agnostic during his twenties, he recrossed the Catholic threshold and resolved to be an "insider" who would devote his life to writing about Catholicism in a way intelligible to those outside the Church. An indication of his success is the fact that in 1955 the prestigious Académie Française elected him to be one of their forty *immortels*. He strove to explain historical events by identifying their connection with the ideas dominant in each epoch and with the inner history of men's aspirations, fears, and uncertainties. He also saw clearly what many historians are understandably blind to—that the turbo engine of the Church's progress lies with each epoch's Christian heroes, the saints, for "to reanimate the inmost forces of the Christian soul is to labour for the most fundamental needs of the Church".[7]

I have sought to present the historical facts in *Heroism and Genius* according to the consensus of historians. However, there are instances when this does not exist. For example, among the several competing theories about the origins of the *troubadour*

---

[5] Christopher Dawson, *Medieval Essays* (Garden City, N.Y.: Doubleday, 1959), p. 53.
[6] Henri Daniel-Rops, *History of the Church of Christ*, 10 vols. (London: J. M. Dent and Sons, 1948–1967).
[7] Henri Daniel-Rops, *The Church in the Eighteenth Century* (London: J. M. Dent and Sons, 1964), p. 300.

culture, there are two that claim it for Christian sources. I decided to close ranks with Christopher Dawson and others who concluded that its source is in the Arabic civilization of eleventh-century Spain.

Heroism and Genius is inspired by the Catholic vision of history as "the essence of innumerable biographies".[8] It rejects the Greek and Hegelian (fatalistic), Nazi, Marxist, and materialist tunnel visions of life as mere fate or destiny in which the individual is a mere clog in the time machine, his freedom chained by a blind, purposeless universe. The builders of the West deciphered the deepest meaning of time's passage by recognizing that because of the creation and the redemption, history is mysteriously both *his story* and ours. "In history the living tissue of events is a compound both of human and divine thoughts and actions, the two elements alternately mingling, contradicting each other, and colliding so as to fulfill the plan of Providence."[9] Hence "we perceive a dignity to the world that is grounded in a destiny from eternity to eternity; we see a story of the world that the world does not begin to suspect is part of its integral identity."[10] To bring this vision of history to contemporary man is to shed light on the untruth of the dominant materialistic ideology in which man is labeled as nothing more than his genetic code, his "now" and "here".

---

[8] Thomas Carlyle, "On History", in *The Works of Thomas Carlyle*, Centenary Edition, ed. Henry Duff Traill, *Critical and Miscellaneous Essays II*, vol. 27 (London, 1896–1899), p. 86.

[9] Henry Marc-Bonnet, *La Papauté contemporaine* (Paris: Presses Universitaires de France, 1946), p. 91, quoted in Henri Daniel-Rops, *A Fight for God, 1870–1939* (London: J. M. Dent and Sons, 1966), p. 73.

[10] Richard J. Neuhaus, "Creating a Culture of Life" (lecture, Toronto, Canada, October 26, 2002).

Part I

The Catholic Matrix
of Western Civilization

Karl Friedrich Schinkel, *Gothic Church on a Rock by the Sea*, 1815.

She [the Catholic Church] saw the commencement of all the governments and of all the ecclesiastical institutions that now exist in the world; and we feel no assurance that she is not destined to see the end of them all. She was great and respected before the Saxon had set foot in Britain, before the Frank had crossed the Rhine, when Grecian eloquence still flourished in Antioch, when idols were still worshipped in the temples of Mecca. And she may still exist in undiminished vigor when some traveler from New Zealand shall, in the midst of a vast solitude, take his stand on a broken arch of London Bridge to sketch the ruins of St Paul's.

— Thomas Babington Macaulay,
"On Ranke's History of the Popes", 1840

Chapter 1

THE WOMB AND THE EMBRYO

Facts are stubborn things; and whatever may be our wishes, our inclinations, or the dictates of our passion, they cannot alter the state of facts and evidence.[1]

—President John Adams

Historians Have Spoken: The Verdict

Within the past hundred years, leading historians have resolutely asserted the Catholic Church's role in the formation of Western civilization. Indeed, to such an extent that the conclusion is now unavoidable: the Catholic Church was its architect and main builder, creating original institutions in Europe in which it embodied the Christian vision and values. The herculean achievement of the conversion of Romans and barbarians to Christianity was the keystone in the arch of this new civilization. The arch had many other stones of Jewish, Greek, Roman, Germanic, and Arab origin that greatly configured its appearance and abilities. However, the wedge-shaped stone that supported and locked all the others into position, allowing it to bear the weight of such an integration, was Catholicism, both as a set of truths and as an institution. At the end of the long night of the Dark Ages, with the dawn of the eleventh century an original civilization came to birth in Western Europe,

All honor to the Cross of the Crucified and Risen Savior, wherefrom radiated the heroism and genius that vitalized with supernatural energies the hearts and minds of both the famed and unsigned founders of the West's Christian civilization—and can do so again. (© Photo of author at 8,100 ft. at the Cross on the Great St. Bernard Pass, Switzerland, the most ancient route through the Western Alps, with the Saint Bernard dog named after St. Bernard of Menthon, ca. 1020-1081, one of the little-known rescuers of Europe amid the Dark Ages.)

one that can only be described as quintessentially Catholic in law, philosophy, art, architecture, and in many other fields, one that brought with it a "new humanism, an authentic 'grammar' of mankind and reality".[2] All this was due to the colossal

---

[1] Charles Francis Adams, *The Works of John Adams, Second President of the United States* (Boston: Little, Brown, 1856), p. 113.

[2] Benedict XVI, "General Audience", November 21, 2012, http://w2.vatican.va/content/benedict-xvi /en/audiences/2012/documents/hf_ben-xvi_aud_20121121.html. All quotations from official papal or conciliar documents are from the Vatican's website.

Raffaelo Sanzio, *Pope Leo X with Cardinals Giulio de Medici and Luigi de Rossi* (detail), ca. 1518.

vitality and dynamism of the previous thousand years. Hence, the Dark Ages led to a naissance, a *birth* of a new culture and civilization, while, by contrast, the fifteenth and sixteenth centuries were merely a renaissance, a *rebirth*, or rather a revival by imitation of the ancient Greco-Roman culture that had been long been dead as a set of patterns of thought influencing the masses.

One by one the bastions of denial crumbled as intellectuals of excellence in the various disciplines spotlighted the Church's preeminent action. The Oxford historian R. W. Southern has shown the guiding role of Catholic Scholasticism in absorbing and integrating the intellectual heritage of the Greco-Roman world for the creation of the rationally coherent worldview of Western civilization. Pierre Duhem, the physicist and historian of science, concluded that the Catholics of the Middle Ages placed the philosophical pillars for modern physics, and contemporary experts like David Lindberg, Stanley Jaki, and Thomas Goldstein have agreed. In the progress of astronomy, Professor J. L. Heilbron recognized the Church's pivotal function. In the development of education, A. F. West attributed a key role to the Church's influence during the reign of Charlemagne, and C. H. Haskins has asserted the Catholic origin of universities. In the discipline of law, the scholar Harold Berman concluded that the template of modern legal systems lies in the Church's own canon law. In economics, John Gilchrist, Henri Pirenne, and Fernand Braudel showed that many of the key features of the free enterprise economic system existed in Catholic medieval Europe, and Joseph Schumpeter has pointed to the group of priest-intellectuals of the School of Salamanca as the thinkers "who come nearer than does any other group to having been the 'founders of scientific economics'".[3] John C. Loudon, Montalembert, and Henry H. Goodell recognized the advances in agriculture made by the Cistercians and other monks. Jean Gimpel and others have revealed the technological sophistication of medieval monasteries. W. E. H. Lecky has shown how the Church introduced social welfare programs with unprecedented organization and intensity. As Newman recognized, "The grace stored in Jerusalem, and the gifts which radiate from Athens, are made over and concentrated in Rome. This is true as a matter of history. Rome has inherited both sacred and profane learning—she has perpetuated and dispensed the traditions of Moses and David in the supernatural order and of Homer and Aristotle in the natural."[4]

---

[3] Joseph A. Schumpeter, *History of Economic Analysis* (London: Allen and Unwin, 1986), p. 97.

[4] John Henry Newman, *The Idea of a University* (London: Longmans, Green, 1907), p. 265.

Hence the ideological prejudice that it is impossible that Catholicism could have been the architect and builder of Western civilization is exploded by the historical facts: *Historia locuta, causa finita* (History has spoken, the case is closed). This assertion goes hand in hand with wholehearted and grateful recognition for the many and splendid contributions made by non-Catholic Christians from the sixteenth century onward—Bach and Handel for instance—and by the Jewish people who have gifted the world with so many scientists, artists, musicians, and statesmen.

Priests: Channels of Lifeblood

In that thousand-year task of construction, maintenance, and reconstruction by the Church, amid the ebb and flow of success and failure, Catholic priests, not only because they numbered so many men of genius and heroism in their ranks, but also because of their triple mission within Catholicism to teach, sanctify, and govern, came to be the front-liners and irreplaceable builders of Western civilization.

Allow me, however, to clearly underline what this assertion about the key role of priests does not mean. It does not assert the untenable claim to some type of monopoly on achievements: priests obviously hold no property rights on all the heroism, nobility, and genius of a thousand years. Many Catholic laypeople contributed enormously to building the new civilization. Christian monarchs like Henry II of Germany, Wenceslaus of Bohemia, and Louis IX of France strove to build Christian nations. Countless Christian women distinguished themselves: the foundresses of orders like Scholastica and Clare of Assisi; the influential queens Theodolinda of the Lombards, Bertha of Kent, Elizabeth of Hungary, Margaret of Scotland, Blanche of Castile, and the empress Cunegonde; the tenth-century abbess Hroswitha, a writer who influenced the development of the German theatre; the abbess Herrad of Landsberg, who wrote one of the best-known encyclopedias of the 1100s, the *Hortus Deliciarum*; and the talented musician Hildegarde of Bingen.

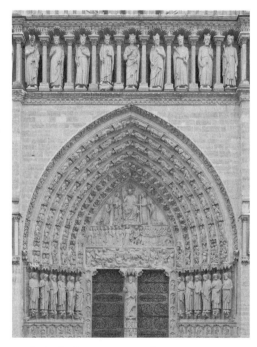

Cathedral of Notre Dame de Paris, main entrance.

While justice requires that history recognize the important contributions of so many women and laymen, it also calls on us to bring to light the number and grandeur of heroes and men of genius in the ranks of the priesthood. In an unbroken line, extending through two thousand years, priests have stood as defenders of humanity and instigators of progress. From cradle to the final frontier unknown priests have been present for everyone who called upon them. In a myriad of ways they have led millions of men and whole countries to Christ and Christian civilization. "The nation's life-blood resided in the clergy", wrote the historian Georges Desdevises du Dézert, referring to Spain in the late 1700s, but the same can be said of other nations and epochs.[5]

Some people, blinded through inherited prejudice, may ask, "What good have priests brought to the world?" To this, one can only answer, "If they had not existed, you would find yourself in quite a different society!" As Pius XI so memorably stated, "All the good that Christian civilization has brought into the world is due, at least in its roots, to the word and works of the Catholic priesthood."[6]

As to the strange criticisms targeting the entire priesthood because of the sins of the few, logic—and pity for the accusers—prompts one to silence. However, when the attacks target priests of heroic grandeur merely because of unfounded suspicions or minor faults, one hardly knows how to respond, except perhaps as Thomas Carlyle: "No sadder proof can be given by a man of his own littleness than disbelief in great men".[7] Or, one could possibly respond in the same vein as the reply that came from the indignation-filled fountain pen of the author of *Treasure Island*, the Scottish Protestant Robert Louis Stevenson. His scathing words were in answer to the smears smudging the reputation of the "Apostle of the Lepers", Father Damien of Molokai: "You are one of those who have an eye for faults and failures; that you take a pleasure to find and publish them; and that, having found them, you make haste to forget the overvailing virtues and the real success which had alone introduced them to your knowledge. It is a dangerous frame of mind."[8]

Elsewhere in the same letter, Stevenson stated:

> But, sir, when we have failed, and another has succeeded; when we have stood by, and another has stepped in; when we sit and grow bulky in our charming mansions, and a plain, uncouth peasant steps into the battle, under the eyes of God, and succours the afflicted and consoles the dying and is himself afflicted in his turn and dies upon the field of honour—the battle cannot be retrieved as your unhappy irritation has suggested. It is a lost battle, and lost forever. One thing remained to you in your defeat—some rags of common honour; and these you have made haste to cast away.[9]

What Stevenson concluded as a result of his own independent investigation of the priest of Molokai could be said about so many of history's priests: "Yet I am strangely deceived or they build up the image of a man, with all his weakness, essentially heroic, and alive with rugged honesty, generosity, and mirth."[10]

So let us not commit the tragic error of disparaging the Church or the priesthood by only looking at wretched and treacherous betrayers. For although any clear-eyed observer of the Church's history recognizes defects, they are the defects on the most magnificent masterpiece that the world has ever known. But, above all, let us not lose sight of the fact that the Church is, in her innermost reality, the Mystical Body

---

[5] Georges Desdevises du Dézert, quoted in Henri Daniel-Rops, *The Church in the Eighteenth Century* (London: Dent, 1964), p. 301.

[6] Pius XI, Encyclical *Ad Catholici Sacerdotii*, December 29, 1935, no. 26.

[7] Thomas Carlyle, *Heroes and Hero Worship* (London: Chapman and Hall, 1869), p. 17.

[8] Robert Louis Stevenson, *Father Damien: An Open Letter to the Reverend Dr. Ed Hyde of Honolulu* (London: Chatto and Windus, 1890), p. 22.

[9] Ibid., p. 11.

[10] Ibid., p. 20.

of Christ. Hence, the Catholic "loves Christ who loves his Church which is his body even if this body is wounded by our sins".[11] As Cardinal Giuseppe Siri remarked:

> [The Catholic] will understand that all the known or unknown betrayals by the few or many members of the Church, the sordidness of soul, the narrow-mindedness, the cruelty, and all the infidelity that the Church may have had and lived within herself, are only the counterpart to the sweat of blood in Gethsemane and to the wounds and blood of the Cross. That is why we must think about the holy being of the God-Man. We may neither change nor desert the Lord because of his wounds.[12]

Let us not, as Pope Leo the Great (ca. 400–461) once murmured, "judge the heritage by the unworthiness of the inheritor".[13] Instead, may the sight of so many heroic figures lead us to the same conclusion as that of the American historian and agnostic Francis Parkman (1823–1893), who, after visiting a Catholic church in Sicily, wrote that the church was "the noblest edifice I have seen. This and others not unlike it have impressed me with new ideas of the Catholic religion. Not exactly, for I reverenced it before as the religion of generations of brave and great men—but now I honor it for itself."[14]

Who else has achieved for mankind what priests like Leo the Great, Jean-Baptiste de la Salle, and Vincent de Paul have accomplished? Among the world's greatest lovers, with hearts aflame from love of the Crucified and Risen Christ, the priests of history have been at the heart of so much that is noble in history: one who became a leper with the lepers on a Pacific island; another who made a vow to take care of the sick even if it meant losing his own life; another who offered himself to substitute a boy as a galley-slave; another who stepped out of the ranks in Auschwitz and said, "Take me!" in order to save a fellow prisoner; another who was the single most important individual in bringing down the Berlin Wall—*no greater love, no greater heroism, no greater achievements!*

Did Alexander the Great, Caesar, or Napoleon ever equal such love with their "greatness"? "What millions died—that Caesar might be great!"[15] Far greater than the political "greats" of history are the men and women who loved heroically: the saints—of whom many were priests—and who "have lit many lights which together form a great path of light over the millennia".[16] For if heroism is not essentially action but suffering, not acquisition but renunciation, not deeds but self-sacrifice, then countless priests through the ages merit the title of hero. It is therefore in the footsteps of giants that we present-day Catholics walk; it is to emulate them that we must strive! And for that we need memory of the ancient saga of Catholic deeds and heroism. What a powerful stimulus is ours in moments of danger or loneliness to

---

[11] Benedict XVI to journalists during the pope's flight to Malta, in "Sexual Abuse Issue Raised as Pope Benedict Visits Malta", BBC News, April 17, 2010, http://news.bbc.co.uk/2/hi/europe/8627429.stm.

[12] Cardinal Giuseppe Siri, *Getsemani* (Roma: *Edizioni della Fraternità della Santissima Vergine Maria*, 1987), pp. 371–72. My translation.

[13] Pope Leo the Great, quoted in Henri Daniel-Rops, *The Church in the Dark Ages* (London: J.M. Dent and Sons, 1959), p. 99.

[14] Quoted in Henry Dwight Sedgwick, *Francis Parkman* (Boston-New York: Houghton, Mifflin, 1904), p. 80.

[15] Thomas Campbell, *The Poetical Works of Thomas Campbell* (Boston: Little, Brown, 1856), p. 35.

[16] Benedict XVI, Homily at the Parish of St. Maximilian Kolbe, Rome, December 12, 2010, http://visnews-en.blogspot.it/2010/12/it-is-god-not-grand-promises-who.html.

remember that we are never alone; that we are surrounded by some of the greatest spirits among men: brothers, who, although their fight on earth is ended, continue to surround us with their protection, prayers, and power from Heaven. Shoulder to shoulder they stand with us against all the forces of darkness in this world.

History as *magistra vitae* (life's teacher) gives important lessons about who the priest is and where his loyalty should remain as heir to an ancient heritage within the world's oldest and greatest institution. It paints a vivid portrait of the priests who led the way in the building of Western civilization. It is in the footsteps of these men that priests of all eras are called to follow: rescuers of the West from barbarianism at the collapse of the Roman Empire; pioneering educationalists; men among the sick and the downtrodden; and defenders of the defenseless. From laying the first stone for legally guaranteed human rights to blazing the trail for the social dignity of women, the priest's fatherhood has had an irreplaceable role in human progress, a peerless and unrivaled place in advancing the well-being of mankind. As Benedict XVI stated, "If we look at history, we can see that many episodes of authentic spiritual and social renewal have been written with the decisive contribution of Catholic priests, animated only by their passion for the Gospel and for man, for his true religious and civil liberty. How many initiatives of integral human promotion began with the intuition of a priestly heart!"[17]

Hopefully these chapters will allow the reader to glimpse not only the well-lit figures of the powerful and the famous but also the silhouettes of the quiet men who changed the course of men's souls in history—and for eternity. Every Catholic priest who was loyal to his triple mission to teach, sanctify, and govern built this civilization; many are the unknown priests whose names are written only in the grateful hearts of individuals and in the "book of life" (Rev 3:5), yet they played a central and procreative role in the building of the West. These are the unsung heroes who, day by day, changed history and, in a certain sense, eternity, at the altar of the Holy Sacrifice, in the confessional, in the catechism class, and at the bedside of the dying.

Let us not forget the grandeur of these lives, for to them we must look in order not to break the line but to continue to stand, shoulder to shoulder with them, in the longest line of self-sacrifice the world has ever known. Through the windows of history we can see clearly the features of these men; in their qualities of spirit we recognize the features of Jesus Christ; in our mystic communion with them we will receive strength for sacrifice unto emulation. Hence, the purpose of this book is not lionizing and nostalgia, a yearning to live in some mythical "good old days", an attempt to find excuses to handcuff progress to obsolete standards. Instead, it is a *shout* to contemporary priests—"Remember!"—as they stand at a crossroads of history and confront the Western civilization of the past and the dictatorship of relativism of the present: *Remember who you are and what you once achieved; recall the crucially important social consequences of your priesthood; remember that the priest, by being truly teacher, sanctifier, and shepherd, changes society and builds Christian civilization—that he simply cannot fail to change the world by being an authentic priest of Jesus Christ!*

Any Catholic committed to the cause of a Christian civilization must be ready, amid the hostility of the post-Western secularized society, to stand for truth against

[17] Benedict XVI, "Angelus Address", June 13, 2010, https://w2.vatican.va/content/benedict-xvi/en/angelus /2010/documents/hf_ben-xvi_ang_20100613.html.

an ideology that would subordinate man to the games of an anonymous relativism. But for a man who enters a seminary and is destined to act as a leader in the institution that built the West, the duty is even more pressing, the sacrifices still deeper, and the risks greater. Yet he must not balk. History summons him to step forward and live with a son's pride; with an heir's sense of responsibility for handing on the tradition received; and with an officer's alertness to the fact that the Church—to a large degree like any merely human institution—will be as effective as its leadership ranks. Vivid memories of the pioneering priests will strengthen his resolve through pride of fellowship, pressure of high expectations, and support through invocation.

Milestones of the Catholic Struggle to Build a New Civilization, circa A.D. 200–1300

These centuries have often been termed the "Middle Ages": a singularly quirky name with which to lump together the thousand years from the collapse of the Roman Empire to the fourteenth century. It would be hard to invent a more pointless, misleading, and naive epithet—pointless since all historical epochs stand in relation to those before and after; misleading because it blinds mankind to the importance of this thousand-year era and to the utterly original nature of the new civilization that had its naissance around the twelfth century, a *birth* that contrasts with the mere *rebirth* (renaissance) of Greco-Roman culture from the fourteenth century onward; and

The Apostles. These statues flank the main east door of Notre Dame Cathedral, Paris.

naive because it hides the distinct phases of evolution of Western civilization from the collapse of Rome to the Renaissance. Firstly, there was the period circa A.D. 200–circa A.D. 400 that saw Roman emperors still managing to defend the frontiers. Then, in the second period during the fifth century, the barbarians took control of the imperial government in the Western Empire. The third epoch was circa A.D. 500–circa A.D. 1050, during which Western Europe experienced "Dark Ages"—a darkness of varying degrees according to place and century, one that was relative to the preceding Roman period and to the subsequent medieval Christendom, an era of monumental heroism and creativity amid barbarism in which the embryo of a new culture gradually coalesced, notably during the reign of Charlemagne (A.D. 768–A.D. 814). The birth of that culture was the beginning of the fourth period, the golden age of an original and decidedly Catholic civilization (ca. A.D. 1100–ca. A.D. 1300). And finally, there came the fifth epoch marked by forebodings of this promising civilization's decline due to complex factors (ca. A.D. 1300–ca. A.D. 1400).

Political Milestones	Catholic Milestones
235–284 Military anarchy within Roman Empire 284–305 Diocletian reigns	250; 257–258 Church under persecution 293–305 Church under persecution ca. 305 St. Anthony organizes monasticism in Egypt
312 Battle of the Milvian Bridge 313 Edict of Milan: toleration of Christians 324 Constantine sole emperor 361–363 Julian the Apostate attempts to restore state paganism	361 St. Martin of Tours founds abbey of Ligugé 361–363 Church under persecution
378 Visigoths defeat Roman army 378–395 Theodosius reigns	
380 Christianity declared to be the official state religion	390 St. Ambrose confronts Theodosius 396 St. Augustine ordained as Bishop of Hippo
402–407 Legions abandon Britain; Saxons, Angles, Jutes invade 406 Vandals, Alans, Suebi cross the Rhine and invade Gaul, Spain, North Africa 410 Visigoths sack Rome 432 Vandals masters of North Africa	410 Monastery of Lérins founded 430 Death of St. Augustine 431 Council of Ephesus 432 St. Patrick begins mission to Ireland 440–461 Reign of Pope St. Leo the Great
455 Vandals seize Rome 476 Last Western Roman emperor, Romulus Augustus, deposed 496 Franks under Clovis rule Gaul	496 Clovis, king of the Franks, baptized 500 Sigismund, king of the Burgundians, baptized 500s Monasticism flourishes in Ireland
527–565 Reign of Emperor Justinian; Italy devastated by war (524–554) 568 Lombards invade Italy	529 St. Benedict founds Monte Cassino ca. 565 St. Columba founds Iona ca. 570 Conversion of the Suevi ca. 585 St. Columbanus founds Luxeuil 589 Reccared I, king of the Visigoths, becomes Catholic
603 Roman Senate meets for last time	590–604 Reign of Pope St. Gregory the Great ca. 599 Ethelbert of Kent converts

Political Milestones	Catholic Milestones
614 Jerusalem captured by Persians	ca. 650–c. 700 Lombards of northern
633–643 Muslim conquest of Syria, Pal-	Italy convert
estine, Persia, and Egypt	
669–708 Muslim conquest of North	716–754 St. Boniface evangelizes
Africa	Germans
	756 Birth of Papal States
771 Charlemagne, sole king of the Franks	782–796 Alcuin at Charlemagne's court
800 Charlemagne crowned emperor	
814 Death of Charlemagne	
ca. 820–ca. 900 Viking invasions	829–865 St. Ansgar in Denmark and
846 Muslims sack St. Peter's	Sweden
871–899 Alfred the Great reigns in	862–ca. 885 Ss. Cyril and Methodius
England	evangelize Slavs
910–955 Hungarian invasion	910 Abbey of Cluny founded
911 Vikings settle in Normandy	ca. 960 Benedictines on site of future
962 Foundation of Holy Roman and	Westminster Abbey
Germanic Empire	982 St. Romuald founds Camaldoli
	988 Conversion of Vladimir, grand duke
	of Kiev
	ca. 1000–1050 Iceland becomes Catholic
	1030–1080 Romanesque church of
	Conques
	1054 Council of Narbonne: "Truce of
	God"
1064 Seljuk Turks capture Armenia	1073–1085 Pope Gregory VII fights
1066 Norman conquest of England	investiture
1077 Henry IV at Canossa	
1078 Seljuk Turks conquer Asia Minor	1080 Two bishoprics established in
	Sweden
	1084 St. Bruno founds La Grande
	Chartreuse
	ca. 1090 Chivalric poem the *Chanson de Roland* written
	1095 Pope Urban II preaches First
	Crusade
1099 Crusaders take Jerusalem	1112 St. Bernard enters Cîteaux
	1126 Diocese founded in Greenland
	1128 Statutes of the Templars
	1135–1144 Gothic church of St. Denis
	built
1215 *Magna Carta* in England	
1226–1270 St. Louis IX, king of France	

Part 2

Laying the Foundations of a
New Civilization, circa A.D. 300–1000

Willem van de Velde the Younger, *The
Gust*, ca. 1680.

The idea that Christianity belongs to the Dark Ages: here I did not satisfy myself with reading modern generalisations; I read a little history.... I found that Christianity ... was the one path across the Dark Ages that was not dark. It was a shining bridge connecting two shining civilizations.

If any one says that the faith arose in ignorance and savagery the answer is simple: it didn't. It arose in the Mediterranean civilization in the full summer of the Roman Empire. The world was swarming with sceptics, and pantheism was as plain as the sun when Constantine nailed the cross to the mast. It is perfectly true that afterwards the ship sank; but it is far more extraordinary that the ship came up again: repainted and glittering, with the cross still at the top. This is the amazing thing the religion did: it turned a sunken ship into a submarine. The ark lived under the load of waters; after being buried under the debris of dynasties and clans, we arose and remembered Rome.

The most absurd thing that could be said of the Church is the thing we have all heard said of it. How can we say that the Church wishes to bring us back into the Dark Ages? The Church was the only thing that ever brought us out of them.

—G. K. Chesterton, *Orthodoxy*

Chapter 2

THE CHURCH AMID DARK AGES

Thought shall be harder,
Heart the keener,
Courage the greater,
As our might lessens.

—*The Lay of Maldon*

Night Falls over Rome

When Peter and Paul went to their martyrdoms in A.D. 67 they left behind a tiny but vigorous Christian community in Rome to which men and women from all levels of society, including the imperial household and the Praetorian Guard, had begun to enter. Slowly, in the midst of admiration, suspicion, and persecution, the young Church went from fragility to strength in an empire that, between the first and fifth centuries, became a white-haired world sinking rapidly into senility.[1]

The causes of Rome's decline were many and complex: falling birthrates, economic factors such as high taxation and absence of a budgetary system, political incompetence, military slackness, barbarian migrations, and, above all, skepticism about life's purpose and a consequent

Partial view of sculpture "Good Defeats Evil" on the grounds of the United Nations headquarters, New York. Created by Zurab Tsereteli, a native of Georgia, the sculpture depicts Saint George slaying the dragon.

moral free fall due to the intellectual bankruptcy of the old pagan state religion. A spiritual cancer gradually enfeebled the formerly austere hearts of the Roman people who became a sensual mob supporting politicians in return for "bread and circuses", as the poet Juvenal remarked, circa A.D. 100.

There was no single event that marked the "fall" of Rome; rather, a series of events are useful milestones along the road of its sociopolitical collapse. The decades 235–284 were years of civil war and constant political upheaval. In 378 the Visigoths defeated the Roman army. In 402 and 407 as a young Patrick, future missionary

---

[1] See Rodney Stark, *Cities of God: The Real Story of How Christianity Became an Urban Movement and Conquered Rome* (New York: HarperOne, 2007), for evidence that the Catholic Faith became the leading religion in the Roman Empire chiefly because of conversion due to personal conviction in the first three centuries and not on account of social pressure after Constantine became sole emperor in 324; also, see Gustave Bardy, *La Conversion au Christianisme durant les premiers siècles* (Paris: Aubier, 1949).

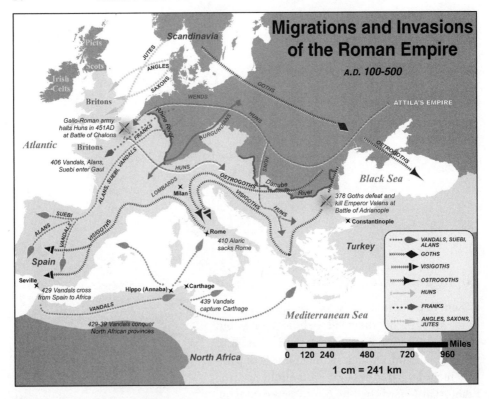

of Celtic Ireland, looked on, the empire's two legions in Britain sailed away while Saxons and Picts came and attacked the Roman settlements. On December 3, 406, Vandals, Alans, and Suebi crossed the frozen Rhine near Mainz after Roman troops had left to defend Italy and began settling in Gaul, Spain, and North Africa. Then, for the first time in almost eight hundred years, Visigoths under Alaric attacked Rome in 410, and the West shuddered as "the City that had taken the whole world was itself taken".[2] By 432 the Vandals were masters of North Africa, and in 455 under Genseric they seized Rome and brought off hostages and treasures. On September 4, 476, the last Western Roman emperor, the teenager Romulus Augustus, took the road to the south after being deposed by the barbarian Odoacer. By 496 the Franks under Clovis were rulers of Gaul. By 554 the thirty-year war between the Eastern emperor Justinian and the Ostrogoths had left behind a devastated Italy, and a proud city of Rome that had once boasted a million-strong population had become a ghost town of forty thousand people. In the midst of relentless butchery and chaos even the possibility of death by plague seemed welcome to the leading figure of the age, Pope Gregory the Great (540–604): "When we consider the way in which other men have died we find relief in thinking about the type of death that is threatening us. What mutilations, what cruelties have we not seen inflicted upon people, for which death is the only cure and in the midst of which life is a torture!"[3]

Night had fallen over Western Europe.

[2] St. Jerome, Letter to Principia, in *Nicene and Post-Nicene Fathers*, 2nd series, ed. Philip Schaff and Henry Wace, vol. 6 (New York: Cosimo, 2007), Letter 127, p. 257.

[3] Pope Gregory the Great, *Epistle* 10.20.

Rescuing from a Burning City

During the fifth to the seventh centuries, Western Europe resembled Mordor, a "dying land not yet dead".[4] Writhing under assaults of transient barbarian populations—yet still reminded of civilization by the remnants and ruins of Roman highways and bridges, aqueducts and amphitheatres—amid nightmarish confusion men thought of yesterday as a dream and despaired of tomorrow. A hodgepodge of barbarian kingdoms, pagan or Arian in religion, established themselves alongside enclaves that called themselves Roman, where there was little else besides lust and impotence.[5]

Men fluctuated between frenzy and hopelessness in their utter disbelief that proud Rome, conqueror of nations, and seemingly eternal in her destiny, could be conquered by a barbarian like Alaric. Even an

Carle van Loo, *Aeneas Bearing His Father Anchises from Burning Troy*, 1729.

intellect like Saint Jerome's fell momentarily into agony in 410: "My voice fails me. Sobs choke my words."[6] What was left of the civilization that had been built over a thousand years? In the face of universal decay and events seemingly masterminded by satanic powers, hope was fast abandoning the hearts of men. In anguish they looked around for a meaning to it all, for an overarching purpose to existence that would give them hope that, somehow, truth and goodness would ultimately vanquish the relentless waves of evil that were lashing the shores of society and their hearts.

The Church did not disappoint them. With her eyes fixed on the North Star of history, the Unchanging One, Jesus Christ, Truth, Life, and Way, she resolutely reminded men to look beyond the immediate fleeting civilizations of this world to the Eternal. Had he not said, "Though heaven and earth should pass away, my words will stand" (see Mt 24:35)? Hence, even if the Divine Author's creation had been warped by the original cataclysmic catastrophe of sin and had been transformed into a dramatic battleground on which the forces of goodness and evil clash, *history* was still *his story*. His providence, which had revealed itself in Jesus Christ to be a providence of pure love, was still ceaselessly and mysteriously acting to overcome the horrors of evil. All was moving toward its God-destined purpose, and the man who played out his role in the act of the drama assigned to him would discover

[4] J. R. R. Tolkien, *The Return of the King: Being the Third Part of the Lord of the Rings* (New York: Houghton Mifflin, 1955), p. 900. Mordor is Tolkien's name for the land devastated by the forces of evil in *The Lord of the Rings*.

[5] See Gregory of Tours, *History of the Franks*, trans. O. M. Dalton, 2 vols. (Oxford: Oxford University Press, 1927), written in the sixth century.

[6] St. Jerome, Letter to Principia, in *Nicene and Post-Nicene Fathers*, Letter 127, p. 257.

that "in everything God works for good with those who love him" (Rom 8:28); he would be united to Jesus Christ, Lord of history, and through the supernatural life of sanctifying grace would begin on earth, in embryonic form, the life that would be his, undyingly, in Heaven.

With these truths the Church showed the men and women of the Dark Ages, whether Roman patricians or Anglo-Saxon chieftains, that her raison d'être was to communicate the divinely revealed purpose of history. She thus restored hope, empowering men to face their present, no matter how terrible, because she assured them there was a future great enough to give reason for withstanding so much evil and pain at hand. Moreover, upon the foundation of these truths there could occur not only a renaissance of the old Roman social order but a naissance of a new and better one: a Christian civilization that would integrate the best of *Romanitas*.[7] However, she pointed out that this construction could only happen by first remaking man in the image of Christ through the truths found in the Catholic Faith and with the supernatural life of the Church's sacraments. Fifth-century writers like Paul Orosius, Salvianus, and Paulinus of Nola all asserted these transcendent truths.[8] But among all of the great Catholic leaders amid the Dark Ages, four stand out as giants of thought and action who did much to lay the foundations of the new Christian order: the "Fathers of Western Culture"—Ambrose, Augustine, Leo the Great, and Gregory the Great. These were the men who ensured that the Church "was the one path across the Dark Ages that was not dark ... a shining bridge connecting two shining civilizations".[9]

Saga of Centuries: The Conversion of Europe

During that long night from the fifth to the tenth centuries, an age of "iron, lead and darkness",[10] the Church achieved the baptism of the barbarian races, thanks to the lucid intelligence and steadfast endurance of devoted bishops, the sweat and blood of pioneering Celtic and Benedictine monks, and the lives spent in prayer by silent hermits.

In 496 Remy (Remigius), Bishop of Reims, christened Clovis, king of the Franks. In 500 Avitus, Bishop of Vienne, friend and mentor of Sigismund, king

---

[7] *Romanitas*: the ensemble of ideas and practices by which the Romans identified themselves as a distinct civilization.

[8] Paulus Orosius, *The Seven Books of History against the Pagans*, trans. Roy J. Deferrari (Washington, D.C.: Catholic University of America Press, 1964); Salvian of Marseilles, *On the Government of God*, trans. Eva Matthews Sanford (New York: Columbia University Press, 1930); Dennis E. Trout, *Paulinus of Nola—Life, Letters, and Poems* (Berkeley: University of California Press, 1999).

[9] G. K. Chesterton, *Orthodoxy* (Mineola, N.Y.: Dover Publications, 2012), chap. 12, p. 140.

[10] Cardinal Caesar Baronius (1538–1607), the Renaissance historian, coined the term "dark age" but limited its application to the period between the demise of the Carolingian Empire in 888 and the beginnings of the Gregorian reform around the middle of the eleventh century. Although writers frequently attribute to him the epigram "an age of iron, lead, and darkness", what Baronius actually wrote is the following: "[N]ovum incohatur saeculum quod, sua asperitate ac boni sterilitate ferreum, malique exudantis deformitate plumbeum, atque inopia scriptorum, appellari consuevit obscurum." ([T]he new age that begins, for its coarseness and barrenness of goodness is usually called iron, for its sordidness and overflowing evil lead, and for its lack of writers, dark.) Caesar Baronius, *Annales Ecclesiastici*, vol. 10, col. 649 (Coloniae Agrippinae: Ioannem Wilhelmum Friessem, 1685). My translation.

GREENLAND
(1000-1100)
Leif the Viking

EUROPE BECOMES CHRISTIAN, 400-1450.

"It was as if the world had shaken herself free,
cast off her old age,
and were clothing herself everywhere
in a white garment of churches."[1]

ICELAND
(874-1050)
Norse Catholic Priests

FINNS
(1100-1300)

ESTONIANS
(1200-1300)

LIVONIANS
(1200-1300)

NORWEGIANS
(950-1100)
St. Olaf Haraldson

LATVIANS
(1200-1300)

PICTS
(563-597)
St. Columba of Iona

SWEDES
(829-1100)
St. Ansgar

LITHUANIANS
(1000-1450)

N. ENGLAND
(635-651)
St. Aidan

DANES
(827-1035)
St. Ansgar

IRELAND
(440-493)
St. Patrick

WALES
(200-400)
Roman Christians

WENDS
(1124-1200)

S. ENGLAND
(597-700)
St. Augustine of C.

FRISIANS
(690-739)
St. Willibrord

SAXONS
(787-805)
St. Boniface

POLAND
(966)
Baptism of Mieszko I

CORNWALL
(500-700)
Welsh and Irish

THURINGIANS
(722-754)
St. Boniface

KIEVAN RUS
(988)

FRANKS
(c.496)
St. Rémy baptizes Clovis

HUNGARIANS
(950-1050)
St. Stephen of Hungary

BURGUNDIANS
(c.500)
St. Avitus baptizes Sigismund

SUEVI
(c.500-600)
St. Martin of Braga

LOMBARDS
(650-700)
Gregory the Great

CROATS
(640-800)

MORAVIA
(862-900)
Sts. Cyril and Methodius

VISIGOTHS
(589)
St. Leander baptizes Reccared

•ROME

[1] Raoul Glaber, Les Cinq Livres de Ses Histoires, III, 4, referring to the springtime of church-building around the year 1000.

The dates on the map refer to the period in which a large part of the population converted. The names indicate important evangelizers.

Etienne-Hippolyte Maindron, *Baptism of Clovis by Saint Remy*, 1865.

of the Burgundians, received him along with thousands of his warriors—as was the mind-set of the barbarians—into the Church. In 575 Columbanus and the Celtic monks disembarked on the shores of Brittany and, like flashes of lightning, crossed France and travelled up the Rhine into Switzerland, then went over the Alps into northern Italy, preaching, founding abbeys, and revitalizing the local churches. In Spain, the magnanimous Visigoth martyr-prince Hermenegild and Bishop Leander of Seville were instrumental in the conversion of the Visigoths under King Reccared I in 589.

To England, in 597, Gregory sent the Roman monk Augustine; within five years King Ethelbert of Kent and several thousand Saxon warriors asked for baptism. The Lombards converted between 653 and 700. Boniface and the Benedictines reinvigorated the Frankish Church and began fostering the conversion of the Saxons and Frisians of Germany and the Netherlands from 716 to 754. Then came that "Indian summer" of the restoration of the Western Roman Empire, transformed through the idealism of Charlemagne, Alcuin, and others into an *imperium Christianum*, at least in valiant aspiration. Cyril and Methodius evangelized the Slavs of Moravia starting in 862. On September 11, 910, the reforming Abbey of Cluny in Burgundy was founded, and by the twelfth century it headed a vibrant order of over three hundred monasteries, a powerful source of renewal for Catholicism.

The north was impenetrable for centuries due to the hostile Vikings who inspired such terror that Catholics of the ninth century added a prayer to the liturgy: *A furore Normannorum libera nos, Domine!* (From the fury of the Northmen deliver us, O Lord!). Finally, one missionary succeeded: the "Apostle of the North", Ansgar (801–865)—whose name means "God's javelin"—penetrated deep into the Norse territories of Denmark and Sweden, using Hamburg as his headquarters. A bold and tenacious individual, he journeyed without any support from Frankish arms, constantly uncertain of the attitude of the Norse kings who wavered between tolerance and persecution. Time and again he met defeat, even the destruction of Hamburg by the Norwegians in 845, but eventually he succeeded in setting up a beachhead at Birka, on Lake Mälaren where the small group of converts included the Swedish king's steward, Hergeir. By 1080 when King Inge wrote to Pope Gregory VII asking for the establishment of two episcopal sees in the nation, Sweden was well on its way to becoming Catholic.

To Iceland Catholics arrived in 874, since at least forty of the original four hundred Viking settlers from Norway under Ingólfur Arnarson included Irish Catholic slaves. Later, from 1000 to 1050, large-scale conversion of the Icelanders occurred. In the fourteenth century the rim of Christendom extended to include Finland, thanks in no small way to the missionary efforts of the Dominicans. Finally, by around 1450, Lithuania also had become part of Christian Europe.

Shouldering Society: Bishops from the Fifth to the Seventh Centuries

During the fifth through the seventh centuries, due to the absence of the political, legal, and military stability of the Roman Empire, Western European society resembled a ship on unknown seas, lashed by high waves. The Church, led by the priesthood, was the only institution capable of taking command of the rudder and navigating because only she knew the direction the ship should be taking to reach a haven of social order. Only the Church had the navigational maps with the knowledge, laws, and traditions from the Old World that had disintegrated. She alone had the vision of history in the light of eternity, and, especially, the supernatural strength that inspirited the stamina necessary to continue at the helm through the long night of centuries during which the storm continued. The priesthood alone, according to both barbarians and Romans, was surrounded by the aura of both religious and intellectual authority as well as by ancient Roman grandeur because Catholic priests were not only the solitary mediators of the sacred but were also the dispensers of Roman law and the holders of the texts of Greco-Roman culture. In this way the Church, led by the priesthood and the monks, had the wherewithal to unite the different peoples of the West within a common culture that would be born from their conversion to the Catholic Faith.

Engelbert Peiffer, *God's Javelin*, Archbishop Ansgar of Bremen, apostle of Denmark and Sweden.

In the vacuum of civil leadership it was particularly the bishops who shouldered responsibility for society because within their ranks were to be found many of the heirs of either imperial officials or converted barbarian leaders. These were the men with the social ascendancy, episcopal authority, training, intelligence, vim, and grit necessary to front the spiritual, moral, social, and economic disorder within the city walls as well as the military menace from without. Although their ancestors had been either Roman aristocrats or barbarian chieftains, these bishops increasingly defined their identity as first and foremost Christian. It is fascinating to see that, generally speaking, one finds in the episcopal ranks the most vital, intelligent, and energetic men of the era: idealists, creators, and organizers. Overachieving youth were drawn to the priesthood as the institution that was on the cutting edge of dealing with the greatest issues of both time and eternity: the defense of all that is truly human in civilization and the leading of men to salvation.

Resolutely they faced toward the future of the Church and not to the past of Rome nor to the increasingly caesaropapist Byzantium. Yet they salvaged all that could be salvaged from the ruins of the ancient city and, with more than a tinge of melancholic admiration, inserted it into the new Christian world they were building. Their grandeur of spirit, devoid of the nationalism that plagues the modern world, can be seen in the way they integrated Burgundians, Franks, Goths, and Romans into a new sociopolitical culture.[11] Acting primarily as *defensores Fidei* (defenders of the Faith), they built up a Church in the West coherent with its divinely established constitution, one which Francis Fukuyama termed "a modern, hierarchical ... and law-governed institution".[12] This task did not estrange them from the everyday physical needs of the people, since well they knew that Catholicism cannot be true to itself without fighting for the integral dignity of each and every person. Consequently these bishops also acted as forceful *defensores civitatis* (defenders of the city).

In their private lives they lived like monks; in their churches they performed the Sacrifice of the Mass with dignity; constantly they reached out to propose the Faith to the pagans of the countryside; and earnestly they cared for the poor and the sick. When armies of Vandals, Huns, Goths, and Lombards appeared on the horizon, these princes of the Church came out of their cathedrals and stood at the head of their people, either negotiating with the enemy as astute rulers or else defending the city walls with the spirit of fearless warriors.

Historical documents show a myriad of such mighty prelates. In Italy, Paulinus of Nola (ca. 354–431), already governor of the region around Naples at twenty-five, on becoming bishop stood up to Alaric the Visigoth when he came to destroy the city. In North Africa, the Bishop of Carthage, Quodvultdeus (died ca. 450), organized resistance to the Vandals who sent him into exile. The list merely in France is lengthy since it is doubtful whether there is a single diocese where the memory of such a priest is not venerated: men like Germanus of Paris, Aignan of Orléans, Felix of Nantes, Didier of Cahors, and Léger of Autun. Rémy of Reims (ca. 437–533) and Vedast of Arras (ca. 463–540), through their friendship, learning, and personal integrity, led Clovis, king of the Franks, to ask for baptism. Exupéry of Toulouse (died ca. 415), besides selling the sacred vessels in order to feed the poor, became such a menace to the Vandals that they exiled him. Anianus of Orléans (358–453) assisted the Roman general Flavius Aetius in resisting the Hunnic army. Germain of Auxerre (ca. 378–ca. 449) went to western France and by his personal prestige succeeded in mitigating the attacks of the Bagaudes and Alans.

Many of them stood before rulers and uttered words like those of Isidore of Seville (ca. 560–636): "You will be king when you act justly, and when you do not act justly you will not be king!"[13] Thomas à Becket was far from being the only bishop to pay with his life for confronting a monarch. He came from a line of men like Praetextatus of Rouen (d. 586), Desiderius of Vienne (d. 607), and one after whom many places in France, Switzerland, and Belgium are named: Saint Léger. This heroic bishop was arrested around A.D. 680 on account of opposition to the tyranny of Ebroin,

---

[11] See Fustel de Coulanges, *Histoire des Institutions Politiques de l'Ancienne France* (Paris: Hachette, 1874), in which the historian recognizes the great open-mindedness and absence of racial prejudice in the Church of those centuries.

[12] Francis Fukuyama, *The Origins of Political Order: From Prehuman Times to the French Revolution* (New York: Farrar, Straus and Giroux, 2011), p. 266.

[13] "Rex eris si recte facies; si non facias, non eris." Isidore of Seville, *Etymologiae*, 9.3.4., col. 342.

mayor of the palace, as well as for demanding moral uprightness from the local elite. His eyes were gouged out and then he was beheaded. But he did not leave the world without leaving a testimony worth gold for the generations to come. For even as he walked to his execution, his only concern was for the salvation of all around him, both friends and enemies.[14]

They offered the Holy Sacrifice, they taught the Faith, they defended the city— and still some. In Nantes, Saint Felix (550–583) organized the city's water supply; at Cahors in southwestern France Saint Desiderius (d. 655) raised fortifications; and in the Rhinelands the prelates built dikes. As a civilization agonized in pain, many Catholic bishops stood like seawalls for humanity, defending the ordinary men and women from both the waves of savage invaders and the incompetence and corruption of native bureaucrats.

Bishops and priests also inspired, educated, and mentored some of the greatest lay statesmen during these centuries. Ouen (609–673) is an outstanding example. During boyhood he had met Columbanus, whose image remained engraved on his heart, inspiring a lifelong pursuit of holiness. As a statesman at the court of King Dagobert of the Franks, where he became chancellor, Ouen, surrounded by power and intrigues, led a life of purity and penance, wearing a hair shirt underneath his robes—a monk without the uniform. After the death of Dagobert he had the chance to follow his heart's desire and became a priest, praying and studying amid solitude—not for long though, since he was named Archbishop of Rouen in 639, where he became a paragon of the true bishop, among other feats restoring peace between Neustria and Austrasia. Another Catholic statesman was Eligius (588–660), who became minister of finance and confidant of King Dagobert and then of Clovis II. His wealth went to the poor and to the foundation of abbeys to where he would escape from time to time until finally his hope of priesthood became reality. Later he was named Bishop of Noyon, about sixty miles north of Paris.

Long is the list of all the outstanding bishops who lived during the Dark Ages and vital their contributions to the safeguarding of the remnants of the old culture and the building of the new one. Perhaps their role can be best summed up and symbolized in the action of Rigobert of Reims (d. 743), who, in order to ensure that the people of his city were safe at night, slept near the ramparts with the keys of the city gate beside him.

Birth of a Remarkable Institution: The Parish

A parish is defined as a part of a diocese that is under the authority of a resident priest, with its church building at the center of the sacramental and liturgical life of the region's Catholics. Up to the third century, there were no parishes anywhere. In the first two hundred years, the Holy Sacrifice of the Mass, the administration of the sacraments, and the care of souls in general were concentrated in the cities where the bishops and clergy lived. It was the cathedral which stood at the center of Christian religious life: this was the church that all Catholics felt was their church although other chapels might exist nearby. In cities where bishops resided, parishes

---

[14] See Joseph Linskill, ed., *La Vie de Saint Leger* ([ca. 980] Paris: Droz, 1937).

only came into existence at the end of the eleventh century. Even then, for a long time, baptism still had to be conferred in the cathedral because no church had its own territory and people. An exception occurred in Rome where, as early as the fourth century, there were quasi-parishes. By the end of the fifth century there were twenty-five of them.

However, beginning in the third century, as the bishops sought to convert the non-Catholic *pagani* (country dwellers), they and their missionaries began leaving the cities where Christianity had first taken root in the largely urban-centered Roman Empire and began penetrating the countryside. There, they established churches with resident priests for the local Christians. The first seem to have been in the east of Europe and the Middle East—about A.D. 320 a decree of the Council of Neocæsarea (Turkey) refers to priests in rural areas and villages as well as in cities. In Gaul during the fourth century, thanks to the missionary thrust begun by Martin of Tours and his monks, increasing numbers of *pagani* converted to Catholicism, churches were built, and priests became resident pastors. A letter from Pope Zosimus in 417 refers for the first time to a rural "*parochia*" in Arles, France.

Many of the parish churches were founded on the lands of great estate owners; others were built close to groups of monks or hermits; others near the tombs of local saints. The choice of location could also be for other motives. For instance, in the area of Alsace in eastern France barbarian tribes often built churches on high ground, frequently on the sites of the local markets and courts of justice. The first church in an area, even after others had been opened, retained a special place in the hearts of the people who would attend the Holy Sacrifice of the Mass there on certain feast days. In Alsace the oldest parishes can often be recognized by the word *kirch* (church), which is sometimes integrated into the name of a village, such as at Kirchberg, where the lovely chapel, with its round tower dedicated to Saint Martin of Tours, still stands. Although initially these parishes had no clearly defined territories attached to them, by the seventh century boundaries had been marked and a priest with authority delegated by the local bishop was resident at each one.

The rural parish was successively called *ecclesia rusticana, parochitana, dioecesis*, and finally, *parochia*, which became *paroisse* in French and "parish" in English. The Latin term *paroecia* is derived from the Greek *paroikia*, which is related to the Greek verb *paroikéin*, meaning to live beside or nearby, a compound of *oikos* (house) and *para* (beside). A *paroikos* was accordingly a neighbor. But it also had another meaning: that of a foreigner living in a country where he has no rights of citizenship. For instance, in the Greek version of the Old Testament Abraham is described as a *paroikos* living in Egypt, and Jacob's sons, since they were a group of foreigners, were called a *paroikia*. In the first two centuries of the Church, Christian corporate self-identity was both *ekklesia* and *paroikia*. *Ekklesia*, a term interpreted to mean "the called-out ones", refers to the nature of the Christian as one who has been called by God to live identified with his salvific plan for humanity. But this necessarily implies becoming a member of the Church, the *paroikia*, the colony of resident "aliens and exiles" in this world (1 Pet 2:11), men and women without citizenship papers because they will not conform to a world that is in opposition to God. In their thoughts and actions they reject the pattern of "this present world but [instead are to] be transformed by the renewal of [their] minds" (Rom 12:2) as they journey resolutely toward the Homeland:

Heaven, the "lasting city" (Heb 13:14). Accordingly, the Church is "*ekklesia* relative to God, *paroikia* relative to the world".[15]

This mystical meaning of "parish" implies that just as groups of exiles care for each other, the *paroikia* of Christians should have the atmosphere of a family where the members, led by the priestly father figure, would care integrally for each other's needs, religious and otherwise—a truly "comprehensive community". In spite of man's perversity this remained the ideal during the Dark Ages, and a very important ideal indeed with great civilizational impact because of the sheer number of parishes. By the eleventh and twelfth centuries, when hardly an inch of ground in Western Europe was not part of some parish, their role in society was well established as the basic cell of the new Christian civilization. Firstly, because it was where men and women went to enlighten and strengthen their souls, often hard-pressed by poverty and pain: "With what serenity one left beautiful gatherings in mysterious churches decorated with inspiring pictures, filled with sweet scents, and enlivened by uplifting sacred music."[16] Secondly, because in a largely rural Europe, the parish became the center of social life—the institution bonding together the population of the countryside into a spiritual family, creating an ethos of solidarity and a sense of belonging for people often living on isolated farms. It became the heart everyone knew they could turn to, the shoulder they could lean on, in the hour of want.

John Emms, *The Saint Bernards to the Rescue* (painted before 1913). The Saint Bernard dogs resemble Bernard de Menthon (ca. 1020–1081), founder of Alpine hospices, and his skillful, great-hearted, and courageous followers who, for a thousand years, have heroically cared for imperiled travellers.

The parish provided not only the sacraments but also for the other needs of soul and body. From the time of Charlemagne and Alcuin in the early ninth century the feature of a school attached to a church became common in the Carolingian Empire; every girl and boy could attend the school free of charge and acquire a basic education. Likewise, if poverty struck at one's door, the parish was a refuge since it was a place where pastors, who were men of the people, showed sensitive compassion to the plight of the suffering.[17]

[15] J. P. Vandenakker, *Small Christian Communities and the Parish* (Kansas City: Sheed and Ward, 1994), p. 16. See also, W. Croce, "The History of the Parish", in *The Parish: From Theology to Practice*, ed. Hugh Rahner (Westminster: Newman Press, 1958), pp. 9–25.

[16] Novalis (Friedrich von Hardenberg), *Christendom or Europe: A Fragment* [1799], in *Novalis: Philosophical Writings*, trans. and ed. Margaret Mahony Stoljar (Albany, N.Y.: State University of New York Press, 1997), p. 138.

[17] This tenderness of priests and bishops toward the poor is illustrated in rather an amusing way by a directive of the Synod of Mâcon in 585: "Bishops' residences should never have dogs lest the poor who come to shelter there be bitten by them." Quoted in Henri Daniel-Rops, *The Church in the Dark Ages* (London: J. M. Dent and Sons, 1959), p. 301.

Throughout many parts of Western Europe from the eleventh century onward parishes institutionalized their ability to bring relief. Pastors placed a quarter of the parochial income from tithes and 50 percent from all donations into a fund that they could draw from to help the needy whose names were written into the parish register, the *matricula*, along with the amount given them. However, not infrequently, the assistance of parish priests went far beyond such aid and sometimes even reached heroic levels. Local histories of countrysides, towns, and villages record the deeds of pastors who gave all for their spiritual sons and daughters during the first millennium.

One of the most colorful of these men, whose sensitivity brought him to high physical altitudes in search of the suffering, was Bernard de Montjou (1020–1081). This offspring of a rich and aristocratic family of Savoy, in spite of the allure of wealth and the offer of a marriage arranged for him by his father, decided to enter the ranks of the clergy in his native diocese of Aosta. By circa 1040, the talented individual was already second-in-command of the diocese. However, when he realized that paganism and nominal Catholicism were still rampant among the Alpine dwellers and in Lombardy, with that restless ardor of the true pastors of souls, he began preaching throughout the region and continued to do so for roughly forty years, bringing about many conversions.

In his diocese there was an Alpine pass that connected the valley of Aosta to the Swiss area of the Valais. The pass, whose highest point is at eight thousand feet above sea level, was at times covered in snow about seven feet deep and with drifts of up to forty feet. Pilgrims travelling to Rome through the pass were at risk from the heavy snowstorms in winter and the avalanches in spring. The enterprising Bernard decided to do something about this. He built a hospice at what is now known as the Great St. Bernard Pass and founded a community of men dedicated to the care of it. From then on, thanks to this diocesan priest of Aosta, the fire of Christlike love blazed amid snow-covered Alpine peaks. For a thousand years, no matter the season, no matter the hour, exhausted and freezing travellers knew they could rely on the chivalrous canons of the Congregation of the Great Saint Bernard, accompanied during centuries by their huge, well-trained dogs named after the daring founder. Symbolic of this millennium-old commitment is the fact that the main entrance of the hospice remains unlocked, day and night. The self-sacrifice of the youths who knocked at the doors of this congregation in order to dedicate their lives to be Christ's watchmen on Alpine heights is astounding. These heroes of the Alps lived in a grim building beside a lake frozen annually during 265 days; where the icy winds of winter do not halt for eight months of the year; where for centuries each winter morning, during the Holy Sacrifice of the Mass, the water to be added to the wine was only brought to the altar from the one heated room of the building immediately before the consecration to avoid it freezing; where, day after day, no matter how harsh the weather, they sent out search parties for travellers in danger and tirelessly cared for the tired, the sick, and all needing shelter.

The valor of such men as Bernard of Montjou is relatively well chronicled. What is far less known is the lifestyle of the ordinary priests who, during that era, spent their lives in parishes. Yet, when plague or famine struck, these priests often proved their mettle. Since we do not have detailed records of such episodes from the first millennium, I will take the liberty of narrating a well-recorded instance of heroism among parish priests during one of the last devastating famines to hit Europe. By seeing how these nineteenth-century priests thought and behaved during the ordeal, we can have an insight into the mentality typical of such a priest. The difference in centuries does not prevent us from attributing the same mind-set to the clergy of the Dark Ages or the medieval period. The truths that shaped the priestly identity and mission had not changed one iota in the course of a millennium: whether in the tenth or the nineteenth century the rank-and-file pastor knew that his God-given role was to live as spiritual father close to his parishioners, no matter the cost.

The insight comes from historical records dealing with the exploits of the clergy of Ireland during the mass starvation of the "Great Famine" of 1845–1850. According to Amartya Sen, the Harvard historian of famines, "[in] no other famine in the world [was] the proportion of people killed as large as in the Irish famines of the 1840s."[18] The cause was a blight that destroyed the potato crop—the staple food for three million of the nation's 8.5 million people—striking down one million persons and forcing another million into exile.

The bravery of Irish priests during those years is a sublime chapter of history. But it was far from being the first one. Others had been written in blood since the early seventeenth century when the British Protestant government began persecuting all Catholics, but especially priests, by means of the Penal Laws. These laws were, according to Edmund Burke, "a complete system, full of coherence and consistency; well digested and well composed in all its parts ... a machine of wise and elaborate contrivance, as well fitted for the oppression, impoverishment and degradation of a people, and the debasement in them of human nature itself, as ever proceeded from the perverted ingenuity of man."[19] For about a hundred years priests were outlawed; they were searched for by informers, bloodhounds, and armed soldiers; they were thrown into prison for the crimes of saying the Mass at "Mass-rocks"; and often they were hung, drawn, and quartered. By the 1840s this type of persecution had ceased. Yet the London government still viewed priests with a mixture of fear and suspicion because of their positions as leaders in an institution that refused to be state-controlled.

When the famine struck, the Irish parish priests, though few in number and with minimal resources, rose to the occasion magnificently,

Sebastiano Ricci, *St. Cajetan Strengthens a Dying Man*, 1727.

---

[18] Amartya Sen (lecture at New York University, 1995), quoted in Cormac Ó Gráda, *Black '47 and Beyond: The Great Irish Famine in History, Economy and Memory* (Princeton, N.J.: Princeton University Press, 1999), p. 3.

[19] Edmund Burke, Letter to Sir Hercules Langrishe, in *The Works of the Right Honourable Edmund Burke*, vol. 6 (London: Thomas McLean, 1823), p. 372.

acting as true spiritual fathers to their suffering children.[20] Their heroism was repeat-edly recognized by non-Catholics and anticlericals. As a British government offi-cial seeking to alleviate the effects of the famine wrote at the time, *"all the Roman Catholic curates* [assistant parish priests] ... *are laboring like tigers for us, working day and night ... [without them] we could not move a stroke."*[21] Even a revolutionary move-ment, the Young Irelanders, although bitter about the Church's refusal to side with them, stated that the priests had cared for the people of their parishes *"with a devotion unsurpassed in the annals of martyrdom"*.[22] One priest, Father Hugh Quigley of Killaloe, narrated his daily existence at the peak of the famine as follows:

> We rise at four o'clock—when not obliged to attend a night call—and proceed on horseback a distance from four to seven miles to hold stations of [the sacrament of] confession for the convenience of the poor country people who ... flock in thousands ... to prepare themselves for the death they look to as inevitable. At these stations we have to remain up to five o'clock p.m. administering both consolation and instruction to the famishing thousands.... The confessions are often interrupted by calls to the dying, and generally, on our way home we have to ... administer the last rites ... to one or more fever patients.
>
> Arrived home, we have scarcely seated ourselves to a little dinner when we are interrupted by groans and sobs of several persons at the door crying out, "I am starv-ing", "if you do not help me I must die", and "I wish I was dead". In truth the priest must either harden his heart against the cry of misery or deprive himself of his usual nourishment to keep victims from falling at his door. After dinner—or perhaps before it is half-over—the priest is again surrounded by several persons, calling on him to come in haste—that their parents, or brothers, or wives, or children are "just depart-ing". The priest is again obliged to mount his jaded pony and endeavor to keep pace with the peasant who trots before him as a guide through glen and ravine and over precipice to his infected hut. This gives but a faint idea of the life of a priest here.[23]

A newspaper account described another priest's schedule: "On last Sunday and Monday week, the broken-hearted clergyman had to drag his own tottering limbs, with scarce an interval of rest, from one corpse to another. In the three subsequent days, exhausted, overcome, feeble and faint, he had still to continue his attendance on the dying; to pass continually from townland to townland; to look on corpse after corpse, to behold, renewed over and over, all the agonies and horrors."[24]

The situation of the clergy in many parts of Ireland was similar to that described in this letter: "The priests are absolutely exhausted having to attend so many sick

---

[20] There were only 2,393 priests in parishes in Ireland in 1845: 1,008 pastors and 1,385 assistant pastors ("curates"); see A. Kerr, *A Nation of Beggars? Priests, People and Politics in Famine Ireland, 1846–1852* (Oxford: Oxford University Press, 1995), p. 48. According to estimates based on the first religious census taken in Ireland by the British government in 1834, Catholics in 1841 were nearly 81 percent of the total population while the combined Protestant total made up most of the remaining 19 percent—in round figures, 6,500,000 Catholics out of the total population of 8,175,000; see "First Report of the Commissioners of Public Instruc-tion, Ireland", *Parliamentary Papers* 33, no. 45 (1835).

[21] Lord Monteagle to Bessborough, October 1, 1846, Monteagle Papers, MS 13, 396, National Library of Ireland, quoted in Kerr, *Nation of Beggars*, p. 48. Italics mine. Lord Monteagle had been Chancellor of the Exchequer in the British government from 1835 to 1839.

[22] *Nation*, July 24, 1847, quoted in Kerr, *Nation of Beggars*, p. 61. Italics mine.

[23] Kerr, *Nation of Beggars*, p. 42.

[24] *Limerick and Clare Examiner*, May 17, 1849. Quoted in the article "Father Thomas Moloney Pleaded for His Starving Flock", Irish Identity, accessed January 20, 2015, http://www.irishidentity.com/stories/molony.htm, courtesy of Matthew Lynch and Austin Hobbs, of *Clare Champion*.

calls and in many instances are obliged to walk, their horses being unable to carry them through want of sufficient feeding and the priest not getting as much as would purchase oats for his horse."[25]

Some priests, perhaps many, even gave away most of their few personal belongings:

> When the terrible scourge of the famine descended upon his [Father Timothy Kelly's] parish from 1845 to 1847, his reaction to the prevailing distress was what one would expect of the pastor and the man sprung from the people. He was in every sense the father of his flock. He organized the provision of meals for the numbers who were starving and when every resource failed he sold all he had, even his horse, to buy food for his people.[26]

It was no surprise, therefore, that as the famine devoured the country many of the clergy became almost as poor as beggars, without decent clothes or even a pair of shoes; indeed, some were almost starving. As a government inspector reported: "In some instances where priests were confined with fever, I found in their cabins nothing available beyond stirabout.... There was no tea, no sugar, no provisions whatever; in some of their huts the wind blew, the snow came in, and the rain dripped."[27]

And yet the Irish priests were not alone in such heroic loyalty. From the frozen landscape of Iceland to the blue waters of the Mediterranean, century after century countless parish priests, whether diocesan or religious, acted as fathers, leaders, organizers, and rescuers of their people when the hour of deadly danger struck. For instance, Father Stefano Bellesini, parish priest of Genazzano, a town in the province of Rome, died during a cholera epidemic on February 2, 1840, while looking after his sick parishioners. When the bubonic plague struck Milan in 1576, the thirty-eight-year-old archbishop, Charles Borromeo, spared no expense and risked every danger in caring for the suffering—and probably paid for it by hastening his own death due to intermittent fever eight years later on November 4, 1584. Mark Twain, describing him as he moved calmly amid the terrified people, stated what could be said of so many unknown parish priests in similar situations through the ages: "He was brave where all others were cowards, full of compassion where pity had been crushed out of all other breasts by the instinct of self-preservation gone mad with terror; cheering all, praying with all, helping all with hand, brain, and purse; at a time when parents forsook their children, the friend deserted the friend, and the brother turned away from the sister while her pleadings were still wailing in his ears."[28]

The parish also exercised a vital role in society from the time of the Dark Ages as a sanctuary of justice. From the sixth century onward, many a man accused unjustly by tyrants or political opponents knew immediately where to find a haven safer than a fortress: the inside of a Catholic church. As soon as he crossed its threshold or held a specified door knocker or rang a certain bell or sat on a certain stone

[25] Letter of Bishop Egan of Kerry to Renehan, April 22, 1846, Renehan papers, MCA, quoted in Kerr, *Nation of Beggars*, p. 170.

[26] Account of the pastorship of Fr. Timothy Kelly, parish priest of Cooraclare and Kilmihil during the Great Famine, in Peter Ryan, *History of Kilmurry Ibrickane* (Old Kilfarboy, County Clare: Old Kilfarboy Society, 2002).

[27] Count P. E. de Strzelecki, agent for the British Association's relief scheme in a letter to Clarendon, August 26, 1848, in *Report and Minutes of Evidence of the Select Committee of the House of Lords on Irish Poor Laws, May 4, 1849*, vol. 16, 979–80, quoted in Kerr, *Nation of Beggars*, p. 171.

[28] Mark Twain, *The Innocents Abroad*, autograph edition (Hartford, Conn., 1869), pp. 231–32.

Ferdinand Georg Waldmüller, *At the Monastery Gate (Am Klostertor),* 1846.

seat near the altar (the "frith-stool"; "frith" meaning peace and freedom), he had gained the "right of asylum" from the state's legal action. There were even certain churches, licensed by the ruler, that offered asylum within a surrounding zone whose boundaries were marked by stones or crosses. This legal right was granted in France by the Council of Orléans in 511 and was confirmed by subsequent councils. In England, King Ethelbert made the first laws of sanctuary-asylum around A.D. 600, and by the eleventh century there were at least twenty-two churches with charters for a sanctuary zone. Bishops and priests defended the right of sanctuary by unsheathing the sword of excommunication for anyone foolhardy enough to violate the sacred threshold. The right was one of the greatest assurances of justice in societies where the poor, then as now, were in great need of protection. It gave the forces of justice time to cool down and, in the case of those who were guilty, offered a breathing space in which they could make their peace with God through sacramental confession.

How many of those priests who during the Dark Ages created and built up parishes—who, Sunday after Sunday, rang the bells of the belfry to call their people to the Holy Sacrifice of the Mass; who ensured that, century after century, their people would have safe havens in stormy hours—would certainly merit the title once given by Pope Saint Gregory the Great to the bishop Melanius of Rennes: "The Father and the Fatherland of all Unfortunates"![29]

> The foundation of rural parishes is therefore a fact of great historical importance, and one which goes far beyond the bounds of religious history alone. As Ferdinand Lot has noticed in his book, *Naissance de la France* [*Birth of France*] ... the parishes were to be the basic cells of the nation until the revolution [of 1789].... Those who see our French village churches as something more than quaint rural scenes, those who see these village communities as represented first and foremost by the belfry and the churchyard, which tell of man's fidelity to the earth and his aspirations to heaven, must pause a long time before this fact. What would our villages be if they were not also parishes? Remote places, miserable slums, lost in the midst of the countryside, bodies without souls. For the folk who lived on the land the foundation of the rural parishes was as important as the emancipation of the communes was for the folk in the towns. In the towns themselves—Pierre Champion has described how it happened in Paris—it was the parishes which created the "quartiers", each with its own distinctive character. *We Western Christians owe a great deal to the men who created these centers of worship.*[30]

[29] Quoted in Daniel-Rops, *Church in the Dark Ages,* p. 265.
[30] Ibid., p. 262. Italics added.

Hence, during long dark centuries and afterward, men, women, and children slept easier at night because of the strong, outstretched arms of these parish churches that served as true havens for humanity. Europe for fifteen hundred years was conscious of how much it owed to this remarkable institution and to those men of the people who watched over them. But do we still realize it? What occurred during the Dark Ages through the parish is today a story seldom thought about. Yet it is worthy of being carefully pondered. Our epoch, like that of the Dark Ages, is also one of cultural turmoil, one in which men and women live atomistic existences amid increasingly soulless megacities. Could the intrinsic vital force of the parish-institution, built on an integral living of the Catholic Faith, not play an analogous role in our times for the Christianization and transformation of secularized societies?

Francisco de Herrera el Mozo, *Pope Saint Leo the Great*, 17th century.

The Hair's Breadth

Today with the advantage of hindsight, we take it for granted that the Catholic Church did step forward into the breach of civilization during the Dark Ages—that its bishops, priests, and monks were those creative minorities who preserved classical literature, christened the barbarian warriors, educated their sons and daughters, instituted the parish, and began seeding the furrows of society with a new culture. But events need not have occurred in this way. Let us not be fatalistic. Just as a recent book of military history, *How Hitler Could Have Won World War II*, points out the moments when the Nazis might have made different decisions that could have led to the swastika's victory, so likewise during the fifth to the eighth centuries only a hair's breadth separated the West from actions or omissions that would have prolonged the age of darkness for one shudders to think how long.[31]

The hair's breadth of a difference was due in no small measure to the thought and action of the Catholic priesthood headed by the four men we shall consider in the next chapter: Ambrose, Augustine, Leo the Great, and Gregory the Great. Standing at the helm of society during the Dark Ages, these extraordinary individuals guided Western Europe with its barbarians and Romans into the harbor of a common culture of Catholic matrix. These four towering giants of genius and government, "the choice and master spirits of this age",[32] sealed the future of the West in so decisive a manner that they merit the title "Fathers of Western Culture".

[31] Bevin Alexander, *How Hitler Could Have Won World War II* (New York: Three Rivers Press / Random House, 2001).

[32] William Shakespeare, *Julius Caesar*, Ignatius Critical Editions, edited by Joseph Pearce (San Francisco: Ignatius Press, 2015), act 3, scene 1, line 164, p. 70.

Chapter 3

FATHERS OF WESTERN CULTURE:
AMBROSE, AUGUSTINE, LEO, AND GREGORY

The breakdown of the political organization of the Roman Empire had left a great void which no barbarian king or general could fill, and this void was filled by the Church as the teacher and law-giver of the new peoples. The Latin Fathers—Ambrose, Augustine, Leo and Gregory— were in a real sense the fathers of Western culture, since it was only in so far as the different peoples of the West were incorporated in the spiritual community of Christendom that they acquired a common culture.

—Christopher Dawson, *Religion and the Rise of Western Culture*

Ambrose: Defender of the City

Born around 338 into one of the patrician families that had been part of the ruling elite of the Roman Empire, Ambrose in his early thirties became governor of the northern Italian provinces of Emilia and Liguria. In 374, by acclamation, the people declared that they wanted him as Bishop of Milan. For over twenty-four years, as a mirror of the ideal shepherd, Ambrose taught, sanctified, and ruled the diocese that was the capital of the Western Empire.

Notwithstanding his admiration and love for ancient Rome, for its literature, art, and law, Ambrose thought of himself first and foremost as Catholic and as a priest of Jesus Christ. Spontaneously he applied to himself the cry of Saint Paul: "None of us lives to himself, and none of us dies to himself. If we live, we live to the Lord, and if we die, we die to the Lord; so then, whether we live or whether we die, we are the Lord's" (Rom 14:7–8). And for him the natural outcome of acknowledging Jesus

Anthony van Dyck, *St. Ambrose Bars Emperor Theodosius the Great from Entering Milan Cathedral,* 1616/1617.

32

Christ as Lord and Savior was Catholicism, the very ground of his existence. There-fore, when he spoke of "our ancestors" he was referring not to Romulus and Remus but to Peter and Paul, and behind them to the Jewish patriarchs and prophets. These convictions resonated in sermons of alternating ardor and tenderness where depth of Christian thought sparkled with the literary style reminiscent of Cicero and Virgil. He also composed numerous hymns and improved the liturgy, efforts motivated by a vehement desire to enlighten men's minds and energize their wills unto deeper Christian conversion.

In the *Hexameron*, his commentary on the creation of the world, we catch a glimpse of the sensitive prelate's love of nature, particularly his fascination with the sea:

> When the sea foams with its surging white caps and mounting billows, or when it bedews the rocks with its snowy spray, or even when under a balmy breeze it shimmers, often in this case presenting itself to the beholder from afar in colors of purple, suggesting serene tranquillity. Such is the aspect of the sea when it does not beat the nearby shores with the onrush of its waves, but when the waters greet them, as it were, in a fond embrace of peace. How gentle is the sound, how pleasing the splash of the water, how pleasant and rhythmic the wave-beats![1]

Ambrose had a special care for the downtrodden. When Augustine, eager to get close to the renowned bishop, first saw him in Milan, he found it difficult to do so on account of the crowds of poor people surrounding him. Moreover, Ambrose vigorously promoted social justice by telling the rich that those in need had a right to their wealth. The same revolutionary Christian spirit, so alien to ancient Rome, showed itself in his sensitivity to the dignity of woman. "Lay aside the inordinate emotions of your heart and the rudeness of your manners when you meet your patient wife. Get rid of your obstinacy when your gentle consort offers you her love. You are not a master, but a husband. You have not acquired perchance a handmaid, but a wife. God designed you to be a guide to the weaker sex, not a dictator. Be a sharer in her activities. Be a sharer in her love."[2] How extraordinary, indeed strange, some of these writings must have appeared to the remnant of old pagan aristocrats and intellectuals! How they must have wondered how a man, born into the ruling class of ancient Rome, could ever have penned such assertions! "Almost unknown to himself, the Gospel had turned this conservative into a revolutionary."[3]

But it was as a man of government in Christ's Church that he made the deepest impression on the imagination of the West for two millennia. By carrying out his duties as bishop to their extreme implications, he showed the Church and society that the Catholic priest is no tool of the state, but a leader who stands on the front steps of the Church to be the voice of Christ and the guide of society in politics,

---

[1] St. Ambrose, *Hexameron* 3.5.21, in *St. Ambrose: Hexameron, Paradise, and Cain and Abel*, ed. John J. Savage, vol. 42, in *The Fathers of the Church: A New Translation* (New York: Fathers of the Church, 1961), pp. 82–83.

[2] Ibid., 5.7.19, p. 174.

[3] Henri Daniel-Rops, *The Church of Apostles and Martyrs* (London: J.M. Dent and Sons, 1960), p. 589. Ambrose thus exemplified what will be seen time and again throughout the Dark Ages, that the "progressives" who laid the foundations of the new Christian civilization were never conservatives but were always traditionalists, i.e., men loyal to the eternally valid and ever vibrantly relevant principles of Catholicism. As Pope St. Pius X stated: "The true friends of the people are neither the revolutionaries nor the innovators but the traditionalists". Pope St. Pius X, *Notre Charge Apostolique*, August 25, 1910, in *Acta Apostolicae Sedis*, Typis Polyglottis Vaticanis, 1910, vol. 18, p. 803.

economics, and culture—that he is *defensor civitatis* (defender of the city) because he is *defensor Fidei* (defender of the Faith). Ambrose, though a man of refined tact, friend to the emperors Gratian and Theodosius, and mentor to the young Valentinian II, was a fighter when it came to claiming the Church's rights. Boldly he proclaimed, "The Emperor is in the Church, not above it", and declared that bishops must not fail to rebuke erring rulers.[4]

Ambrose burnt the lesson into the memory of the West through his confrontation with Emperor Theodosius the Great. For in November 390 Ambrose excommunicated the generally upright but rather hotheaded ruler for his massacre of thousands of innocent people in Thessalonica, telling him that it would only be after he had done penance for his sin that he could again cross the threshold of the basilica and receive Holy Communion. His letter to Theodosius combined utmost finesse with unflinching firmness:

> You shall then make your offering when you have received permission to sacrifice, when your offering shall be acceptable to God. Would it not delight me to enjoy the favour of the Emperor, to act according to your wishes, if the case allowed it? ... Are not those who condemn their own sin, rather than those who defend it, the true Christians? ... He who accuses himself when he has sinned is just, not he who praises himself.... Thanks be to the Lord who wills to chastise His servants that He may not lose them. This I have in common with the prophets, and you shall have it in common with the saints.... I follow you with my love, my affection, and my prayers. If you believe me, be guided by me; if, I say, you believe me, acknowledge what I say; if you believe me not, pardon that which I do in that I set God before you. May you, most august Emperor, with your holy offspring, enjoy perpetual peace with perfect happiness and prosperity.[5]

After a month's delay in which shocked courtiers urged the emperor not to give in, the ruler of the Roman Empire took off his imperial robes at Christmas and donned the penitent's clothing, walking through the square of Milan to the cathedral where Ambrose welcomed him. "He threw to the ground all the royal attire he was wearing," said Ambrose in his sermon at the emperor's funeral in 395, "he wept publicly in church over his sin.... What private citizens blush to do the emperor did not blush to do: to perform public penance; and afterwards not a day passed on which he did not grieve for that fault of his."[6] When Theodosius was on his deathbed he called for Ambrose. Commenting on his relationship with the emperor, the bishop stated with emotion: "I have loved a man who, in his last moments and with his last breath, kept asking for me. I have loved a man who, in the very moment he was being set free from the body, was more anxious about the state of the churches than about his own dangers. Yes, I have loved, I admit it, and for that reason my grief has pained me to the core of my being."[7]

---

[4] St. Ambrose of Milan, *The Sermon against Auxentius*, in *Patristica Latina*, 217 vols. (Paris: J. P. Migne, 1841–1855), 16:1018b (the first number is that of the volume, the second of the column); hereafter cited as *PL*.

[5] St. Ambrose of Milan, Letter 51, in *Nicene and Post-Nicene Fathers*, 2nd series, ed. Philip Schaff and Henry Wace, vol. 10 (Buffalo, N.Y.: Christian Literature Publishing, 1896), p. 452.

[6] Ambrose of Milan, "Oration on the Death of Theodosius I", *Ambrose of Milan: Political Letters and Speeches*, trans. with an introduction and notes by J. H. W. G. Liebeschuetz (Liverpool, England: Liverpool University Press, 2005), p. 193.

[7] Ibid.

The submission of Theodosius was one of the most stunning and symbolic moments of Western civilization. The painting of the event by Subleyras depicts men looking on in staggered amazement at what is occurring. As indeed they might! That dramatic scene of a bishop's hand raised in absolution, and an emperor dressed in penitential purple kneeling before him, showed the social pyramid of the ancient world turned upside down. The successors of bishops, who only a century before had been executed in amphitheatres by emperors, now judged these emperors within their basilicas. The Caesars who had often behaved as if *L'État, c'est moi* (I am the state) now recognized themselves as subjects of the natural law and accepted the Catholic Church as its custodian. It was nothing less than a revolution, one that was mightier and deeper than the French Revolution of 1789 and its like. Thus Ambrose, faithful to his priestly duties as teacher, sanctifier, and man of government, sealed the conscience of Western man in a way unknown to other civilizations for almost two thousand years.

Pierre Subleyras, *Bishop Ambrose of Milan Absolves Emperor Theodosius*, 1740.

The great bishop died in Milan during the night of Good Friday in 397. Right unto the end he worked at a rhythm that astonished his contemporaries. The day after his death, five bishops struggled to baptize the crowd of catechumens that Ambrose had normally brought into the Church singlehandedly. On his deathbed, with his arms wide open in the form of a cross, his lips moving in silent prayer, his dying became the final act of a lifelong thrust for mystical identification with Jesus Christ, Crucified and Risen, through fulfillment of the priestly mission.[8]

Augustine: Converter of Culture

Man of His Century and of Every Century

Augustine was born on November 13, 354, in the area of modern-day Algeria at Thagaste, now Souk-Ahras, a town close to the Mediterranean. Surrounded by mountains with holly-oak forests where lions and leopards roamed, Thagaste, with its high white walls that glistened in sunlight, was in a valley of olive groves, lush vineyards,

---

[8] This interpretation of the death of Ambrose is from Benedict XVI, "General Audience", October 24, 2007, http://w2.vatican.va/content/benedict-xvi/en/audiences/2007/documents/hf_ben-xvi_aud_20071024.html. See Benedict XVI, *The Fathers of the Church: Catecheses: St. Clement of Rome to St. Augustine of Hippo* (New York: K.S. Giniger, 2009), p. 99.

Ary Scheffer, *Augustine with Monica*,
ca. 1846.

and flourishing cornfields through which flowed the Mejerda. He was a Berber, a Numidian, and thus, although we have no description of his appearance, it is not unlikely that he was a typical member of his people—tall, long-limbed, with bronzed skin, a high forehead, and striking black eyes. As a child he soon showed his hot-blooded, wild temperament as well as a brilliant mind. He tolerated no restraint on his passions, except, sometimes, that of his gentle and intensely Catholic mother, Monica, whom he dearly loved.

His father, hoping the youth would make his reputation as a public speaker and teacher, sent him to study at Madaura and Carthage. In the latter, "the city of Venus", amid the seething excitement of a world of forbidden pleasures, the eighteen-year-old Augustine took a mistress and had a child by her—rather exceptional for someone so young even there. But the city also lit other fires in him—for philosophy, by putting in his hands the *Hortensius* of Cicero, and for religion, by enmeshing him in the circles of the esoteric, confused, and pseudo-Christian sect of the Manichees. From 374 to 383 in Thagaste and Carthage he worked as a rhetorician. Then he headed for Rome, where he failed to find a job with an adequate salary and ended up living in a hovel for several months. His Manichee friends came to the rescue by securing for him an excellent position as professor of rhetoric in Milan.

It seemed that finally, at thirty years of age, his ambitions were about to be achieved; and yet, interiorly, a rising sense of having reached a dead end was gnawing at his mind and heart, for by then he had recognized Manichaeism to be a hollow religion, and his own lifestyle as unworthy of one who sought wisdom.

In Milan he met one of the men who publicly embodied the grandeur of Catholicism in that century. As he listened to Ambrose preach in the cathedral, he began to understand the Catholic Faith as the wisdom that calls on man to travel to the utter frontiers of reason in the quest for life's ultimate meaning. Yet he also came to realize that on reaching those borders it is necessary to accept that only by a revelation from the Creator of the universe can the ultimate truths about God and man, time and eternity, be known; and only through an authoritative institution with divine credentials, the Church, can such a revelation be preserved and rightly interpreted. Thus, the Bible and the Catholic Church, for so long objects of derision to him, turned into subjects for reverential and intense reflection. The more his brilliant mind came to understand, the more it seemed that all his experiences up to that moment had led him toward Catholicism as the answer to his raging desires for truth, love, and happiness. And from then on, new ideas that he encountered in his studies of Plato and the Neoplatonists were viewed through the prism of the Faith.

But yet he held back from crossing the Church's threshold—or, rather, he was held back by semi-enslavement to the pleasures of the body. The combat between "the two men in me" grew ever more violent. The passions led him, even then, to take a new mistress. However, divine providence placed people on his path who encouraged him to cross the Rubicon for the sake of Christ—Pontitian, his compatriot who inspired him with the examples of other converts to Catholicism like the imperial officials of Trèves who had left everything to devote their lives to God; and a priest who described the conversion of the great Victorinus, the famous Neoplatonist.

Then came the moment when divine grace mysteriously broke through the barriers of darkness in Augustine's soul. It was probably in the spring of 386 amid the peaceful gardens of his friend's villa outside Milan, at Cassiciacum, beside serene Lake Como, with the Alps on the horizon. "And thou, O Lord, how long? How long, O Lord?" the anguished man cried out. "How long, how long? Tomorrow and tomorrow? Why not now? Why not this very hour make an end to my uncleanness now?"[9] It was then that he heard a child singing nearby and the words were "Pick it up, read it; pick it up, read it."[10] Rising to his feet he quickly went to where his friend Alypius sat with the letters of Saint Paul alongside him. The pages fell open on chapter 13 of the Letter to the Romans: "[L]et us conduct ourselves becomingly as in the day, not in reveling and drunkenness, not in debauchery and licentiousness, not in quarreling and jealousy. But put on the Lord Jesus Christ, and make no provision for the flesh, to gratify its desires" (Rom 13:13–14). Light flooded his soul; supernatural strength entered his will—his prayer had been answered.

On the evening of April 24 or 25, in 387, together with his son, Adeodatus, and his friend Alypius, Augustine received baptism at the hands of Ambrose.

All of these dramatic events that shaped his soul were laid bare with transparent sincerity in the *Confessions*, written about ten years later. It is, above all, an "Epistle to God" (Papini), a passionate cry of gratitude from a soul of genius conscious of all that he had received, disclosing intimate secrets as evidence of God's providential love. Alongside a few other works such as the *Summa Theologiae* of Saint Thomas Aquinas and the *Divina Commedia* of Dante, it ranks as one of the great intellectual masterpieces produced by Western civilization. It marked the beginning of a new literary genre, the autobiography of deep introspection alerting man to the cosmos within him: "Men go forth to marvel at the heights of mountains and the huge waves of the sea, the broad flow of the rivers, the vastness of the ocean, the orbits of the stars, and yet they neglect to marvel at themselves."[11] The *Confessions* have placed Augustine among history's great psychologists, but unlike Freud and others, he pointed to the soul's relationship with the God of Christianity as the ultimate meaning that answers so much anguish and heals so many wounds.

These memoirs only bring us to the start of Augustine's life as a Christian. Another thirty-four years would follow in which this man of fragile health, suffering from terrible insomnia, asthma, and chronic bronchitis, accomplished projects that leave one astounded. As his life on earth came to an end, Augustine listed no fewer than

---

[9] St. Augustine, *Confessions and Enchiridion*, trans. and ed. Albert C. Outler (Philadelphia: Westminster Press, 1955), 8–12, p. 131.

[10] Ibid.

[11] St. Augustine, *Confessions* (Mineola, N.Y.: Dover Publications, 2002), 10.8, p. 180. Unless otherwise indicated, all subsequent quotations from the *Confessions* are from this edition.

232 books he had authored. Alongside these are over 300 sermons and 250 letters that have come down to us out of a total that probably runs into thousands. He had an analytic mind capable of swiftly pinpointing truth and error; the range of themes went from the most abstract metaphysical problems to extremely practical questions in litigations. Philosopher, poet, mystic, man of government—one stands in admiration before such an intellect reinforced by a powerful memory and a seemingly endless ability to work.

And yet there is something else in Augustine that attracts men and women of every century: his deep humanity. To read the *Confessions*—one of the clearest portraits of the new type of man shaped by the convergence of classical and Christian culture—is to feel a warm empathy with this passionate priest who knew the burning emotions of the soul and the extraordinary ardor required to live out genuine love. "To love and to be loved was sweet to me",[12] he said of his youth, a love sought amid the mysteries of sexuality, deep friendships, and philosophy, as well as amid the beauties of nature. Love is the key to understanding him, his conversion to Catholicism, and his vision of society. Even as old age crept over him, his love for God and people—not a nameless mankind but concrete individual persons—remained sensitive. But it was the passionate love of God that penetrated and transformed his love for others, a love born from the power of divine light and energy that had rushed upon his soul in the foothills of the Alps, had penetrated his being at baptism, and had flourished amid the natural grandeur of his fiery and enthusiastic spirit. His phrase "Only love, and do what you will!",[13] so often quoted and so often misunderstood, means that for the man who loves God and neighbor unto self-sacrifice, life is sheer freedom for excellence through the emancipation it brings from enslavement to disordered passions.

One is left with no doubt that for Augustine God is no abstract idea but a living reality whom he has come to know personally. His sermons and books are distilled from his own intensely lived experience—there is no gap between thought, expression, and lifestyle. The God whom he had come to know in Jesus Christ was the axis of his existence. All he wanted was to be with the One who had rescued him so unexpectedly from his misery and whom he loved as the Great Lover of humanity, dwelling within him by grace, and enlightening every dimension of his existence.

Intellect and Heart Forged by Priesthood

After his entry to the Church, Augustine returned to North Africa, sold off his inheritance, giving much of it to the poor, and in the autumn of 388 established an informal monastery at Thagaste, where he, along with his talented seventeen-year-old son, Adeodatus, and his friends Alypius and Evodius, could study, contemplate, pray, and write. Thus would he have happily spent the rest of his life. But it was not to be: after three years, in 391, during a sermon in the basilica of Hippo in which Bishop Valerius spoke of his pressing need for a priest, the Catholics of the city surrounded Augustine, demanded that he be the one, then seized him and forced him toward the bishop's throne. Such spontaneity was common in the Church of those

---

[12] Ibid., 3.1, p. 31.
[13] St. Augustine, *Homily 7 on the First Epistle of St. John*, 8.

Carle van Loo, *St. Augustine Preaching before Valerius, Bishop of Hippo*, 1755.

days, as Ambrose had already discovered. The reluctant candidate, recognizing in this *vox populi* a sign of God's providence, assented to the capture and agreed to ordination. In 395 he succeeded Valerius as bishop.

Entrance to the Church's priesthood was a dramatic change for Augustine. While still at Thagaste he compared his intellectual life to the priestly lifestyle, remarking, "There is nothing better or more exquisite than to be able to search in the solitude of silence for the divine treasure ... [but] on the other hand, preaching, reproving, correcting, building—worrying about this and that—what a dreadful responsibility and effort! Who would not run from a task of this kind?"[14] Nevertheless, it was the priesthood, especially in its highest degree of the episcopacy, that would decisively forge the character and intellect of Augustine. Were he to have remained in his monastic-style oasis, he would probably still have authored impressive works of literature, the West would still have had her literary genius, and the Church might, presumably, still have acknowledged a saint. But it would have been a different type of genius and a dissimilar form of saint, one resembling Cassiodorus (ca. 500–ca. 585), who composed his educational philosophy and helped preserve classical literature in the seclusion of the school and library at Vivarium in southern Italy, or like Cassian (360–435), who had written on monasticism and mysticism from his monastery at Marseilles.

The priesthood forged Augustine because its mission of teaching, sanctifying, and governing in the Church vigorously thrust him away from any tendency to make

[14] Quoted in Henri Daniel-Rops, *The Church in the Dark Ages* (London: J. M. Dent and Sons, 1959), p. 22.

culture an end in itself, remote from the urgencies of the moment, and from the overarching purpose of life. It perfected his ardent, turbulent power for love, transforming it into energy at the service of the people since the priesthood exists not for the fulfillment of the individual who receives it but for the benefit of those whom he shepherds. "Another Christ" is the ideal placed before him; the embodiment of Christian virtue is what the people expect of him. No matter the century, the priest or bishop is at the center of the Catholic community and must live close to it, in body and spirit since, in the sight of God, he bears the responsibility for doing everything possible to ensure the salvation of his flock. Hence, the sacrament of Holy Orders vitalized dimensions of Augustine that would otherwise have remained dormant; it widened his vision, extended the radius of his influence, and burdened him with innumerable tasks that placed the intellectual at the hub of ordinary life. All of the responsibilities that came with ordination impelled him with even greater urgency to penetrate the meaning of the Catholic Faith not just for himself but for the people who looked up at him expectantly each Sunday desiring to hear words of light and strength in that terrible age.

The bishop in the fifth century was no distant figure to the rank-and-file Catholic but one who fathered all the material, moral, and spiritual responsibilities for his flock, including the administration of the Church's wealth. Not one of these dimensions did Augustine shirk even if, in order to allot more time elsewhere, he delegated the economic management to others, merely reviewing annual reports. The poor were a special concern of his; he even took on heavy debts for their sake, would even occasionally melt down sacred vessels in order to redeem captives—something he knew that Ambrose had also done—and encouraged each parish to provide clothes for its poor once a year. The bishop's social importance was acknowledged by the state; since Constantine's reign he held judicial authority and was called upon to decide numerous legal disputes. This obliged him at times to stand between any oppressed members of the Church and the despotic imperial machine of decadent Rome. All such needs and cares, loaded onto his heart by those around him, must have flung him to his knees to pray with even greater intensity.

There in Hippo—the modern Algerian town of Annaba—with its enchanting bay and its hillsides covered with olive groves and tall pines, he was everyone's bishop. His affectionate and attractive personality drew non-Christians close, and he would invite them to eat with him. But he brooked no compromise or appearance of compromise with evil—Catholics who publicly sinned in a serious matter and would not repent were not to be seen at his table, and he rigorously applied the penalties of the Church to them, although always with courtesy and inviting them to a change of heart. This winning combination of moral coherence, great-heartedness, and modesty marked all his dealings with others. It grieved him to see fellow Catholics like Jerome and Rufinus quarreling, for he reckoned that such disputes often occur "not because it is true but because it is their own. Otherwise they could equally love another true opinion, as I love what they say when what they speak is true—not because it is theirs but because it is true, and therefore not theirs but true".[15] When the gruff Saint Jerome became angry with him, even remarking on Augustine's

---

[15] St. Augustine, *Confessions* 12.25, p. 260.

ignorance of Greek, the Bishop of Hippo wrote back: "And again, I beseech you to correct boldly whatever you see needful to censure in my writings. For although, so far as the titles of honor which prevail in the Church are concerned, a bishop's rank is above that of a presbyter, nevertheless, in many things Augustine is inferior to Jerome."[16] Jerome was won over.

Each Sunday the crowds of Hippo went to the Basilica of Peace to hear him preach. They loved their bishop and knew that he loved them: "I do not wish to be saved without you", he told them. "What is the purpose of my life? My only purpose is that we should live together in Christ. This is my passion, my honor, my riches; this is my joy and my glory."[17] Seated in his *cathedra*, at a distance of only fifteen feet from the first row of his audience, Augustine well knew that his fellow Numidians would only enter into his ideas if he first entered into their passions. So he would start with the problems worrying them, talking in a straightforward manner in a Latin they could well understand; pleasing their North African love of subtlety in language, holding them spellbound with his ability to reason out a biblical text as if it were a riddle; becoming emotional about what moved both them and him: happiness, love, fear, guilt, peace; and more than once reducing them to tears. At times they would interrupt him to finish off one of his biblical quotations; other times they applauded; on occasion they would quietly gripe when he called for an end to some semipagan practices. As the sermon went on, Augustine would ask for a moment of silence because his frail voice tired quickly.

The love of God and the hope springing from union with Jesus Christ were the leitmotifs of all his preaching. Frequent was his call to reflect on the goal of life, for "even if the Lord's day, the Last Judgment, be some distance away, is your day of death far off?"[18] Urgency about conversion marked his sermons: "God, who has promised pardon to the penitent sinner, has nowhere promised to one who delays his conversion a morrow to do penance in."[19] Sincerity of Christian life should be seen in outreach to the poor, one of the great questions at man's final judgment. Sixty-nine of his sermons are about the saints whom Christians are called to honor and invoke as intercessors. Prayer for the souls in Purgatory he often recommended.[20]

Augustine, convinced that he would fulfill his duties toward his people in the measure of his own interior strength, turned the episcopal residence into a type of monastery. There, he and the priests, deacons, and clerics who lived with him adopted a community lifestyle committed to pursuing Christian excellence. They renounced personal property and lived austerely: plain furnishings, no silver cutlery except spoons; dishes of wood, stone, or earthenware; eating together their meals of bread and vegetables with a little wine while listening to a reading or discussing matters of the spirit. Augustine, who made the adoption of this lifestyle a condition for ordination to the priesthood, laid out its principles in two sermons and in a letter written in 423. Later generations would order them into a program

---

[16] St. Augustine, Letter 82 to St. Jerome, in *Nicene and Post-Nicene Fathers*, 1st series, ed. Philip Schaff and Henry Wace, vol. 1 (Buffalo, N.Y.: Christian Literature Publishing, 1896), p. 361.

[17] St. Augustine, Sermon 17.2.

[18] Ibid., 1.

[19] St. Augustine, Sermon 39.

[20] St. Augustine, Sermon 172.

for religious life known as the "Rule of St. Augustine", which became the core of the statutes for important orders of the Middle Ages like the Augustinians, Dominicans, and Norbertines.

Blueprints for a New Culture

As the barbarians broke through the imperial frontiers in the fifth century, Roman civilization, already in decay, went into a free fall. Augustine had come to recognize more and more clearly as he got closer to Catholicism that not only was the sociopolitical structure of Rome inept to protect life and liberty but that its culture offered no propaedeutic for man's salvation. Cicero, Virgil, and Plato provided pillars of wisdom rich in literary excellence but not foundations for the soul or society. Only on the truths of Jesus Christ, Augustine realized, could the mind of man and the structures of a new civilization be built. Christ must be the Lord of one's intellect; everything considered valuable in the old order must be reappraised in the light of his teachings; nothing could be left outside of his dominion. His powerful intellect and fine sensibility were now focused on the person and truth of the God-Man with consuming passion. To a friend who had sent him some literary bagatelle he replied: "What do these verses matter? In them I only see a soul and a mind that I cannot offer to God."[21]

The implications for culture and civilization were drawn out, one after the other, from the overarching Christian vision of man and history. The most important branch of knowledge was theology since it "begets, nourishes, defends and strengthens that most wholesome faith".[22] Augustine was emphatically clear: reason was to be respected and pushed to its limits in order to clarify man's understanding of the Catholic Faith. There was no clash between philosophy and Christianity. Augustine showed how reason fortified faith in his masterpiece *On the Trinity* by using the philosophies of Plato, the Neoplatonists, and Aristotle to clarify the meaning of Christian doctrines. "Before faith you must understand in order to believe, after faith you must believe in order to understand."[23] But philosophy by the fifth century was stagnant. Christianity, through the genius of Augustine, reinvigorated it with monumentally original insights in metaphysics, epistemology, ethics, and psychology. The North African bishop pioneered new trails of thought that, through two millennia, have inspired intellectuals whose differing and often discordant interpretations of so many of his ideas witness to its complexity and grandeur, equaled in the history of philosophy only by Aristotle, Plato, and Thomas Aquinas. Medieval thinkers particularly built upon his theories. Thomas Aquinas, for example, using Augustine's theology, defined sin as "a word, deed, or desire contrary to the eternal law".[24] Even when the Dominican largely disagreed with the great North African on topics such as the divine illumination in man's normal mode of cognition, he always sought to incorporate as many of Augustine's insights as he deemed to be true.[25] Another medieval theologian whose work shows the

---

[21] St. Augustine, Letter 26 to Licentius.
[22] St. Augustine, *De Trinitate* 14.1.3.
[23] St. Augustine, Sermon 43.7.
[24] St. Thomas Aquinas, *Summa Theologiae* Ia–IIae, q. 88, a. 1.
[25] St. Thomas Aquinas, *Summa Theologiae* I, qq. 75–89.

imprint of Augustine is Anselm of Canterbury, notably in his ontological argument for God's existence.[26] In *The Journey of the Mind to God*, a work of the Franciscan theologian Bonaventure, one sees a wholehearted admirer of Augustine's integration of philosophy and theology.

The prestige of Augustine was immense during the millennium after his death. Popes and councils regarded him as one of the great champions of orthodoxy in the face of heresies such as Pelagianism, Donatism, Arianism, and Manichaeism: "It is Augustine", declared John II in 534, "that the Roman Church follows and [thereby] safeguards her doctrines."[27] But even long after medieval Christendom had disintegrated, he remained an important point of reference among Western intellectuals. To cite just one instance: his powerful influence on the conversion to Catholicism of the English intellectual John Henry Newman (1801–1890). While reading an article in which the position of the African Donatists of Augustine's time was likened to that of the Anglicans, Newman came across a quotation from the Bishop of Hippo that utterly stunned him since it showed that doctrinal conflicts in the ancient Church had been resolved on the basis of the principle of universality (catholicity)—that Augustine had appealed to the *securus judicat orbis terrarum*, the secure judgment by the Catholic (universal) Church as the infallible criterion:

> "Securus judicat orbis terrarum!" [a phrase whose meaning is elsewhere stated by Newman as, "The universal Church, in her judgments, is sure of the Truth"]. What a light was hereby thrown upon every controversy in the Church! ... The deliberate judgment, in which the whole Church at length rests and acquiesces, is an infallible prescription.... For a mere sentence the words of St Augustine struck me with a power which I never had felt from any words before.... They were like the "Tolle, lege, Tolle, lege," of the child which converted St Augustine himself. "Securus judicat orbis terrarum!" By those great words of the ancient Father, interpreting and summing up the long and varied course of ecclesiastical history, the theology of the Via Media [Anglicanism] was absolutely pulverised.[28]

Twentieth-century philosophers and theologians were also influenced by him. Ludwig Wittgenstein's *Philosophical Investigations* began with an extensive quotation from the *Confessions*.[29] Bertrand Russell was impacted by Augustine's reflections in the *Confessions* on the nature of time.[30] Edmund Husserl, the founder of the school of phenomenology, stated: "The analysis of time-consciousness is an age-old crux of descriptive psychology and theory of knowledge. The first thinker to be deeply sensitive to the immense difficulties to be found here was Augustine, who laboured almost to despair over this problem."[31] Martin Heidegger referred to the great North African several times in his work *Being and Time*.[32] The political theorist Hannah Arendt began her philosophical career with a doctoral thesis

---

[26] St. Anselm of Canterbury, *Proslogion*, chaps. 1–4.

[27] Quoted in Daniel-Rops, *Church in the Dark Ages*, p. 51.

[28] John Henry Cardinal Newman, *Apologia pro vita sua* (New York: W. W. Norton, 1968), p. 488.

[29] Ludwig Wittgenstein, *Philosophical Investigations* (Oxford: Wiley-Blackwell, 2009), Part I, 1–3, 32.

[30] Bertrand Russell, *History of Western Philosophy* (London: George Allen and Unwin, 1979), pp. 352–53.

[31] Edmund Husserl, *Phenomenology of Internal Time-Consciousness*, trans. James S. Churchill (Bloomington, Ind.: Indiana University Press, 1964), p. 21.

[32] Martin Heidegger, *Being and Time*, trans. John Macquarrie and Edward Robinson (New York: Harpers, 1964), p. 171.

entitled *The Concept of Love in Augustine* (1929). Pope Benedict XVI's 1953 dissertation was likewise on the writings of the Bishop of Hippo: *The People and the House of God in Augustine's Doctrine of the Church*.

Thus, by personifying the harmonious union of classical learning, philosophical genius, and the Catholic Faith, the saintly sage of Hippo became a prototype of the Christian "converter of culture".

> Augustine not only describes but illustrates in his own person the work of Christ as converter of culture. The Roman rhetorician becomes a Christian preacher who not only puts into the service of Christ the training in language and literature given him by his society but, by virtue of the freedom and illumination received from the Gospel, uses that language with a new brilliance and brings a new liberty into that literary tradition. The Neo-Platonist not only adds to his wisdom about spiritual reality the knowledge of the Incarnation which no philosopher had taught him, but this wisdom is humanized, given new depth and direction, made productive of new insights by the realization that the Word has become flesh.... The Ciceronian moralist does not add to the classical virtues the new virtues of the gospel, nor substitute new law for natural and Roman legislation, but transvalues and redirects in consequence of the experience of grace the morality in which he had been trained and which he taught. In addition to this Augustine becomes one of the leaders of that great historical movement whereby the society of the Roman Empire is converted from a Caesar-centered community into medieval Christendom. Therefore, he is himself an example of what conversion of culture means; in contrast to its rejection by radicals, to its idealization by culturalists, to the synthesis that proceeds largely by means of adding Christ to good civilization, and to the dualism that seeks to live by the gospel in an unconquerably immoral society.... Christ is the transformer of culture for Augustine in the sense that he redirects, reinvigorates, and regenerates that life of man expressed in all human works, which in present actuality is the perverted and corrupted exercise of a fundamentally good nature.[33]

In this way Augustine drew up the blueprints of culture that intellectuals, popes, bishops, and rulers of the Dark Ages and medieval society used as they created the Christian ethos at the heart of the new sociopolitical order of Christendom, a society wherein the truths of the Catholic Faith enlightened and strengthened human institutions for the sake of man's overarching purpose: eternal salvation in Christ.

Blueprints for a New Sociopolitical Order

In the autumn of 410, Hippo was flooded by refugees bearing the unbelievable news that Rome, eternal Rome, had been captured and sacked by the Goths. Dazed by the event, men feverishly looked for an explanation and almost immediately the pagans pointed accusing fingers at the Christians, attributing the catastrophe to the abandonment of the old gods for the new religion. As a refutation, but going far beyond the limits of a response, Augustine, toward the end of 412, began writing his monumental vision of Christian civilization, the *City of God*, a work that would only be completed in 426.

It is hard for us nowadays to imagine the mental collapse caused by the storming of Rome; it seemed as if the world was about to fall into an abyss of barbarianism.

---

[33] H. Richard Niebuhr, *Christ and Culture* (New York: Harper and Row, 1951), pp. 208–9.

Philippe de Champaigne, *St. Augustine*, 1650.

Many contemporaries, numbed with horror, could see no future for society. But for Augustine, his genius now fully infused with the Christian vision of life, it was the provocation to present the relationship between the Catholic, the Church, and civilization on the basis of the biblical text: "For here we have no lasting city, but we seek the city which is to come" (Heb 13:14). Neither Rome nor Greece nor any civilization is immortal, he wrote, for our destination is an eternal homeland; our paramount task is to reach it by building and rebuilding on earth civilizations that will help, not hinder, progress to our destination—societies that will be the closest possible imitations of the archetype: the heavenly society, the City of God.

Systematically, Augustine's work unfolds the idea that Christianity is no mere "religion", a purely private relationship between the individual and God hidden within the conscience, but rather a revolutionary force capable of transforming society in all its dimensions—the answer to all the great questions about the purposes of history, human nature, marriage, family, education, justice, and the relationship of the individual and the state to the Church. In the measure in which civilization is built according to the divine blueprints offered it by Catholicism, it will be a society eminently worthy of man. But the efforts to build will occur in wartime, for history is essentially a great drama, an unending battlefield until the world's last night, on which the visible and invisible forces of good and evil fight for the conquest of man's soul. Each individual must decide on which side he will combat, which city he will construct: "Two cities have been formed by two loves: the earthly by the love of self even to the contempt of God; the heavenly by the love of God, even to the contempt of self."[34]

Knowledge of God's will is to be found in the truths revealed by Christ and conserved through the Church he founded and in the natural law within man's conscience. Yet, as Augustine well knew from his own experience, the moral conscience by itself is incapable of rescuing man from the gravitational pull of his disordered passions; only the truth and grace of Christ could empower man to rise above his wretched inclinations to evil—solely by using freedom to live according to the pattern of Christ's earthly life, Passion, death, and Resurrection as a tireless "revolutionary of the Cross"[35] would a new man be born, capable of building a rough-hewn, earthbound version of the City of God.

Nevertheless, for the Christian on pilgrimage to the heavenly city, even such an ideal earthly society would always be eyed warily for fear that one might be allured by one's own shortsightedness and anarchic passions to forget about one's destination.

[34] St. Augustine, *City of God* 14.28, trans. Marcus Dods, from *Nicene and Post-Nicene Fathers*, 1st series, ed. Philip Schaff, vol. 2 (Buffalo, N.Y.: Christian Literature Publishing, 1887), p. 430.
[35] Daniel-Rops, *Church in the Dark Ages*, p. 297.

The earthly city had to be built as a reality existing to care for the pilgrim's travel needs—there to offer roadside hospitality to men on the march to their true homeland. Its main function for the embodied and wounded spirit that constitutes man is preventive and therapeutic. As none other than Baudelaire once stated in a terse phrase in his diary that Nietzsche afterward transcribed in one of his own notebooks: "Genuine civilization ... does not lie in gas nor in steam nor in turntables. It lies in the lessening of the marks of original sin."[36] This does not imply any disdain for man, nature, or reason; it is simply raw realism about ever-present danger from within. Once this alertness has become part of one's personality, a remarkable transformation occurs in the interior of the Christian. His will, freed from domineering passions, protects the clear-sightedness of his intellect and the refinement of his sensibility so that the beauty of the world, nature, and man are better understood and admired through their relation to God. As Augustine told his people in Hippo: "Question the beauty of the earth, question the beauty of the sea, question the beauty of the air expanding and spreading, question the beauty of the sky.... Question all these realities. All respond: "See, we are beautiful." Their beauty is an acknowledgment. These beauties are subject to change. Who made them if not the Beautiful One who is not subject to change?"[37]

This new insight into beauty makes man long for the undying Beauty, the source of all this fleeting loveliness. He senses that immersed in the Eternal Beauty is where he will find utter, transforming happiness. And at times he has a mysterious, remote foretaste of what this will mean:

> Late have I loved you, O Beauty ever ancient, ever new, late have I loved you! You were within me, but I was outside, and it was there that I searched for you. In my unloveliness I plunged into the lovely things which you created. You were with me, but I was not with you. Created things kept me from you; yet if they had not been in you they would not have been at all. You called, you shouted, and you broke through my deafness. You flashed, you shone, and you dispelled my blindness. You breathed your fragrance on me; I drew in breath and now I pant for you. I have tasted you, now I hunger and thirst for more. You touched me, and I burned for your peace.[38]

One principle and priority was to underlie all of man's daily living: love! "[Y]ou shall love the LORD your God with all your heart, and with all your soul, and with all your might" (Deut 6:5), and should love one's neighbor as oneself. And since man is loved by God to the extent that he wants him to reciprocate his love, every man and woman has a dignity that in itself surpasses that of the very universe. Accordingly, all of society's institutions and laws must protect the sanctuary of each person's dignity. Everything must further, or at least not impede, man's ability to love God and his fellow man. Hence, Augustine's program is that of a civilization of love wherein the individual is at the center, the brotherhood of man is a necessity, union with God the purpose, and true freedom the implication. Society would thus be a space wherein

[36] Charles Baudelaire, *Mon Coeur Nis a Nu*, 32 (1866), in *Oeuvres Posthumes*, ed. Louis Conard, vol. 2 (Paris: Louis Conard, 1952), p. 109.

[37] St. Augustine, Sermon 241.

[38] St. Augustine, *Confessions* 10.27, in *Liturgy of the Hours* (Totowa, N.J.: Catholic Book Publishing, 1975), p. 1357.

man would find support for his journey to the eternal Homeland; in it he would transform himself into a fitting citizen for Heaven by making himself a fitting citizen of earth through the sacred liturgy and through the development of his talents unto the greater glory of God in concrete action benefiting his fellow men.

Though Augustine's thinking soared to metaphysical peaks, it returned to the valleys with concrete applications regarding personal relationships, patriotism, government, and Church-state dealings.

Powerfully novel and practical was his portrayal of the relationship between love, sexuality, and marriage. While many in his day emphasized Saint Paul's statement about marriage as a moral and social necessity—"better to marry than to be aflame with passion" (1 Cor 7:9)—they neglected the apostle's other words: "Husbands, love your wives, as Christ loved the Church and gave himself up for her" (Eph 5:25). On the truth of Christ's salvific love and on the truth of procreation as the first purpose of marriage, Augustine built his conception of the conjugal bond as "sacramental love", a communion of hearts that symbolizes divine love, is expressed in physical intimacy, and should lead the spouses toward greater union with God—a highly influential idea that would mark the Western psyche.

The nation or homeland Augustine considered to be an extension of the family, a motherland that nourishes man, a love that flows in his blood, and that therefore can ask for sacrifices. Astonishingly, the genius of the fifth century envisioned the birth of nation-states imbued with the Christian sense of international fraternity and thus functioning as a family of nations.

Augustine's sociopolitical ideal subordinates the state to the principles of the natural law, assigning to government only a protective role over the individual, the family, and the common good. Its duty is to assist the members of society in their quest for spiritual and material well-being through upholding public order, education, and freedom of enterprise, stepping in only to protect justice and ensure that everyone has life's necessities. Hence, the state for Augustine is merely the sum total of administrative accessories. It must never be regarded by citizens as the source of its own authority, which is derived only from adherence to the natural law, to which rulers owe obedience. Indeed, there is no authentic society and no legitimate state where natural law is absent—only a mob.

> Thus, where there is not true justice there can be no assemblage of men associated by a common acknowledgment of right, and therefore there can be no people, as defined by Scipio or Cicero; and if no people then no weal [sociopolitical order] of the people, but only of some promiscuous multitude unworthy of the name of people. Consequently, if the republic is the weal of the people, and if there is no people if it be not associated by a common acknowledgment of right, and if there is no right where there is no justice, then most certainly it follows that there is no republic where there is no justice.[39]

Catholic theologians of later centuries drew out the consequences from Augustine's thought: government ought to be kept in its place, unjust laws should not be obeyed, and tyrants could be ousted. In Western Europe there would be no caesaropapism and the "divine right" of kings never became an official Church teaching.

---

[39] St. Augustine, *City of God* 19.21, in *Nicene and Post-Nicene Fathers*, 1st series, ed. Philip Schaff, vol. 2 (New York: Cosimo, 2007), p. 414.

No other civilization ever sought to break the state to harness with such a firm line of argument:

> Justice being taken away, then what are kingdoms but great robberies? For what are robberies themselves but little kingdoms? The band itself is made up of men; it is ruled by the authority of a prince, it is knit together by the pact of the confederacy; the booty is divided by the law agreed on. If, by the admittance of abandoned men, this evil increases to such a degree that it holds places, fixes abodes, takes possession of cities and subdues peoples, it assumes the more plainly the name of a kingdom because the reality is now manifestly conferred on it not by the removal of covetousness but by the addition of impunity. Indeed, that was an apt and true reply which was given to Alexander the Great by a pirate who had been seized. For when that king had asked the man what he meant by keeping hostile possession of the sea, he answered with bold pride, "What thou meanest by seizing the whole earth; but because I do it with a petty ship I am called a robber, whilst thou who dost it with a great fleet art styled emperor."[40]

The Church-state relationship in Augustinian thought rested on his awareness of the Church's transcendent mission to empower man to reach his eternal destiny. Such a mission was superior to that of the state, and, therefore, while each had its own specific authority, the Church had the right to supervise the state in order to ensure it fulfilled its role. Throughout the following centuries enough priests and laity would remember this principle to ensure an ongoing tension between state and Church, thus helping to prevent or tear down totalitarian regimes. Frequently misinterpreted, however, was Augustine's idea that the state had a duty to assist the Church. He never argued for any role of the state in fostering conversions to Christianity through pressure and violence—truth and charity were to be the only weapons. Toleration of non-Catholic religions was acceptable; though the "secular arm" should protect the Church's efforts to evangelize, never did he propose the burning of heretics.

The *City of God* would inspire and frame not only the Church's sociopolitical doctrine but also its legal thought. For although Catholic jurists certainly borrowed procedures from Roman law, purified and incorporated customs found among the Germanic peoples, and sought guidance from the Old Testament, Aristotle, and Justinian, at the end of the day the Catholic legal system was an original synthesis. This was due in no small way to Augustine, who had fused Christian truths with the definition of natural law as given in the *De Legibus* of Cicero. By asserting that law must be in accord with human nature, he built a theory that later Catholic thinkers would place at the heart of Western civilization's legal mentality and would export internationally as the basis for global law.

During the Dark Ages, only the recognition by reason of a divinely constituted natural law that was protected by the overarching Christian vision and the sanctions of the Church had the power to tame barbarian tribes accustomed to solve disputes by vendettas and bloodbaths. On this foundation, in the eighth century, Alcuin and the statesmen around Charlemagne sought to construct, however imperfectly, a society according to Augustine's principles. By the thirteenth century it was evident that a legal revolution had taken place in Western Europe. Strange to ancient

---

[40] Ibid., 4.4, p. 66.

ears were the rights guaranteed not only to women but to children; unheard of was the protection given to widows, the poor, and orphans; and wide-ranging were the boundaries set to state power and the exercise of war. Unknown to the ancient world were the laws elevating the status of woman to a par with man, protecting her right to choose a spouse and gain a declaration of annulment. Slaves were to be treated as fellow men and brothers in Christ, with all the respect with which a father treats his children—all of which implied for any committed Christian that they should be given their freedom. Augustine's thought went on to play a crucial role in the formulation of a universally viable set of legal principles by the Renaissance priest Francisco de Vitoria (ca. 1483–1546), the "Founder of International Law", and with these in mind the Spanish Empire promulgated decrees to protect the Native Americans. Only in the past hundred years has this legal structure been assaulted and largely replaced worldwide by the new legal positivism that is the ever-so-fragile product of political consensus and the ever-so-dangerous tool in the hands of certain lobbying groups and budding dictators.

Standing Upright to the End

Augustine's final days were spent in overcrowded Hippo, whose streets were jammed with refugees seeking a safe haven from the fury of Genseric's red-haired Vandals who, wherever they went, burned fields, looted towns, massacred, maimed, and raped. On August 28, 430, in the third month of the siege of his beloved city, Augustine, his weary body racked by a high fever, died. As death approached, he had prayed, asking pardon from God for having done so little for him, time and again reading aloud the words of the penitential psalms that he had nailed to the walls of his room. By standing erect in a city filled with fear, his physical strength failing but his will steadfast, his frail voice preaching the hope of Christ to the multitude packing the basilica, urging the citizens to a hardy defense, putting nerve into priests who were tempted to flee, he became the model of so many bishops during the darkness of the following centuries.

Augustine, as the thousand-year-old civilization of Rome burned, experienced the drama of it all in his own flesh yet never surrendered to despair but pointed in his writings and in his life to a possible new world order. Thus he became the guide for Catholic leaders during the long night before the Middle Ages, immediately influencing the two outstanding pontiffs of his era: Leo the Great, who, as a young priest, had once met him, and Gregory the Great.

Leo the Great: Rome at the Center

Twenty-two years after Augustine's death, Italy was in turmoil. The Roman armies were in retreat; the emperor and the imperial court had fled from Ravenna; and panic set in among the population of Rome as Attila and his army of Asiatic Huns invaded the peninsula. In desperation, the emperor Valentinian III turned to Pope Leo I to ask him, somehow, to halt the enemy.

Leo (ca. 400–461), a Tuscan by birth, had arrived to the city on the banks of the Tiber as a youth and had adopted it as his native soil. Ordained quite young, the promising cleric was sent on a mission to Saint Augustine by the future Pope

Raffaello Sanzio, *The Meeting between Leo the Great and Attila*, 1514.

Sixtus. By 430, he was already archdeacon of Rome and respected well beyond the boundaries of the city. In September 440, the Roman clergy and people elected the forty-five-year-old to the See of Saint Peter. A born leader of men, Leo was serene and inspired serenity. He was generous, compassionate, accessible, and modest. As an orator his words moved both the learned and the uneducated. When faced with complex problems, his swift and penetrating mind identified concrete solutions. This was the man who rode out, unarmed, to confront Attila on the banks of the Mincio River near the city of Mantua:

> Attila was just preparing to cross the Mincio when he saw a strange procession advancing toward him, shrouded in a cloud of gold-tinted dust: priests in dalmatics, monks in drugget [coarse wool clothing], two patricians on horseback, and a host of deacons and choristers bearing crosses and banners and lifting high gold monstrances which gleamed in the sunlight, were marching slowly to meet him. From the entire column the rhythmical responses of hymns and psalms rose on high, swelling into a formidable chorus. In the midst of the procession rode an old man with a white beard, praying as he rode. The Hun galloped toward the river, urged his horse into it, and halted on a sandy islet, within hailing distance of the strangers. "What is your name?" Attila shouted to the old man. There came the answer: "I am Leo, the Pope." The singing had stopped. Attila hesitated for a moment, then, urging his horse forward into the water again, gained the far bank. And the Pope came forward to meet him.[41]

Leo won from Attila the promises that he would depart from Italy and would seek a peaceful agreement with the emperor. His achievement had momentous implications. It showed Italy that a new defender of its cities and countryside had appeared in place of the emperors whose political power was decaying in the West.

[41] Daniel-Rops, *Church in the Dark Ages*, pp. 99–100.

The papacy was now consciously society's protector with Leo fully exercising his role, influencing the imperial court through his counsels and rebukes to Galla Placidia, Valentinian, Theodosius II, and Emperor Leo I, and going forth again in 455 to face Genseric and the Vandals. To the conservative Romans who still clung to paganism and accused the Church of bringing about the downfall of the empire, Augustine had replied in the parchments of the *City of God* but Leo had answered on horseback at the Mincio River.

Within the Catholic Church, Leo the Great's papacy was enormously important because of its confirmation of the authority of the Roman See, a truth that had been previously asserted by Ambrose, "Where Peter is, there is the Church",[42] and also by Augustine, whose declaration had been paraphrased to "*Roma locuta, causa finita*" (Rome has spoken, the case is closed).[43] By his wisdom and excellence in government he merits the epithet "organizer of the historic papacy".[44] Nothing that affected the Catholic Church was foreign to his eyes and ears. Vigorously he acted in a thousand directions, as we know from his correspondence, refusing to tolerate any betrayal, even tiny, on tradition, principles, and papal authority. "The Lord ... wanted His gifts to flow into the entire body from Peter himself as if from the head, in such a way that anyone who had dared to separate himself from the solidarity of Peter would realize that he was himself no longer a sharer in the divine mystery."[45] Elsewhere he stated: "Although bishops have a common dignity, they are not all of the same rank. Even among the most blessed Apostles, though they were alike in honor, there was a certain distinction of power. All were equal in being chosen, but it was given to one to be preeminent over the others ... the care of the universal Church would converge in the one See of Peter, and nothing should ever be at odds with this head."[46] He corrected bishops who acted independently; sought worthy candidates for the episcopacy; and fought against heresy. With regal language the modest Leo asserted the rights of the papacy to insiders and outsiders and declared that the true grandeur of Rome lay not in her political past but in being forevermore the seat of the successors of Saint Peter.

Always available to his own Roman people, Leo frequently left the Lateran Palace to care for their needs, ensure corn was stored in case of famine, and put finances in order. He kept up relations with the barbarians. He supervised excavations in the catacombs. He channeled his concern for the souls of his flock by preaching awe-inspiring, elegant, and accessible sermons and by stating clear definitions of Church doctrine. And in 441, he gave his support to a priest evangelizing a distant island in the north of Europe, sending him three helpers—the priest's name was Patrick.

By establishing a papacy that exercised its prerogatives, Leo placed it in a position of such prestige that in the hands of his preeminent successor, Gregory the Great, and other pontiffs, it was in a strategic position to ensure Catholic unity, impulse

---

[42] St. Ambrose, "Ubi ergo Petrus, ibi Ecclesia", *In Psalmum XL Enarratio* (PL 14:1134).

[43] "Iam enim de hac causa duo concilia missa sunt ad sedem apostolicam; inde etiam rescripta venerunt; causa finita est." (For already on this matter two councils have sent to the Apostolic See whence also rescripts have come. The case is closed.) St. Augustine, Sermon 131.10 (PL 38:734).

[44] Pierre Batiffol, *Le Catholicisme de Saint Augustin*, 2 vols. (Paris: Gabalda, 1920), quoted in Daniel-Rops, *Church in the Dark Ages*, p. 104.

[45] Pope Leo I, Letter to the Bishops at Vienne, July, A.D. 445, in *The Faith of the Early Fathers*, ed. and trans. William A. Jurgens, vol. 3 (Collegeville, Minn.: Liturgical Press, 1970), p. 269.

[46] Letter to Bishop Anastasius of Thessalonica, ca. A.D. 446, in Jurgens, *Faith of the Early Fathers*, vol. 3, p. 270.

missionary penetration of barbarian nations, and act as the arbiter of justice in Europe. Later on, in the first half of the eighth century, it would also be capable of forging an alliance with the Frankish Pepin that would promote the Christianization of the only nominally Christian masses of the Franks. This alliance would have two important consequences. Firstly, it would enable the application to much of Western Europe of the emerging synthesis of the Catholic Faith, Greco-Roman law, and classical and Teutonic culture that was assembled under Alcuin and the other Catholic intellectuals in the second half of the eighth century. Secondly, it would empower the monks' missionary thrust to expand the rim of the future Christendom northward and eastward.

Gregory the Great and the Thrust toward the Barbarians

According to the mathematician and philosopher Alfred North Whitehead, Gregory the Great (540–604) was "a man whose high official position is surpassed only in the magnitude of his services to humanity".[47] He belonged to an ancient Roman family, the Anicii, to whom grandeur clings like bark to a tree, since in its lineage were not only two emperors but also the philosopher Boethius. As a child he lived with his parents, Gordian and Sylvia, and two aunts, Aemiliana and Tharsilla, who were consecrated virgins, in a villa on the Caelian Hill with a view of some of ancient Rome's majestic buildings. The talented youth rose rapidly in the city's government to become prefect (governor) in 572. Then he turned his back on the world's honors to become a monk, giving his

Peter Paul Rubens, *The Ecstasy of St. Gregory the Great* (detail), 1608.

estates in Sicily to establish six monasteries and transforming his mansion on the Caelian into the Abbey of St. Andrew. There, Gregory named someone else as abbot and lived as one of the rank and file, serenely fulfilled as Augustine had been in his villa at Thagaste, dedicated to prayer and study.

It was not to last. Pope Pelagius II obliged Gregory to abandon his peaceful life in order to assist him in governing the Church. In 579 he sent the reluctant monk as papal ambassador to the imperial court at Byzantium in order to ask for military reinforcements to defend Rome against the approaching Lombards. In 585, on his return, he became the Pope's close collaborator. After Pelagius' death, the Romans sought out Gregory, demanded he be their pontiff, successfully blocked his escape, and carried him to St. Peter's Basilica, where they cheered mightily at his consecration on September 3, 590.

> Was there any pontificate which was fuller than this one? Although delicate in health (he was ashamed not to be able to obey the rules of fasting lest he swooned), Gregory

---

[47] Alfred North Whitehead, *Science and the Modern World* (New York: Macmillan, 1931), p. 272.

was one of those men who by rigorous self-discipline are able to obtain more from a sickly body than most of us obtain from a healthy one. Ambitiously bold in his ideas, resolute in their application, following through every task which he undertook to the last detail, he was a worthy son of those great administrators whose endeavors had created the Empire. Gregory was a hot-tempered man, somewhat inclined to intransigence, but he radiated such boundless generosity of spirit that, without trying to please, he made people love him. His intellect matched his character: it was lucid, penetrating, and quick to assess men or to judge situations; there was no danger of him mistaking weakness for charity, illusion for hope; the art of government came to him naturally, and it had been further matured by his long official employment. He was a tireless worker, always busy dictating letters (we still possess nearly nine hundred, dealing with the most varied topics), receiving visitors, and vastly increasing the scope of a pope's duties.[48]

Indeed, his biographer, Paul the Deacon, informs us that "he never rested" (*Vita*, 15). Ceaselessly he built up Rome. He saved the city from intrusions by the Lombards and Byzantines; founded a highly organized relief system benefiting the poor for whom, as one eyewitness exclaimed, "the Church was like a great open granary";[49] and, in the universal Church, made his voice heard at the councils of Carthage and Arles. His relentless and vigorous action was marked by the wise sense of direction springing from the infra-eternal vision of Augustine's *City of God*: all sociopolitical efforts should be directed toward helping the individual man and woman live at the deepest level of earthly existence where eternity, in a mysterious, initial, and imperfect measure, begins through union with God by sanctifying grace. For Gregory was first and foremost a priest for whom the papacy revolved on the priestly axis of teaching, sanctifying, and governing. His sense of priesthood had been forged amid the silence, study, self-conquest, and prayer characteristic of monasticism. As pontiff he penned the *Pastoral Rule* in which he outlined this challenging vision of priestly identity.

When Gregory ascended the throne of Peter, nostalgia for the past still lingered in the air and many a Roman around the new Pope may still have harbored the hope that somehow the empire would be restored through the efforts of Byzantium and the inbuilt greatness of the thousand-year-old society. After all, how could such a powerful civilization cease to exist? Such men found it hard to accept that history had long been tracing its verdict on the walls of the West. Indeed, during Gregory's reign, in 603, after thirteen hundred years of existence, the Roman Senate met amid the ruins of the Roman Forum for the last time and then pulled shut the heavy bronze doors. From the Atlantic to the Rhine, from Scandinavia to North Africa, the lands had already become largely barbarian both in population and culture. Moreover, Catholics had still not accomplished their mandate to propose the Faith to these new races. The Church was waiting for a pope of clear vision and steel determination who would, with a sense of urgency, decisively cross the Rubicon in order to go northward—a leader who would leave behind any nostalgia for a revival of the old *imperium Romanum*, end the Catholic Church's gaze toward weak and caesaropapist Byzantium, and resolutely focus all corporate energies on the conversion of the barbarian world.

---

[48] Daniel-Rops, *Church in the Dark Ages*, pp. 225–26.
[49] Quoted in ibid., p. 226.

In Gregory the Church had such a pontiff: "Now Rome is desolate, worn down, full of sorrows. No one comes to it to get on in the world.... The city which has lost its inhabitants, in losing its feathers, has enlarged its baldness as the eagle. Shrunk also are its wings with which it used to fly to the prey, for all its men of might, by whom it ravened, are extinguished."[50] The new pontiff also saw clearly that missionary work should no longer be left only to the spontaneous efforts of individual bishops or monks but should be inspirited and impelled by the successors of Saint Peter. Missionary efforts fanning out from Rome across Europe would streamline the out-

Francisco de Goya, *St. Gregory the Great* (detail), 1797.

reach to the barbarians, foster the cohesiveness of Christ's Church in doctrine and discipline, and favor her "catholic" (universal) identity.

This strategy, born from the sense of urgency for man's salvation, became action as Gregory gave marching orders to bands of Benedictine monks to set out for various immigrant peoples of the continent. Indeed, the oils of consecration were still wet on Gregory's hands when he began pursuing the conversion of the troublesome Lombard warriors of King Agilulf in northern Italy. He found an ally in the beautiful Theodolinda, a Bavarian princess who, as Lombard queen, raised her children in the Catholic Faith, built churches, enabled Columbanus to found his monastery at Bobbio, and patiently guided her husband to the threshold of the Church. The letters of the queen to the Pope testify to her grandeur of soul and remind us of the quiet but powerful feminine role in the conversion of Europe. With time their joint efforts led to the conversion in the seventh century of the Lombard nation under Bertarid (671–688) and decisive progress under Liutprand (712–744) toward a common Christian culture for both the Lombards and the peoples they had subjugated in Italy.

Simultaneously, Gregory pursued the growth of the Church in Gaul (France) and Spain, as can be seen in his correspondence with the Frankish king Childebert II and with the Visigoth ruler, Reccared I. The latter had converted to Catholicism in 589 and had begun to lay the juridical foundations for the end of racial divisions and the creation of a Christian society. And then there was the conversion of England. "The Rome of St. Peter began her conquests where the Rome of Augustus had left off: with Britain and Germany."[51] To the shores of Kent ruled by King Ethelbert, Gregory sent Augustine and a band of monks in 596:

> The meeting of the saint and the king was a wonderful one; sitting under a tree, surrounded by his warriors, Ethelbert watched the forty Roman monks coming toward him in slow procession, bearing a great silver cross and the figure of Christ painted on

[50] Pope St. Gregory the Great, *Homilies on the Book of the Prophet Ezekiel*, quoted in Thomas W. Allies, *The Holy See and the Wandering of the Nations from St. Leo I to St. Gregory I* (London: Burns and Oates, 1888), p. 283.
[51] Ernest Lavisse, *General View of the Political History of Europe* (New York: Longmans, Green, 1891), p. 22.

wood, singing Gregorian hymns. Referring to this scene Bossuet wrote: "The history of the Church contains nothing finer".[52]

Augustine spoke to Ethelbert of the God who had so loved men as to die on the Cross for their salvation. Ethelbert's queen, the lovely Bertha, a Parisian princess, supported Augustine's efforts. Within five years the king and a large number of warriors became Catholic. In Rome, Gregory, now continuously sick and confined to bed because of typhoid fever and gout, was overjoyed. In characteristic spirit he began laying out plans for the organization of Britain's dioceses and the future of a completely Christian island. Gregory's letters to missionaries included wise instructions for the toleration of everything within the customs of the Germanic peoples that was compatible with the natural law and the Catholic Faith—a decisive part of the blueprints for a common Christian European culture. In his guidelines for the first Benedictine missionaries to the Anglo-Saxons of Britain, he ordered that idols be destroyed but not the temples, which were to be converted into churches; and pagan festivals were to be discouraged not merely by prohibitions but by replacing them with Christian feasts and feasting. "There is no doubt", he wisely remarked, "that it is impossible to cut away everything immediately from their hardened minds. He who strives to climb to the highest position rises by degrees or steps and not by leaps."[53]

During his fourteen-year reign, Gregory's wise, forceful, and daring strategies defended and expanded the rim of the future Christendom in spite of savage Lombards to the north and south of Rome and incompetent Byzantines in the northeast. All was done amid an Italian landscape of burning towns and unsafe highways. The decisive new thrust for the conversion of Anglo-Saxons, Lombards, and Visigoths showed the ancient world that a new empire was coming into existence, independent and distinct from the political power of Byzantium, using stones from the ancient Roman world but with its own pillars, power, authority, and instruments. By the end of the reign of Gregory the Great, men knew that papal Rome had indeed succeeded the imperial city, and the most clear-sighted among them sensed that the seeds of a new West were being planted amid the centuries of winter.

The seed sowers were the Benedictine and Irish monks whom Gregory had impulsed directly and indirectly throughout his reign. Indicative of the spiritual closeness between the Roman pontiff and the Celtic monks is the preface to Saint Columba of Iona's hymn, *Altus Prosator* (High Creator). It describes the arrival from Rome to the windswept island at the distant edges of the northern world of Pope Gregory's messengers, bearing the gift of a set of hymns for evening prayer, and, in return, the sending by Saint Columba of his own compositions to the pontiff. To these creative minorities, the monks of the West, we will now turn our attention.

---

[52] Daniel-Rops, *Church in the Dark Ages*, p. 231.

[53] Letter of Pope Gregory the Great to Abbot Mellitus, written in A.D. 601, in Venerabilis Baedae, *Historia Ecclesiastica Gentis Anglorum*, ed. Georgii H. Moberly, bk. 1, chap. 30, p. 74. My translation.

Chapter 4

CREATIVE MINORITIES: THE BENEDICTINE AND IRISH MONKS

> Usually it is the creative minorities who determine the future, and in this regard the Catholic Church must understand that she is a creative minority who has a heritage of values that are not things of the past but are a very lively and relevant reality.
>
> —Benedict XVI, September 26, 2009

The soul of Gregory the Great had been molded by monasticism. As pope he encouraged the spread of Benedictine abbeys that, together with those founded by the Irish monks, became the training centers for many of the most gifted and dedicated of the Church's bishops and priests during the Dark Ages. These monasteries became the launching pads for the missionary penetration of the barbarian races as well as the oases for the preservation of Greco-Roman culture. In their cloisters, ever so silently, ever so gradually, these men sketched the blueprints of a new cultural synthesis that, in the eighth century, began to take shape in the society of Charlemagne's empire. This became the foundation of the Christendom that would emerge in the twelfth century when the ethos and institutions characteristic of Western civilization became clearly visible.

Alexandre Cabanel, *The Roman Monk*, 1848.

Benedict and the Shaping of the Western Mind

On September 4, 476, the barbarian Odoacer deposed the last Roman emperor Romulus Augustus—an episode that has come to symbolize the collapse of the proud Roman Empire. Fifty-three years later, in 529, halfway along the road between Rome and Naples, on a mountaintop with the ruins of a temple to Apollo, another empire was founded when a youth named Benedict, who had turned his back on the decadence of Rome, started the monastery of Monte Cassino.

Benedict (480–547) was born in Norcia, a town located on a plain within view of some of the highest peaks of the Italian Apennines, among people legendary for their ruggedness, austerity, and energy, *severissimi homines* ("the sternest of men"—Cicero). As a youth he travelled to Rome, then under barbarian rule, for studies. In those years much was stirring within his soul—a radical Christian idealism was awakening that would make no compromise with the forces of darkness either in self or in the world around him. Sickened by the debauchery of Roman society, the

Fra Angelico, *St. Benedict* (detail), 1438–1440.

roughly nineteen-year-old Benedict obeyed the words from the Gospel of Saint John that he would afterward place at the beginning of his Rule for monks: "Run while you have the light of life so that the darkness of death may not overtake you" (see Jn 12:35). Thirty miles eastward to Subiaco he went, determined to find a place of silence where *tranquillitas ordinis* (the serenity of order) reigned, indispensable for a Christian contemplative life. For three years he endured the solitude of a cave on the rocky flank of the mountain cliff in that isolated valley, engaging in that hardiest of combats, the combat of self against self. The outcome of this interior warfare was a new man who, although he would never be ordained to the priesthood, built his entire existence around the axis of the tripartite priestly mission to teach, sanctify, and shepherd others toward deeper union with God. His first attempt to institute a community of like-minded men failed, but he persisted and within a few years twelve monastic communities were born, all regarding Benedict as their father.

Of this man, the Patriarch of Western Monasticism, we have neither a contemporary portrait nor a detailed biography. Perhaps the best image of him was drawn by Pope Gregory the Great in his impersonal description of the ideal pastor:

> The conduct of a prelate should so far surpass the conduct of the people as the life of a pastor sets him apart from his flock. For one who is so regarded that the people are called his flock must carefully consider how necessary it is for him to maintain a life of rectitude. It is necessary, therefore, that he should be pure in thought, exemplary in conduct, discreet in keeping silence, profitable in speech, in sympathy a near neighbour to everyone, in contemplation exalted above all others, a humble companion to those who lead good lives, erect in his zeal for righteousness against the vices of sinners. He must not be remiss in his care for the inner life by preoccupation with the external; nor must he in his solicitude for what is internal fail to give attention to the external.... The ruler should ever be pure in thought. No impurity should stain one who has undertaken the duty of cleansing the stains of defilement from the hearts of others as well as from his own. For it is necessary that the hand that aims at cleansing filth should itself be clean, lest, sordid with clinging dirt, it fouls for the worse everything it touches.[1]

Word reached Rome about this extraordinary Christian mentor of men's souls. Soon, old aristocratic families took the road to Subiaco, entrusting the education of their sons to him, boys such as Maurus and Placidus, who would later be in the forefront of spreading the Benedictine ideal.

After Benedict had founded Monte Cassino, he put the wisdom of his Subiaco years on parchment—what the world now calls the Rule of Saint Benedict. If geniuses are judged by the magnitude of their ideas, Benedict ranks among the greatest—and yet disconcertingly so at first glance. For his program for a new lifestyle, the Rule, one of the landmark documents of Western civilization, can be

---

[1] Pope St. Gregory the Great, *Pastoral Rule*, bk. 2, in *St. Gregory the Great: Pastoral Care*, Ancient Christian Writers, trans. Henry Davis, S.J., vol. 11 (Westminster, Md.: Newman Press, 1950), pp. 45–46.

The young Benedict amid bare rock in the cave of Subiaco, with his eyes fixed on Jesus Christ Crucified; his heart shielded from the world by the sign of the cross; his mind raised in sublime and life-giving prayer. From the overhanging rock, by a long rope, the monk Romanus used to let down some food to him in a basket. (Sculpted by Antonio Raggi, disciple of Bernini, 1657.)

condensed in a mere one hundred pages. Nor is it original as regards the individual ideas, since he took much from Saint Basil, Cassian, Saint Augustine, and others. His creative ability was rather that of the synthetic genius founded upon deep wisdom, inspired intuition, and also maturity of years at the moment of penning it in Cassino. It is marked by extraordinary knowledge of the human heart and of his era, sensitive *humanitas*, and a spirit marked by Roman concreteness and practicality. Benedict successfully drew up a program for a way of life singularly in harmony with the requirements of human nature, "a guide to life equal to man's capabilities, and one which could be offered to anyone who wished to follow the way of God without forcing his nature artificially in doing so."[2]

It signaled the arrival of a new type of monk and established a new ascetic framework for the formation of priests—after Benedict's death significant numbers of monks were ordained—who would be focused men, with hearts detached from riches, power, and sensuality, and thus capable of spearheading the Church's missionary thrust. In the Benedictine converged the genius of Roman realism and order with Christian supernatural loftiness, producing a man who harmonized prayer and asceticism with study and manual work. A sense of balance was evident in the Rule's prescriptions about the austere daily existence: "For the daily meals ... should it happen that the work is heavier than usual, the abbot may decide ... to grant something additional, provided that it is appropriate.... The superior will determine when local conditions, work, or the summer heat indicates the need for a greater amount."[3]

The monastery, in order to be "a school for the Lord's service",[4] was a community, a micro-state, self-sufficient and agrarian, with its chapel, refectory, dormitory, workshops, mill, garden, guesthouse, and library. Self-contained it might well be, but it was certainly not designed to create men with "ingrown eyeballs". The Benedictines, like their Celtic and Egyptian brothers, were supposed to be men who entered the monastery not only for their own salvation but for the salvation of their fellow men. The ideal was therefore neither Nirvana nor narcissism but rather the following of Jesus Christ the Savior, who, from Bethlehem to Gethsemane and

[2] Henri Daniel-Rops, *The Church in the Dark Ages* (London: J. M. Dent and Sons, 1959), p. 273.
[3] Rule of St. Benedict, chap. 40, in Timothy Fry, ed., *The Rule of St. Benedict in Latin and English with Notes* (Collegeville, Minn.: Liturgical Press, 1981), pp. 62–63.
[4] Ibid., p. 18.

Calvary, had brought about the rescue of humanity from eternal darkness by becoming the prototype of human love and fulfillment through rejection of the world's allurements toward self-aggrandizement.

For this reason the life of the Benedictine naturally thrust outward, transformation of self requiring transformation of one's relationships and environment. This outcome had been prefigured during Benedict's years in Subiaco. For he had not only prayed and reflected in the cave, but with some frequency used also to go out onto the mountainside where local shepherds would

Giovanni Antonio Bazzi, *Saint Benedict Instructing the People in Sacred Doctrine*, from a series of paintings completed between 1497 and 1508. A scene repeated countless times, nation after nation, throughout the Dark Ages.

be waiting to hear him explain the truths of Christianity. Marking that spot is a poignant inscription on rock, placed there by Pope Pius IX, listing the names of the Benedictine monks who, having lit the flame of Christian idealism at Subiaco, became the torchbearers of the Catholic Faith from Sweden to Andalusia, thus playing a major role in laying the groundwork for a new civilization.

Down that mountainside came a trickling stream of Christian life that, with the centuries, began to grow and swell until it became a mighty river of grace and culture irrigating the plains and valleys of Europe. Benedict and his monks can rightly be called "Fathers of European Civilization", for during the Dark Ages their monasteries became "the storehouse of the past and the birthplace of the future",[5] "kinds of fortresses in which civilization sheltered beneath the banner of a saint: all that was noblest in learning and in culture was preserved in them".[6]

> St. Benedict found the world, physical and social, in ruins, and his mission was to restore it in the way not of science, but of nature, not as if setting about to do it, not professing to do it by any set time, or by any rare specific, or by any series of strokes, but so quietly, patiently, gradually, that often till the work was done, it was not known to be doing.... Silent men were observed about the country or discovered in the forest, digging, clearing and building; and other silent men, not seen, were sitting in the cold cloister, tiring their eyes and keeping their attention on the stretch, while they painfully copied and recopied the manuscripts which they had saved. There was no one who contended or cried out or drew attention to what was going on, but by degrees the woody swamp became a hermitage, a religious house, a farm, an abbey, a village, a seminary, a school of learning and a city.[7]

[5] John Henry Newman, "The Tradition of Civilization: The Isles of the North", chap. 10 in *Historical Sketches*, vol. 3 (London: Longmans, Green, 1897), p. 124.

[6] François-René de Chateaubriand, quoted in Daniel-Rops, *Church in the Dark Ages*, p. 278.

[7] Newman, *Historical Sketches*, vol. 3, p. 410.

Christ's paradoxical words regarding "whoever would save his life will lose it" (Mt 16:25) had been shown to be true not only for Benedict's determination to save his own soul, but also for his ability to save society's soul. He had become capable of changing the world by having first turned his back on it.

> The very word "monk" is a revolution, for it means solitude and came to mean community. This communal life became a sort of reserve and refuge behind the individual life; a hospital for every kind of hospitality.... Monks and nuns stood to mankind as a sort of sanctified league of aunts and uncles ... [who] kept the poor from the most distant sight of their modern despair.... The abbots were elective. They introduced representative government, ... in itself a semi-sacramental idea.... Mile by mile, and almost man by man, they taught and enriched the land.[8]

If the map of Europe would not be recognizable without the action of these men, even less so would the European mind-set. Here we shall allude briefly to three ways in which the role of the Benedictines turned out to be crucial for the shaping of the Western mind—as guardians of memory, in the formation of economics, and in the creation of what would become the modern scientific mentality.

Firstly, in the history of the West the chain linking ancient Greece and Rome with the modern world would have been broken if it had not been for the monks who guarded the classical manuscripts from destruction during the decline, fall, and aftermath of the Roman Empire. Our knowledge of the Greek and Roman cultures—their philosophies, principles of law, social organization, literatures, and history—depends almost exclusively on the copies of texts made by the monks and on their chronicles. The same can be said regarding our knowledge of the history of the European peoples during the Dark Ages. As the non-Catholic philosopher and historian David Hume recognized:

> It is rare that the annals of so uncultivated a people as were the English, as well as the other European nations, after the decline of Roman learning have been transmitted to posterity so complete and with so little mixture of falsehood and fable. This advantage we owe entirely to the clergy of the Church of Rome, who, founding their authority on their superior knowledge, preserved the precious literature of antiquity from a total extinction.[9]

Most of these monks, whether Benedictine or Celtic, are unknown to us with a few exceptions like Saint Isidore of Seville (ca. 560–635), the author of *Etymologiae*; the Celt Gildas the Wise (ca. 516–570), who wrote *The Ruin and Conquest of Britain*; and, of course, the Venerable Bede (ca. 673–735), "Father of English History", author of *The Ecclesiastical History of the English People*. Not only did they preserve the classical Greco-Roman heritage, but they also collected and transmitted to posterity so much of the oral and written traditions of the Germanic, Celtic, and Nordic peoples. In the case of Scandinavia, its gradual conversion to the Catholic Faith from the ninth century onward brought with it knowledge of the Latin alphabet and language. By the twelfth century this bore fruit for the preservation of the region's history in works such as *Gesta Danorum*, composed by Saxo Grammaticus under the patronage

[8] G. K. Chesterton, *A Short History of England* (Auckland, New Zealand: Floating Press, 2011), pp. 38–39.
[9] David Hume, *The History of England from the Invasion of Julius Caesar to the Revolution of 1688*, vol. 3 (London: J. McCreery, 1807), p. 297.

of Bishop Absalon Hvide, the founder of Copenhagen. The Benedictine monks of medieval Catholic Iceland gathered together Norse poetry and sagas, a literature that has influenced writers such as Tolkien.

Secondly, in the groundwork for economics—a topic that will be studied in greater detail further on—Benedict's influence has been recognized as foundational for modern Western economic prosperity. "Through Saint Benedict's Rule," stated Toynbee, "agrarian life was restored to health first in Italy and then in the rest of the derelict domain of the Roman Empire in Western Europe. . . . It is no exaggeration to say that the whole of the extraordinary economic development of our modern Western society . . . can be traced back to Saint Benedict's initiative."[10]

Thirdly, science, in a more subtle way, also owes an immense debt to the genius of Subiaco. As Duhem, Jaki, and others have pointed out, the odds in favor of science being born in the landmass called Europe were slim.[11] Pitiful indeed was Europe's appearance alongside the sophisticated civilizations of India, China, Egypt, Babylon, and the Arab empire. The Chinese, for instance, had a far longer history of civilized society, and the scholars at their imperial courts had made discoveries such as gunpowder; India had a school of atomism; Babylon's astronomers were second to none; Ancient Egypt had first-class geometry; and the medieval Arabs had done much to perfect medicine. Yet, astonishingly, in every one of these advanced cultures, science was "stillborn". And something utterly unexpected took place: in the primitive Catholic Middle Ages, the baby that would grow into modern science was born alive and healthy.

Why? The causes are complex, but chief among them is the fact that modern science is not a disconnected series of discoveries owed haphazardly to individual genius but is, above all else, a *mentality*. However, the mentality of a civilization is the outcome of the worldview of its educated elite. Such a mind-set does not appear overnight; for centuries it is being fashioned underground in the minds of individuals and subcultures until, finally, just as in springtime, society one day awakens to recognize its changed mental landscape. To understand the new scenery one needs to know the type of seeds that had been planted, and what had been happening underground in the secret springs of the imagination, in the treasuries of memory, and in the tone of thought.

The two most important seeds of the scientific outlook of Western man came from Catholicism.

The first was the Christian idea of God. Unlike in the predominant Asiatic religions, he was not an impersonal, arbitrary, and inscrutable deity but a personal God, a Creator who is Creative Reason and who brings the universe into existence sealed with a causal structure identifiable by man intuitively and rationally. Hence, reason is the way to understand a world that, from the movements of the stars to the micro-cosmos, has been rationally organized. No reality is haphazard; no event is mere chance. Furthermore, the Creator-God remains intimately involved in the universe and in the evolution of humanity, providentially guiding history through that mysterious union of his action and man's freedom. In fact, God's Creative

---

[10] Arnold J. Toynbee, "Man at Work in God's World", speech at the Royal Institute of International Affairs, London, October 19, 1955.

[11] Stanley L. Jaki, *The Savior of Science* (Grand Rapids, Mich.: Wm. B. Eerdmans, 2000).

The Conversion of King Ethelbert by Saint Augustine. Detail of a mosaic by
Clayton & Bell in the chapel of Saint Gregory and Saint Augustine in Westminster Cathedral.

Reason, the Second Person of the Blessed Trinity, had entered into time in the
Incarnation and had willingly suffered crucifixion for love of man. Thus, God
confirmed that he, the Creator, is Love as well as Reason, and that the universe
is a product of his goodness for the well-being of humanity. This recognition
of the universe's rational structure and its inherent goodness freed Catholics from
the intellectually paralyzing fear of the cosmos that was inherent to paganism and
pantheism; it functioned as the common sense of Western man long before it
triggered the scientific revolution.

The second crucial influence for the birth of science was "an active interest in
the simple occurrences of life for their own sake".[12] This seemingly banal statement
comes from Alfred North Whitehead, the twentieth-century mathematician and
philosopher who in *Science and the Modern World* stated that it was amid the barbarism
of the sixth century that "every action is laying the foundation for the tremendous
rise of the new European civilization":[13]

> The two outstanding men, who, in the Italy of the sixth century, laid the foundations
> of the future were St. Benedict and Gregory the Great. By reference to them we can
> at once see how absolutely in ruins was the approach to the scientific mentality which
> had been attained by the Greeks. We are at the zero point of scientific temperature. But
> the life-work of Gregory and of Benedict contributed elements to the reconstruction
> of Europe which secured that this reconstruction, when it arrived, should include a
> more effective scientific mentality than that of the ancient world.

[12] Alfred North Whitehead, *Science and the Modern World*, Lowell Lectures, 1925 (New York: New American Library, 1959), p. 20.
[13] Ibid., p. 21.

The Greeks were over-theoretical. For them science was an offshoot of philosophy. Gregory and Benedict were practical men, with an eye for the importance of ordinary things; and they combined this practical temperament with their religious and cultural activities. In particular, we owe it to St. Benedict that the monasteries were the homes of practical agriculturalists, as well as of saints and of artists and men of learning. The alliance of science with technology, by which learning is kept in contact with irreducible and stubborn facts, owes much to the practical bent of the early Benedictines. Modern science derives from Rome as well as from Greece, and this Roman strain explains its gain in an energy of thought kept closely in contact with the world of facts.

But the influence of this contact between the monasteries and the facts of nature showed itself first in art. The rise of Naturalism in the later Middle Ages was the entry into the European mind of the final ingredient necessary for the rise of science. It was the rise of interest in natural objects and in natural occurrences, for their own sakes. The natural foliage of a district was sculptured.... Every art exhibited a direct joy in the apprehension of the things which lie around us.... The simple immediate facts are the topics of interest and these reappear in the thought of science as the "irreducible stubborn facts".

The mind of Europe was now prepared for its new venture of thought. It is unnecessary to tell in detail the various incidents which marked the rise of science: the growth of wealth and leisure; the expansion of universities; the invention of printing; the taking of Constantinople, Copernicus; Vasco da Gama; Columbus; the telescope. The soil, the climate, the seeds were there, and the forest grew.[14]

In 1953, the historian Arnold J. Toynbee made a "long-meditated pilgrimage" to the cave at Subiaco. He was conscious that the Western civilization for which Benedict had laid important seeds was dead and had been replaced by a secularized culture whose influence was swiftly expanding worldwide. *Time* magazine, on October 9, 1956, reported that the "tall, white-haired Englishman with gentle eyes stood in silent prayer", praying, as he himself afterward disclosed "that the spirit which had once created a Western Christian Civilization out of the chaos of the Dark Age might return to re-consecrate a latter-day Westernizing World".[15]

Columbanus and the Irish Monks

D-Days: Disembarking of Columbanus in France and of Columba in Scotland

Due to the missionary impulse given to the Benedictines by Gregory the Great, they began to emerge from Italy, spreading northward. In 595 forty monks headed by Augustine, prior of the Abbey of St. Andrew's in Rome, were sent to evangelize England. As they travelled through Gaul (France), they brought their form of monasticism to the attention of the influential monastery of Lérins and to Gallic churchmen, possibly leaving behind copies of Saint Benedict's Rule. As a result, in the 600s, Benedictine influence began penetrating already-existing abbeys, firstly at Lérins, and then gradually all over Gaul, through bishops formed at that nursery of churchmen.

---

[14] Ibid., pp. 22–23.
[15] Arnold Toynbee, *An Historian's Approach to Religion* (London: Oxford University Press, 1956), p. 151.

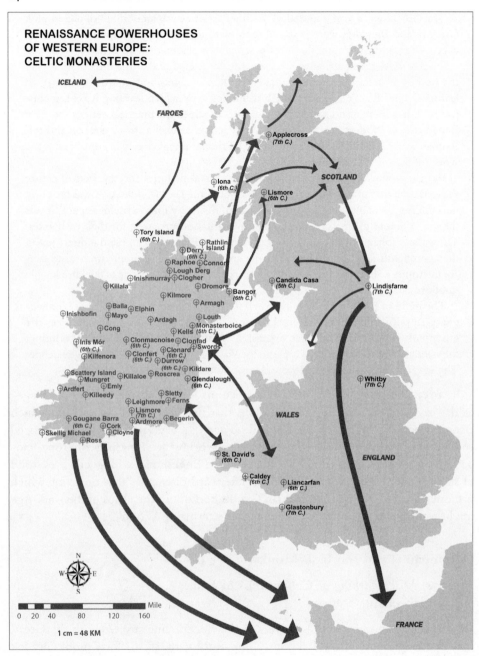

RENAISSANCE POWERHOUSES
OF WESTERN EUROPE:
CELTIC MONASTERIES

But twenty years before the sons of Saint Benedict had arrived from the south, there had landed on the shores of northern France bands of fiercely austere but winsome monks who came from the *finis terrae* (end of the earth), the mist-covered island lashed by Atlantic waves on the westernmost regions of the known world. On the coast of Brittany at Guimorais, between Saint-Malo and Mont-Saint-Michel, there is a granite cross to recall that day in 575 when the Irish priest Columbanus, accompanied by twelve monks, disembarked. These men blazed a trail across France, the Rhinelands, Switzerland, and northern Italy—the area that would largely comprise the heartlands of the eighth-century Carolingian Empire—founding or inspiring some two hundred monasteries before 730. These abbeys would have a far-reaching impact. They became the chief nurseries of a Catholic priestly and lay elite for the ongoing Christianization of northern France, Belgium, the Netherlands, Luxembourg, and Switzerland in the seventh century; the basis for the Anglo-Saxon evangelization in Western Germany in the first half of the eighth century; the launching pads for further missionary thrusts into Scandinavia and the Baltic lands in the ninth century; and, finally, they were the oases in which there occurred the renaissance of learning and the birth of a new Christian culture under Alcuin and Charlemagne that did much to pave the way for the golden age of medieval Christendom.[16]

It is hard to know which quality to admire most in this Father of Europe—his daring spirit or the sublime and tender sensitivity evident in his letters and poetry, his tenacity and austerity, or his depth of culture. By all accounts Columbanus had a larger-than-life personality. Already as a youth he cut a striking appearance and had attracted, and been strongly attracted by, the female sex. As his first biographer, Jonas, narrated:

St. Columba and His Brother Missionaries Land on the Isle of Iona. Detail from a window in Holy Trinity Church in Stratford-upon-Avon. This image accurately portrays the attire typical of Columbanus and Columba and also insightfully captures something of the intense Christian spirit that motivated these men to leave their homeland and embark for foreign shores.

> Columbanus, once childhood was over, dedicated himself enthusiastically and productively throughout his youth to studies of the humanities and sciences until he reached manhood. But since his handsome figure, and especially his splendid color and noble bearing, made him attractive to everyone, the ancient enemy finally began to turn his deadly weapons upon him in order to catch in his nets this youth whom he saw growing so swiftly in grace. He aroused against him the lust of sensuous young women, mainly those whose fine figure and shallow beauty normally turn the minds of wretched men mad with passion.[17]

As he travelled through Europe, like all the Celtic monks he was easily identifiable. He wore a long white habit, carried a curved staff, and had a water bottle and pouch containing relics of the saints hanging from around his neck. Whether before kings or simple countryfolk, the man whose "eyes were the color of gray sea water", whose voice was "strong and melodic", and whose hair, tonsured in the Celtic style, fell behind onto his shoulders, inspired awe:

---

[16] Travels and Influence of a "Father of Europe": "Columbanus is to be ranked among those truly great and extraordinary men whom divine providence is accustomed to raise up at the most difficult moments for mankind to restore causes almost lost." Pope Pius XI to Cardinal Franz Ehrle, August 6, 1923. Cardinal Ehrle was papal legate to the 13th centennial celebrations marking the death of St. Columbanus held at Bobbio, Italy. Published in *La Civiltà Cattolica* (Rome, 1923), p. 453. My translation.

[17] Jonas, *Vita Sancti Columbani*, 7, in D. Johannes Mabillon, *Acta Sanctorum Ordinis S. Benedicti*, vol. 1 (Venice, 1733), n. 7, p. 5. My translation.

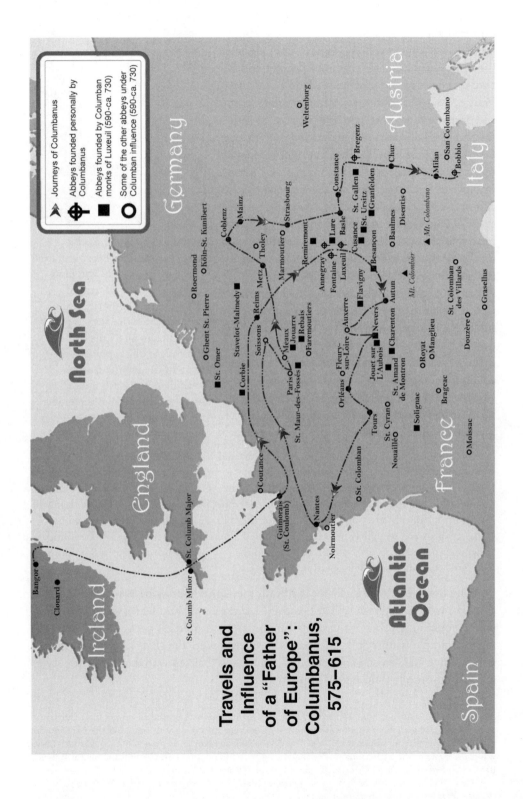

Travels and Influence of a "Father of Europe": Columbanus, 575–615

This bearded, gnarled giant, with muscles of steel, who could fell a tree with one blow of his axe and dig the soil for fifteen hours on end without showing any signs of fatigue. Yes, it was a rugged man who landed at Guimorais! A kind of Israelite prophet, walking the sixth-century earth, as plain-spoken as Isaiah or Jeremiah, on whose face, so his biographer assures us, "the might of God was clearly visible", a great walker and preacher, a tireless pioneer, a healer, and almost a soothsayer, and yet a man whose Irish ancestry had left him his sense of poetry and mystery, his love of nature and of day-dreaming.[18]

Chamnoald, royal chaplain at Laon, who occasionally accompanied Columbanus when the latter went for walks in the forest, never forgot how the monk used to call the animals and birds, and when they came would stroke them as they frisked and gamboled about him; how often he would call a squirrel from the top of a tree, "take it into his hand, put it on his neck and let it go up and down his chest".[19]

Columbanus founded his first monastery at Annegray amid the Vosges country of Burgundy. Then, in 590, on account of the large numbers donning the monastic uniform, he transformed an abandoned Gallo-Roman fortress at *Luxovium* (present-day Luxeuil-les-Bains), located in a wild, forested region, into a second abbey. Luxeuil rapidly became the most flourishing Christian center in Gaul, one of the great lighthouses of Catholic life in Europe. Its membership would shoot upward to six hundred, making it the monastic metropolis of the north.[20] But after Columbanus bluntly condemned the immorality of vicious King Thierry, he was forced to leave this family of monks whom he loved as a father, and go via Besançon, Autun, Auxerre, Nevers, Orléans, and Tours to Nantes, on the Atlantic coast of France, to embark for Ireland. Before boarding the ship he penned his adieu to these spiritual sons in a letter that expresses the ardor and tenderness that were so characteristic of him: "Wherever God will build with you, go and multiply, you and the myriads of saints who will be your offspring." But he immediately reminded them of the price they must pay for building up Christ's Church:

> If you get rid of enemies, you get rid of combat; if you get rid of combat, you also get rid of the crown. Where there is struggle with the adversary, there is courage, vigilance, zeal, patience, fidelity, wisdom, steadfastness, good judgment. Without [spiritual combat] destruction follows—and, I add, without freedom, no honor ... a messenger has arrived to tell me the ship is ready ... the end of my parchment forces me to finish my letter. Love is not orderly; it is this that has made it [my letter] muddled.... Farewell, dear hearts of mine, pray that I may live for God.[21]

But once at sea a storm drove the ship ashore, and the captain refused to set sail again with the Irish monks aboard. After a short stay in France, Columbanus and his band then went up the Rhine—Coblenz, Mainz, into the area of modern-day Switzerland to Basle, and then to Bregenz on the shores of Lake Constance, where they set up another monastery. As the oars dug into the strong currents of

---

[18] Daniel-Rops, *Church in the Dark Ages*, p. 216.

[19] Jonas, *Vita Sancti Columbani*, 7, n. 30, p. 26. My translation.

[20] The statutes established by St. Columbanus for Luxeuil and his other monasteries can be read in *Patrologia Latina*, vol. 80 (Paris: J.P. Migne, 1863), pp. 201ff.

[21] St. Columbanus, Letter 4, in *Sancti Columbani Opera*, in G.S.M. Walker, ed., *Scriptores Latini Hiberniae*, vol. 2 (Dublin: Dublin Institute for Advanced Studies, 1957). My translation.

the mighty Rhine, the resonant voice of Columbanus may have been heard giving rhythm to the strokes of the oars as he sang the verses—and everyone else repeated the refrain—of a rowing song, *En Silvis Caesa*, that he had composed.

Behold, the boat from forest hewn
journeys o'er the waves of twin-horned Rhine,[22]
and anointed through the waters glides.
Heave, men! Let the echo of our "heave" resound thundering!
The wild winds swell, the slashing rains whip,
But manly strength conquers and routs the storm.
Heave, men! Let the echo of our "heave" resound thundering!
To enduring effort clouds and storms do yield,
Zeal conquers adversity, tireless toil triumphs o'er all.
Heave, men! Let the echo of our "heave" resound thundering!
Hold fast! Endure! And look ahead toward better times,
You who have worse endured; an end to this too God will give.
Heave, men! Let the echo of our "heave" resound thundering!
When the unseen foe tires the heart,
Tempting and startling with passion its depths,
Let your souls, men, remembering Christ, cry "heave"!
Steadfast be in will, scorn the enemy's guile,
With virtues armed, defend yourselves with valor.
Let your souls, men, remembering Christ, cry "heave"!
Strong faith and holy ardor conquer all.
The ancient foe, defeated, breaks his arrows.
Let your souls, men, remembering Christ, cry "heave"!
The majestically virtuous One, the origin of all, the Supreme Power,
To the fighter pledges, to the victor gives reward.
Let your souls, men, remembering Christ, cry "heave"![23]

With Thierry still breathing threats they continued further south. One of the monks accompanying him, Saint Gall, fell seriously ill on the journey and stayed behind in the Swiss area that would soon proudly name itself after him. Crossing the Alps, the great lover of Christ founded his final abbey amid the Lombards at Bobbio, one that would become the Christian lighthouse of northern Italy. There, in A.D. 615, his lifelong prayer was definitively answered: "Wound our souls with your love so that the soul of each one of us may be able to say in truth, 'Show me him whom my soul has loved' for by love am I wounded."[24]

His achievement was colossal. Columbanus had found the Church in northern France, the Lowlands, and the Rhinelands sinking in a sea of moral squalor. Like a

[22] "Twin-horned" is a description of the Rhine made both by Columbanus and the Roman writer Virgil on account of the two branches of the river near Koblenz.
[23] Translation is mine. For the original Latin text, see James Carney, ed., *Medieval Irish Lyrics* (Berkeley: University of California Press, 1967), pp. 8–10. My translation "resound thundering" corresponds to the meaning of the verb used by St. Columbanus, *reboare*, which was used by Ovid and other classical writers to indicate the powerful echo given by mountains.
[24] Walker, *Sancti Columbani Opera*, pp. 120–21. My translation.

comet he had passed overhead, radiating the light of Christ and, as a contemporary remarked, "hurling the fire of Christ wheresoever he could, without concerning himself with the blaze it caused".[25] And blaze it did. For centuries the noblest Burgundian, Frankish, and Lombard parents earnestly took the road to the Columban abbeys in order to entrust their children to these oases of holiness and learning. Among the youth who graduated were many who became outstanding leaders in Church and state. Almost all of the great churchmen, missionaries, and founders of monasteries in seventh-century France were either immediate disciples or spiritual heirs of his: Saints Omer (Audomar), Wandrille, Ouen, Bertin, Philibert, Eustace, Fara, Valery, and Romaric. No less than twenty-one men from Luxeuil have been acclaimed as saints, according to Montalembert.[26] Some 250 European place-names recall him and the Celtic monks who followed in his footsteps.

With the passion of a man in love, he had instilled in these sons by word and example the desire for a Church faithful to its identity and therefore in constant reform. As Henri Daniel-Rops remarked: "In the heart of the Dark Ages the spirit of reform, or, to phrase it differently, the idea of 'perpetual revolution'—for we should remember that Christianity is, essentially, the 'Revolution of the Cross'—was made incarnate in two mighty individuals. These were St. Columbanus at the end of the sixth century and St. Boniface in the eighth."[27] However, they were reformers who, although capable of reprimanding popes for what they considered their errors and omissions, nevertheless loved Church and papacy with inseparable loyalty. "We Irish", wrote Columbanus to the reigning pontiff, "are especially bound to the See of Peter ... the chariot of the Church came to us across the western waves with Christ as its charioteer and Peter and Paul as its swift and strong horses."[28]

Among the Irish monks, next to Columbanus in degree of impact during the Dark Ages was Columba (521–597), who founded the monastery on the island of Iona, off the coast of Scotland, in 563. According to the ninth Abbot of Iona, Adomnán (627–704),

> From his boyhood Colum Cille [Columba] devoted himself to the Christian combat and to the search for wisdom. By God's grace he preserved integrity of body and purity of soul so that he seemed like one ready for the life of heaven though still on earth; for in appearance he was like an angel, refined in his speech, holy in his works, preeminent in character, great in counsel. In the forty-second year of his age he sailed away from Ireland.... During his life of thirty-four years as a soldier of Christ on the island of Iona, he could not let even one hour pass that was not given to prayer or reading or writing or some other good work. Night and day he so unwearyingly gave himself to fasts and vigils that the burden of each single work seemed beyond the strength of man. Yet through all he was loving to everyone, his holy face was always cheerful, and in his inmost heart he was happy with the joy of the Holy Spirit.[29]

[25] Quoted in Brendan Lehane, *Early Celtic Christianity* (London: Continuum, 1968), p. 166.

[26] The twenty-one men from Luxeuil acclaimed as saints are listed in Count de Montalembert, *The Monks of the West from St. Benedict to St. Bernard*, vol. 1 (New York: P.J. Kenedy and Sons, 1912), p. 591.

[27] Daniel-Rops, *Church in the Dark Ages*, pp. 296–97.

[28] St. Columbanus, Letter to Pope Boniface, Letter 5, in Walker, *Sancti Columbani Opera*, pp. 120–21. English translation here as found in Christopher Dawson, *The Making of Europe: An Introduction to the History of European Unity* (Washington D.C.: Catholic University of America Press, 2003), p. 175.

[29] Adomnán, *The Life of Columba*, preface 2, quoted in *The Divine Office: The Liturgy of the Hours according to the Roman Rite*, vol. 3 (London: Collins, Dwyer, and Talbot, 1974), pp. 444–45. See Adomnán, *The Life of Columba*, Alan Orr Anderson, ed. (London: Thomas Nelson and Sons, 1961).

With Iona as his base he pioneered the conversion of the districts of Caledonia, from the region of the wild Picts in the north beyond the Grampians to that of the Dalriadian Scots in the south, as well as the islands along the western coast. His declaration against Scots paying tribute to the High King of Ireland was an important step in the forging of Scotland's national identity. Even more so was his decision to crown Aidan, who had been educated on Iona, as the first king of Dalriada in 574. Seating him on the "Stone of Destiny"—an oblong block of red sandstone—Columba solemnly anointed him and received his vow to remain true to the Catholic Faith. From then on, all of the Scottish kings were crowned in this way until 1296, when King Edward Longshanks of England took the "Stone of Destiny" away from Scone to Westminster where it has remained the coronation stone for British monarchs. For all of this, Scots of old cherished the memory of Columba, frequently baptizing their children with the name Malcolm, "Servant of Columba".

Dorothy Burrows, *Saint Columba Arrives to Iona*

After his death, Iona became the training ground for bishops and missionaries who pioneered the conversion of northern England. Outstanding among them for his effectiveness was Saint Aidan (ca. A.D. 600–651), "a man of singular gentleness, piety, and moderation, having a zeal of God".[30] King Oswald of Northumbria, a devoted friend of Aidan, helped him to found the great abbey of Lindisfarne, destined to become the bridgehead for the evangelization of northern and central England—Northumbria and Mercia—while from Kent Saint Augustine of Canterbury (530–604) and the Benedictines would bring the Catholic Faith to the south. Due to the conversion of Britain, many Anglo-Saxon monks in the seventh and eighth centuries would in turn become torchbearers of the Faith to Europe, men like Saint Willibrord of Utrecht (ca. 658–739), "Apostle of the Frisians", and the "Apostle of Germany", Saint Boniface (672–754), who restored discipline in the Frankish Church and fostered the conversion of many Thuringians, Saxons, and Frisians. He would be followed by his compatriot, Alcuin of York (ca. 730–804), who, alongside Charlemagne, initiated the forging of a Christian synthesis of the Roman and Teutonic cultures.

Hence, the continent owes much to the Celtic monks who became "the benefactors of almost every nation in Europe"[31] between the sixth and tenth centuries.

---

[30] A.M. Sellar, ed., *Bede's Ecclesiastical History of England* (London: George Bell and Co., 1907), bk. 3, chap. 3, p. 139.

[31] The German historian Johann Joseph Ignaz von Döllinger, quoted in John Henry Cardinal Newman, "The Tradition of Civilization: The Isles of the North", in *Rise and Progress of Universities and Benedictine Essays*, ed. Mary Katherine Tillman (Leominster, Herefordshire; Gracewing and Notre Dame: University of Notre Dame Press, 2001), p. 126.

Although most of them were from Ireland, some also came from the Celtic regions of Wales, Scotland, Cornwall, the Isle of Man, and Brittany. Frequently they left an indelible mark on the regions they evangelized: Saint Kilian at Würzburg in Bavaria, Saint Virgil at Salzburg in Austria, Saint Cathaldus in southern Italy, and Saint Minnborinus in Cologne. In Brittany almost every town claims for itself a Celtic holy man: Saints Malo, Brieuc, Tudwal, Cadoc, Guenhael, Samson (founder of Dol), and Corentinus (Cury), the first Bishop of Quimper.

Some went as far east as Kiev in the Ukraine; others went northward to Iceland. When the Viking longboat bearing Ingólfur Arnarson and the first permanent Norse settlers came ashore in Iceland in A.D. 874, they discovered they were not the first to disembark on the island. According to the accounts of the *Íslendingabók* of Ari Thorgilsson and other Icelandic histories, the Celtic monks had arrived ahead of them but at the approach of the anti-Christian Norsemen they departed. Another account supportive of their Icelandic presence is to be found in the geography book *Liber de Mensura Orbis Terrae*, written around 825, wherein the Celtic monk-author Dicuil describes both the Faroes and what is probably Iceland. He narrates that as early as the seventh century Irish monks had sailed to the subarctic island group of the Faroes (the name meaning "Sheep Islands")—distant only 261 miles (420 km) from Iceland—in order to live a life of prayer and penance: "[A] set of small islands, nearly all separated by narrow stretches of water; in these, for nearly a hundred years, hermits sailing from our country, Ireland, have lived. But just as they were always deserted from the beginning of the world, so now because of the Norse pirates they are emptied of hermits and are filled with countless sheep and very many diverse kinds of seabirds".[32] Then he goes on to describe another island, *Thule*, north of the Faroes, where the water is often ice-free and the sun barely goes below the horizon around the summer solstice so that at midnight it is still as bright "as in broad daylight".[33] This description could well refer to Iceland, which had also often been named *Thule* on medieval maps. The source of his information, states Dicuil, is from the Irish monks who had been going there since around A.D. 795.

"Who Are These Men?"

Even from a distance of centuries, one can still understand the awe of the barbarians when they first met these Celtic monks: "Who are these men? Where have they come from? What makes them who they are?"

It was similar to the wonder that had already been aroused at the sight of the first monks in Gaul, where monasticism had existed since the fourth century when Saint Martin (316–397) had founded monasteries at Ligugé and Tours around 360; Saint Honoratus had started another on one of the Lérins islands off the French

---

[32] Dicuil, *Liber de Mensura Orbis Terrae*, cited in Jonathan Wylie, *The Faroe Islands: Interpretations of History* (Lexington: University Press of Kentucky, 1987), p. 7. However, the *papar* (the "fathers" in Old Gaelic, as the Irish monks were called) have returned to these wild windy regions! Since 1999, Gregorian chant has again filled the air as the Holy Sacrifice of the Mass has been offered on the island of Papa Stronsay in the Orkneys, to the south of the Faroes, by a new traditional order, the Congregation of the Sons of the Most Holy Redeemer; see http://www.papastronsay.com/.

[33] Dicuil, *Liber de Mensura Orbis Terrae*, cited in Njörður P. Njarðvík, *Birth of a Nation: The Story of the Icelandic Commonwealth* (Reykjavik: Iceland Review History Series, 1978), p. 13.

A.D. 564: King Brude of the Picts meeting Columba for the first time at his stronghold on the summit of a crag near Inverness. Columba, when confronted by locked gates on his arrival, had made the sign of the cross, after which the gate bolts fell to the ground, allowing him to enter, much to the royal astonishment. The Irish monk became friend and mentor to the powerful Pictish ruler who decided to become Catholic. This wood carving on oak panels commemorating the event is at St. Columba's Cathedral, Oban, in the Diocese of Argyll and the Isles and is the work of Donald Gilbert of Sussex. The cathedral stands on the edge of Oban Bay, looking west across the Firth of Lorne to Iona.

Riviera around 370; and John Cassian had established the Abbey of St. Victor, near Marseilles, about 415. The barbarians, whether pagan or nominally Christian, were perplexed in the presence of such a hitherto unknown type of man. They intuited a spiritual strength, purpose, and intensity beside which they began to recognize their own savage, unrestrained ferocity as weakness. Admiration grew within them as they watched these monks striving to live without appeasing mediocrity, with no pause for comfort beyond the utterly necessary, and rebuffing any compromise with the lust of the flesh.

All of this they saw in the Celts, and indeed their degree of rugged asceticism, surpassing that of the Gallic monks, left them thunderstruck. But the Celtic missionaries also possessed qualities that distinguished them from most of their Frankish or Gallo-Roman confrères. The native monks—with the exception of some of the members of Saint Martin of Tour's communities—were largely isolated from the ebb and flow of social life; theirs was the Egyptian monastic ideal that considered the hermit's existence to be the goal of monastic aspiration, with fasts and vigils of prayer as the method to attain it. The Celts, however, were recognized as outwardbound. They had crossed the sea, abandoning their homeland, in order to bring the new religion to strangers. There was no personal material benefit to be gained; they carried no arms, had no political protectors, and sought no power. Their leader, Columbanus, already in his late forties, was relatively old in an age when so many died young from disease and privations. The Franks, Bretons, Lombards, and others were gladdened when they saw that these inspiring men set each monastery in the heart of the community. The monks wanted to interact with the local people; they wanted to educate the young, train the men in agricultural techniques, care for their sick, strengthen justice, stand between them and tyrannical rulers, and, in all and above all, bring every person to the truth and peace of Christ.

They were also extraordinarily cultured due to their knowledge of Latin, Greek, philosophy, and astronomy, a quality to be found in Gaul only amid members and graduates of the monastic "university" on the island of Lérins and among some of the Gallo-Roman artistocrats. Since the sixth century they were almost alone in Western Europe in their knowledge of Greek. By the eighth century the most important centers preserving and copying the manuscripts of Greece and Rome were almost all Celtic in origin or had been strongly influenced by Celtic monasticism. Besides the Irish monasteries of Kells, Durrow, and Bangor, there were the Anglo-Saxon abbeys of Lindisfarne and York, as well as the continental centers of Luxeuil, St. Amand, Corbie, Autun, Soissons, Echternach, St. Gall, Bobbio, and Nonantola.

The effects of this new type of monk and monasticism overflowed into society. In education, the Celtic monastic schools spearheaded what became under Charlemagne and Alcuin a mass-literacy movement, creating a society of educational opportunities rare in history. This they achieved by teaching children from about seven to seventeen years of age, providing them with manuscripts of the Gospels, the Psalms, and classical authors. They also taught reading and writing in the vernacular languages; indeed, Irish Gaelic became the first vernacular language in Europe to develop a written form during the sixth century. This educational drive was accomplished with such reckless generosity that any youth keen to study knew that he could just knock on the door of any abbey and he would be admitted: "The Scots [*Scoti*, Irish] willingly received them all, and took care to supply them with daily food without cost, as also to furnish them with books for their studies, and teaching free of charge."[34] In the face of obstacles their generosity was creative, as for instance in Brittany where, due to warfare in the region, they established their school on an island off the coast and built a four-hundred-foot bridge to enable the students to attend.

In agriculture the Irish monks were highly competent. They turned many a wilderness into fertile farmland by clearing forests or by draining and damming riverbed land. Around their abbeys they built up communities of farmers, artisans, blacksmiths, and other workers. They popularized the horse-collar that enabled better ploughing and may have invented the corn kiln, which played an important role in cereal production. They brought about a revival of agriculture, and their own abbey estates grew enormously. For instance, the monastery of Bobbio in northern Italy, by 643, held some 150 monks housed in ten multistoried buildings as well as lay cooperators in thirty other houses. In that year the monastery had the following surpluses for resale: "2,100 bushels of corn, 1,600 cartloads of hay, 2,700 litres of oil, 5,000 pigs, large and small cattle; to which must be added the production of around 650 farms, roughly 3,600 bushels of corn, 800 amphoras of wine and other products".[35] And all of this, according to their rules, they sold at a lower price than that charged by others. Moreover, the noblemen who joined the Columban abbeys often either freed their serfs or allowed them to become part of the monastic estate where they could live and work in peace.

The Celtic monasteries also became fortresses of justice, protecting the poor from their often brutal overlords. The Irish monks had brought with them from Ireland a tradition of law codes such as the *Lex Innocentium* (Law of Innocents) also known as

[34] A. M. Sellar, ed., *Bede's Ecclesiastical History of England* (London: George Bell and Co., 1907), bk. 3, chap. 27, p. 204.

[35] Jean Decarreaux, *Monks and Civilization: From the Barbarian Invasions to the Reign of Charlemagne* (New York: Doubleday, 1964), p. 360.

the *Cáin Adomnáin* (Law of Adomnán), on account of its leading promoter, Adomnán of Iona, ninth Abbot of Iona. It legislated protection for children, students, and clerics, as well as decreeing that "whoever slays a woman ... his right hand and his left foot shall be cut off ... and then he shall be executed".[36]

And what missionaries they were! For instance, during the forty-year reign of Walbert, Abbot of Luxeuil (ca. 628–668), groups of monks set out *every* day from the abbey to either propose the Faith to non-Christians or else to strengthen those already baptized.

But *why*? Why did they do all this? And at such heights of self-sacrifice? Why had they abandoned their homeland to live among foreigners? Why such a rugged, indeed severe lifestyle?

The ultimate explanation lay in their Christian vision of life, nuanced and shaped by the Celtic culture. God for them was the Creator of an immensely beautiful world of sky, land, and ocean, all of which reflected his own radiant splendor and goodness. Man, created to share in God's happiness, had lost his filial inheritance by abusing his freedom, with the result that he had enslaved himself to the powers of darkness and sin. Yet, God, in an act of awesome love, had entered the world to rescue man; heroically he had liberated him on Calvary; and he had empowered the restoration of man's intimate union with him by instituting the Church with her sacraments, through which a new supernatural life could spring up in man's interior. Due to this life the Christian was never alone during his journey on earth; he was united with his Eternal Father, the all-powerful but gentle "High King" (*Ard Rí*) of Heaven; with the Holy Spirit, the Protector; and with Jesus Christ, the Rescuer, the Savior-Hero of the Cross, "the victorious one", "lord of victories", "mighty warrior", but, above all, the intimate and beloved Friend of the soul. To him the young Celt, aspiring to be a monk, pledged his manhood with enthusiastic, undying loyalty. A modern-day Irish poet, Joseph Plunkett, succinctly expressed this passionate love for Christ that was united to the Celtic sensitivity for nature, in his poem "I See His Blood upon the Rose": "I see his blood upon the rose / And in the stars the glory of his eyes, / His body gleams amid eternal snows, / His tears fall from the skies. / I see his face in every flower; / The thunder and the singing of the birds are but his voice / And carven by his power rocks are his written words. / All pathways by his feet are worn, / His strong heart stirs the ever-beating sea, / His crown of thorns is twined with every thorn, / His cross is every tree."[37]

In their love for Christ these men found the strength for the self-sacrifice implied by chastity, obedience, and the renunciation of so much that men hold dear, as can be glimpsed in a prayer of Columba, composed on the shores of his exile, the Isle of Iona, off the coast of Scotland: "Lord, Thou art my island; in Thy bosom I rest. Thou art the calm of the sea; in that peace I stay. Thou art the deep waves of the shining ocean; with their eternal sound I sing. Thou art the song of the birds; in that melody is my joy. Thou art the smooth white strand of the shore; in Thee there is no gloom. Thou art the breaking of the waves on the rock; Thy praise is echoed in

---

[36] Henry Frowde, ed., *Cáin Adamnáin: An Old-Irish Treatise on the Law of Adamnan* (Oxford: Clarendon Press, 1905), p. 25.

[37] Joseph Mary Plunkett, "I See His Blood upon the Rose", in *The Oxford Book of English Mystical Verse*, ed. D. H. S. Nicholson and A. H. E. Lee (Oxford: Clarendon Press, 1917), n. 342.

the swell. Thou art the Lord of my life."[38] We can better gauge the depth of their love when we glimpse something of the pain, springing from their sacrifice, that these sensitive men felt at times. Such an insight is given us by Columba, his heart breaking within him, as he spoke of his longing to return to Ireland from Alba (Scotland) and to see once more his mentor, Comgall: "And watch the waves break upon the Irish shore! / What joy to row the little bark, and land amid the whitening foam upon the Irish shore! / Ah! How my boat would fly if its prow were turned to my Irish oak-grove! / But the noble sea now carries me only to Albyn [Scotland], the land of ravens. / My foot is in my little boat; but my sad heart ever bleeds! / There is a gray eye which ever turns to Erin; / But never in this life shall it see Erin, nor hear her sons nor her daughters! / From the high prow I look over the sea; / And great tears are in my gray eye when I turn to Erin. / To Erin, where the songs of birds are so sweet, / And where the clerks [clerics] sing like the birds; / Where the young are so gentle, and the old are so wise; / Where the great men are so noble to look at and the women so fair to wed! / Young traveler! carry my sorrows with thee; / Carry them to Comgall of eternal life. . . . / My heart is broken in my breast . . ."[39]

It was therefore a passionate and steadfast love for Jesus Christ that transfigured pain and sacrifice, indeed life and death, for the Celtic monk. They made their own the leitmotif of Saint Paul: "For to me to live is Christ, and to die is gain. If it is to be life in the flesh, that means fruitful labor for me. Yet which I shall choose I cannot tell. I am hard pressed between the two. My desire is to depart and be with Christ, for that is far better" (Phil 1:21–23).

The road to deeper union with the God-Man, the prototype of human grandeur, was through the transforming of one's personality unto Christlikeness. However, there were three major obstacles to this Christification: man's wounded nature, with its disordered inclination to pleasure; the social milieu that sin had made toxic to some degree; and the Prince of Darkness, a real, personal, and powerful spirit bent on man's damnation. Overcoming these enemies to attain salvation required the supernatural life, channeled through the

Window of Iona Abbey, Scotland.

Church's sacraments and strengthened by prayer. But it also demanded man's free cooperation through an exertion to pattern one's life on the salvific pattern of Jesus Christ's death and Resurrection. This implied self-combat in order to eradicate sin and foster the growth of Christ's virtues in one's thoughts and actions. Thus the Celtic monks adopted the motto of Saint Paul: "I have been crucified with Christ; it is no longer I who live, but Christ who lives in me; and the life I now live in the

---

[38] Quoted in Andrea Skevington, *Wise Sayings of the Celts* (Oxford: Lion Hudson, 2012), p. 6.
[39] Quoted in Charles Forbes, Comte de Montalembert, *Saint Columba: Apostle of Caledonia* (Edinburgh-London: William Blackwood and Sons, 1868), pp. 40–41.

flesh I live by faith in the Son of God, who loved me and gave himself for me" (Gal 2:20). And so they loved, adored, and cherished the Cross, not only because in it was the answer to tragedy, pain, and death, but above all because it was "the center of the fire in which they were to be changed".[40] The pain that seared through their hearts at different moments when life showed them what they had renounced was accepted and united with love, tinged by sorrow, to the self-offering of Jesus Christ Crucified for the salvation of humanity. Through this doorway, repeatedly passed through, they knew they would come to ever-increasing intimacy with the Friend of their souls. For this reason Celtic monks frequently practiced the "cross-vigil", praying with arms outstretched, sometimes for hours on end. And for the same motive they erected beautiful, intricately carved, and tall crucifixes, some of them fifteen feet high.

Hence, the Celtic monastic ideal required men of exceptional strength of character, capable of lifelong ascetic campaigning. For the Celtic male who crossed the monastic threshold there was accordingly no question of leaving behind his dream of warriorhood: it was merely a matter of shouldering a different type of militancy. The love of warfare that ran through his blood would rise to a more sublime level, joining passionately in the cosmic conflict between the forces of darkness and light for the sake of the eternal salvation of souls. To enter Ardmore, Glendalough, Bangor, or Iona was to join a regiment of Christ's army in order to wage conflict against the High King's enemies, the satanic powers. Make no mistake about it: underneath the white habits of these monks was the ancient Celtic warrior spirit.[41] As one of them, possibly Faustus of Riez (ca. 408–ca. 492), in a sermon to his fellow monks

Celtic cross at Monasterboice, Ireland, with a monastic round tower in the background.

on the island of Lérins, said: "To this place, dearly beloved, we have gathered, not for peace and security, but for confrontation and combat. It is for struggle that we have advanced hither. It is to wage wars with vices that we have embarked.... What we need, brothers, is ever watchful focus and untiring vigilance since this battle never ends; no ceasefire is possible with the enemy. He can be conquered but he cannot be received in friendship. Hence, this warfare to which we have committed ourselves is extremely hard and most dangerous since it is waged within a man, and it is not brought to a conclusion unless by the man himself."[42]

---

[40] Benedicta Ward, *High King of Heaven* (Kalamazoo, Mich.: Cistercian Publications, 1999), p. 96.

[41] The Celtic love of war had already been noticed centuries before by the Greek historian, Strabo (ca. 64 B.C.–ca. A.D. 24), who remarked: "The whole race is war-mad ... high spirited, and quick to battle, but otherwise straightforward and not of evil character. And so when they are stirred up they assemble in their bands for battle quite openly and without forethought.... They are ready to face danger even if they have nothing on their side but their own strength and courage." Strabo, *The Geography*, ed. H.L. Jones (Cambridge, Mass.: Harvard University Press, 1917–1932), vol. 2, p. 235.

[42] Bishop Faustus of Riez, "Sermo Primus" (*PL* 58:869).

When this struggle was waged heroically, it merited the laurels of martyrdom of which there were three types, according to the Irish monks. Red martyrdom was heroic love through suffering a violent death for Christ's sake. Iron-grey (blue) martyrdom was extraordinary love through engaging steadfastly in long-term combat for the sake of conquering one's disordered will, perhaps especially in its tendency to pride. White martyrdom was the victory in the struggle with the body's disordered passion of sensuality. The red implied that one had already attained the iron-grey and the white; and all three surged from a singleminded love sealed by purity of heart and a hard-won conquest of one's will through deep and prolonged personal prayer flanked by fasting and other ascetic practices. A high point in this struggle to love and bear witness ("martyrdom") to Christ was to leave behind one's beloved *patria* and set sail for foreign lands.[43]

Hence, it was with the vitality of athletes that these ardent Celts committed themselves to the cause of Christ. Moreover, their austerity did not thwart but rather refined their humanity, as can be seen in the descriptions of men like Columba. The austerity of these ascetic superstars with their habits of intense work, fasting, and long hours of prayer went unchanged even when they were at the courts of rulers, as can be seen in the life of the mild Aidan of Lindisfarne, cherished friend of King Oswald of Northumbria.

> He was one to traverse both town and country on foot, never on horseback, unless compelled by some urgent necessity; and wherever on his way he saw anyone, either rich or poor, he invited them, if infidels, to embrace the mystery of the Faith, or, if they were believers, to strengthen them in the faith and to stir them up by words and actions to alms and good works.... This [praying and reading of sacred Scripture] was the daily employment of himself and all that were with him, wheresoever they went; and if it happened, which was but seldom, that he was invited to eat with the king, he went with one or two clerks, and having taken a small repast, made haste to be gone with them, either to read or write.... At that time, many religious men and women, stirred up by his example, adopted the custom of fasting on Wednesdays and Fridays, till the ninth hour, throughout the year ... whatsoever gifts of money he received from the rich, he either distributed them, as has been said, to the use of the poor, or bestowed them in ransoming such as had been wrongfully sold for slaves.[44]

For those monks who had been ordained, the standards were even higher because of the Celtic reverence for the dignity of the priesthood: "It is right to show reverence to ordained priests and to fulfill their commands as if they were God's angels among men; seeing that it is through them that the Kingdom of Heaven is to be won by baptism and communion and intercession, and by the Sacrifice of the Body and Blood of Christ, and by preaching of the Gospel, and by building up the Church of God, and unity of law and rule; and this is what is pleasing to God on earth."[45]

---

[43] The three types of Celtic martyrdom are explained in a collection of ancient Gaelic glosses, scholia, prose, and verse, the "Cambrai Homily", written around the end of the seventh century. "Iron-grey" is one of the possible translations of the Gaelic word *glas*, which can comprise various tints between sky blue, grey, and green. In clothing it stood for the color derived from the dye *glaisia*, "woad". See Whitley Stokes and John Strachan, eds., *Thesaurus Palaeohibernicus*, vol. 2 (Cambridge, Mass.: Harvard University Press, 1903), pp. 246–47.

[44] Venerable Bede, *Ecclesiastical History of the English Nation*, bk. 3, chap. 5, quoted in Alban Butler, *Lives of the Saints* (Montreal: Palm Publishers, 1956), pp. 406–7.

[45] *The Rule of the Céli Dé*, par. 64, quoted in *The Divine Office: The Liturgy of the Hours according to the Roman Rite* (London-Sydney-Dublin: Collins-Dwyer-Talbot, 1974), p. 470.

Therefore, the priest's obligation to pursue self-conquest was more urgent: "When is a person competent to answer for the souls of others? When he is competent to answer for his own soul first. When is he capable of correcting others? When in the first place he can correct himself. A person who corrects his own soul to life everlasting, how many souls could he convert? The people of the whole world: provided that they were willing, he could convert them to life everlasting so that they would belong to the Kingdom of Heaven."[46]

Accordingly, sacrifice of all that men cherished on earth was possible because engraved upon the hearts of the Celtic monks were the words: "[Y]our merciful love is better than life" (Ps 63:3). This was what had motivated them to enter monastic solitude where, daily, amid prayer and silence, they offered themselves to God as co-workers in the mysterious conspiracy of divine providence for man's salvation. Yet though their spirits dwelt on mystic peaks, their hearts burned with a practical love for their fellow men that was global in a way the world had never known until the arrival of Christianity. When they learned of the barbarians who did not know the Savior, these Celtic mystics could not resist leaving their island fortress to become *peregrini pro Christo* (pilgrims for the sake of Christ). The ancient chronicles tell us of the young Irishmen who, as they boarded the boats to cross the sea to Europe, vowed never to return to the lovely land of their birth. Their motive was evident: blazing within them was a fire that a man had once passionately expressed in his leitmotif, "[T]he love of Christ urges us" (2 Cor 5:14). And urge them it certainly did, as can be seen in the never-a-pause existence of their paragon, Columbanus, who, even at seventy years of age, crossed the Alps and at death's door wanted to set out again to the Slavs. In their youth, these priests' love for Christ and humanity resembled the fiery flames shooting up into the air from a mighty wood fire. As the years went by, diminished were the flames by the body's exhaustion, but more intense became the heat that radiated all around them amid the cold and darkness of the night of those centuries.

So, when youth and warriors visited Luxeuil, Bobbio, and the other Columban monasteries, they noticed one thing above and beyond the austerity and scholarship of these men: their supernaturally motivated happiness. And that was the chief reason why they joined in such large numbers abbeys in France, Germany, Switzerland, and Lombardy.

The Silent Revolution

Plight of Church and Society at the Arrival of Columbanus

When Columbanus and his fellow monks landed on the shores of northern Gaul (France) in A.D. 575, they found a land that had been devastated by wars, massacres, and, from about A.D. 550, a series of plagues. The population of Gaul in the sixth century had shrunk to a quarter of its size in the second century.[47] Villages had been abandoned and shrouded in forest darkness; the soil went untilled for want

---

[46] *The Alphabet of Piety*, chap. 2, par. 18, ascribed to the Lismore monk Colmán mac Béognae (d. 611), a text regarding the fundamentals of monastic commitment, quoted in *The Divine Office*, p. 471.

[47] Xavier de Planhol and Paul Claval, *An Historical Geography of France* (Cambridge: Cambridge University Press, 1994), p. 68.

CELTIC TORCHBEARERS
OF EUROPEAN RENAISSANCE
(SIXTH–NINTH CENTURIES)

Ireland

England

Wales

Spain

ST. WILLIBRORD
Utrecht
(8th century)

ST. WIRO
Roermond
(8th century)

ST. MAILDUF
Malmesbury
(675)

ST. FEUILLIEN
Namur
(7th century)

ST. ROMBAUT
Malines
(8th century)

J. S. ERIUGENA,
DICUIL
Aachen
(9th century)

ST. CLEMENT, DUNGAL
Paris
(8th-9th century)

ST. FRICOR
Picardy
(7th century)

ST. LIVINUS
Brabant
(7th century)

ST. FEUILLIEN
Namur
(7th century)

ST. PAUL AURELIAN
Batz
(6th century)

ST. TUDWAL
Tréguier
(6th century)

ST. MALO
(6th century)

ST. SAËNS
(ca. 680)

ST. ABEL
Reims
(8th century)

ST. TRESSAN
Chalons-en-Champagne
(7th century)

ST. KILIAN
Würzburg
(7th century)

ST. DISIBOD
Disibodenberg
(7th century)

ST. RONAN
Locronan
(ca. 7th century)

ST. BRIEUC
(5th century)

ST. SAMSON
Dol
(6th century)

ST. FURSEY
Lagny-sur-Marne
(ca. 650)

ST. GOBAIN
(7th century)

ST. TRUDPERT
Münstertal
(7th century)

ST. ALTO
Altomünster
(8th century)

ST. GILDAS THE WISE
Rhuys
(6th century)

ST. FIACRE
Breuil
(7th century)

ST. COLUMBANUS
Luxeuil
(590)

ST. FRIDOLIN
Säckingen
(ca. 480-540)

ST. SÉZIN
Guisseny
(6th century)

ST. DESLE
Lure
(ca. 611)

ST. URCISIN
St. Ursanne
(7th century)

ST. GALL
St. Gall
(ca. 550-640)

ST. MARCELLUS
(9th century)

ST. VIRGILIUS
Salzburg
(ca. 700-784)

ST. HÉLIE
Angoulême
(9th century)

ST. FINTAN
Rheinau
(9th century)

ST. ÉMILION
Saint-Émilion
(8th century)

ST. COLUMBANUS
Bobbio
(614)

ST. FREDIANO
Lucca
(ca. 510-588)

ST. DONATO
Fiesole
(ca. 800-876)

ST. CATALDO
Taranto
(ca. 7th century)

"The renaissance of Christian wisdom and culture over several regions of France, Germany, and Italy is due to the toil and zeal of Columbanus; a fact that reveals the merits of the priesthood and, especially, of Catholic Ireland." Pope Pius XI's letter to Cardinal Franz Ehrle (August 6, 1923), papal legate to the 13th centennial celebrations in honor of St. Columbanus, held at Bobbio, Italy. *La Civiltà Cattolica* (Rome, August 1923), pp. 453–54. My Translation.

of laborers; culture and education withered to the point that it was difficult to find anyone who could even read and write. Gallic scholars had abandoned their land to sail to Western Europe's haven of peace, Ireland, and there amid the enthusiasm of an entire nation that had embraced the Catholic Faith, they taught all they knew of classical learning to the native monks.[48]

---

[48] For a description of society in Gaul during the sixth century, see Gregory of Tours, *History of the Franks*, trans. O. M. Dalton, 2 vols. (Oxford: University Press, 1927).

Moreover, Gaul was a bestial society. Chroniclers of the fifth and sixth centuries don't mince their language as they describe either the Gallo-Romans or the barbarians. Both rulers and ruled lived lives of debauchery, corruption, and savage brutality; atrocities went unpunished; and bloody vendettas were the methods of justice after the triumph of the Visigoths and Franks had led to the widespread adoption of Germanic laws.

Complex were the causes of this moral decadence, but one very important one was the absence, practically speaking, of the sacrament of confession, the sacrament conveying the horror of sin, the grandeur of God's love, and the possibility of ongoing conversion to ever higher degrees of virtue—keystone dimensions of the Christian identity. Due to the method of administering it since ancient times, it had become a reality on the frontiers of existence, for most Christians only to be met at death's door. Its absence showed in the lifestyle of the masses: their sense of evil was numbed, laymen felt no need to repair injustice, and even many priests had only vague memories of asceticism, a by-product from use of the sacrament, as a thing of the past.

One could justify the practice of seldom allowing confession in the pre-Constantinian centuries of Christianity, when its peripheral place was largely compensated by the intensely religious life of Christians who lived in a Church composed of small, tightly knit, and deeply committed communities. But after Constantine, especially from the fifth century onward, due largely to the conversions en masse of the barbarians and to the sociopolitical chaos of the epoch, both knowledge and practice of the Faith had dramatically plummeted, and immorality among Christians had risen. By the sixth century the old method was well and truly obsolete, made inaccessible for the masses because of the way it was designed.

First of all, it often gave only one opportunity: "Just as there is one baptism, so also there is one confession."[49] It was allowed twice or possibly several times in the East under bishops such as St. John Chrysostom (ca. 349–407), and in the West by bishops like Caesarius of Arles (502–542).[50] The thinking behind this mentality is certainly understandable: in the light of reverence for God and the grandeur of the supernatural life received in baptism and strengthened by the Eucharist, the Christian has all the necessary strength for vanquishing temptation to mortal sin, and therefore a once-off access to confession should be enough.

Secondly, the ancient method, by its very structure, even if administered by the gentlest of bishops, was humiliating for most people. As regards the actual confession of sins, at least in some places during the first centuries, it seems that the penitent actually stood before the community and exposed them, no matter how secret they were, even though without going into details. Historians agree that over time this practice gave way universally to private and secret disclosure to a bishop or priest. Indeed Pope Leo the Great, in a letter of 459, sternly condemned the custom, still in force in some places, of obliging Christians to read a detailed list of their sins publicly. But the second dimension of the sacrament, penance (reparation for sin), remained public: the bishop or priest publicly assigned the penalty such as fasting,

---

[49] St. Ambrose, Sermon 258.

[50] For the practice under Caesarius of Arles, who taught that the sacrament may be administered twice, see Oscar Watkins, *A History of Penance: Being a Study of the Authorities*, vol. 2 (London: Longmans, Green, 1920), pp. 550–62.

wearing sackcloth, reciting special prayers, or prostrating oneself on the ground in church. Hence everybody knew of one's wrongdoing—it was obviously a matter of being labeled for life.[51]

For many people the sting of the severity lay in the shame of joining a segregated group within the community, the "order of penitents". In certain areas, sinners in the third and fourth centuries were divided into four classes for attendance at the Holy Sacrifice of the Mass. In the measure in which they fulfilled their penance, they moved closer to the altar until, finally, the bishop received them back into full union with the Church. The first group, the "weepers", didn't even enter the building but remained outside the doorway; the "hearers" stood in the vestibule but had to leave after the sermon; the "kneelers", with ashes on their heads and dressed in sackcloth, were in the rear of the congregation—while everyone else stood, they remained on their knees; and, lastly, the "co-standers" mingled with the congregation but could not yet receive Holy Communion. Such severity was too much for both Romans and barbarians in the fifth and sixth centuries. However, it must be said that it was not as if the Church acted unreasonably in this publicizing of penance. Arguably, the open and serious nature of offenses headed by apostasy from the Faith, murder, adultery, and other more generic sins that grievously harmed one's neighbor, such as severe instances of greed, justified it. Moreover, with the exception of the gravest offenses, it was up to the bishop to decide in each case whether public penance was necessary, and what form it would take. Nor did the Church require public penance of young people.

Thirdly, the penance for sins was severely burdensome whether in the amount of prayer, almsgiving, fasting, or other works to benefit the poor.

Fourthly, this form of confession was not pedagogy for growth in holiness. In saying this, there is no question of denying the intrinsic power of the sacrament for the forgiveness of sins and the bestowing of sanctifying grace, irrespective of the format used. However, the old structure was not the best tool for enlightening the intellect and motivating the will to cooperate with grace in overcoming tendencies to sin so as to ascend toward the highlands of Christlikeness. Understandably so, since it was usually limited to one's deathbed or after committing a notoriously grave sin, and therefore it did not occur often enough to be a method suitably tailored to the individual's needs for a pedagogy of virtue. It offered no constant irrigation for souls suffering drought due to the scorching heat of moral decadence which, by the late sixth century, had created a spiritual desert in much of Western Europe.

The Engine of Renewal: The Irish Method of Confession

The Irish priests were able to remedy this urgent problem because they had designed a new method of confession. When Columbanus and companions came ashore in Brittany, inside waterproof leather bags they brought penitential manuals containing detailed instructions about its use. With these they instigated nothing less than a quiet revolution in the Church that would have purifying and transforming effects on society.

---

[51] Emile Amann, "Pénitence-Sacrement", in *Dictionnaire de Théologie Catholique*, vol. 12 (Paris: Letouzey et Ané, 1933), cols. 783–837.

Domenico di Niccolo dei Cori, *The Confession*, ca. 15th century.

This new method of confession was born in the monasteries of Ireland, thanks to Saint Finnian of Clonard (A.D. 470–549) and his peers.[52] Such great importance was given to this sacrament that the ability to be a capable confessor was a prerequisite for ordination: "Therefore, any bishop who confers Holy Orders on a person who is deficient in learning and devotion, or who is incapable of hearing confessions, or is ignorant of law and rule and the appropriate remedies for every kind of sin—that bishop is guilty before God and man, for what he has done is an insult to Christ and His Church."[53]

When Irish confession arrived to continental Europe with Columbanus, the reaction in Burgundy and elsewhere was enthusiastic. For both Gallo-Romans and barbarians, nature and the Christian life seemed to come together and bond with relative ease in the new format. Its qualities made confession a far more welcome knocker on the door of reticent human nature since its gentle demeanor assured man that he would not be humiliated and that the restoration of his soul would be accomplished amid serenity. It must have been a most unexpected answer for many an anguished soul longing to encounter God's mercy but fearing the severity of the ancient method. Now, within a sanctuary of secrecy, through priests who were hard on themselves but gentle with others, learned but also down-to-earth, they were able to have the same experience as that of the woman publicly accused of sin to whom Jesus Christ had said simply: "Has no one condemned you? ... Neither do I condemn you; go and do not sin again" (Jn 8:10–11).

The first quality about the new method that people noticed was its confidential nature. Walls of secrecy protected the sinner's reputation. From beginning to end, Celtic confession was a private matter: the Irish knew nothing of a public acknowledgment of sins in church; nothing of a public penance; nothing of a segregated "order of penitents"; and rarely any public incurring of ecclesiastical or civil consequences. The admission of sins was made privately, and the penance was assigned confidentially even if, because of its content (for example, a pilgrimage), people could well suspect a penance. Even in the case of excommunication, reconciliation at the end of the term occurred privately, and it seems that generally any delegated priest could do so, without the need to recur to the bishop. To no one else could men turn amid the anguish of their sins, guilt, and moral questions with such assurances of utter confidentiality. Unrivaled was the status of the priest-confessor as "man of secrets" because the Church sealed his lips unto death, with the warning of the

---

[52] For the practice of confession under St. Finnian of Clonard, see Watkins, *History of Penance*, vol. 2, 606–12.
[53] *The Rule of the Céli Dé*, par. 59, quoted in *The Divine Office*, p. 470.

second and eternal death if the seal were ever broken.[54] Indeed, the Irish Church laid down that to reveal information heard in confession was one of the four deadly offenses for which absolution would not be given—a terrifying prospect indeed.[55]

As Columbanus' monks founded monasteries in France, Switzerland, the Lowlands, and Lombardy, and Columba of Iona's spiritual sons did likewise in Scotland and England, and, subsequently, Boniface did in Germany, they spread the Celtic culture of privacy and absolute confidentiality, safeguarded by severe penalties, throughout the Western European Church. This does not imply that the obligation of confidentiality associated with private confession did not already exist. When private confession occurred, Church authorities naturally insisted on secrecy. For instance, in A.D. 554, the Church in the East, at the Second Council of Dvin in Armenia, warned that a priest who revealed a secret of confession would be deposed and excommunicated.[56] In the West, during the fifth century, Pope Leo the Great had stated that whenever confession was made in private, it was forbidden to disclose its contents.[57] However, it seems that only in the ninth century did the Church in the West decree heavy penalties for breaking the seal.[58] In 1151, Gratian, in his "Decretum", a compilation of the edicts of previous councils and other ecclesiastical laws, states, "Let the priest who dares to make known the sins of his penitent be deposed and during all the days of his lifetime let him continue wandering as a disgraceful individual."[59] In 1215, canon 21 of the Fourth Lateran Council made the obligation of secrecy a universal norm: "Let the priest absolutely beware that he does not by word, or sign, or by any manner whatever, in any way betray the sinner ... For whoever shall dare to reveal a sin disclosed to him in the tribunal of penance we decree that he shall not only be deposed from the priestly office but that he shall also be sent into the confinement of a monastery to do perpetual penance".[60]

Secondly, penances given in the Celtic form of confession were mild by comparison with the severer continental system. A synod of Saint Patrick decreed that "forgiveness is more in keeping with the examples of Scripture; let penance be short, with weeping and lamentation ... rather than long and tempered with relaxations".[61]

Thirdly, Celtic confession was also "user-friendly" in that as often as you needed it you got it, since the priests were keen to restore men to Christian life and to lead

---

[54] Of course, as a phrase, "seal of confession" is an anachronism when applied to the epoch of St. Columbanus. The image of the seal was first used with regard to confession in the twelfth century by the secretary of St. Bernard, Nicolas of Clairvaux, in *Sermo in festo sancti Beato Andreae* (see *PL* 184:1054A–1054B).

[55] See John Thomas McNeill, *The Celtic Penitentials and Their Influence on Continental Christianity* (Paris: Librarie Ancienne Honoré Champion, 1923), p. 96. Evidence for the existence of the penalty is to be found, for instance, in the early ninth-century work the *Félire Óengusso* (*The Martyrology of Óengus*), which survives in at least ten manuscripts; see Whitley Stokes, ed., *The Martyrology of Oengus the Culdee*, vol. 29 (London: Henry Bradshaw Society, 1905), p. 223, n. 5.

[56] See Bertrand Kurtscheid, *A History of the Seal of Confession* (London: B. Herder, 1927), p. 56.

[57] Ibid., pp. 51–55.

[58] Ibid., p. 87, n. 32.

[59] "Deponatur sacerdos, qui peccata penitentis publicare presumit, et omnibus diebus vitae suae ignomiosus peregrinando pergat." See "Decretum Gratiani", Decreti Pars Secunda, causa 33, questio 3, *Tractatus de Penitencia*, distinctio 6 at http://geschichte.digitale-sammlungen.de/decretum-gratiani/online/angebot (accessed on January 23, 2015).

[60] Quoted in Abigail Firey, *A New History of Penance* (Leiden, Netherlands: Koninklijke Brill NV, 2008), p. 241.

[61] See David Wilkins, ed., *Concilia Magnae Britanniae et Hiberniae, a synodo verolamiensi A.D. CCCC XLVI. ad londinensem A.D. M DCCXVII*, vol. 1 (London: Gosling, 1737), p. 4.

them higher toward Christlike perfection. They institutionalized this in their penitential manuals. The penitential ascribed to Saint Columbanus legislates in canon
30 "that confessions be given with all diligence".[62] Under the Celtic regime, more
priests were available to hear confessions than in the Mediterranean system where
only the bishop and a few designated clerics did so. Statutes of Celtic monasteries
explicitly stated that priests were even to be excused from the sacrosanct duty of
singing the Psalms in community if needed by penitents.

Fourthly, any sin, great or small—and not just one of a limited number as in the
Mediterranean form—could be confessed.

Fifthly, there was the personal guidance that the priests linked to the sacrament.
They gave spiritual guidance because they first took it themselves. For these monks
were not satisfied simply with receiving absolution from the guilt of serious sin; no,
they wanted much more. Passionately they wanted to purify the soul from even the
scars of evil in order to allow the new supernatural life received in baptism and
the other sacraments to transform their thoughts, aspirations, and actions. They
wanted Christian perfection, a transformed personality, Christlikeness—and being
Celts, they wanted it fast. But, naturally, such an arduous task and such a subtle
surgery of the soul could not be done on one's own. Since *nemo est iudex in causa
sua* (no one is a judge in his own case) and since self-knowledge is even more difficult for those blinded by years of labyrinthine self-deception, a wise guide is vitally
urgent. A master physician is needed, and where else to seek one, and where else
to undergo such surgery, than in confession? After all, who knew the soul better
than the priest who had just listened to the tale of one's sins and evil inclinations?
And who was better equipped to be a master surgeon than the priest who was
already so knowledgeable? Was he not himself a man who had spent years living
amid the peaks of Christian self-conquest? Thus, Celtic confession provided the
trustworthy guide who could lead the sinner through the jungle of his own soul,
at times preventing self-knowledge from becoming an occasion for despair, and at
other moments removing the blindness of pride and shallowness in order to see all
the suffering caused to those around him.

The Celtic format of confession with spiritual guidance made it a powerful and
subtle tool for the pedagogy of transforming raw human nature into the new Christlike man. For it was personalized like a tutoring system, able to take each one where
he was at, helping him both to appreciate God's unique love for him as an individual
as well as the importance of an energetic response. It was an effective surgical instrument for a successful "heart transplant" because it facilitated three conditions for
the operation: self-knowledge, wise decision making, and practices of self-mastery
(asceticism).

Firstly, it provoked greater self-knowledge. Since it allowed the acknowledgment
of any and every sin, mortal or what we now call "venial", it implied a sensitive
examination of one's lifestyle and motives. With frequent use—as was encouraged
by the Celtic system—the habit of such self-questioning led to increasing clarity
about one's defects, qualities, and opportunities for Christian growth. With this
incisive self-knowledge men were better equipped to make wise judgments for

---

[62] For a description of the penitential system of St. Columbanus and his monks, see Watkins, *History of
Penance*, vol. 2, pp. 612–20.

the transformation of their character. Thus Celtic confession did for the interior of man what Gothic architecture would do for the interior of medieval churches—it allowed the light of Christ to flood the mind and heart, thus shattering darkness and enabling men to see both insidious evil and hitherto unrecognized goodness hiding amid nooks and crannies.

Along with self-knowledge one could also receive a plan of ascetic action, tailored to one's temperament, from keen-eyed priests who willingly gave counsel on the practices that would enable one to avoid occasions of sin, pray more deeply, overcome character flaws, and acquire virtues. These surgeons of souls were men of subtle psychological insights, as the instruction manuals for priest-confessors, the penitentials, insinuate:

> But this is to be carefully observed in [the determination of] all penance [to be imposed on the sinner]: the length of time anyone remains in his faults; with what learning he is instructed; with what passion he is assailed; with what courage he stands; with what tearfulness he seems to be afflicted; and with what oppression he is driven to sin. For Almighty God who knows the hearts of all and has bestowed diverse natures will not estimate [various] weights of sins as [worthy] of equal penance.[63]

The attractiveness of these rugged Irish priests for the barbarians and Gallo-Romans cannot be exaggerated, for they truly loved and sought to empathize with the Christians who came to them. In the midst of their penitential manuals one finds the most heart-warming recommendations to priests about the attitude to hold toward sinners:

> As often as we assign fasts to Christians who come to penance, we also ought to unite ourselves with them in fasting for one or two weeks or for as long as we are able.... For nobody can raise up one who is falling beneath a weight unless he himself bends towards him in order to extend his hand to him; and no physician can treat the wounds of the sick unless he comes into contact with their foulness. So also no priest or pontiff can treat the wounds of sinners or take away the sins from their souls except through the urgency with which he brings attentive concern, prayers, and tears. Therefore we must be considerate towards sinners, since we are "members one of another" [Rom 12:5] and "if one member suffers anything all the members suffer with it" [1 Cor 12:26].... When, therefore, anyone comes to a priest to confess his sins, the priest ought first to pray alone in the secret depths of his heart: "Lord God Almighty, be favorable unto me a sinner in order to make me, on behalf of sinners and those who confess their sins, a worthy mediator between you and them. I implore you, who wants not the death of sinners but only that they convert and live, to accept the prayer of your servant which I pour forth before the face of your glory for your men-servants and maid-servants who desire to do penance: that you may rescue them from sin in the future and keep them unharmed from every temptation."[64]

No wonder that the Irish began calling the priest-confessor with that poignantly beautiful title, *anam chara* (soul-friend) or *animae carus* (beloved of my soul). The qualities of Celtic confession forged a type of relationship between men hitherto unknown.

---

[63] *The Penitential of Cummean* (ca. A.D. 650), ascribed to the Irish Abbot Cummean, quoted in John T. McNeill and H. M. Gamer, *Medieval Handbooks of Penance: A Translation of the Principal libri poenitentiales and Selections from Related Documents* (New York: Columbia University Press, 1938), p. 116.

[64] *The Tripartite Penitential of St. Gall* (ca. A.D. 800), quoted in McNeill and Gamer, *Medieval Handbooks of Penance*, pp. 283–84.

The sheer confidentiality between priest and penitent was peerless; it gave birth to trust, which in turn fostered transparency and depth of communication. Seldom do men reveal their souls to the same degree outside that sanctuary, for here—and only here—is where men have such powerful motives to utterly discard masks and pull aside curtains of iron. Thus, Irish confession was a quantum leap from all that the great Roman and Greek writers such as Cicero and Aristotle had written about the friend as the other half of one's soul. These authors were thinking about those friendships between individuals who, bound by a common and intense pursuit of virtue, open the doors of their hearts to each other for mutual guidance and encouragement. Yet, sublime as these friendships are, they do not rival the relationship between priest and penitent since this is transformed by the supernatural. For in the person and functions of the confessor we are dealing with something surpassing human grandeur. Here it is God's love that faces the sinner, respects him, and loves him by destroying the guilt of sin and invigorating his soul anew.

Men sought guidance from these Celtic monks because they looked up to them as men of grit, guts, and culture; they trusted them as spiritual fathers; they loved them as *anam chara*. How could they not? Many a Gallo-Roman or barbarian on first experiencing Celtic confession must have been somewhat puzzled. Its gentleness contrasted not only with the harshness of the old method but also with the hardihood with which these Irish priests treated themselves. They saw that these Celts—individuals such as Columbanus and Fridolin—were men who had made the sacrifice of marriage and family, and they reckoned that this must have cost them mightily in their youth. They saw them live with reckless contempt for egotism. And so they suspected that the empathy and wise counsel experienced during confession came largely from their own hard-fought victories with temptations of the spirit and the flesh. As regards the severe penances, well, how could they refuse them when they saw the priest-confessor living a lifetime of heroic renunciation? Moreover, they saw that the penance came from the heart of a selfless friend; such a friend may advise, cajole, console, and sternly correct the other because he is seen as both God's representative and the other's most loyal companion.

Thus the Picts and the Saxons, the Gallo-Romans, Franks and Lombards, all saw a new type of priest coming from the westernmost land. Certainly, in preceding centuries there had been instances of wise spiritual guides amid the Desert Fathers and among so many dedicated priests and bishops. But it was different. Different because it was not bonded to the revolutionary new pattern of the sacrament of confession as practiced by the Irish priests. And because it was not readily available to the masses of people.

Irish confession spread like wildfire and gained the upper hand over its Mediterranean counterpart—not however without opposition, even from the Council of Toledo (589). Its spread was aided by the manuals of the Irish monks that were copied far and wide. They were in use throughout France in the sixth century and in England by the late seventh when Archbishop Theodore of Canterbury (appointed in A.D. 668) adopted them.[65] By the ninth century they were common in Italy and among the Spanish Visigoths. Eventually, the method won a worldwide

---

[65] For a description of the penitentials in use on continental Europe in the seventh century, see Watkins, *History of Penance*, vol. 2, pp. 643–65. For details of the expansion of the Celtic system, see ibid., pp. 622–27.

triumph: the Church's decision was sealed at Lateran Council IV in 1215 and then at the Council of Trent in 1551. Catholics everywhere will always be thankful to the priests of Ireland for this magnificent gift of the secret meeting between the soul and God's representative, wherein he is touched by divine mercy and guided as a unique individual to the shores of Eternity.

The effects of these secret meetings rippled and surged throughout society, invigorating the men and women who would build the new civilization. They strengthened marriage, bonded fathers and sons and mothers and daughters, reconciled bloodthirsty rivals, and prevented or mitigated wars. A new and powerful instrument of civilizational change had been born. For the roots and resolutions of the small and great social conflicts do not occur first and foremost in parliaments or palaces but in the secret recesses of men's souls, whence all injustice arises. It is on this secret battlefield where the struggle with temptation to sin, the enemy par excellence of a truly human civilization, rages. It is here, and nowhere else, that the keystones of a just social order are laid or destroyed.

The practice of private confession also burned onto the Western soul a principle that is not native to the other influential civilizations of humanity: that the individual man, woman, or child is above the tribe, nation, state, and collectivity. Because men were willing to spend hours on end, in huge city cathedrals or tiny rural chapels, amid the coldness of winter and the heat of summer, attentive to the woes of both king and beggar, listening compassionately in order "to make known to his people their salvation through forgiveness of all their sins, the loving kindness of the heart of our God who visits us like the dawn from on high ... to give light to those in darkness, those who dwell in the shadow of death and guide ... into the way of peace" (Lk 1:68–79), the concept of the dignity of the individual hit home. It became clear through this one-on-one dialogue that God, through his representative, loved each man as an individual—regardless of race or rank. The Western paradigm on human dignity—the necessary first step toward any just sociopolitical reform—was being forged in a way that neither all the empty verbosity of the Enlightenment nor all the stormings of the Bastilles of this world could ever have achieved. For all were equal as they knelt. Indeed all were equal as they waited for the sacrament, and if someone tried to alter this egalitarian state of affairs, priests were quite capable of calling the violator to order. One such incident from the seventeenth century occurred when a wealthy white lady in Cartagena, Colombia, jumped the queue, going ahead of a black slave, but found that it was all to no avail since the confessor, Father Peter Claver (1580–1654), insisted on hearing the slave's confession first.

The waves of Celtic confession's influence rose, swelled, and spread through society according to the rank of the men and women who knelt in the confessional. During centuries it must be said that all social levels in Europe had their confessors. Indeed, the precise format of Irish confession contributed greatly to the popularizing of the institution of the court chaplain: a priest who acted as confessor–spiritual director to a ruler or aristocrat. History records that as early as the sixth century Saint Columba was *anam chara* to Aidan, king of Dalriada in Scotland, and that the priest Adamnan around 675 was soul-friend to Fínsnechta, High King (*Ard Rí*) of Ireland. Who knows how much injustice was avoided or mitigated and how many conflicts or even wars were prevented thanks to these chaplains, through their behind-the-scenes guidance of emperors, kings, queens, and nobles along the time line of the West?

Edwin Longsden Long (1829–1891), *Confession*, 1862.

The position of royal confessor was often a risky and rough occupation for the priest who conscientiously fulfilled his duty. Instances of priests who paid in the flesh for their spiritual guidance are numerous. When King Louis XIII's confessor, Father Nicholas Caussin, roused the royal conscience about excessively heavy taxation policies and the monarch's treatment of his bride and the queen mother, he attracted the fury of Prime Minister Richelieu, who had the priest banished in December 1637. Likewise Father Claude de la Colombière (1641–1682), confessor to Duchess Mary of Modena— afterward queen of England as wife of King James II—ended up in prison before being banished in 1679, accused of conspiring against the government.

Another who walked along the cliff-edge of death for years was Father Henry Essex Edgeworth de Firmont (1745–1807), confessor of King Louis XVI. Born in Ireland, at about four years of age his family moved to France where he became a priest and a close friend to members of the royal family. During the French Revolution of 1789, his courageous and steadfast loyalty to the imprisoned King Louis, Queen Marie Antoinette, and their children merited him respect even from the revolutionaries. It was he who said the final Mass for the condemned king, and on January 21, 1793, while the Paris mob looked on and the drums beat, it was on his arm that King Louis leaned as he walked to the guillotine. On the death of the priest in 1807, King Louis XVIII wrote to his brother, Ussher Edgeworth: "You will regret the best and tenderest of brothers. I weep for a friend and comforter, a benefactor, who guided the King, my brother, on his way to Heaven, and pointed out the same path to me.... My family and all the loyal French by whom I am surrounded feel as I do, as if we had lost a father."[66]

Mission Accomplished

The following painting portrays the "Father of English History", the polymath, poet, and biographer, the Venerable Bede (672–735), in his final hours during which he translated the Gospel of Saint John into Old English, dictating it to one of his students. He died in a manner characteristic of the monks of the Dark Ages, whether Celtic or Benedictine: upright and in action unto the end. Bede's student

[66]Letter of King Louis XVIII of France to Ussher Edgeworth, quoted in M. V. Woodgate, *The Abbé Edgeworth* (Dublin: Browne and Nolan, 1945), pp. viii–ix.

Cuthbert the Deacon in a letter to another cleric, Cuthwin, described his last weeks on earth as follows:

> When it came to the Tuesday before Ascension Day, his breathing became very much worse, and a slight swelling had appeared on his feet; but all the same he taught us the whole of that day and dictated cheerfully and among other things said several times: "Learn your lesson quickly now; for I know not how long I may be with you, nor whether after a short time my Maker may not take me from you." But it seemed to us that he knew very well when his end should be. So he spent all that night in thanksgiving, without sleep; and when day broke, which was the Wednesday, he gave instructions for the writing, which we had begun, to be finished without delay. We were at it until nine o'clock; at nine o'clock we went in procession with the relics, as the custom of that day required.
>
> One of us stayed with him and said to him: "There is still one chapter short of that book you were dictating but I think it will be hard on you to ask any more questions." But he replied: "It is not hard. Take your pen and mend it and write fast." And so he did.... [H]e said: "It is time, if it so please my Maker, that I should be released from the body and return to Him who formed me out of nothing, when as yet I was not. I have lived a long time, and the righteous Judge has well provided for me all my life long. The time of my departure is at hand, and my soul longs to see Christ my King in all His beauty." ... And so upon the floor of his cell, singing "Glory be to the Father and to the Son and to the Holy Spirit" and the rest, he breathed his last.[67]

Like Bede, so many monks of the Dark Ages must have crossed the final frontier with joy in their hearts, serene in the awareness that they had done their part in the Church's mission to "[g]o make disciples of all nations" (Mt 28:19). They had not sought first and foremost to build a new society; their focus was on the individual man and woman whom they looked upon with the eyes of Jesus Christ as a soul and body of priceless, indeed eternal, value. Deep down, they knew that if the individual soul could be remade in the image of the God of Love, a new social order would, somehow, be born.

Strengthening the spirits of so many of the Irish monk-missionaries in their final earthly moments was the presence at their sides of monastic sons from among the Lombards, Franks, and other races who had joined the Columban abbeys. Luxeuil, the principal one in northern Europe, had so many members

James Doyle Penrose, *The Last Chapter* (detail), 1902.

that choir followed choir in chanting the Psalms, day and night, in *laus perennis* (unceasing praise of God). During the seventh century Luxeuil gave birth to

---

[67] Letter of Cuthbert the Deacon to Cuthwin, circa June 735, in A. M. Sellar, ed., introduction to *Bede's Ecclesiastical History of England* (London: George Bell and Co., 1907), pp. xli–xliii.

daughter monasteries, which, by the middle of the eighth century, had adopted the Benedictine rule. This empowered Benedictine monasticism, not only numerically and territorially but also culturally, due to the adoption of the Irish monastic traits of dedication to scholarship and education. From these abbeys, during the ninth century, came forth the reforming bishops and abbots who vigorously sought to strengthen the Church's priesthood in order to awaken the masses to the grandeur of Christian life.

These monasteries were therefore able to function as the indispensable instruments of the Anglo-Saxon Alcuin for launching the campaign to make education better and more widespread in the late eighth and early ninth centuries in Charlemagne's empire—the "First Europe"—a prelude to the dawn of the great medieval culture in the twelfth. This is why no less a personage than Pope Pius XI, whose specialization as a paleographer had been ancient and medieval Church manuscripts, was able to assert: "The more scholarly investigation throws light upon the unknown dimensions of the so called 'Middle Ages', the clearer it becomes that the renaissance of Christian wisdom and culture over several regions of France, Germany, and Italy is due to the toil and zeal of Columbanus; a fact that reveals the merits of the priesthood and especially of Catholic Ireland."[68] Rightly therefore can Christopher Dawson call this seminal epoch of Western civilization the "Age of the Monks" due to the accomplishments of both the Celtic and Benedictine branches of Western monasticism.[69]

The Celtic monks continue to inspire and provoke us in the twenty-first century. Benedict XVI remarked that "along with the Irishmen of his time ... [Columbanus] with his spiritual energy, faith, love for God and neighbor truly became one of the Fathers of Europe: he shows us even today the roots from which our Europe can be reborn."[70] This was also the conviction of Robert Schuman, a founding father of the European Union, first president of the European Parliament, and twice prime minister of France: "St. Columbanus, this illustrious Irishman who departed from his own country into voluntary exile, sought and achieved a spiritual union between the principal European countries of his time. He is the patron saint of all those who now seek to build a united Europe."[71]

Of course, Columbanus brought about that "spiritual union" by convincing Burgundians and Lombards of the truth of Christianity and by baptizing or confirming them as members of the Mystical Body of Christ, the Catholic Church. His work was a part of what Daniel-Rops called the "Irish miracle": "'The Irish miracle', as we like to call it, is this second setting out of Christianity from a country which had only just been baptized, and which was immediately dreaming of giving Christ back to the world. Ireland, between the fifth and the eighth century, was like a second Palestine, like a new cradle of the Christian faith."[72] This saga can awaken us to the dynamism and power of rejuvenation within Catholicism. It should lead us to hope that something similar may occur once more. Why not? Since

[68] Pope Pius XI to Cardinal Franz Ehrle, August 6, 1923. Published in *La Civiltà Cattolica* (Rome, 1923), pp. 453–54. My translation.

[69] Dawson, *Making of Europe*, p. 5.

[70] Benedict XVI, "General Audience", June 11, 2008.

[71] Robert Schuman, speech at Luxeuil, July 23, 1950.

[72] Henri Daniel Rops, ed., *The Miracle of Ireland* (Baltimore: Helicon Press, 1959), p. 7.

"Jesus Christ is the same yesterday and today and for ever" (Heb 13:8), all that is required of us is to "[r]emember your leaders, those who spoke to you the word of God; consider the outcome of their life, and imitate their faith" (Heb 13:7). Unchanging identity; fidelity to Catholic Tradition whereby we hold the same Faith as Columbanus and Benedict, Peter and Paul; an infra-eternal vision; a lifestyle of self-conquest in private and courageous action in public—these will ever be the keystones for Catholic creative minorities, builders of Christian civilization.

Boniface: Seed Sower of Civilization in Germany

From the newly converted Anglo-Saxons of Britain came an individual who strikingly exemplified that "union of Teutonic initiative and Latin order",[73] welded together and transformed by the spirit of Christ, that became "the source of the whole medieval development of

Werner Henschel, *Statue of St. Boniface* (ca. 680–754), 1830, in Fulda, Germany.

culture":[74] Saint Boniface (ca. 680–754). He, more than any other, laid the solid foundations for the Catholic Church and her culture in Germany. The grandeur of his achievements looms even larger in the light of his complex personality:

> Whose irresistible attraction we still seem to feel ... an attraction combining simplicity and nobility of character, gentleness and steadfastness of nature, the same attraction which during his lifetime gathered such a cluster of youthful vocations around him. Perhaps there is no other saint who touches us more closely through those aspects of his character in which sanctity and human weaknesses mingle as through those in which the miseries which are our own are dissipated in the love of Christ. He had a restless, unsteady, complex nature, dangerously wracked by the black humours of despair, and he was extremely self-effacing and timid. Although St Boniface accomplished an immense work, it was done almost reluctantly and without his ever having had the slightest desire to push himself to the forefront of events. The superior interests of the Church alone guided him, but when they were in play this timid man was carried away by his enthusiasm, and his boldness knew no bounds. He hewed down the sacred oaks, hunted the heretics, had unworthy bishops deposed, and went so far as to make observations to the Pope. A magnificent type of missionary, both prudent and enterprising, an organizer as well as an apostle ... he was a creator, a man who founded a church, and whose work was to be lasting. Above all, he was a wonderfully priestly man, penetrated to the core by the living water of the Church, unreservedly faithful to the Holy See, and a man in whom Christ's charity was so great that it could

---

[73] Dawson, *Making of Europe*, p. 212.
[74] Ibid.

overcome all his scruples and make him able to find a brother in the most ferocious of the Barbarians as well as in the most fallen of the Christians.[75]

Born about 680 in the village of Crediton in Wessex, he was given the baptismal name of Winfrid. Educated from the age of seven at the Benedictine abbeys of Exeter and Nursling, his brilliant mind soon became evident and would have made it possible for him to spend a lifetime studying and teaching amid tranquil cloisters. But no, his heart longed to bring the Faith to the pagans of the continent, so at thirty-eight years of age he travelled to Rome in order to ask Pope Gregory II for a precise mission. Their conversations during the winter of 718–719 were decisive since the pontiff, impressed by the spirit of the Anglo-Saxon priest, made him his representative in Germany, renaming him "Boniface". He swore an oath of allegiance to the papacy on the tomb of Saint Peter, one that he would resolutely uphold until death; a clear testimony to this are his letters to Gregory and the two succeeding pontiffs, asking for guidance on everything from the naming of bishops to missionary organization, thus giving a clearly Roman seal to the fledgling Germanic Church.

His mission was arduous and complex. Although Columbanus and other predecessors had heroically pioneered Christianity in these perilous barbarian lands from the late sixth century, pagans were still numerous, many Christians were still only nominally so, sacrifices to Wotan still occurred amid "sacred groves", and there yet remained the task of building up a stable Church organization. The biggest obstacle to progress was the decadence of the clergy. "Religion is trodden under foot", wrote Boniface. "Benefices are given to greedy laymen or unchaste and publican clerics. All their crimes do not prevent their attaining the priesthood; at last rising in rank as they increase in sin they become bishops, and those of them who can boast that they are not adulterers or fornicators are drunkards, given up to the chase, and soldiers who do not shrink from shedding Christian blood."[76]

Then there was the political complication. Boniface, immediately recognizing the determination of the Franks to conquer the other Germanic peoples, and reckoning that no stable organization of the Church could occur without their cooperation, came to an agreement with the Frankish leader Charles Martel and his successors, Pepin and Carloman, whereby they supported his missionary efforts.[77] But, at the same time, he maintained his independence, especially in the choice of co-workers who were either monks from England, or, later on, native Saxons.

Boniface from 719 to 723 organized the chaotic Church in the area of Belgium and the Netherlands before he went straight to the fortress of paganism in Hesse and Thuringia. For thirty years, amid danger and poverty, travelling with companions all as ardently dedicated to the mission as himself, Boniface penetrated into Saxon and Frisian lands. From his correspondence with friends in England we can only admire the winsome style of his method.[78] Attentively, he listened to the pagan explanations of their religion; calmly, he pointed out the inconsistencies; and persuasively, he unfolded the truth and beauty of Christianity. His organizational genius led him to

[75] Daniel-Rops, *Church in the Dark Ages*, pp. 237–38.

[76] Abridged from Epistle 49 (to Pope Zacharias), as quoted in Dawson, *Making of Europe*, pp. 190–91.

[77] For more detail on the political and military history of Charles Martel and his successors, see Warren H. Carroll, *The Building of Christendom* (Front Royal, Va.: Christendom College Press, 1987), pp. 275–332.

[78] See Edward Kylie, *The English Correspondence of Saint Boniface* (London: Chatto and Windus, 1911).

establish monasteries and bishoprics on sites of old pagan sanctuaries, preeminent among which was Fulda, the future "Monte Cassino of the North". These became the nurseries of a new Teutonic Christian culture which was integrated during the ninth and tenth centuries by Charlemagne, Alcuin, and associates into the cultural unity of Catholic Western Europe. Germany's first towns also grew up around them in what had been up to then a totally rural landscape.

Like Columbanus he never looked back at past achievements. Even at eighty he set off to convert the Frisians in the Zuiderzee region of the Netherlands where, on June 5, 754, a martyr's death crowned a hero's existence. At Fulda one can still see the gashed copy of the Gospel he was reading when attacked and which he spontaneously raised to shield his head from the blows of the swords and axes of the assailants. But, in a sense, he had already since his youth been pouring out his lifeblood for Christ and for those violent barbarian souls whom he dearly loved.

Three years before his death, by anointing to kingship a young prince whom history would know as Charlemagne, he had helped pave the way for another Anglo-Saxon missionary who would continue to build on his foundations: Alcuin.

Chapter 5

ALCUIN AND THE IDEALISTS BEHIND
THE FIRST EUROPE

> The Roman Catholic Church was then, as it is now, a great democracy. There was no peasant so humble that he might not become a priest, and no priest so obscure that he might not become Pope of Christendom.... What kept government alive in the Middle Ages was this constant rise of the sap from the bottom, from the rank and file of the great body of the people through the open channels of the priesthood.
>
> —President Woodrow Wilson, *The New Freedom*, 1913

The New Alliance: Papacy-Monasticism-Frankish Monarchy

In the sixth and seventh centuries, while the Celtic and Benedictine monks were engaged in strengthening and spreading Christianity in northern Europe, ominous threats arose to the Church's future in the Mediterranean area. By 632, year of the death of Muhammad, most of the Arabian Peninsula had converted to Islam, and a decade later Islamic armies conquered Mesopotamia and Persia, Byzantine Syria and Egypt. By 698 the rest of North Africa had fallen. In 711 Tariq ibn Ziyad landed in Gibraltar with around ten thousand men. Within a few years Islamic forces swept through Spain and Portugal, barring a few mountainous areas of Galicia, Asturias, and among the Basques—even crossing the Pyrenees into France. Hence, to the south and east of Rome boundaries had been set to the Church's expansion and the threat of invasion loomed large. From where could the popes find support? Little or no help was to be expected from

Alcuin at the Court of Charlemagne.
Engraved by an unnamed artist from a painting by Magaud.

the Eastern Roman Empire of Byzantium; even in Italy where it still had territory around Ravenna its rulers did nothing but burden the peninsula with taxes and interfere with papal elections and projects. Accordingly, it was northward that the more farseeing among the popes, bishops, and monks increasingly looked both for the defense of Christian territories and for expansion.

94

The "First Europe": Charlemagne's Empire, circa 800

The Frankish ruler's territories included all of modern-day France, Switzerland, Belgium, Luxembourg, the Netherlands, the western parts of both Germany and Austria, northern Italy, and part of northeastern Spain: a million square kilometres. Although the word "Europe" referring to a geographical reality appeared in the seventh century B.C., it was only under the grandfather of Charlemagne, Charles Martel, that it acquired a sociocultural and political meaning. A few decades later, the Irish cleric Cathulf, in a letter to the young Charlemagne, recommended that he thank God for having given him lordship of "Europe". In 799, one of Alcuin's students, Angilbert, called Charlemagne the "venerable leader of Europe" and "king, father of Europe": "Charles, learned, modest ... master of the world, beloved of his people ... the pinnacle of Europe ... [who] is in the process of redrawing the walls of the new Rome".[1]

[1] *Encyclopædia Universalis Online*, s.v. "Europe: Histoire de l'idée européenne", accessed December 4, 2015, http://www.universalis.fr/encyclopedie/europe-histoire-de-l-idee-europeenne/. My translation. See also Jean-Baptiste Duroselle, *L'Europe: Histoire de ses Peuples* (Paris: Hachette, 1998); J.K. Sowards, ed., *Makers of the Western Tradition: Portraits from History*, 6th ed., vol. 1 (New York: St. Martin's Press, 1994), pp. 152–74; C. Delisle Burns, *The First Europe: A Study of the Establishment of Medieval Christendom A.D. 400–800* (London: G. Allen and Unwin, 1949).

Since the conversion of Clovis, king of the Franks, on Christmas Day 496, Rome knew that the conversion of the barbarians was no impossible task. It is true that the conversion *en masse* had created only nominal Christians, and that by the middle of the sixth century Gaul was still a savage society. However, Columbanus and the Celtic monks had made a powerful breakthrough by establishing monasteries that became seminaries of ascetic, learned, and missionary-minded priests. Then came the Anglo-Saxon Boniface (680–754), who expanded the frontiers of Catholicism by his inroads into the territories of the Saxons, Frisians, and other ethnic groups beyond the Rhine, and who had structurally reformed, at least to some degree, the Church in the Frankish lands of northern France and the Lowlands. All this he had achieved, firstly, by resting his authority, not on local episcopates, but on his status as the Pope's personal representative; and, secondly, by gaining the protection of the powerful Mayor of the Palace of the Frankish monarchy, Charles Martel (688–741). The latter, though officially only second-in-command to the Merovingian king, functioned as the de facto ruler.

Boniface inaugurated the alliance in 722, when he presented Charles Martel with a letter from Pope Gregory II asking his support for the missionary work in Germanic lands. After Charles Martel had halted the Muslim invasion of France by his victory at the Battle of Tours in 732, both Gregory and Boniface increasingly looked on this successful warrior—grandson of the saintly Bishop Arnulf who became a Colomban monk in his final years—as a possible new Constantine, a protector for the sorely besieged Church. Charles lived up to their expectations by effectively ensuring the safety of missionaries in Frankish lands. His two heirs, Carloman—who became a monk at Monte Cassino after several years in power—and his other son, Pepin (741–767), continued to support Boniface as he restored discipline in the local church. In 751, Pepin, still second-in-command to King Childeric III, who took no part in public business, wrote to Pope Zachary I asking whether it was good that a man be called king despite the fact that another held and exercised the royal power. The Pope replied that the name should correspond to the reality. Shortly afterward the Merovingian king quietly retired to a monastery, and in 751, with papal approval, Boniface solemnly consecrated and anointed Pepin as king at Soissons, thereby guaranteeing the Christian identity of the new dynasty.

The anointing occurred none too soon. In the autumn of 753 the Lombards prepared to attack Rome, and the city was defenseless after the Byzantines had refused military support. Desperate, Pope Stephen II made a decision that would have momentous consequences in papal history. Leaving the Lateran Palace, he rode to the north of Italy, crossed the Alps through the Great St. Bernard Pass, and headed for Ponthieu in northern France, where King Pepin was residing. Alerted about the unexpected arrival of the august visitor, the monarch sent his son, the future Charlemagne, and his prime minister, Fulrad, Abbot of Saint-Denis, to greet him. When the papal group was about five miles from the palace, the king himself rode out to welcome the Pope, dismounted, prostrated himself before him, and then, taking hold of the bridle of his horse, led the pontiff to his residence.

There followed on July 28, 754, a magnificent ceremony at the Basilica of St. Denis during which the Pope himself anointed Pepin, bestowing on him the additional title of Patrician of the Romans, a title that carried with it the duty to defend the Eternal City. It is history's first recorded crowning by a pope of a civil ruler.

In the same ceremony he also anointed Pepin's two sons, Carloman and the future Charlemagne. And immediately Frankish warriors crossed the Alps, speedily bringing the Lombards into submission. To ensure the independence of the papacy, Pepin offered the Pope the territories around Rome and Ravenna connected by a slender slice of land containing Perugia; thus the Papal State was born. Fulrad, Abbot of Saint-Denis, reverently laid the documents of Pepin's donation and the keys of the new papal cities on the tomb of Saint Peter. The emperor in Byzantium protested, but to no avail. The alliance of papacy and Franks that had been inaugurated by Boniface—who was martyred only weeks before the papal coronation of Pepin— was now sealed.

Charlemagne: "Rough-Hewn from Gnarled Germanic Wood"

Pepin died in 768 and was succeeded by his two sons, Charlemagne and Carloman. But after the latter's death in 771, Charlemagne annexed his brother's heritage, forming one Frankish kingdom.

Charlemagne! Charles, king of the Franks, already named *Carolus Magnus* in his own life-time, was the man whom many Catholics of his age hailed as the "new reborn Constantine", a second King David, the political leader who could bring about the great ideal of Augustine's *City of God*. But who exactly was this man underneath the layers of mystique? Contemporary documents such as Alcuin's letters and especially the *Vita Karoli Magni* written by his first biographer, Einhard, a member of the royal court who had lived close to the ruler for twenty-three years, allow us to assemble a mosaic image of the empire builder.[2]

Charlemagne mounted the throne in 768 at the age of twenty-six and would reign for forty-five years—a complex personality, to say the least. Physically, it seems that he was of higher than average height for his epoch—of sturdy build, with a round face and a long thick beard, "his eyes very large and animated, nose a little long, fair hair, and face laughing and merry", "his appearance always stately and dignified",[3]

Albrecht Dürer, *Charlemagne*, ca. 1512.

---

[2] See Einhard, *The Life of Charlemagne*, trans. Samuel Epes Turner (New York: Harper and Brothers, 1880), http://legacy.fordham.edu/halsall/basis/einhard.asp. Einhard's life was written circa A.D. 829–836; see Paul E. Dutton, *Charlemagne's Courtier: The Complete Einhard* (Peterborough, Ontario: Broadview Press, 1998). The "Monk of St. Gall" who wrote the *Life of Charles the Great* (*De Carolo Magno*) for King Charles the Fat in A.D. 883–884 was probably Notker "the Stammerer". See Monk of St. Gall, *The Life of Charlemagne*, in *Early Lives of Charlemagne*, by Eginhard and the Monk of St. Gall, trans. and ed. A.J. Grant (London: Chatto and Windus; Boston: John W. Luce, 1907).

[3] Einhard, *Life of Charlemagne*, no. 22, "Personal Appearance".

self-assured, with an energetic voice and an iron constitution. Besides hunting, he liked to swim in the spa at Aachen, together with his sons, dozens of the nobles, and his personal escort of soldiers. He had a hearty appetite capable of consuming a whole hare along with four other courses, "not counting the roast which his huntsmen used to bring in on the spit, for he was more fond of this than of any other dish".[4] Indeed, in his old age, he hated his physicians, according to Einhard, "because they wanted him to give up roasts, to which he was accustomed, and to eat boiled meat instead."[5] And yet, for Christian reasons, fasting was also a regular part of his life—no small sacrifice for someone with such a huge gusto for food. He dressed plainly "like the common people", despising "foreign clothes, however fine-looking, and never allowed himself to be robed in them",[6] except on two occasions during his visits to Pope Hadrian and his successor. He hated any gaudy display of wealth, pomp, and ceremonial, and also abhorred drunkenness, wasting time on long banquets, and excessive entertainment. Charlemagne, according to Einhard, kept his children close by him, both at mealtimes and on journeys, his sons riding alongside him and his daughters following behind.[7]

Impetuous action was normally foreign to his behavior. Although affectionate, he was normally in control of his emotions. Yet, there were exceptions, as when some of his sons and one of his daughters died; or when he heard of the death of Pope Hadrian, "whom he had loved most of all his friends".[8] He "not only made friends easily but clung to them persistently".[9] Highly intelligent, far-sighted, energetic, and a born administrator, he could simultaneously take interest in the reform of liturgy as well as wage war on the Saxons and Avars. Although he knew how to read, he was otherwise a largely unschooled warrior up to his adult years, when he vigorously set himself to learn, rising at dawn for classes with "Alcuin, a man of Saxon extraction, who was the greatest scholar of the day."[10] He investigated "the motions of the heavenly bodies with a great curiosity and with an intelligent scrutiny"; his attempts at learning to write ultimately failed, although he "used to keep tablets and blanks in bed under his pillow so that at leisure hours he might accustom his hand to form the letters".[11]

Indeed, his thirst for learning was unquenchable. Although normally he spoke in the Germanic tongue, he insisted on learning Latin; while eating, or resting in the spa, he liked to listen to poems read aloud; Augustine's *City of God* was his bedside book; and, notoriously, he collected scholars for the royal palace the way other rulers gathered artworks.

Einhard recalls that Charlemagne "cherished with the greatest fervor and devotion the principles of the Christian religion, which had been instilled in him from infancy."[12] This was due largely to the example of his father, a wise ruler with a stable personality, who had shown his willingness to stand up for the Church's

---

[4] Ibid., no. 24, "Habits".
[5] Ibid., no. 22, "Personal Appearance".
[6] Ibid., no. 23, "Dress".
[7] Ibid., no. 19, "Private Life".
[8] Ibid.
[9] Ibid.
[10] Ibid., no. 25, "Studies".
[11] Ibid.
[12] Ibid., no. 26, "Piety".

rights on more than one occasion. One document tells how Pepin refused to give in to the demands of the Byzantine emperor who asked him to take away territory from the papacy; it narrates how he had affirmed under oath that he had gone to war not for political motives but "only for the love of St. Peter and for the remission of his sins, and he declared that no enrichment of his treasury would persuade him to take back what he had once offered to St. Peter".[13]

Another influence on Charlemagne was the powerful prime minister in his father's government, Fulrad (710–784), the saintly Abbot of St. Denis, friend of Saint Boniface and the popes Stephen II, Hadrian I, and Paul I. As king, Charlemagne asked him to continue as his chief statesman. There was also the Irish priest Cathulf, who motivated Charlemagne to keep a copy of the Bible at hand and to read a passage from it daily. Perhaps it was from him that Charlemagne acquired a love for praying the liturgical hours:

> He was a constant worshipper at this church [of Aachen] as long as his health permitted, going morning and evening, even after nightfall, besides attending Mass; and he took care that all the services conducted therein should be administered with the utmost possible propriety, very often warning the sextons not to let any improper or unclean thing be brought into the building or remain in it. He provided it with a great number of sacred vessels of gold and silver and with such a quantity of clerical robes that not even the doorkeepers who filled the humblest position in the church were obliged to wear their everyday clothes when on duty. He was at great pains to improve the church reading and psalmody for he was well-skilled in both, although he neither read in public nor sang except in a low tone and with others.[14]

He was convinced of his mission to be a warrior-king: "Throughout his whole reign the wish that he had nearest at heart was to re-establish the ancient authority of the city of Rome under his care and by his influence, and to defend and protect the Church of St. Peter."[15] For forty-five years he sallied forth on fifty-five campaigns with his legendary sword *Joyeuse* (Joyful) in hand, against Saxons, Bavarians, the Mongolian Avars in the area of Hungary, and the invading Muslims in southern France.

His high Christian ideal as statesman was not exactly matched by his standards of sexual morality, since over the years he probably had a minimum of ten mistresses. He also prevented his daughters from marrying, probably for political reasons, and tolerated their cohabitations with courtiers at the imperial court. However, it must be admitted that he never explicitly condoned his or their immorality and legislated Christian moral values regarding marriage and family life for his empire. He energetically assisted the poor not only at home but also abroad, notably in the Middle East and North Africa, where he engaged in diplomatic relations with Islamic rulers in order to assist the suffering Christians under their jurisdiction.[16] Hence, though hardly Christian in some ways—"rough-hewn from gnarled Germanic wood"[17] —he had an unbending conviction that political position and military prowess were in function of achieving good for others, above all, for their souls. This he declared

---

[13] See *Vita Stephani II*, in *Liber Pontificalis*, ed. L. Duchesne, vol. 1 (Paris, 1886), pp. 452–54. Quoted in Brian Tierney, *The Crisis of Church and State, 1050–1300* (Englewood Cliffs, N.J.: Prentice Hall), pp. 20–21.

[14] Einhard, *Life of Charlemagne*, no. 26, "Piety".

[15] Ibid., no. 27, "Generosity".

[16] Ibid.

[17] Henri Daniel-Rops, *The Church in the Dark Ages* (London: J.M. Dent and Sons, 1959), p. 390.

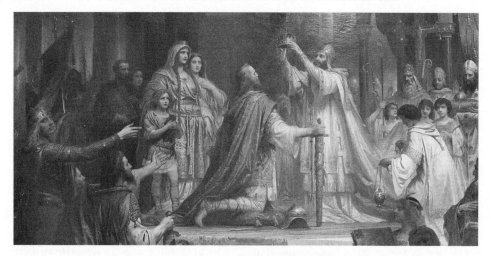

Friedrich Kaulbach, *Coronation of Charlemagne*, 1861.

publicly to be the axis of his government in the legislation of 789, whereby he set the attainment of peace and the struggle against cruelty, injustice, and hunger as his priorities. He passed laws to protect the common man from lying merchants and unjust landowners. In order to ensure that people would have guaranteed food supplies during crop failures, he outlawed the export of corn; and in 807 he put restrictions on army recruitment in order to guarantee a workforce for farmers.

At the death of Charlemagne, the ordinary Frankish men and women felt they had lost their paternal guardian who had guaranteed social stability and had protected them from injustice. Nevertheless, when dealing with enemies, he could be as brutal as any barbarian, and within the empire he acted unjustly in applying the death penalty for petty crimes. Yet, the overall image left to posterity, even though exaggerated, raised the standard for anyone claiming to be a Christian monarch. What Charlemagne attempted, others would attain: Louis IX of France, Henry II of Germany, Stephen of Hungary, Godfrey de Bouillon, Casimir of Poland, Wenceslaus of Bohemia, Edward the Confessor, Robert II of France, Alfred the Great of England, and, in modern times, Emperor Karl von Habsburg of the Austro-Hungarian Empire.

The Ideal behind Charlemagne's Empire

From 768 to 800 Charlemagne ruled as king of the Franks. Then, on Christmas Day 800, in St. Peter's Basilica, Pope Leo III crowned him as emperor, the first with the imperial title in Western Europe since Romulus Augustus had been deposed in 476.

The man who more than any other prepared the ground for the ideal of a Christian Carolingian empire was Charlemagne's close friend and "Minister of Culture", Alcuin. He and others, mostly bishops and priests, had held long discussions in monastic cloisters about their ideals, the problems of Western Europe, and how to resolve them. The writings of the Anglo-Saxon in the years before A.D. 800 tell of a heart and mind increasingly uneasy: Viking longships were off the coasts, the Saxons were still largely pagan, the Adoptionist heresy had gained influence, and, in Rome, the Pope had been physically assaulted and imprisoned by the city's aristocrats.

In June 799, from the monastery at Tours, Alcuin proposed his solution in a letter to Charlemagne. He argued that since the Eastern Roman emperor, the "titular holder of the imperial dignity", was no longer capable of militarily defending the Church from so many ominous dangers, Catholics relied on him (Charlemagne) providentially "to govern the Christian nation.... Now it is upon you alone that the Churches of Christ rely, to you alone that they look for salvation, you who are the avenger of crimes, the guide of the erring, the consoler of the afflicted and the support of the godly".[18] In other letters the term *imperium Christianum* appeared. The coronation of the Frankish king as emperor, he urged the powerful circle around him, would be the logical way not only to address present urgencies but to resolve an ongoing need for a political protector of the Church who would clear away obstacles to her mission for the well-being, eternal and temporal, of souls.

Alcuin and the others proposed to build a new type of society, in which law would be both Roman and Christian, the state forming a harmonious unity with the Church in the common quest to create a social order according to the blueprints of the Gospel. Although nostalgic for the grandeur of the old Roman Empire, the idealists' notion of *imperium* was radically different: they wanted to give birth to a Christian family of nations united under a powerful, peace-loving ruler who would guarantee that all dimensions of society would be Christian. Such was the program that appeared after the coronation of Charlemagne in the laws of the Capitulary (a set of Frankish royal decrees) in 802.

No one was under any illusion about the challenges facing the creation of what men by 1000 would call "Christendom". As they looked around, they saw barbarian kingdoms ruled by monarchs with only a veneer of Catholicism, all fiercely jealous of their independence. Savagery, ignorance, and violence were widespread among the masses. To attempt to forge a Christian society out of such raw material would require generations of heroic endeavor. Yet, for these Catholic idealists there was no other solution: in their minds this was the only road for society to travel in order to be faithful to the Christian principles as unfolded by Augustine. Only a strong Christian state would have the capacity to fight against the centrifugal forces of tribalism and nationalism that imperiled the unity of the Church, held up social progress, and jeopardized peace; and peace was the necessary condition for the creation of Christian culture, a sense of brotherhood among Christians, and the uplifting of the poor from their misery and moral squalor.

The Carolingian attempt at embodying Christianity in the sociopolitical order was a new framework for the relations between Church and society. The Church had always recognized that the Gospel of Jesus Christ was not some esoteric doctrine about prayer and inner transformation to be lived on the edges of social life. As soon as Constantine had officially ended the persecution of Christians, men like John Chrysostom and Ambrose intuitively applied Christian truths to the social order. But it was Saint Augustine in his *City of God* who pioneered the systematic application of Christian principles to the creation of a new social order—and this became the bedside book of Charlemagne.

Although it is unlikely that the Frankish emperor's rudimentary education enabled him to grasp the book's highly nuanced explanation of Church-state relations, he was

---

[18] Quoted in Robert Folz, *The Coronation of Charlemagne* (London: Routledge and Kegan, 1974), p. 125.

deeply influenced by some of its key ideas that he adopted as personal convictions. Dear to him was Augustine's portrayal of the ideal Christian ruler:

> For neither do we say that certain Christian emperors were therefore happy because they ruled a long time, or, dying a peaceful death, left their sons to succeed them in the empire, or subdued the enemies of the republic, or were able both to guard against and to suppress the attempt of hostile citizens rising against them. These and other gifts or comforts of this sorrowful life even certain worshippers of demons have merited to receive, who do not belong to the kingdom of God to which these belong; and this is to be traced to the mercy of God who would not have those who believe in Him desire such things as the highest good. But we say that they are happy if they rule justly; if they are not lifted up amid the praises of those who pay them sublime honors, and the obsequiousness of those who salute them with an excessive humility but remember that they are men; if they make their power the handmaid of His majesty by using it for the greatest possible extension of His worship; if they fear, love, worship God; if more than their own they love that kingdom in which they are not afraid to have partners; if they are slow to punish, ready to pardon; if they apply that punishment as necessary to government and defence of the republic, and not in order to gratify their own enmity; if they grant pardon, not that iniquity may go unpunished, but with the hope that the transgressor may amend his ways; if they compensate with the lenity of mercy and the liberality of benevolence for whatever severity they may be compelled to decree; if their luxury is as much restrained as it might have been unrestrained; if they prefer to govern depraved desires rather than any nation whatever; and if they do all these things, not through ardent desire of empty glory, but through love of eternal felicity, not neglecting to offer to the true God, who is their God, for their sins, the sacrifices of humility, contrition, and prayer. Such Christian emperors, we say, are happy in the present time by hope, and are destined to be so in the enjoyment of the reality itself when that which we wait for shall have arrived.[19]

Hence, Charlemagne's soul was infused with the vision of himself, not as another Caesar, but as the Christian ruler of an empire entrusted to him by God and intimately united with the Church of Rome.

The Reality

Notwithstanding all their idealism, Charlemagne and others fused and confused what the great genius of North Africa in his complex writings had made separate and distinct.

For them the bonding between state and Church occurred with the coronation ceremony's anointing ritual. Unlike in Byzantium, where it happened after the sovereign was already in power and then only as a ceremonial, in the West it was this rite, developed in Anglo-Saxon England and Visigothic Spain under the Church's influence, that gave the ruler his authority. It sealed him as sacred, with the mission of guaranteeing a sociopolitical order that would protect the Church as she sought to fulfill her mission of bringing men to God. However, how was this royal duty to be interpreted? Was the monarch still a servant of the Church, and the exercise of his authority subject to the interpretation of the pope and bishops? Or somehow,

---

[19] St. Augustine, *City of God*, trans. Marcus Dods, *Nicene and Post-Nicene Fathers*, 1st series, ed. Philip Schaff, vol. 2 (Buffalo, N.Y.: Christian Literature Publishing, 1887), bk. 5, chap. 24.

Charlemagne and His Counsellors at Aix-la-Chapelle (engraving).

because of his protectorship of the Church, was he entitled to intervene in the Church's internal affairs?

Pope Stephen IV, who anointed Louis as Charlemagne's successor, was succeeded by Pope Gregory IV who intervened in the politics of the empire. Both of these popes, as well as their successors, were of the opinion that the empire was built upon the Church: the crown and the imperial apparatus were not an end but a means to the establishment of a Christian society under the tutelage of the successors of the apostles. It was therefore the Church that ultimately mattered; the emperor was a servant–guardian. In as much as he fulfilled his mission he should have the Church's support, but since her authority was superior to his, she had the duty to judge him if he were unable, or otherwise unfit, to fulfill his task. The pope would then be obliged to intervene because, as Vicar of Christ on earth, it was his responsibility to judge all men in matters of faith and morals. Indeed, this authority belonged to all bishops in as much as they, like the pope, as successors of the apostles, were responsible for ensuring that society was ordered in function of man's eternal salvation. Hence the bottom line was that just as the ruler had received kingship at the hands of the bishop, so likewise he could be deposed by him. Charlemagne probably recognized this implication. Einhard his biographer states that he was quite uneasy after the coronation on that Christmas Day of A.D. 800, and later he insisted on personally crowning his own son. A thousand years later, on December 2, 1804, Napoleon would do likewise in Notre Dame de Paris when he himself placed the crown on his head rather than allow the Pope to do so (in this instance we can suppose that Pius VI was quite happy to have nothing to do with it).

There was, however, another quite ominous interpretation of the emperor's status. According to an anonymous monk of the influential Swiss monastery of St. Gall, the king's principal role was not only to defend the Church's safety by force of arms but also to be "the *'episcopus episcoporum'* [the bishop of bishops], their overseer in the government of the Church".[20]

Charlemagne immediately began giving the Church a headache because he reckoned that he had the authority to intervene for the sake of the Church's security whenever the pope or the bishops were either unable or unwilling. Roadblocks put up by Alcuin would be swept aside by both Charlemagne and his successors who would remember that the Anglo-Saxon monk had defined the emperor as one called by divine providence to guide the pope but would forget that he had also declared the emperor to have no right ever to sit in judgment on the Holy See.[21]

---

[20] Monk of St. Gall, *Life of Charlemagne*, bk. 2, chap. 25, p. 157.

[21] See Alcuin, Letters 27 and 174, in Alcuin, *Opera Omnia* (*PL* 100). Unless indicated otherwise, all of the letters of Alcuin are numbered according to this collection.

During the lifetime of Charlemagne, the state, embodied in a patriarchal monarch, was plainly in charge of the Frankish Church. This fusion of powers could be seen in action at the court in Aachen where the chancellery, composed of clerics and headed by the archchaplain and the chancellor, ran state and Church as one organism. In a single meeting they could go from selecting a candidate for the episcopacy to deciding on defense of the imperial borders, from issuing a decree on monastic discipline to legislating on education and Sunday rest from work. And after the meeting one could see them processing into the imperial chapel, where they and the emperor sang the Divine Office together. Local government in the three hundred counties into which the empire was divided was also highly influenced by bishops and clerics. Moreover, Charlemagne oversaw the local administrators through teams of travelling supervisors, the *missi dominici*, consisting of a nobleman and a bishop or abbot. The churchman, however, was usually more influential because of his ecclesiastical status and level of education.

For the Church there were certainly drawbacks to this arrangement: bishops could be called away from their dioceses to act as imperial statesmen, diplomats, and judges; Church property was often viewed as imperial property; ecclesiastics who were not of the Christian excellence of Alcuin and his brother idealists were tempted to live like the wealthy nobles. But the advantages were also numerous: the great abbeys became hubs of educational and economic growth with farms, mills, hospitals, schools, and workshops; new monasteries, favored by rich donations from Charlemagne, were founded; and even Charlemagne's nomination of bishops was a blessing because the monarch and those around him sought only orthodox, morally upright, intelligent, and vigorous priests. A splendid sight indeed was the front line of the episcopate of the Carolingian Empire: Theodulf of Orléans, Hincmar of Reims, Saint Lullus of Mainz, Arno of Salzburg, and Paulinus of Aquileia. Thanks to these bishops and imperial support, the Church began to awaken out of her slumber. Priests became better educated; concubinage diminished among them; and they taught the laity enough rudiments of the Faith to enable them to fulfill Aachen's requirements for godparents: "that no one presume to receive another from the sacred font of baptism before he can recite the Lord's Prayer and the Creed".[22]

The Idealists around Charlemagne

An International Group

The leading idealists who sought to integrate the Catholic Faith, Greco-Roman learning, and the Germanic culture of the Franks into a sociopolitical ethos for Charlemagne's empire were mostly connected with the Palace Academy. This school, so integral to the emperor's plans for the growth of both Christianity and culture in his lands, educated himself and his sons and daughters, as well as the scions of noble families. The teachers, headed by Alcuin, also functioned as an unofficial "Ministry of Culture", a think tank or policy institute for everything ranging from public education to liturgy, theology, moral questions, the arts, and literature. It was so vital a part of Charlemagne's government that when he left Aachen to

---

[22] Letter of Charlemagne, quoted in Owen M. Phelan, *The Formation of Christian Europe: The Carolingians, Baptism, and the Imperium Christianum* (Oxford: Oxford University Press, 2014), p. 159.

travel, the Academy went with him. The members formed a tightly knit group, for they shared the same ideal for society and lived with all the excitement of pioneers of culture in a largely barbarian society. Even when teachers and students departed to take up positions in Church or state elsewhere, they stayed in contact by correspondence.

Who were these intellectuals who, in the history of civilization, have rarely, if ever, been equaled in the degree of power that they exercised for the molding of an empire?

Firstly, it is noteworthy that the Frankish king chose them without any racial prejudice. From Spain came Theodulf the Visigoth (ca. 760–821), who had trained as a monk under the saintly and austere

Jean Victor Schnetz, *Charlemagne and Alcuin,* 1830.

Benedict of Aniane in southern France and would later be appointed Bishop of Orléans. He insisted on keeping the door of his home open to welcome the poor or pilgrims in need of food and lodgings for the night. For he was of the opinion that if a man wanted to be offered a seat at God's heavenly banquet, he had firstly to provide a place for the needy at the earthly dinner table. A man of fresh and daring ideas, he never forgot the public schools he had seen in Rome during his youth; he became firmly convinced that every child had the right to an education, and that money should not be an obstacle. Energetically he contributed to the boom in public education for the masses that began under Charlemagne and Alcuin by building schools on monastic lands or alongside parish churches. However, in his final years, amid the tumult after Charlemagne's death, he was exiled and died in such a way that poisoning was suspected.

Then there was Paulinus of Aquileia, a Roman, recognized by the Church as a saint, who became the "master of grammar" (*grammaticus magister*) at Aachen for about ten years. In 787 he was appointed patriarch of the Italian city of Aquileia, located at the head of the Adriatic. A strong defender of the Church's freedom from undue imperial interventions, Paulinus opposed Charlemagne's decree forcing the Saxons to convert, even confronting the emperor personally. Due to his efforts in favor of the peaceful Christianization of the Asiatic Avars and the Alpine Slavs, he merited to receive the title "Apostle of the Slovenes".

Peter of Pisa, who taught Latin and grammar, was a Lombard. So was Paul the Deacon (ca. 720–799), who probably worked as secretary to the Lombard king Desiderius and lived at the court of Benevento before entering a monastery on Lake Como. By 782 he was a resident of Monte Cassino, and it was there that he met Charlemagne, who, impressed by his literary achievements, invited him to the Palace Academy. There, he became the imperial tutor of Latin grammar and the topography of Rome. However, his heart was in the cloister and he never ceased to hope that one day he would be able to return there, as indeed he did in 787. His contributions to the cultural renaissance included a history of the Lombards and a compilation of sermons, which, on Charlemagne's orders, were used for preaching in parishes.

The Frank Angilbert (ca.760–814), a cleric in minor orders, was an imperial official and diplomat who spent some years working in the government of Italy. Educated under Alcuin, he was a member of the Palace Academy and was renowned as a skillful poet. He cohabited with Charlemagne's daughter, Bertha, a fact accepted by monarch and court, from which at least two sons were born, one of whom, Nithard, became a notable historian in the mid-ninth century. His principal biographer states that he did serious penance for his sins before his death.

Einhard (770–840), also a Frankish layman, was educated by the monks of Fulda and by Alcuin. The latter, impressed by his mathematical and architectural talents, recommended him to Charlemagne who put him in charge of the construction of Aachen's cathedral and the palaces at Aachen and Ingelheim. He also acted as imperial diplomat, was a poet and artist, and wrote the *Life of Charles the Great*. He was deeply in love with his wife, Emma, with whom it seems he had a son, Vussin. It is said that these two souls in their later years decided to offer their lives more intensely to God's service by vowing continence and dedicating their energies to religious activities. After Emma's death in 835, the grief-stricken Einhard wrote to a friend that he was reminded of her "every day, in every action, in every undertaking, in all the administration of the house and household, in everything needing to be decided upon and sorted out in my religious and earthly responsibilities".[23] He spent his final years as abbot of a Benedictine monastery that he had founded.

Others around Charlemagne included Fardulf, the Lombard priest who acted as his chaplain; Rado, the chief royal notary; Odo, the Armenian architect of the Palace Chapel; Arno, one of the imperial supervisors and later Archbishop of Salzburg; and Lullus, an Anglo-Saxon Benedictine from Malmesbury Abbey who became Boniface's successor at Mainz. Also present were Lombard disciples of Boethius and Cassiodorus; Spanish spiritual sons of Saint Isidore of Seville, "the last scholar of the ancient world"[24]; and Smaragdus of Saint-Mihiel, perhaps the most original writer of the group, authoring the *Royal Road*, a manual of asceticism and mystical theology for rulers.

Alcuin

The Man Whom Charlemagne Called "My Mentor"[25]

Alcuin (ca. 730–804) held a special position among these scholars as the empire's unofficial "Minister of Culture", a man for whom Charlemagne held deep admiration, whose friendship he cherished, and to whom he gave an important role in

---

[23] Einhard's letter to Lupus of Ferrières, April 836, quoted in Julia Smith, "Einhard", *Transactions of the Royal Historical Society* (Cambridge, England, 2003), p. 55.

[24] Comte de Montalembert, *Les moines d'Occident depuis saint Benoît jusqu'à saint Bernard*, vol. 2 (Paris: Jacques Lecoffre, 1860), p. 228.

[25] "Alcuin, Mentor of Charlemagne", in *History of the English Speaking Peoples: Based on the Text of "A History of the English-Speaking Peoples" by Sir Winston Churchill*, ed. Mortimer Wheeler, Hugh Redwald Trevor-Roper, Alan John Percivale Taylor (London: B.P.C. Publishing, 1970), p. 177. See also Monk of St. Gall, *Life of Charlemagne*, bk. 1, n. 2, p. 61.

formulating policy and in drafting official documents.[26] Thanks to Einhard's biography of the emperor and Alcuin's own correspondence, we can picture both his personality and achievements in spite of his modest nature. And achievements there certainly were, for this truly Christian soul, of penetrating and encyclopedic mind, warmhearted and gutsy—more than once the owl stunningly became a roaring lion—was the chief architect of the cultural renaissance in much of Western Europe in the late eighth and early ninth centuries.

Alcuin was born into an Anglo-Saxon family in Northumbria. As a child he attended the cathedral school of York founded by Archbishop Ecgbert, a student of the Venerable Bede.[27] The bright, devout, and studious youth flourished under the attentive prelate who recognized his potential. The air he breathed was both Celtic and Roman. Vibrant still was the influence of the Irish apostle of northern England, Saint Aidan of Lindis-

Frederic Wilson, *Alcuin and Charlemagne*, 1898. This Tiffany window portrays the emperor and Alcuin consulting an astronomy book in the Palatine Chapel. Beside them is a volume of the writings of the Venerable Bede.

farne (d. in 651), a monk trained at St. Columba's abbey on the Isle of Iona. The zeal and learning that he and other Celtic monks had brought to England was largely responsible for triggering the golden age of Northumbrian culture from the seventh through the eighth centuries, whose leading representative was Egbert's mentor, the Venerable Bede (ca. 672–735) of Jarrow Abbey. York inherited Jarrow's preeminence along with its Roman culture derived from the influence of the School of Canterbury founded by Archbishop Theodore and his colleague, Abbot Hadrian, who had both been sent to England by Pope Vitalian in 669. This Roman dimension would influence Alcuin's lifelong convictions about the role of the papacy, the universal character of the Church, and the importance of Catholicism's Latin heritage. Under Ecgbert, spiritually forged in the school of the Venerable Bede, he also learned the importance of uncompromising moral standards in the priesthood. Bede, in a letter of 734, had urged Ecgbert to revitalize the Church in Northumbria by studying Gregory the Great's *Pastoral Care* and by taking Aidan of Lindisfarne and Cuthbert as examples of model bishops. He had also reminded his former student of the gravity of his responsibility: "But if any one, which God forbid, should receive the rank of bishop, and should take no pains either by a righteous life to save himself from evil or [to save] his people by punishing and admonishing them—what shall happen to him when the Lord comes at an hour that he knows not of is declared

---

[26] See Donald A. Bullough, *Alcuin: Achievement and Reputation* (Leiden and Boston: Brill Academic Publishers, 2004).

[27] See Peter Hunter Blair, *The World of Bede* (Cambridge: Cambridge University Press, 1990), p. 305.

plainly in that Gospel sentence addressed to the unprofitable servant, 'Cast him into outer darkness where there shall be weeping and gnashing of teeth'."[28]

Alcuin, named head of the cathedral school in 767, successfully guided and enlarged it for fourteen years. In March 781, during a stop in Parma while returning to England from Rome, the Anglo-Saxon cleric met Charlemagne whose achievements he already admired.

The Frankish king was keen to attract such a brilliant scholar to his capital and offered the Anglo-Saxon intellectual the position of Master of the Palace School. Although reluctant to leave his beloved Northumbria, Alcuin, after a delay, accepted, intuiting the potential for the creation and spread of Christian culture through Aachen—the "new Athens ... only much more excellent".[29] "And", as the monk of Saint Gall wrote, "Charles received Albinus [Alcuin] kindly and kept him at his side to the end of his life, except when he marched with his armies to his vast wars: nay, Charles would even call himself Albinus's disciple; and Albinus he would call his master."[30]

Although Alcuin would often sign off on personal letters as *Albinus, humilis Levita* (the humble deacon), at some point he was ordained to the priesthood.[31] A biographer remarked about his final years in Tours, "Celebrabat omni die missarum solemnia"[32] (he used to celebrate a solemn Mass every day). Also, in one of his letters he acknowledged the gift of a chasuble, which he promised to use at the Holy Sacrifice of the Mass.[33] Historians generally agree that even if he was not a monk, he lived like one, with monastic austerity. He never sought either a bishopric or a rich abbey—either of which could have been his with a mere hint to Charlemagne. Indeed, at the moment of his retirement, he only accepted the abbey of Tours because the emperor insisted upon it.

Although Alcuin was ascetic, he was a Catholic ascetic and therefore very sensitive to beauty, as can be glimpsed in these charming verses about the countryside around his monastic cell:

> Beloved cell, sweet habitation [of] mine, girt around with whispering trees, and all hidden by the foliage green, before thee stretch the meadows, blooming with fragrant flowers and life-giving herbs; babbling at thy door, the stream meanders by, on whose banks, all embowered in flowers, the fisherman loves to sit and tend his net. The lily pale, the blushing rose, mingle their odors with the sweet-smelling fruit hanging in rich profusion from thy orchard trees while all around, the feathery denizens [inhabitants] of the wood swell out their matin song in praise of their Creator.[34]

All the chroniclers agree that Alcuin was a likeable personality, for though he was as unbending as cold steel on principles, he had great warmth, empathy, and the ability to take himself lightly and to be interested in others. In one of his verses, one glimpses

[28] Venerable Bede, Letter to Ecgbert the Bishop, in J.A. Giles, *The Biographical Writings and Letters of Venerable Bede* (London: James Bohn, 1845), p. 139.
[29] Alcuin, Letter to Charlemagne 86 (*PL* 100:282).
[30] Monk of St. Gall, *Life of Charlemagne*, bk. 1, no. 2, p. 61.
[31] Alcuin, Letter to Charlemagne 7 (*PL* 100).
[32] *Beati Flacci Alcuini Vita*, in Alcuin, *Opera omnia*, vol. 100, chap. 13, n. 26.
[33] Alcuin, Letter 203.
[34] Carmen 23, "O mea cella, mihi habitatio dulcis amata", quoted in R.B. Page, *The Letters of Alcuin* (Charleston, S.C.: Bibliolife, 2009), p. 77.

a youthful spirit when he describes himself as "rubbing the sleep of night from his eyes and leaping from his couch as soon as the ruddy charioteer of dawn imbues the deep waters with the new light of day".[35] Or those tenderly Christian lines of the poem "In Dormiturio", written as an inscription for the dormitory of the young students at the Palace School: "May he who stills the roaring winds and raging seas, the God of Israel who has never slept throughout the ages, may He who allots the day for work and the night for rest grant to the weary brothers sweet refreshing sleep and dispel with all-powerful hand the fears that disturb their slumbers".[36]

His correspondence and poetry—although bloated at times with literary clichés and exaggerations typical of court literature—nevertheless reveal the sincerity and ease with which he gave and won friendship. Open was the heart of Alcuin—venerated as a saint after his death—but high indeed was his ideal of friendship, as he stated in a letter to Charlemagne:

> A friend is so called because he is the custodian of the soul. He strives with all his loyalty to keep the soul of his friend harmoniously integrated so that no point of the sacred law of friendship may be violated. Rare are those who understand it. For almost everyone strives to comply with this duty of friendship by attending to the character of his own soul, [and] not [to] that of another who is his friend. And if it lies heavy on a friend and coequal to preserve the integrity of his friend's mind inviolate, how much more so on a lord, on one who loves to raise up and govern his subjects in all honor.[37]

However, what gave depth to Alcuin's intellectual brilliance and cordiality was the virtue that he esteemed most of all, "the chief adornment of the soul": wisdom. To be wise was "to care for the soul more than the body since the former remains, the latter perishes"; it meant travelling along the rugged trails of self-conquest, disregarding "worldly praise, honor and the deceitful pleasures of wealth.... Wisdom is, however, not to be lightly won; there is no royal road; her heights will not be attained until the intervening plains and slopes have been crossed and ascended."[38]

These truths were deep convictions that he spent his life communicating to those around him, as can be seen in his letters. To fellow Anglo-Saxons in Northumbria he urged: "Stand manfully, fight bravely, defend the camp of God", counseling them not to "glory in showy clothing" and not to allow "drunkenness to blot out the word of prayer" nor to "go after luxuries for the body and worldly greed".[39] Indeed, as the years went by, instead of life amid power and a licentious imperial court enfeebling his principles and asceticism, they seem to have indirectly toughened them.

Alcuin was, above all, someone for whom existence was centered on the Catholic Faith which he knew to be inseparably bonded to the Church, a reality that he passionately loved not as a cold institution, but as the Mystical Body of Christ. Moreover, he loved the Church and souls as a priest whose triple mission is to teach, sanctify, and govern by word and witness. From this love flowed tireless efforts to

---

[35] Quoted in ibid.

[36] Alcuin, *In Dormiturio*, quoted in Page, *Letters of Alcuin*, p. 78.

[37] Alcuin, Letter 4, quoted in C. Stephen Jaeger, *Ennobling Love: In Search of a Lost Sensibility* (Philadelphia: University of Pennsylvania Press, 1999), p. 50.

[38] Alcuin, *Grammatica* (PL 101), quoted in Page, *Letters of Alcuin*, pp. 78–79.

[39] Alcuin to Bishop Higbald of Lindisfarne, A.D. 793, quoted and translated in G. F. Browne, *Alcuin of York* (London: S.P.C.K., 1908), p. 132.

defend the Church's unity through upholding orthodox doctrine, as witnessed by his writings against the heresy of Adoptionism. On one occasion he compared the unity of the Church with the "seamless robe of Christ which even the soldiers near the cross did not dare to divide".[40]

An excerpt of a prayer composed by him allows us a glimpse into the Christian sentiments of his soul: "O King of Glory and Lord of Valor, our warrior and our peace, who said 'Trust, for I have conquered the world'. Triumph also in us your servants, for without you we can achieve nothing. Grant unto your servants to speak your word with boldness and to show in eloquent witness what we set forth in speech. Give us to will and to accomplish. Grant your mercy to go before us and your mercy to follow us. May it go ahead of our initiative, may it follow us to its completion. And what shall I now say unless that your will be done, you who will that all men be saved? Your will is our salvation, our glory, and our joy."[41]

His own high standards of virtue can be seen in the friends who surrounded him: saintly priests like Arno of Salzburg, Leidrad, Paulinus of Aquileia, and Theodulf; women like the beautiful Gundrada, lady of the imperial court, "noblest of the noble", whose reputation for chastity radiated in that den of impurity; laymen such as Megenfrid the Treasurer, Duke Eric of Friuli, and Gerald of Bavaria. It can also be seen through those for whom he reserved his deep admiration: Saints Martin of Tours, Vedast, Riquier, and Willibrord, about all of whom he wrote.

In his own quiet, usually pleasant, but nevertheless determined Anglo-Saxon manner, he was a moral reformer, convinced that both priests and laity should do their utmost to live up to their Christian identity. His efforts started with the entourage around Charlemagne, many of whom were ill at ease with the austere priest, but whom they had to tolerate because of his friendship with the emperor. To the pure Gundrada he urged that she be an example to the other women; in a letter to his pupil Nathaniel he warned about protecting his chastity in dealings with the females of the court; Magharius, Charlemagne's wise advisor, is cautioned to keep pleasures of the body at a distance; Angilbert, whose concubinage with Bertha was in broad daylight, received stinging counsel as did Pepin, king of Italy. Even Charlemagne was corrected for his sexual immorality: "Behold our Solomon, resplendent in his diadem and crowned with virtue; imitate his virtues and avoid his vices".[42] On at least one occasion he even spoke publicly to the emperor about the value of sexual self-control—though without alluding to the monarch's poor performance in this area—stating that intemperance destroyed both physical health and mental strength. He even urged that in everyday life self-discipline should be evident in a man's speech, which should be chaste, straightforward, clearly pronounced, and unspoiled by undue brusqueness of tone or laughter. And one of his final letters before dying was to remind Charlemagne to prepare himself for his own death and God's judgment.

Alcuin insisted with Charlemagne that he carefully choose the right men for positions of power: "Let no one tarnish your good name by dishonesty, for the faults of

---

[40] Alcuin, *Adversus Felicem* (*PL* 100:132). My translation.
[41] Letter from Alcuin to Arno, Bishop of Salzburg, in A.D. 797 (*PL* 100), Letter 69. My translation. Alcuin's scriptural references have been omitted.
[42] Alcuin, Letter 309, in Page, *Letters of Alcuin*, p. 58.

the servants are often blamed on the prince."[43] Both Alcuin and Theodulf of Orléans sought to eliminate unjust judges who were quite numerous. As Theodulf scathingly remarked: "I have seen judges who were slow to attend to the duties of their office though prompt enough to take its rewards. Some arrive at the fifth hour and depart at the ninth; others, if the third hour sees them on the bench will rise therefrom at the sixth. But if there is a bribe to receive the same men will be in court before the *prima* [first hour]".[44]

His wise words of guidance also crossed the North Sea to Anglo-Saxon rulers. In an urgent tone he penned letters to four Anglo-Saxon kings—Offa, Ecgfrith, Cenwulf, and Æthelred I—warning them that the sinful king endangered his kingdom and his crown; that history has no shortage of examples of monarchs who lost their dominions because of sins of luxury and greed; that the only king who governs his kingdom well is the one who governs himself well.

Toward the reform of the priesthood went the greatest efforts of Alcuin and others in the imperial circle, for they realized that the moral, cultural, and Christian strength of the empire would be made or broken by the clergy. Alcuin waged a constant struggle, aided by imperial power, to reform priests who had sunk to abysmal depths of corruption and incompetence. Large numbers of them were immoral individuals allured to ordination by the sight of the Church's wealth. Simony was on all sides; priests partied, hunted, attended dramas and entertainments, dressed extravagantly, and drank until they were incapable of rising the following day to perform their duties. They were haughty, lewd, and foulmouthed—to one archbishop Alcuin bluntly remarked that he should allow neither "vain babblings nor scurrilous language [to] proceed out of his mouth".[45] Their corruption, ignorance, and sloth were impeding the urgent efforts of Charlemagne, Alcuin, and associates to raise the Christian, educational, and economic standards of the masses.

In 789 imperial legislation that bore the fingerprints of Alcuin urged higher moral standards among the clergy and called for greater selection in the recruitment of candidates for ordination. Other decrees ordered priests to learn the *Pater Noster, Credo*, the manual of penances, the rites of exorcism, the Church calendar, Sunday and other main liturgical texts, and "Roman singing" (plain chant). They were to make their sermons more catechetical in order to resolve the massive ignorance among the laity; therefore the main topics were to be the Blessed Trinity, the life of our Lord Jesus Christ, the Christian virtues of charity, humility, chastity, self-restraint in eating and drinking, and the dedication of Sunday to worship and rest. All sermons were to be given in the language of the people.[46]

All this reforming zeal came from the heart of a man who dubbed himself a "seed sower of peace".[47] But peace for Alcuin meant neither absence of conflict nor appeasement nor political correctness, but rather the establishment of *tranquillitas*

---

[43] Alcuin, Letter 217, quoted in Page, *Letters of Alcuin*.

[44] Theodulph of Orléans, *Versus Contra Iudices*, vv. 391–96, quoted in Page, *Letters of Alcuin*, pp. 58–59.

[45] Alcuin, Letter 114, quoted in Page, *Letters of Alcuin*, p. 56.

[46] Alessandro Barbero, *Charlemagne: Father of a Continent* (Berkeley: University of California Press, 2004), p. 106.

[47] "Let us be seed-sowers of peace among Christian peoples" ("Pacis enim seminatores simus inter populos Christianos"). Alcuin's letter, in A.D. 790, to Abbot Adelard of Corbey, quoted in *Alcuini sive Albini Epistolae*, Letter 9, in E. Dümmler, *Epistolae IV, Epistolae Karolini Aevi II* (Berlin: Monumenta Germaniae Historia [MGH], 1895), p. 35.

ordinis (the harmony due to order), an order achieved when man lives in obedience to God's commands expressed through the natural law and the laws of the Church. In a world of fallen men, war was an unfortunate necessity that had to be engaged in at times as a last resort for the sake of justice. He tried to persuade Charlemagne to reduce the number of his military conflicts—and was possibly the only one who dared to do so.[48] However, it was with regard to Charlemagne's handling of the Saxons, whom the Franks had been fighting on and off from 772, that his efforts became noticeably forceful, indeed fierce.

Charlemagne's wars against his eastern neighbors usually lasted one or two years and would normally end in a Frankish victory and with the Saxons swearing oaths of allegiance to the emperor—only to betray them as soon as the monarch had returned to Aachen. In 782 Charlemagne's patience ran out and he beheaded forty-five hundred Saxon rebels at Verden. After further uprisings, around 792, the incensed monarch issued the decree *Capitulatio de Partibus Saxoniae* (Ordinances concerning Saxony), ordering that Saxons either become Christian or face death.[49] There is no evidence of any attempt to implement the law. It had been made without consulting Alcuin, who was probably in Northumbria at the time, making an unsuccessful attempt to stay there permanently. When the Anglo-Saxon priest heard about it, he was outraged. His letter to the monarch was a crescendo of vehement opposition culminating in a clarion call to quash the law. He told the ruler that faith is always a free act and must never be forced, reminding him that Augustine had stated that conquered barbarians should be treated as a blessing from God and should be guided to Christ through gentleness, charity, and preaching. He also urged Charlemagne to put a stop to Church taxation on the conquered Saxons, "even at the expense of the public need": "You may gather hence whether or not it is wise to impose on these savage tribes, in the commencement of their faith, the yoke of tithes [the ecclesiastical tax]; whether the Apostles, taught by the Lord Christ himself, and sent forth to preach by him, ever demanded tithes or ordered them to be demanded."[50]

To other men of influence around the emperor he indignantly pounded home his opinion, which, of course, was, and is, official Catholic doctrine. In a letter to Maginfred, an imperial privy counsellor, he wrote: "If the same pains had been taken to preach to them the easy yoke and light burden of Christ as has been done to collect tithes and to punish the slightest infringement of the laws on their part, then they would no longer abhor and repel baptism."[51] In the same vein he addressed Arno, Archbishop of Salzburg, regarding the conversion of the Avars: "What avails baptism without faith?... How can a man be compelled to believe what he does not believe? Men may indeed be forced to the font but not to the faith. Man, endowed as he is with

---

[48] See Luitpold Wallach, *Alcuin and Charlemagne: Studies in Carolingian History and Literature* (Ithaca, N.Y.: Cornell University Press, 1959), p. 24.

[49] *Capitulatio de partibus Saxoniae* (A.D. 775–790), in Alfred Boretius, ed., *Capitularia regum Francorum*, vol. 1 (Hannover, 1883) nn. 26, 68–70; for an English translation, see Paul E. Dutton, ed., *Carolingian Civilization: A Reader*, 2nd ed. (Peterborough, Ontario, and London: Broadview Press, 2004), 66–69. The decree itself is an undated document so the date is disputed by historians. Circa A.D. 792 is the conclusion of the Israeli historian Yitzhak Hen; see "Charlemagne's Jihad", in *Viator: Medieval and Renaissance Studies*, vol. 37 (Turnhout, Belgium: Turnhout, 2006), pp. 33–51. Although a minority position among historians so far, this date seems to be the one that fits in best with the other circumstances known about Charlemagne's decree.

[50] Alcuin, Letter 110; translation from Wallach, *Alcuin and Charlemagne*, p. 252.

[51] Alcuin, Letter 113; translation from Page, *Letters of Alcuin*, p. 53.

reason, must be instructed and educated at length before he can perceive the truth of the Faith."[52]

Alcuin proposed another method for proposing the Catholic Faith to the Saxons in a letter to Charlemagne:

> Now, in your wise and godly concern, may you provide good preachers for the new people, sound in conduct, learned in the Faith and full of the teaching of the Gospel, intent on following the example of the apostles in the preaching of the word of God. For they gave their hearers milk, that is, gentle teaching, when they were beginners in the faith, as the Apostle Paul said "... I fed you milk to drink, not meat, as babies in Christ..." [1 Cor. 3:1–2], meaning that new converts to the Faith must be fed on gentler teaching as babies on milk, lest minds too weak for harder teaching vomit what they have imbibed.... Careful thought must also be given to the right method of preaching and baptizing that the washing of the body in baptism not be made useless by lack in the soul of an understanding of the Faith.[53]

His efforts triumphed: in 797, five years after the promulgation of the infamous decree, Charlemagne abolished the death penalty for paganism.[54] Therefore, this legislation of enforced conversions had been a short-lived aberration, and one only existing on paper. The Church continued its peaceful missionary work among the Saxons, many of whom voluntarily decided to become Christian.

But there were also other areas where Alcuin and the emperor did not agree. Charlemagne's way of enforcing Christian legislation on his own Frankish and Christian people was at times nauseating, with capital punishment meted out not only for serious crimes like murder but also for violations of the law of fasting. The powerful friend of the ruler patiently sought to change things through patient prodding, although, on at least one occasion, with boldness he went so far as to tell the emperor that just as God's providence had given him an empire, so too could he strip him of it: "I know in whose hands are the powers of all kings and kingdoms."[55] Who knows how much more intolerant the monarch would have been had priests like Alcuin, Paulinus of Aquileia, and others not been at his side, reminding him in one way or another that the emperor was under and not above the law; that his power was delegated by God and had limits; that moral strength, forgiveness and peace were the pillars of a Christian society; and that only by observing them would an empire flourish.

The two men also disagreed over the monarch's decision to oblige Pope Leo III to swear an oath regarding the accusations made against him by his enemies in 800, with Alcuin arguing that no man could sit in judgment upon Christ's Vicar.[56] Later, during his retirement at Tours, the Anglo-Saxon priest also opposed the emperor by refusing to hand over to imperial law enforcers a man on the run from justice who had sought asylum at his monastery; instead, he demanded, in a stiff letter, that

---

[52] Alcuin, Letter 107; translation from Augustus Neander, *Light in the Dark Places; Or, Memorial of Christian Life in the Middle Ages* (New York: Lane and Scott, 1851), pp. 253–54.

[53] Alcuin, Letter 110; translation from Stephen Allott, *Alcuin of York: His Life and Letters* (York: William Sessions, 1974), p. 73.

[54] See the second Saxon capitulary, dated October 28, 797, in *Capitularia regum Francorum I*, ed. Alfred Boretius (Hanover: Monumenta Germaniae Historica [MGH], 1883), n. 27, pp. 71–72. Also, see Alcuin, *Epistolae*, ed. Dümmler, Epp. 174, 177, and 184, pp. 288–89, 292–93, and 309–10, respectively.

[55] Quoted in Allott, *Alcuin of York*, p. 75.

[56] Alcuin, Letter 102, in Alcuin, *Epistolae*, in *Epistolae karolini aevi II, Epistolae IV*, ed. Ernst Dümmler (Berlin: Weidmannos, 1895).

Scholarly Monks, engraving by Hermann Vogel, 1880–1883.

the accused be tried by Charlemagne personally. This confrontation took its toll on the aged abbot's frail constitution and hastened his death.

Educator of an Empire's Educators

When Alcuin arrived to Aachen in 782, cultural standards were at freezing temperature in the Frankish territories, an area roughly corresponding to what is now France, Belgium, the Netherlands, Luxembourg, and the Rhinelands. He, Charlemagne, and others were convinced of the importance of culture and resolved to engineer a renaissance. For Alcuin, to whom fell the chief role in designing the program, the central purpose was clear: to create the rich soil and favorable climate in which the seeds of the Catholic Faith could grow naturally into a Christian culture and society.

With Charlemagne's support, Alcuin and those around him developed a strategy that bore the marks of both the farsightedness and sense of detail characteristic of the Anglo-Saxon monk. It was designed to operate in four concentric circles. "He thought in centuries. He knew that his work was akin to that of planting oaks, raising a forest of faith that would be resilient, hardy, slow-growing but strong, able to withstand a hostile climate."[57] In the inmost circle was the Palace School of Aachen, where he trained the torchbearers who would carry the spirit, ideals, and methods of the new culture into episcopal chancelleries and monastic classrooms. But it was also the headquarters where he, the other teachers, and some of the leading students discussed, argued, prayed, and planned about how to restore the practical tools of culture (literacy, quantities of books, art, architecture, liturgy, and music) throughout the empire. The second circle was composed of a small number of monasteries where higher education was given to the most talented monks and clerics. The third circle consisted of the majority of abbeys and cathedral schools where most young monks

[57]Pierre de Cointet, Barbara Morgan, and Petroc Willey, *The Catechism of the Catholic Church and the Craft of Catechesis* (San Francisco: Ignatius Press, 2008), p. 10.

and nobles studied. Finally, in the fourth circle lay the cherished horizon of all their efforts: the creation of schools for universal primary education, located either on monastic grounds or in the parishes, directed by monks or parish priests.

In the imperial palace at Aachen (Aix-la-Chapelle), a fine city of some forty thousand people, Alcuin and others educated those who would be the principal agents of cultural transformation: the emperor himself, his wife and children, members of the imperial household, certain clerics, and sons of the nobility. It was no ideal setting: the students were a mixed bag of young and old, some of them rather uncouth, flippant, and given to interrupting the teacher.

But they had, in many ways, an ideal teacher. The words "Alcuin is my name, Wisdom I always loved" were no mere rhetoric on his epitaph.[58] He personified his motto: *Disce ut doceas* (Learn in order to teach).[59] The Anglo-Saxon priest's overarching faith had deepened and widened a natural enthusiasm for learning until it encompassed everything from mathematics to geography and theology, the movements of the stars and the "tremors of the earth and sea, the natures of men and cattle, of birds and wild beasts".[60] The man who once remarked that "you know very well how sweet arithmetic is in its reasoning"[61] had a brilliant and incisive mind. It was not, however, an original, creative one, and although he was an excellent theologian well able to dispute about complex questions, his strongest abilities lay in pedagogy, compilation, and organization, qualities brought to perfection by an ardent ambition to communicate the Faith to others.

An educationalist in every fiber of his body, Alcuin threw himself singlemindedly into the teaching of the students at the Palace Academy and later at Tours. He organized schooling on a modern plan: "Provide masters both for the boys and the clerics; arrange into separate classes those who practice the chant, those who study the books, and those who do the copying [of manuscripts]".[62] Grammar, arithmetic, logic, rhetoric, music, astronomy, and geometry formed the core of the curriculum. Each class had its own teacher who was in charge of discipline "so that the boys be not allowed to run about in idleness nor engage in silly play".[63] An inscription over one of the school doorways recommended students to be diligent—and educators to be kind! A superb teacher himself, Alcuin became for his students the embodiment of learning, patience, and excellence in pedagogy through setting high goals, arousing interest, and awakening imagination. Many of the students reciprocated by revering and loving him as a spiritual father and later as a friend, remaining in contact with him by correspondence long after they had graduated.

Under Alcuin, the Palace School became the nursery of leaders for Church and state in the Carolingian Empire, many of the alumni vigorously impelling the growth of the Catholic Faith, education, and culture. "Wherever", wrote Wattenbach, referring to the Carolingian epoch, "anything of literary activity is visible, there we can

---

[58] Ethel Mary Wilmot-Buxton, *Alcuin* (New York: P.J. Kenedy, 1922), p. 185.

[59] *Disce ut doceas*, or variants thereof, can be found throughout Alcuin's writing, e.g., Letter 270, in Alcuin, *Epistolae*, p. 429. It was very likely inspired by the great intellectual of his homeland, the Venerable Bede; see *Histoira ecclesiastica gentis Anglorum*, V, 24.

[60] A verse from a poem of Alcuin's, *De pontificibus et sanctis Ecclesiae Eboracensis*, in Peter Godman, ed., *The Bishops, Kings, and Saints of York* (Oxford: Clarendon Press, 1982), verse 1448, p. 115.

[61] Alcuin, Letter 148, in *Epistolae*, p. 239.

[62] Alcuin, Letter 114, quoted in Page, *Letters of Alcuin*, p. 97.

[63] Ibid.

with certainty count on finding a pupil of Alcuin's."[64] To name but a few: Theodulf of Orléans, who became Alcuin's successor as Charlemagne's right-hand advisor on all educational matters; Arno, who was named Archbishop of Salzburg; Fridugis, who would succeed Alcuin in Tours; Aldrich, who became Abbot of Ferrières; and Adelard, Abbot of New Corbie in Saxony.

Adelard (ca. 751–827) is representative of the finest members among the new class of Catholic priests-statesmen who were so powerful during the Dark Ages. While still a teenager, Charlemagne, his first cousin, made him Count of the Palace, an influential government position. But Adelard had other ambitions: at twenty he entered the abbey at Corbie, and then, for the sake of guaranteeing his monastic vocation, sought refuge further south in Monte Cassino. To no avail. The monarch, who rarely took no for an answer, pursued him and ordered his return to Corbie, naming him prime minister of his son Pepin, king of Italy. After Charlemagne had died, Emperor Louis suspected him of intrigue and banished him to the island of Noirmoutier in 817, but after several years, recognizing he had made a mistake, recalled him and made him one of his trusted counselors. In 822 Adelard and his brother Wala founded New Corbie Abbey in Westphalia. The Church venerates him as a saint, and in art he has often been portrayed digging in a garden, his abbot's mitre lying on the ground beside him.

Among the heirs of Alcuin, preeminent for intellectual influence was the celebrated Rabanus Maurus (ca. 780–856), who studied for twelve months in Tours under the aged but ever-inspiring "Master of the Vineyards". Then he returned to his abbey at Fulda, the sanctuary of Catholicism in Germanic lands that had been founded in 744 by Saint Sturm, disciple of Saint Boniface. Under Rabanus it became the leading center of culture in Germany, open to laymen as well as candidates for the priesthood, all of whom studied the seven liberal arts along with theology and the German language. Among his most distinguished students were Walafrid Strabo, Servatus Lupus, Otfried of Weissenburg, and Rudolf of Fulda. Their heirs in turn included the cultured group of ecclesiastics who taught and counseled the remarkably intelligent young emperor Otto III (980–1002): Notker of Liège, Bernward of Hildesheim, Heribert of Cologne, and the most illustrious of all, Gerbert of Aurillac, who went on to become Pope Sylvester II (999–1003), famed for his wisdom and encyclopedic knowledge. When Rabanus became Archbishop of Mainz, he sought to improve the quality of priestly preaching and the use of German, meriting the title bestowed upon him by historians: "Teacher of Germany".[65] Notable also was his love for the poor—the *Annales Fuldenses* state that during the famine of 850 he daily fed more than three hundred people.

Alongside the intellectuals and prelates directly formed by Alcuin or his disciples, there were also the Irish monks who played an important role in cultural renaissance and the creation of a new Christian culture in the ninth and tenth centuries. Charlemagne appointed one of them, Clement, as regent of the imperial school in Paris from 774 to 818. The school, which was open to any talented youth, whether noble

---

[64] Quoted in Jane S. F. Leibell and Helen D. Leibell, *Anglo-Saxon Education of Women: From Hilda to Hildegarde* (Washington, D.C.: Georgetown University, 1922), p. 131.

[65] See Frank N. Magill, *The Middle Ages: Dictionary of World Biography*, vol. 2 (Oxford: Routledge, 1998), p. 768.

or working class, planted the seeds of intellectual excellence that would ultimately grow into Europe's greatest medieval university. Another monk, Dougal, working mainly at the monasteries of Saint-Denis, Pavia, and Bobbio, in a letter to Charlemagne answered the monarch's question about why two solar eclipses occurred in the year 810, showing an extraordinary knowledge of astronomy for his epoch. Others were the grammarian Cruindmelus; the poet Dungal of Bobbio; Bishop Donatus of Fiesole; the geographer Dicuil; and the poet and scribe Sedulius Scottus, who founded the school at Liège; Elias, who taught at Laon; Dunchad at Reims; and Israel at Auxerre. Then there was Johannes Scotus Eriugena (ca. 815–877), one of Europe's outstanding early medieval philosophers who became master of the Palace School. Through his translations of Pseudo-Dionysius the Areopagite, he transmitted Neoplatonic theology to medieval intellectuals. One of these intellectuals was Abbot Suger (ca. 1081–1151), the developer of the first authentically Gothic building, the Basilica of St. Denis, partly inspired by Pseudo-Dionysius' theology in which God's causality is compared to the emanation of light from the sun. Eighth-century and ninth-century Irish monks were especially active at Reichenau, St. Gall, and Bobbio. "Almost all of Ireland, despising the sea, is migrating to our shores", wrote Heiric of Auxerre in 870, adding ruefully, "with a herd of philosophers".[66] Every monastery or cathedral school at which they appeared soon showed their influence. To the curriculum already in place they added the study of Greek and stamped their teaching of philosophy and the Bible with commentaries drawn from the writings of the Greek Fathers and the Neoplatonists. One of the last of the renowned Irish scholars on the European mainland was Petrus Hibernicus, "the theologian who had the supreme task of educating the mind of the author of the Scholastic apology, *Summa contra Gentiles*, St. Thomas Aquinas, perhaps the keenest and clearest mind that human history has ever seen".[67]

By the middle of the ninth century, the renaissance had spread throughout the empire, channeled largely through the network of monasteries founded or inspired by Columbanus, other Celtic monks, and their Benedictine counterparts. In France, Orléans was followed by Reims, Auxerre, Laon, and Chartres; in southern Germany and Switzerland, before the close of the eighth century, it was centered in Rheinau, Reichenau, and St. Gall; and a few decades later it had penetrated northern Italy, especially through Bobbio and Pavia. Under Charlemagne's heirs, the movement established itself in Belgium and the Netherlands at Utrecht, Liège, and St. Laurent.

Restorer of the Tools of Intellectual Culture

To enable the seeds of the Catholic Faith and Christian culture to grow and flourish among the peoples of the empire, Alcuin, ever practical, realized that the soil

---

[66] Quoted in Ted Byfield, *Darkness Descends: A.D. 350 to 565, the Fall of the Western Roman Empire* (Canada: Christian History Project, 2003), p. 253.

[67] James Joyce (lecture, Università Popolare di Trieste, Italy, April 27, 1907); rep. in *The Critical Writings of James Joyce*, eds. Ellsworth Mason and Richard Ellmann (New York: Viking Press, 1964, 1966), p. 157. More precisely, the role of Petrus Hibernicus was that of introducing St. Thomas to philosophy. Elsewhere, in a poem entitled "The Holy Office" (1904), Joyce (best known as the author of *Ulysses*) spoke of himself as "steeled in the school of old Aquinas"; see A. Nicholas Fargnoli and Michael Patrick Gillespie, *James Joyce, A to Z: The Essential Reference to His Life and Writings* (Oxford: Oxford University Press, 1995), p. 8.

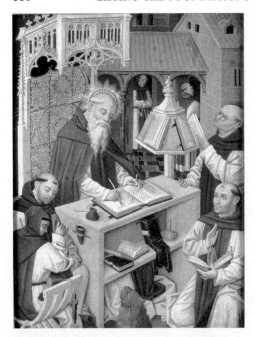

Maestro del Parral, *St. Jerome in the Scriptorium*, ca. 1485. "And other silent men, not seen, were sitting in the cold cloister, tiring their eyes and keeping their attention on the stretch, while they painfully copied and recopied the manuscripts which they had saved" (John Henry Newman, *Historical Sketches*, vol. 2 [London: Longmans, Green, 1903], p. 410).

required cultivation, and that the cultivators needed to receive the necessary tools for the task. This "restoring the tools of labor to intellectual culture"[68] implied books and pens—and therefore parchment and bristles! So Alcuin went to Charlemagne and asked that he stock the forests with enough deer for making vellum, enough boar for getting the bristles for brush pens, and possibly with the recommendation that oak trees be preserved since they provided the oak gall purple-brown or brownish-black ink.

In the same practical vein, he saw that if reading and writing were to become popular, it was important to make reading as easy as possible and therefore writing as uniform as possible. For this purpose he developed a school of calligraphy, and it is largely due to him and his student Abbot Fredegise that an easily readable handwriting, the Carolingian minuscule, reached its definitive form. This was the forerunner of our modern script, with its clear and distinct lowercase letters, capital letters, spaces between words, paragraphs, and other elements of punctuation. It was easier both to write and read, thus contributing to a civilization based on the written word and speeding up the spread of classical culture.

With reading and writing in place, books could be produced more swiftly and manuscripts copied more accurately. Few books existed at the beginning of the Carolingian period, and the process of copying a book was lengthy, the Bible requiring several years. Any one monk replicated perhaps a mere ten books in his lifetime. Alcuin and his associates collected the ancient texts—joining the ranks of the greatest collectors in history—and assembled, organized, conserved, copied, and disseminated them. Vital work indeed, since we owe the tiny remnant of ancient Roman manuscripts of authors such as Virgil that we possess today to the Carolingian copyists. The "Minister of Culture" ensured that every monastic school would have its scriptorium where books were copied and recopied by the monks and the most advanced students. Because Alcuin facilitated this multiplication of literature, over the following two hundred years Western Europe acquired enough books to make learning more widespread, thus stimulating the qualitative leap in culture that happened in the twelfth-century and thirteenth-century universities. Had Alcuin not stocked the forests with deer and wild boar in the eighth century, as one author clear-sightedly

---

[68] Daniel-Rops, *The Church in the Dark Ages*, p. 421.

remarked, the young Thomas Aquinas might have lacked the excellent library he used at Naples in the thirteenth.[69]

Alcuin set a standard curriculum for the liberal arts in the monastic and cathedral schools, with the priority of enabling youth to study the doctrines of the Catholic Faith. Such a goal may seem rather narrow to those who do not know the internal dynamism of Catholic theology. However, with its bipolar structure of the truths of divine revelation and veneration for human intelligence, Catholic theology pushes reason to its uttermost limits in an effort to clarify the meaning of God's revealed truths. Hence, the implications of the curriculum were far-reaching. It stimulated rational inquiry firstly in theology and philosophy and then extended centrifugally into other disciplines, much as a V-shaped wake streaming from its source in the back of a ship spreads outward.

Thus, the Carolingian intellectual thrust, coalescing and building upon the labors of the previous three hundred years, actually laid the foundations for the rise of the institution that more than any other became the powerhouse of Western civilization's intellectual progress: the university. This connection between Catholicism, medieval monasticism, and the historical growth of European intellectual life was the theme of Benedict XVI's address to intellectuals at the Collège des Bernardins, a former monastery in Paris. He explained that, historically, the renewal of Western intellectual dynamism lay in the culture of the Church's abbeys, those places where, during the first millennium and the medieval epoch, men came not to preserve or create culture but to adore God and dedicate themselves more exclusively to the ultimate purpose of existence.

> Their goal was: *quaerere Deum* [to seek God]. Amid the confusion of the times in which nothing seemed permanent, they wanted to do the essential—to make an effort to find what was perennially valid and lasting: life itself. They were searching for God. They wanted to go from the inessential to the essential, to the only truly important and reliable thing there is. It is sometimes said that they were "eschatologically" oriented. But this is not to be understood in a temporal sense, as if they were looking ahead to the end of the world or to their own death, but in an existential sense: they were seeking the definitive behind the provisional. *Quaerere Deum*: because they were Christians this was not an expedition into a trackless wilderness, a search leading them into total darkness. God himself had provided signposts, indeed he had marked out a path which was theirs to find and to follow. This path was his word which had been disclosed to men in the books of the sacred Scriptures. Thus, by inner necessity, the search for God demands a culture of the word ... we must learn to penetrate the secret of language, to understand it in its construction and in the manner of its expression. Thus it is through the search for God that the secular sciences take on their importance, sciences which show us the path towards language. Because the search for God required the culture of the word, it was appropriate that the monastery should have a library pointing out pathways to the word. It was also appropriate to have a school.... The monastery serves eruditio [learning], the formation and education of man—a formation whose ultimate aim is that man should learn how to serve God. But it also includes the formation of reason—education—through which man learns to perceive, in the midst of words, the Word itself.[70]

---

[69] De Cointet, Morgan, and Willey, *Craft of Catechesis*, p. 11.

[70] Benedict XVI, "Address to Representatives from the World of Culture at the Collège des Bernardins in Paris", September 12, 2008.

To ensure common standards throughout the empire, Alcuin restored Latin, which had been disfigured by barbarian usages. The Germanic language, for the sake of the education of the masses, and due to Charlemagne's interest in his native tongue, was also promoted.

Music in the empire might well have been dominated by the native Frankish and pagan heroic sagas and war ballads if Charlemagne's personal tastes had prevailed. Instead, Gregorian chant became fashionable and schools were set up at many monasteries for the training of young musicians. Since a nation's music powerfully forges its soul, this was of no minor importance. Something of the Anglo-Saxon monk's influence on Frankish music can be seen in these words he wrote to the emperor: "[Your letter] also admonished me to mix a sweet melody ... amidst the horrible din of clashing weapons and the raucous blare of trumpets, since a sweet and gentle musical refrain can mollify the savage impulses of the mind ... you wished that the fierceness of your boys might be softened by the sweetness of some song or other."[71]

Aachen cathedral and other churches of the era show that "Charlemagne founded a 'Holy Roman' architecture as well as a Holy Roman Empire".[72] Styles from East and West converged: Byzantine influences from Ravenna and Constantinople; Arabic art from Baghdad and Cordoba; and geometric art with intricate tracery and stylized animal motifs from the Celts. The Romanesque began to appear in this epoch as vaulting replaced flat wooden roofing. Carolingian mosaic art, borrowed from Ravenna and Byzantium, can still be seen today at Germigny-des-Prés in the oratory built by Theodulf. Sculpture in the form of elegant ivory-work also developed. The art of illumination and miniature, imported largely from the Anglo-Saxon monasteries, added new decorative elements from the East and the ancient world, as can be seen in the Gospel Books of Vienne. From the tenth century on, these miniaturists influenced the artistic schools of the Rhineland and, through them, the painters of the Middle Ages.

Charlemagne was a lover of the sacred liturgy and during his visit to Rome in 781 had been struck by the beauty and clarity of the Roman Rite. Circa 785 he obtained from Pope Hadrian a copy of the Gregorian sacramentary containing the ancient Roman Rite and determined, with Alcuin as his principal agent, to model the Frankish missal upon it. The resulting Romano-Frankish missal, often called "Alcuin's Missal", bore "witness to the intense spiritual life with which the Carolingian epoch was filled, a spiritual life which sparkled especially in the monasteries and in the cathedrals".[73] Its beauty was swiftly appreciated and led to uniformity throughout the empire in the offering of the Holy Sacrifice of the Mass, with only a few dioceses like Lyons and Milan retaining their own usages.

Thrust toward Universal Education

Around A.D. 787, Charlemagne put his signature to a letter usually referred to as *De Litteris Colendis* (On the Promotion of Literary Culture), one of the landmark

---

[71] Alcuin, Letter 149, *Epistolae*, pp. 242–43. English translation from C. Stephen Jaeger, "Alcuin and the Music of Friendship", in MLN [Modern Language Notes], vol. 127, no. 5 (Baltimore: Johns Hopkins University Press, 2012), p. S106.

[72] Christopher Dawson, *The Making of Europe: An Introduction to the History of European Unity* (Washington, D.C.: Catholic University of America Press, 2002), p. 202.

[73] Joseph A. Jungman, *The Mass of the Roman Rite*, vol. 1 (Notre Dame, Ind.: Christian Classics, 1951), p. 91.

documents of his reign.[74] Although addressed to Abbot Baugulf and the monks of Fulda, it contained directives for the entire Frankish kingdom.[75] The monarch stated that abbeys and dioceses were to provide academic training for monks and priests so that they might better understand the sacred Scriptures, profess orthodox doctrine, and communicate the Catholic Faith effectively. "Let there, therefore, be chosen for this work men who are both able and willing to learn and also desirous of instructing others; and let them apply themselves to the work with a zeal equalling the earnestness with which we recommend it to them."[76] The monarch concluded by expressing his hope in these educators: "It is our wish that you may be what it behooves the soldiers of the Church

Eugen von Blaas (1843–1931), *Charlemagne and His Scholars.*

to be—religious in heart, learned in discourse, pure in act, eloquent in speech; so that all who approach your house in order to invoke the Divine Master or to behold the excellence of the religious life may be edified in beholding you and instructed in hearing you discourse or chant, and may return home rendering thanks to God most high."[77]

Charlemagne's strategy was clear. He wanted the abbots and bishops to establish schools in order to train teachers from among the monks and the clergy of the episcopal residences who, in turn, would educate the crucially important parish priests: this was to be the first stage toward achieving widespread educational and social reform. A wise policy indeed: "It was at this level, after all, where the reform of society had to begin, with rural priests serving as the point men, the 'soldiers of the Church' (in the words of the *Epistola de Letteris Colendis*) of the new society".[78]

Although the letter contained no implementation guidelines, around the same time, presumably at Alcuin's prompting, the emperor obtained a corps of instructors of grammar, arithmetic, and Gregorian chant from Rome, whom he sent to several monasteries to implement his decisions and set certain benchmarks of quality.[79]

---

[74] See *Epistola De Litteris Colendis*, in the series *Monumenta Germaniae Historica* (MGH), Alfredus Boretius, ed., *Legum Sectio II. Capitularia regum Francorum*, vol. 1 (Hannover: Hahn, 1883), p. 79; translation in H.R. Loyn and John Percival, *The Reign of Charlemagne: Documents on Carolingian Government and Administration* (New York: St. Martin's Press, 1975), pp. 63–64.

[75] See J. Bass Mullinger, *The Schools of Charles the Great and the Restoration of Education in the Ninth Century* (New York: G.E. Stechert, 1911), p. 97.

[76] *De Litteris Colendis*, in *Legum Sectio II*, p. 99.

[77] Ibid.

[78] John J. Contreni, "The Pursuit of Knowledge in Carolingian Europe", in Richard E. Sullivan, *The Gentle Voices of Teachers: Aspects of Learning in the Carolingian Age* (Columbus: Ohio State University Press, 1995), p. 111.

[79] Mullinger, *Schools of Charles the Great*, p. 100.

In most monastic schools the curriculum was the *trivium*—grammar, rhetoric, and logic—while a small number of abbeys, such as Tours, had the *quadrivium*, advanced studies of geometry, arithmetic, astronomy, and music.

De Litteris Colendis was so innovative that the French historian, Ampère, referred to it as the *"Charter of Modern Thought"*.[80] This "manifesto of the Carolingian educational reform movement"[81] was the outcome of several years of intense reflection and discussion by Alcuin and his associates about the religious and educational reform of the empire. Although Alcuin's name does not appear on the purple imperial legislative parchments, we can surmise, as Gaskoin remarked, that "the voice is the voice of Charles, but the hand is the hand of Alcuin".[82] Such is the conclusion from our knowledge of Alcuin's role in the formulation of Charlemagne's policies and in the drafting of official documents, but, in this instance, it is also due to spotting the Anglo-Saxon cleric's convictions throughout the letter: the bond between education and Christian virtue; the link between thought and language; and the need to select teachers from among students with a love for educating.[83]

The follow-up came in A.D. 789 when Charlemagne signed into law an *Admonitio Generalis* (General Directive), a vast program of ecclesiastical and educational reform outlined in eighty-two articles, addressed to all ranks of the clergy and laity.[84] Chapter 72 specified how to implement *De Litteris Colendis* by mandating all monasteries and bishops throughout the Carolingian Empire to open up schools and to teach the sons of serfs and free laymen a medieval form of shorthand, grammar, arithmetic, singing, and the Psalms.[85]

De Litteris Colendis and the *Admonitio Generalis* were groundbreaking in that, for the first time, a ruler sought to implement educational reform throughout his domains, systematically and energetically; one which, although focused on the formation of candidates for the priesthood, offered the opportunity for any child, no matter how poor, to obtain an education. Thus, monasteries such as those of St. Gall, Fulda, and Reichenau began to operate two schools, an "internal" school (*schola claustri*) and an "external" (*schola canonica* or *schola externa*). The internal was for future members of the order, some of whom enrolled as children. The external was for all other children or youths, whether villagers, farmers, or offspring of the local nobility. All were to be treated equally, stated the monastic codes. Documentary evidence for monastic schooling in more than seventy Carolingian monasteries has survived.[86]

---

[80] M. J-J. Ampère, *Histoire littéraire de la France avant le douzième siècle*, vol. 3 (Paris: Hachette, 1839), p. 25.

[81] Contreni, "Pursuit of Knowledge", p. 106.

[82] Charles J. B. Gaskoin, *Alcuin: His Life and His Work* (London: C. J. Clay and Sons), p. 182.

[83] *De Litteris Colendis* bears Alcuin's literary style; see Luitpold Wallach, "Charlemagne's *De litteris colendis* and Alcuin: A Diplomatic-Historical Study", in *Speculum*, Medieval Academy of America, vol. 26, no. 2 (April 1951), pp. 228–305. For Alcuin's role in the formulation of Charlemagne's policies and in drafting official documents, see Donald A. Bullough, *Alcuin: Achievement and Reputation* (Leiden and Boston: Brill Academic Publishers, 2004), pp. 379–88.

[84] See *Admonitio Generalis*, in *Monumenta Germaniae Historica* (MGH), Alfredus Boretius, ed., *Legum Sectio II. Capitularia regum Francorum*, vol. 1 (Hannover: MGH, 1883), pp. 52–62; translation in P. D. King, *Charlemagne: Translated Sources* (Kendal, Cumbria: P. D. King, 1986), pp. 209–20.

[85] See Contreni, "Pursuit of Knowledge", p. 108.

[86] See Pierre Riche, *Education and Culture in the Barbarian West, Sixth through the Eighth Centuries* (Columbia, S.C.: University of South Carolina Press, 1978).

The thrust toward universal primary education continued in successive legislations, whether at the level of the entire Carolingian Empire or in individual dioceses.[87] In 797, Alcuin's successor as "Minister of Culture", Theodulf, Bishop of Orléans, ordered in his own diocese "that priests establish schools in every town and village, and if any Christian wishes to entrust their children to them to be educated they must not refuse to accept them but should lovingly teach them ... and let them exact no fee from the children for their schooling, nor receive anything from them except what parents may voluntarily and affectionately offer".[88] An imperial capitular law of 802 ordered that "everyone should send his son to be educated, and the child should remain studying diligently at school until he has become well qualified".[89]

Girls as well as boys were educated in the Carolingian era before, during, and after Charlemagne's reign. As one historian remarks: "the general picture of female participation in Carolingian educational and intellectual life is quite clear".[90] This was due to a tradition, predating the arrival of Alcuin, springing largely from the mentality of the Irish and Anglo-Saxon missionaries. Colomban monasteries such as Annegray, Luxeuil, and Fontaines were forged by an Irish heritage that sealed them not only with a strong intellectual ethos but also with esteem for the role of women in society and the importance of both educating them and having them as educators.[91] Female abbeys in Ireland at Kildare, Sliabh Cuilinn (Killeevy, county Armagh), and elsewhere educated both sexes. One of them, at Cluain-Credhuil (Killeedy, county Limerick), had a school for boys that trained so many bishops and priests that the foundress, Ita (ca. 480–570), became known as the foster mother of Irish saints.[92] Irish churchmen, like Brendan of Clonfert, respected the minds of women like Brigid of Kildare and turned to them for guidance.[93] The Anglo-Saxon missionaries, who had also been influenced by Irish monasticism through Aidan of Lindisfarne, included in their ranks highly educated nuns who, in turn, took care to educate the Frankish girls entering their convents.

Some of these women come to our attention through the correspondence of leading figures such as Alcuin, whose letters to individuals like Tetta, Abbess of Lindisfarne, provide evidence for erudite nuns and lay women among Franks and Anglo-Saxons.[94] Some were socially prominent such as as Gisla (ca. 757–810) and Rotrud (ca. 775–810), the sister and daughter of Charlemagne. Many others like the expert scribes in convents such as Corbie, Soissons, and Noinnoutiers have left little or no trace of their personal identity.[95] Yet, among both cloistered and lay women there were outstanding intellectuals. Hroswitha of Gandersheim (ca. 935–

[87] See Rosamond McKitterick, *The Frankish Church and the Carolingian Reforms, 789–895* (London: Royal Historical Society, 1977), pp. 45–79.

[88] Bishop Theodulf of Orléans, *Capitula ad presbyteros parochiae suae* (PL 105:196), chap. 20.

[89] See Mullinger, *Schools of Charles*, p. 102.

[90] Contreni, "Pursuit of Knowledge", p. 114.

[91] For the influence of Irish monasticism on the development of culture among the Franks, see M. T. W. Laistner, *Thought and Letters in Western Europe A.D. 500 to 900*, 2nd edition (Ithaca, N.Y: Cornell University Press, 1976), pp. 141–52.

[92] See Patricia Ranft, *Women and the Religious Life in Premodern Europe* (New York: St. Martin's Press, 1996), p. 11.

[93] See ibid., p. 17.

[94] See Page, *Letters of Alcuin*.

[95] See Patricia Ranft, *Women in Western Intellectual Culture, 600–1500* (New York: Palgrave Macmillan, 2008), p. 10; Contreni, "Pursuit of Knowledge", p. 114.

1002) wrote two historical epics, *The Deeds of Otto* and *The Founding of Gandersheim Monastery*; as a hagiographer she authored eight biographies; and she is reckoned to be the first person since antiquity to compose drama in the Latin West.[96] Others were Hugeberc, an eighth-century abbess "who created a new approach to geographical writing, the travelogue … [and] Dhuoda, a ninth-century Carolingian lay woman, [who] wrote a sophisticated educational manual for her son which includes lessons in scriptural exegesis, pastoral theology, political ideas, grammar, and numerology".[97]

Dhuoda, born into a wealthy family, married Duke Bernard of Septimania, son of William of Gellone, cousin of Charlemagne, in 824. Bernard, frequently away from the family due to his court duties in Aachen, left his wife to administrate and militarily defend the family territories in the region of what is now southeastern France. In the warfare among the Frankish leaders after Charlemagne's death, Dhuoda's husband and her two sons were all murdered for political reasons. For the eldest son, William, Dhuoda had authored the *Liber Manualis*, a manual of wise counsel on how to live a Catholic existence. The seventy-three chapters cover topics as varied as success in society, the love of God, the evil of sin, how to pray, the helpfulness of praying the Psalms, the role of fathers, and how to raise children. Throughout the book, she shows her knowledge of Hebrew, Greek, and Latin, as well as familiarity with the Bible, and with a representative group of classical and medieval authors, ranging from Ovid and Prudentius to Saint Augustine and Venantius Fortunatus. As Ranft points out, this widely-read woman had so imbued her memory, understanding, and imagination with biblical and classical thought that spontaneously she expressed her own ideas in their phraseology.[98] Thanks to the *Liber Manualis*—the lone survival out of probably many such books produced by women of the epoch—we have a window into the high educational level of the lay aristocrats, both male and female.[99] For Dhuoda was not an exception. Contemporary historians have rejected the opinion, prevalent for decades, that the schooling of girls was neglected during the Carolingian centuries.[100] Dhuoda's scholarship level was representative of the typical education of her century, as recent historical research into the era's literacy has shown through its identification of the writers, copyists, and illuminators of the epoch's manuscripts.[101]

The convents were the main centers for educating girls—with boys also present, and indeed, even young men. So common was it for nuns in the Carolingian Empire to educate both sexes that one abbess, Eangtha, could casually mention in a letter to Boniface that it was a formidable task to be "ministering to so many minds … of either sex and of every age".[102] We have far less documentary information about parish schools but it is probable that most, if not all, educated girls as well as

[96] See Katharina M. Wilson, *Medieval Women Writers* (Manchester: Manchester University Press, 1984), pp. 30–63.

[97] Ranft, *Women in Western Intellectual Culture*, p. 1.

[98] Ibid., p. 13.

[99] M. A. Claussen, "God and Man in Dhuoda's *Liber manualis*", in *Women in the Church*, Studies in Church History, 27 (1990).

[100] See Elizabeth van Houts, *Memory and Gender in Medieval Europe* (Toronto: University of Toronto Press, 1999); Stephen Stofferahn, "Changing Views of Carolingian Women's Literary Culture: The Evidence from Essen", *Early Medieval Europe* 8, no. 1 (1999): 69–97.

[101] Rosamond McKitterick, *Books, Scribes and Learning in the Frankish Kingdoms, 6th–9th Centuries* (Cambridge: University of Cambridge, 1994); Pierre Riché, "Les bibliothèques de trois aristocrates laïcs carolingiens", in *Le Moyen Age* 69 (1963): 87–104.

[102] Ranft, *Women in Western Intellectual Culture*, p. 10.

boys. We have documentary evidence, for instance, that before the end of the ninth century both boys and girls attended the schools attached to the parish churches in the Diocese of Soissons.

Hence, the work of Charlemagne and Alcuin, built upon the educational ethos that had disembarked on the shores of continental Europe with Columbanus and Boniface, led to a bold thrust toward universal free primary education in the Carolingian Empire. Amid the rough-and-ready classrooms of the monastery and parish, seated on the schoolroom floor which was strewn with straw, any and every child, from farm, forge, or castle, received an education. Certainly, it was rudimentary. The monk or cleric, with his small collection of liturgical and homiletic books, mainly offered an education in the Catholic Faith to the children. But in the process he taught them how to read, write on wax tablets or on pieces of slate, along with some arithmetic. He explained the rudiments of Latin since it was the Church's language; opened young ears to the sounds of Gregorian chant so that they could sing at Mass as well as in the processions in honor of the local saints; and, in some places, taught some type of manual trade. The hand of Alcuin can be detected in the regulations governing these schools for they even concerned themselves with the health and comfort of the students, laying down the hours to be given to work, standards of neatness—and provision for a midday siesta. It is heartening to think of the good this education achieved for so many children growing up in the midst of so much barbarism; and how dear this achievement must have been to men like Charlemagne, Alcuin, and Theodulf. It is said that the emperor personally visited some of the schools, talking to the students and, with that thoroughness characteristic of both him and Alcuin, ensuring they had everything necessary. Thus, the eyes of innumerable children were opened to new dimensions of life; every peasant child was presented with the keys of learning, keys that opened the doorways for the more talented among them to continue at a monastic or cathedral school and reach the highest positions in Church and state, as occurred, for instance, in the ninth century when a poor orphan, Paschasius Radbertus (785–865), became Abbot of Corbie; Ebbo (ca. 775–851) became Archbishop of Reims; Gerbert (ca. 946–1003) became Pope Sylvester II; and a serf's son became Abbot Suger (1081–1151), prime minister of France and the "Father of Gothic Architecture".

After Alcuin and Charlemagne (814–1000)

Relations between Church, State, and Society

Alcuin had always hoped that he would die on his favorite feast day, Pentecost. His prayer was answered. On the spring day of May 19, 804, just as dawn broke and the chanting of the monks could be heard from the abbey lying amid the vines of the Loire valley, the "Father of the Vineyards",[103] after a life poured out for God and humanity, crossed the final frontier. The truths that had guided him were on his epitaph:

> O thou who passest by, halt here a while, I pray, and write my words upon thy heart,
> that thou mayst learn thy fate from knowing mine. What thou art, once I was, a

---

[103] Alcuin graciously attributed the title "Father of the Vineyards" to his successor in the post of Charlemagne's "Minister of Culture"; see Andrew Fleming West, *Alcuin and the Rise of the Christian School* (London: W. Heinemann, 1903), pp. 78–79.

wayfarer not unknown in this world; what I am now, thou soon shalt be. Once was I wont to pluck earthly joys with eager hand; and now I am dust and ashes, the food of worms. Be mindful then to cherish thy soul rather than thy body since the one is immortal, the other perishes. Why dost thou make to thyself pleasant abodes? See in how small a house I take my rest as thou also shalt do one day. Why wrap thy limbs in Tyrian purple, so soon to be the food of dusty worms? As the flowers perish before the threatening blast, so shall it be with thy mortal part and worldly fame. O thou who readest, grant me in return for this warning one small favor and say: "Give pardon, dear Christ, to thy servant who lies below." May no hand violate the sacred law of the grave until the archangel's trumpet shall sound from heaven. Then may he who lies in this tomb rise from the dusty earth to meet the Great Judge with his countless hosts of light. Alcuin, ever a lover of Wisdom, was my name; pray for my soul, all ye who read these words.[104]

Alcuin: the man whom Charlemagne, whose influence enters into every modern European state, acknowledged as his mentor; the modest, genial, penetrating mind who had no desire to be in the limelight; wielding only the sword of the

Vilhelm Bissen, *Bishop Absalon Hvide*, 1901. Bishop Hvide was founder of Copenhagen, statesman, defender of his countrymen, and promoter of the Gregorian reform in Denmark, ca. 1128–1201.

spirit in order to bring about true peace through fostering the reign of Christ in hearts and in the social order; the priest who, along with Saint Boniface, brought about that union of the Catholic Faith, Roman order, and Teutonic drive that was crucial to the formation of medieval culture.

Ten years later, at dawn on January 28, 814, Charlemagne, struck by a sudden attack of pleurisy, tried to raise his hand to make the sign of the cross, realized he was in his final agony, asked to receive Holy Communion, and a few hours later was dead.

And almost immediately his fragile empire began to crack and totter. As it collapsed, the half century of light gave way to dusk that descended and covered Western Europe until the restoration of political order under the Ottonian emperors circa 960–1002. Three main causes lay behind the breakdown. Firstly, Charlemagne, faithful to the Frankish habit of splitting kingdoms among the male offspring, divided the empire between his three sons in 806, making all equal in rank and giving none of them the imperial title. Consequently, dynastic wars ensued and in 843 three kingdoms replaced the empire, occupying the areas of modern-day France, Germany, and an area from Holland to central Italy. Secondly, the new rulers lacked the charisma of their father. Thirdly, barbarian hordes increased their assaults, ravaging the countryside, burning cities and looting monasteries: Magyars and Wends from the east, Saracen pirates from the Mediterranean, and Vikings from Scandinavia. Charlemagne had foreseen this. During a tour of the Atlantic coast, while gazing at Viking longships on the horizon, he had emotionally told those around him that he greatly feared the harm the Norsemen would cause after

[104] See Wilmot-Buxton, *Alcuin*, p. 185.

his death. Likewise, Alcuin, in 797, grieving about the horrors of the Norse raids in Northumbria, had written: "It somehow seems that the happiness of the English is nearly at an end".[105]

Too weak to resist, Western Europe relapsed into semianarchic chaos for over a century with famines raging in countrysides further disturbed by marauding bands of thugs. Under weak rulers the imperial apparatus became too feeble to ensure justice or even food supplies. To make matters worse, the monarchs intruded into Church government by nominating as bishops and abbots individuals who often brought decadence inside cathedrals and cloisters.

However, some of the leading churchmen, spiritual sons of those nominated under the influence of Fulrad and Alcuin, were fully conscious of their own authority vis-à-vis that of the state. The Pope's anointing of Charlemagne on Christmas Day 800 had bonded the Church and State together, a union symbolized in Aachen by the imperial palace and cathedral standing side by side. During the formidable emperor's reign, bishops and priests stood behind the throne. But after his death, in a collapsing society wherein only the Church remained standing, there was a reversal of roles: her de facto submission to the emperor ended, and there was a vast transfer of authority and power to the leading bishops. And they meant to use it.

The Church did not acquire this power—contrary to what caricatures would have us believe—because ambitious prelates wanted to dominate for egotistic reasons, although there is no doubt that such ecclesiastics were not lacking. The chief cause was sociological. The age shoved the Church into the center, for men saw her to be order in the midst of chaos, purpose amid aimlessness, and the upholder of marriage and family, the poor, and the defenseless in a society in free fall into savagery. The masses looked at priests standing in front of them, teaching them how to read and write; from monks, covered in sweat, they learned how to clear forests, drain swamps, and improve tillage; to bishops they could turn and ask for protection from despotic nobles. This grassroots closeness of people and Catholicism during these centuries is the real explanation for the episcopal power.

Hence, the masses gave power to the Church because this was *their* Church! Catholicism in the West was not an isolated esoteric religion on the edges of society but an earthy, gritty way of living, in which men and women changed the social order! Moreover, although the priesthood was a distinct class, it was not a distant one. Even if many bishops and abbots were from the aristocracy, the prelate could just as well be the woodcutter's son as the king's, due to an open system of promotion.

When Charlemagne's empire began to sway, bishops, priests, and monks generally sought to prop it up. Even as late as the 840s, after the death of Emperor Louis, Bishop Drogo of Metz, the bastard son of Charlemagne, and Archbishop Rabanus Maurus, former student of Alcuin, were still championing the ideal of a united Christian empire. However, the groups in favor of various kingdoms were already gaining the upper hand, with a consequent and intolerable increase of social injustice and suffering. It was then that some of the bishops stepped in to fill the vacuum of effective leadership, courageously so at times, restraining kings and aristocracy, and even helping to overthrow rulers in extreme instances.

---

[105] Alcuin's letter to Osbert, quoted in Douglas Dales, *Alcuin: His Life and Legacy* (Cambridge: James Clarke, 2012), p. 60.

Jules Breton, *The Blessing of the Wheat in the Artois*, 1857.

They explained the legitimacy of their political interventions by reminding aristo-crats that the state was subordinate to the Church. Hincmar (806–882), Archbishop of Reims, stated: "This world is chiefly ruled by the sacred authority of bishops and the power of kings.... But the episcopal dignity is greater than the royal, for bishops consecrate kings, but kings do not consecrate bishops."[106] He, Archbishop Agobard of Lyons (regarded as the most cultured man of his epoch), Abbot Wala of Corbie (first cousin of Charlemagne), Paschasius Radbertus, Ebbo of Reims, Bernard of Vienne, and others wanted the good of both state and Church under an emperor who would be loyal to the mission received at his anointing. The bishops gained increasing influence because the society was becoming Christian in its culture with the consequence that all its citizens, whether priests or laymen, believed in the supernatural authority of the Church. For instance, when opponents threatened to oust Charles the Bald in 859, he appealed to the Church as his last line of defense, asserting that no one else could legitimately dethrone him.

By the middle of the ninth century the power of the Church's authority became evident in Pope Nicholas I (858–867), who became the preeminent figure in Western Europe. This pontiff, winsome in personality, steadfastly upright, and magnanimous of heart, with no army worth mentioning, sustained solely by an unfaltering convic-tion about his role as St. Peter's successor, withstood both the Eastern and Western emperors.[107] His enemies claimed he was arrogant and power hungry, but the poor peasants and the unjustly treated rejoiced in this protector who sought nothing for himself and risked death itself for the sake of justice.

The conflict between Church and state continued into the Middle Ages, result-ing in a topsy-turvy situation of cooperation for the benefit of society, tension, and conflict. Bishops in the Middle Ages were not above using strong-arm tactics to defend the Church's independence. Between 1073 and 1085, Pope Saint Gregory VII fought the lunge toward totalitarianism hidden within the policy of investiture—the control of episcopal and other clerical appointments by feudal lords—going so

---

[106] Quoted in R. W. Southern, *Western Society and the Church in the Middle Ages* (New York: Penguin, 1970), p. 176.

[107] See Daniel-Rops, *Church in the Dark Ages*, p. 457.

far as to excommunicate Emperor Henry IV of Germany, over whom he gained a short-lived victory at Canossa when the deposed ruler knelt in the snows, asking for forgiveness and the restoration of his throne. Afterward, however, Gregory was forced into exile to Salerno, where he died, the epitaph on his tomb summing up the raison d'être for his lifelong struggle: "I have loved justice and hated iniquity; therefore, I die in exile". The clash continued under his successors, ending in a partial victory for the Church and enabling all concerned to understand better the distinct roles and responsibilities of both Church and state in society. As the political scientist Francis Fukuyama remarked:

> By Huntington's categories, autonomy is a hallmark of institutional development, and here law in the West became far more developed than its counterparts elsewhere. No other part of the world experienced the equivalent of the Gregorian Reform and the investiture conflict in which the entire hierarchy of the Church engaged in a prolonged political conflict with the temporal ruler and ended up stalemating the latter. The resulting settlement, the Concordat of Worms [1122], ensured autonomy for the Church as an institution and gave it considerable incentive to develop its own bureaucracy and formal rules. Thus, in premodern times, the rule of law became a far more powerful check on the power of temporal rulers in Western Europe than was the case in the Middle East, India, or in the Eastern Orthodox church. This had significant implications for the later development of free institutions there.[108]

The Flame Kept Burning: Renaissance of Culture, Naissance of Christendom

Although Charlemagne's political empire followed him to the grave, his empire of cultural achievements lived on. Through the long harsh winter from 814 to around the year 960, amid the darkness of those centuries of Viking, Muslim, and Magyar terror, with a papacy so often under siege, and an empire disintegrating into feeble kingdoms, culture, nevertheless, "like a fire in dry grass passed here and there, always alive at this or that monastic center".[109] Charlemagne and Alcuin, by placing the Church at the very center of the Carolingian Empire as educator of both the elites and the masses, had set in motion a movement with immense impetus. Amid quiet cloisters, the keepers of the torches of Christianity and culture continued to train the youth of Western Europe; monks in summer and winter kept copying the ancient manuscripts; and missionaries set out northward and eastward to expand the rim of the future Christendom.

The thrust of the Carolingian effort to educate every Frankish child in the smallest of hamlets slowed down considerably but never halted. Gradually, at the grassroots level, it shaped a new cultural synthesis of the Roman and Teutonic cultures with the Catholic Faith. Barbarians who until then had lived with one foot on the threshold of the new religion and the other on soil that was strongly pagan now came inside the Church because of the Carolingian integration of their Germanic language and the best of their customs with the Catholic Faith. One of their own, Charlemagne, personally embodied this unity, and in the centuries after his death the people

---

[108] Francis Fukuyama, *The Origins of Political Order: From Prehuman Times to the French Revolution* (New York: Farrar, Straus and Giroux, 2011), pp. 288–89.

[109] David Knowles, *The Evolution of Medieval Thought*, 2nd ed. (London: Longman, 1989), p. 69.

Harry Mileham, *Alfred Translates "Pastoral Care"* *("Liber Regulae Pastoralis")* by Pope Gregory the Great, 1909. King Alfred the Great (849–899) is depicted with his collaborators, who could well represent Plegmund, Grimbald the Fleming, Asser the Welshman, and John, a monk from Corbey Abbey in Saxony. The translation, which they distributed to the Anglo-Saxon bishops for the training of priests, was part of their program for the revival of learning and the creation of a Christian culture in Viking Age England. *Pastoral Care* is the oldest known book written in English.

looked back with nostalgia and pride to a ruler who was both Teutonic and Christian. Moreover, the monasteries and parish churches in the largely agrarian society with few urban nerve centers became hearths for the common people, their belfries pointing heavenward but their sturdy walls stretching outward to encircle the countryside, providing agricultural techniques, hospitality, education, and, above all, the peace of Christ. Thus Catholicism became the religion of the people, and its power to forge culture over the two centuries before A.D. 1000 was assured.

Nevertheless, in 814, Charlemagne's empire was only part of Western Europe. Britain and Ireland, Scandinavia, Spain, Portugal, southern Italy, and Sicily were all outside its political and cultural boundaries. Therefore, it is necessary to explain how the Carolingian culture spread and became the dominant formative ethos of European and Western civilization. It occurred firstly through the thrust of Frankish missionaries northward into Scandinavia and eastward through Hungary, the rest of Germany, and the Baltic states. Secondly, Anglo-Saxon England began to move outside the sphere of the Nordic culture; firstly, under King Alfred the Great, who invited monks from the Carolingian Empire to work alongside him to promote education in England; and then, definitively, with the Norman invasion of 1066. Likewise, Sicily and the rest of southern Italy came under Carolingian influence through the Norman conquest that occurred in the late eleventh and through much of the twelfth centuries. In Spain, Frankish influence penetrated through their conquest of the northeastern region between the Pyrenees and the Ebro River in modern-day Catalonia, conquering Girona in 785 and Barcelona in 801. There they established the *Marca Hispanica*, a group of counties functioning as Frankish feudal fiefdoms, of which Andorra is the sole autonomous survivor. Out of these counties emerged the principalities of Catalonia, Navarre, and Aragon, the latter uniting with Castile in the fifteenth century to become the core of a unified Spain. Thus, the formative hub of European civilization was located in the homeland of the Carolingian Empire, the area that is now France, Belgium, the Netherlands, western Germany, and Lombardy in Italy. Here its components came together during the Dark Ages, went into gestation for several hundred years, and then, in the twelfth century, emerged from a cocoon-like existence as the new culture at the basis of the new civilization.

Its matrix was Catholic due to the crucial educational project of Charlemagne and Alcuin in the eighth century that made the Carolingian Empire the heir of the hitherto leading European educators: the Celtic monks in Ireland, Scotland, Wales, and England whose monastic schools were in decline due to the Viking destruction. Elsewhere, even in southern Italy and Spain, few cultural centers existed. Thus, the future of Western culture lay largely within the cloisters of the Carolingian abbeys. The Germanic warrior and the Anglo-Saxon priest had changed the intellectual course of European history by bonding Catholicism and education through fostering intellectual life at the monastic and cathedral schools. From their classrooms arose the intellectual elite who prepared the ground for the twelfth-century universities that coalesced the patterns of thought configuring the Western mentality. The new overarching vision of life created a society wherein men recognized the authority of the Church in religion, morality, and education. In a fallen and flawed world, a springtime of Christian civilization erupted: warriors had a new ideal of manhood in Christian chivalry; women enjoyed unprecedented rights and respect; new patterns of trade and commerce were taking the shape of free-market economics; national monarchies, Christian in ethos, took the political lead; cities came alive; the Crusades began as an idealistic just war to defend the Byzantine Empire from Seljuk Muslim aggression and to free the Holy Land from a Muslim occupation that had led to a period circa 1073–1098 characterized by "a whirlpool of anarchy and insecurity ... of slaughter and vandalism, of economic hardship, and the uprooting of populations".[110]

Any culture must ultimately be judged by what it does for its masses and not merely for its elites. Alcuin and the Carolingian idealists had sought to create a Christian culture among the Franks, who, due to their shallow conversion en masse, retained their Germanic tribal and kinship bonds by which they lived on a perpetual wartime footing with constant feuding and bloodshed, homicide, and vengeance. The efforts to replace such savagery with the selfless forgiveness of the Cross and the Sermon on the Mount was an uphill struggle. Barbarousness was curbed but not cured by Charlemagne, a monarch who was imbued with more than a little of the brutality himself, and it would take two more centuries before a noticeable difference could be seen among the population, proof that the Christian "Revolution of the Cross",[111] within the limitations of fallen human nature, had triumphed.

Perhaps the most striking illustration of the change that Christianity brought to people's lifestyles is to be seen among the Vikings of Scandinavia, the fierce marauders who had haunted men's nightmares during the ninth and tenth centuries but who by the late eleventh century had become Catholic. Adam of Bremen, the eleventh-century German chronicler, described the "new" Vikings, even if with a touch of overstatement:

> But after their acceptance of Christianity, they have become imbued with better principles and have now learned to love peace and truth and to be content with their poverty; even to distribute what they have stored up and not as aforetime to gather up what was scattered.... Of all men they are the most temperate in their food and in their habits, loving above all things thrift and modesty. Yet so great is their veneration for priests and churches that there is scarcely a Christian to be found who does not make

---

[110] Moshe Gil, *A History of Palestine, 634–1099* (Cambridge: Cambridge University Press, 1997), p. 420.
[111] Daniel-Rops, *Church in the Dark Ages*, p. 296.

an offering on every occasion that he hears Mass.... In many places of Norway and Sweden the keepers of the flocks [bishops] are men of noble rank who, after the manner of the patriarchs, live by the work of their hands. But all who dwell in Norway are most Christian with the exception of those who dwell far off beside the Arctic Seas.[112]

Speaking about the Vikings of Iceland, Adam remarked:

Blessed is the people, say I, of whose poverty no one is envious, and most blessed in this—that they have now all put on Christianity. There is much that is remarkable in their manners, above all charity, whence it comes that all things are common among them not only for the native population but also for the stranger. They treat their bishop as if he were a king for the whole people pay regard to his will, and whatever he declares from God, from the scriptures, and from the customs of other nations they hold as law.[113]

Another benchmark for the revolutionary changes brought by Christianity is the elimination of racism in the Dark Ages. Missionaries made it clear to Greeks, Romans, and barbarians that a Catholic's "whole religion is rooted in the unity of the race of Adam, the one and only Chosen Race",[114] that humanity is meant to be a brotherhood, and that every Christian must be a Good Samaritan to every person. Even if Christian behavior often failed to match the ideal, it did lead to a difference in the patterns of thought among the Romans, Franks, Saxons, and other races. Since the Church was Catholic, truly and universally open like a harbor, the idea of an Anglo-Saxon, Celtic, or Frankish Church became inconceivable, indeed repugnant, to the minds of many. An artistic representation of this all-embracing spirit can be seen in Charlemagne's Breviary, where there is a charming and artistically perfect miniature of the Church symbolized as a fountain, welcoming everyone who has come to ask for her "living water". This new vision inspirited the Church's fusion of the races in the European landmass through fostering marriage between Burgundians and Gallo-Romans, Visigoths and Hispano-Romans, Saxons and Britons, Lombards and Franks. Besides diminishing racial strife, thus allowing men and women in a largely rural society to peacefully live, love, and honor God, the Church's insistence on the principles of racial equality and the necessity of freedom of choice for the validity of marriage had another, more subtle, implication: it asserted the rights of the individual over those of the family, community, race, and state. This revolutionary principle of the individual's dignity would shape the new social bedrock of emerging Christendom, radically configure the Western psyche, and survive even decades of Nazi, Fascist, and communist brainwashing.

European society was, in other words, individualistic at a very early point, in the sense that individuals and not their families or kin groups could make important decisions about marriage, property, and other personal issues. Individualism in the family is the foundation of all other individualisms. Individualism did not wait for the emergence of a state declaring the legal rights of individuals and using the weight of its coercive

[112] Adam of Bremen, *Descriptio Insularum Aquilonis* (Description of the Northern Islands), nos. 30–31. This is an appendix to his chronicle *Gesta Hammaburgensis Ecclesiae Pontificum* ("Deeds of the Bishops of the Church of Hamburg"), a history of the Church in Hamburg and its work in bringing the Catholic Faith to northern Europe. It was written between 1072 and 1081 in Bremen. Quoted in Christopher Dawson, *Religion and the Rise of Western Culture* (New York: Image, 1991), p. 98.

[113] Adam of Bremen, *Descriptio Insularum Aquilonis*, no. 35, quoted in Dawson, *Religion and the Rise of Western Culture*, p. 99.

[114] G. K. Chesterton, *The Catholic Church and Conversion* (New York: The Macmillan Press, 1926), p. 52.

power to enforce those rights. Rather, states were formed on top of societies in which individuals already enjoyed substantial freedom from social obligations to kindreds. In Europe, *social development preceded political development*. But when did the European exit from kinship occur, and what, if not politics, was the driving force behind this change? The answers are that the exit occurred very shortly after the Germanic tribes that overran the Roman Empire were first converted to Christianity, and the agent was the Catholic Church.[115]

All this the Church achieved by keeping her gaze fixed on the polar star of the purpose for which she had been founded: the salvation of the individual soul—a strange paradox indeed to modernists and others who deny the supernatural. But it is precisely because the supernatural enlightens, heals, and invigorates the natural in man that this otherworldly fixation was the effective route to building the new social order. What the missionary Augustine explained to Ethelbert, king of Kent, under the trees at Canterbury in 597, was the bedrock on which the Church began building the new West: that God so loved humanity as to create the first man and woman from whom all are descended; in his sight, therefore, all are brothers and sisters—no matter their race—and are equally loved, indeed to the sheer "madness" of God the Son's agony for man's redemption on Calvary. On this sublime foundation the Church gave barbarians and Romans a religion that was not just a private belief but a social institution, bonding them together with a common culture that inspired a new social order.

That Catholic social order—Christendom—had a brief springtime of life in the twelfth and thirteenth centuries before corrupt and incompetent clergy, philosophical nominalism, the rise of nationalism, the Black Death, and the Hundred Years' War undermined its foundations in the following two hundred years. Then began the era of "modernity" which, although spanning five centuries, is an ideologically coherent unity. The unifying factor is the assault on the cultural and socio-political ethos of Christendom. This onslaught, due to its philosophical roots in socio-political gnosticism, its socio-cultural pervasiveness, and its frequent use of violence in order to pursue a utopian world order, increasingly rejected not only Catholicism but also the Natural Law and any sense of cultural heritage from previous generations to the extent that the world witnessed the arrival of a new phenomenon—the *socio-cultural revolution*. The successive stages and agents of change of the revolutionary process can be identified emblematically by the years in which crucial events occurred: the outbreak of the Protestant revolution in 1517, the foundation of the first Grand Lodge of Freemasonry in London in 1717, the French Revolution of 1789, the October Marxist-Leninist Revolution of 1917 in Russia, and the 1968 cultural-Marxist revolution which is currently eradicating the remnants of the Catholic social order.[116]

---

[115] Fukuyama, *Origins of Political Order*, p. 231.

[116] Christopher Dawson, *The Gods of Revolution* (Washington, D.C.: Catholic University of America Press, 2015); Eric Voegelin, *Modernity Without Restraint: The Political Religions, The New Science of Politics, and Science, Politics, and Gnosticism* (Columbia: University of Missouri Press, 2000); Augusto del Noce, *The Crisis of Modernity* (Montreal: McGill-Queen's University Press, 2014). For an instance of the use of violence in the revolutionary ideology, see the analysis of the first genocide of modern times, the 1793–1794 massacre of the Catholics of the Vendée by the French revolutionaries whose motto was "liberté, égalité, fraternité" in Reynald Secher, *A French Genocide: The Vendée* (Notre Dame: University of Notre Dame Press, 2003); Michael Davies, *For Altar and Throne: The Rising in the Vendée* (Forest Lake: Remnant Press, 1997). For the Catholic vision of freedom, equality, and fraternity, see Roberto de Mattei, *Blessed Pius IX* (Leominster: Gracewing, 2004), pp. 147–68; also H.J.A. Sire, *Phoenix from the Ashes: The Making, Unmaking, and Restoration of Catholic Tradition* (Kettering, Ohio: Angelico Press, 2015), pp. 166–69.

Since Christian values breathe with the lungs of Catholicism, both their intellectual justification and the moral stamina necessary to keep them alive as social transformers depend on adherence to the Catholic Faith by a large enough number of creative minorities. This is the logic behind Hilaire Belloc's provocative utterance, "In such a crux there remains the historical truth: that this our European structure, built upon the noble foundations of classical antiquity, was formed through, exists by, is consonant to, and will stand only in the mold of the Catholic Church. Europe will return to the Faith, or she will perish. The Faith is Europe. And Europe is the Faith."[117] Belloc later clarified: "I have never said that the Church was necessarily European. The Church will last forever on this earth until the end of the world; and our remote descendants may find its chief membership to have passed to Africans or Asiatics in some civilization yet unborn. What I have said is that the European thing is essentially a Catholic thing, and that European values would disappear with the disappearance of Catholicism."[118] Christopher Dawson gave the principal historical reason for this identification:

> It is this, above all, that distinguishes the Western development from that of the other world civilizations. The great cultures of the ancient East, like China and India, were autochthonous growths which represent a continuous process of development in which religion and culture grew together from the same sociological roots and the same natural environment. But in the West it was not so. Primitive Europe outside the Mediterranean lands preserved no common centre and no unified tradition of spiritual culture. The people of the North possessed no written literature, no cities, no stone architecture. They were, in short, "barbarians"; and it was only by Christianity and the elements of a higher culture transmitted to them by the Church that Western Europe acquired unity and form.[119]

Even a historian as unsympathetic to Catholicism as Edward Gibbon (1737–1794) recognized that "the growing authority of the Popes cemented the union of the Christian republic; and gradually produced the similar manners and the common jurisprudence which has distinguished from the rest of mankind the independent and even hostile nations of modern Europe."[120] Francis Fukuyama also gives a reason favoring Belloc's assertion, an important point that many historians, even Catholics, either ignore or downplay in their analysis of the genesis of Western institutions, the fact that "it was not Christianity per se, but the specific institutional form that Western Christianity took, that determined its impact on later political development".[121] Catholicism brought to birth a very different sociopolitical order than that of either the Eastern Orthodox churches or Protestantism.

The European, or indeed anyone seeking to understand his identity in an increasingly Westernized world, will discover much by opening the pages of the epic saga

---

[117] Hilaire Belloc, *Europe and the Faith* (Charleston, S.C.: BiblioLife, 2011), pp. 260–61.

[118] Hilaire Belloc, *Catholic Herald*, Letters to the Editor, March 20, 1936, quoted in R. Speaight, *The Life of Hilaire Belloc* (New York; Farrar, Straus and Cudahy, 1957), p. 387.

[119] Christopher Dawson, *Religion and the Rise of Western Culture* (New York: Doubleday, 1991), pp. 23–24.

[120] Edward Gibbon, "The Conversion of the Barbarians", *Decline and Fall of the Roman Empire* (London: Joseph Ogle Robinson, 1830), chap. 37, ii.

[121] Fukuyama, *Origins of Political Order*, p. 275. Hilaire Belloc had stated: "[T]he religion which created our European culture was the Catholic Church; not an indefinable nothingness called 'Christianity,' but a definite institution with a known name and position in time and place." Hilaire Belloc, letter to the editor of the *Catholic Herald*, March 20, 1936.

of the Church's integration of the Roman, the Teutonic, and the Christian before the dawn of medieval Christendom in the eleventh century.

> Every man of us today is three men. There is in every modern European three powers so distinct as to be almost personal, the trinity of our earthly destiny. The three may be rudely summarized thus. First and nearest to us is the Christian, the man of the historic Church, of the creed that must have colored our minds incurably whether we regard it (as I do) as the crown and combination of the other two, or whether we regard it as an accidental superstition which has remained for two thousand years. First, then, comes the Christian; behind him comes the Roman, the citizen of that great cosmopolitan realm of reason and order in the level and equality of which Christianity arose. He is the Stoic who is so much sterner than the anchorites. He is the republican who is so much prouder than kings. He it is that makes straight roads and clear laws, and for whom good sense is good enough.
>
> And the third man—he is harder to speak of. He has no name, and all true tales of him are blotted out; yet he walks behind us in every forest path and wakes within us when the wind wakes at night. He is the origins—he is the man in the forest. It is no part of our subject to elaborate the point; but it may be said in passing that the chief claim of Christianity is exactly this—that it revived the pre-Roman madness yet brought into it the Roman order. The gods had really died long before Christ was born. What had taken their place was simply the god of government—*Divus Caesar* [divine Caesar]. . . . Christianity called to a kind of clamorous resurrection all the old supernatural instincts of the forests and the hill. But it put upon this occult chaos the Roman idea of balance and sanity. Thus, marriage was a sacrament, but mere sex was not a sacrament as it was in many of the frenzies of the forest. Thus wine was a sacrament with Christ; but drunkenness was not a sacrament as with Dionysius.
>
> In short, Christianity (merely historically seen) can best be understood as an attempt to combine the reason of the market-place with the mysticism of the forest. It was an attempt to accept all the superstitions that are necessary to man and to be philosophic at the end of them. Pagan Rome has sought to bring order or reason among men. Christian Rome sought to bring order and reason among gods.[122]

After centuries of struggle, upon the anvil of Charlemagne's sociopolitical order, the Catholic priesthood had led the way in forging the union of the Catholic Faith, Roman order, and Teutonic impetus that was crucial to the formation of medieval culture, the society of Christendom, and the ethos of Western civilization.

---

[122] Chesterton, *William Blake*, pp. 106–8.

Part 3

Distinctive Features of Western Civilization That Budded in the Dark Ages

The role of Catholic priests in the creation of some of the landmark social, artistic, and economic institutions that mark Western civilization as both original and originating in the Catholic matrix

Carl Friedrich Lessing, *Romantic Landscape with Monastery*, 1834.

The end of the Dark Ages was not merely the end of a sleep.... It was the end of a penance; or, if it be preferred, a purgation. It marked the moment when a certain spiritual expiation had been finally worked out and certain spiritual diseases had been finally expelled from the system ... by an era of asceticism, which was the only thing that could have expelled them. Christianity had entered the world to cure the world; and she cured it in the only way in which it could be cured.

—G. K. Chesterton, *St. Francis of Assisi*

Chapter 6

GUARDIANS OF THE ANCIENT RITE: THE TRADITIONAL MASS AND THE CULTURE OF CHRISTENDOM

[The Ancient Rite] is the most beautiful thing this side of heaven. It came forth out of the grand mind of the Church and lifted us out of earth and out of self, and wrapped us round in a cloud of mystical sweetness and the sublimities of a more than angelic liturgy, and purified us almost without ourselves, and charmed us with celestial charming so that our very senses seem to find vision, hearing, fragrance, taste, and touch beyond what earth can give.

—Frederick W. Faber[1]

The Ancient Rite

The priesthood's role in creating the new culture of Christendom—with its patterns of thought expressed in original philosophy, theology, music, art, architecture, literature, and drama, as well as in the everyday lifestyle of the population—was exercised largely through the sacred liturgy, especially by fulfilling Christ's command given at the Last Supper: "Do this in remembrance of me" (Lk 22:19).

By the reign of Pope Gregory the Great (590–604), the clergy had already designed the essential structure of the sublimely beautiful rite that would become over the following three hundred years in Western Europe the principal form of enacting the Holy Sacrifice of the Mass, the rite that is now called the "Traditional Mass", the "Traditional Latin Mass", the "Tridentine Mass", or, more recently, the "Extraordinary Form of the Roman Rite".

The Master of Saint Giles, *The Mass of Saint Giles*, ca. 1500, with possibly either the emperor Charlemagne or Charles Martel present.

[1] Quoted in Nicholas Gihr, *The Holy Sacrifice of the Mass* (St. Louis: B. Herder, 1908), p. 337.

In the history of civilizations, cult (public worship of God or liturgy), constituted by interrelated words, symbols, gestures, and chants that form a ritual order, has always embodied a world vision for its adherents. This configures all dimensions of society from education to agriculture, architecture, music, the arts, defense, and warfare. Thus, *cult* has been the root and soul of *culture*, the only exception being our contemporary post-Western civilization of Europe and the Americas, which is rapidly becoming the dominant global culture.[2]

From a historical and sociological perspective Catholicism brought to birth a new culture in Europe, chiefly because its most influential doctrines were embodied in the word form, symbolism, and ceremonial of *the Mass according to the Church's most ancient rite.*

In these pages I will refer to this rite as "the Ancient Rite" (usually without quotation marks) because it is the *most* ancient rite by which Mass has been enacted that is still in use as the "Extraordinary Form of the Roman Rite": "There is no existing Eastern liturgy with a history of continual use stretching back as far as that of the Roman Mass".[3] For although the Church in the East also has ancient rites, they continued to develop into the medieval centuries, whereas the Traditional Latin Mass has remained largely unchanged since the sixth century and is therefore undoubtedly the most antique rite.[4]

The Ancient Rite's impact is due not only to the fact that it is the *Mass* but to the fact that it is this concrete rite, this *"Ancient Rite"*, a clearly defined complex ceremonial embodying "everything that the [Western] Christian world possessed of doctrine and poetry, music and art [that] was poured into the liturgy, moulded into an organic whole which centered round the Divine Mysteries."[5]

The Ancient Rite was born in Rome. Between the reign of Pope Gregory the Great (590–604) and the eleventh century, the influence of the Roman Rite of the Mass spread until it became the principal way of enacting the Holy Sacrifice of the Mass in Western Europe. However, during those centuries it did undergo changes, which, while respecting its ethos, significantly enriched it. Crucially important were the modifications it underwent when Charlemagne decided to adopt the Roman Rite as the official way of offering the Holy Sacrifice of the Mass in the lands of his empire, the heartlands of the future Christendom. After visiting the Eternal City in 781, the Frankish ruler wrote to Pope Hadrian, asking for a copy of the Roman Rite's sacramentary, which was sent to him sometime between 784 and 791. However, this eighth-century sacramentary was incomplete, and so Alcuin and his associates sensitively completed it with sections from the sixth-century Gelasian sacramentary (also Roman) and from the Gallican Rite. By

---

[2] See Christopher Dawson, *Progress and Religion: An Historical Inquiry* (Washington, D.C.: Catholic University of America Press, 2001), pp. 81–193. The post-Western civilization of Europe and the Americas is, however, in demographic decline.

[3] Adrian Fortescue, *The Mass: A Study of the Roman Liturgy* (London: Longmans, Green, 1914), p. 213.

[4] Klaus Gamber, *The Reform of the Roman Liturgy* (San Juan Capistrano, Calif.: Una Voce Press, 1993), p. 10. Of course, the Ancient Rite includes not only the Holy Sacrifice of the Mass but also the rituals for administering the sacraments, praying the *Divinum Officium*, and performing other ecclesiastical actions such as blessings. However, while recognizing the role of the latter in the creation of Christendom's culture, this chapter will focus on the Mass of the Ancient Rite since its cultural importance far outweighs that of all the other components.

[5] Christopher Dawson, *The Formation of Christendom* (San Francisco: Ignatius Press, 2008), p. 147.

the tenth century, through the influence of Charlemagne's successors, this Roman-Gallican Rite returned to Rome, where it became the unique rite in Rome itself, taking the place of the original pure Roman Rite.

By the eleventh century this Roman-Gallican Rite was in use throughout most of Western Europe. Only a few relatively minor additions were made to it from then on. During the reign of Pope Innocent III (1198–1216), the Franciscans spread the use of the book containing it, the *Missale Romanum*, throughout Europe, and, after 1492, in the New World. It contained all the necessary texts and rubrics (instructions) for the performance of the Mass in the Ancient Rite. Although the opening prayers at the foot of the altar, the priest's prayers at the Offertory, and the Last Gospel were inserted later, this twelfth-century form of the rite is almost identical to that codified and published, with only minor changes, by Pope Saint Pius V after the Council of Trent (*Concilium Tridentinum*) in 1570.

Thus, the "Tridentine" Mass was the millennial "Ancient Rite" with merely slight changes. The priests assigned to produce the Tridentine missal, with profound veneration for a thousand years of ceremonial, symbol, and text embodying the spirit of their forefathers, carefully avoided interfering with its structure. As Jungmann recognized, "All in all, the changes thus made within the Mass-liturgy are very few indeed."[6] Or, as another expert remarked about the

"So our Mass goes back without essential change to the age when Caesar ruled the world and thought he could stamp out the Faith of Christ, when our fathers met together before dawn and sang a hymn to Christ as God. . . . There is not in Christendom a rite so venerable as ours" (Adrian Fortescue, *The Mass: A Study of the Roman Liturgy* [London: Longmans, Green, 1914], p. 213).

prayer preceding the epistle (the "collect"), the reformers of Trent simply "adopted *en bloc* a corpus of Mass collects that had been used for *at least* 800 years".[7]

The Ancient Rite is a magnificent marriage between the self-restrained and intellectually precise Roman prayers, accompanied by ceremonial austerity and structured by the ancient Roman sense of practicality with the dramatic tone, emotion-laden symbols, and impressive gestures of the Gallican rite of the fiery Celts and Teutons. It is to the latter that the Roman Rite owes so much of the

---

[6] Joseph Jungmann, *The Mass of the Roman Rite*, vol. 1 (Notre Dame, Ind.: Ave Maria, 2012), p. 140.

[7] Lauren Pristas, *The Collects of the Roman Missals of 1962 and 2002* (London-New York: Bloomsbury T&T Clark, 2013), p. 207. Italics mine.

sense of the *mysterium tremendum et fascinans* (awe-inspiring and fascinating mystery) conveyed by the vivid touches in her prayers, the richly symbolic ceremonies of Holy Week, and the blessings of candles, palms, ashes, and other elements. Accordingly, the fusion of the wild Celtic and Teutonic spirit with the refined and ordered Greco-Roman ethos makes the Ancient Rite both complex, intricate, and intellectual as well as earthy and cosmic.

The amalgamation of the Gallican and Roman rites into the "Ancient Rite" had important sociocultural effects, for it happened at the crucial moment when "*Europa*" was coming into existence due to a new distinctive culture that was coalescing in the Carolingian Empire—the sociopolitical framework for Christendom and Western civilization—caused by the merging of the three most important formative influences on the Western mind-set: the Greco-Roman, the barbarian, and the Christian. The Ancient Rite gave a powerful impulse to the new social order by becoming the chief cultural instrument for communicating the Catholic ideals at the heart of the emerging civilization.[8] Thus, in the "Mass of the Ages" every Western man and woman can enter into contact with the instrument that forged the characteristically Western psyche, coalescing the barbarian, ancient Roman, and Gospel mentalities.

This is the rite that remains in place today. A contemporary Catholic who attends the "Mass of the Ages" in London or Washington, D.C., would feel quite at home if carried back to a twelfth-century Romanesque church. The language is Latin; the core of the text is the Canon (largely similar to the "First Eucharistic Prayer" of the Ordinary Form of the Roman Rite);[9] the same Vulgate version of the Bible, authored by Saint Jerome, is in use; and the ceremonial and air of silence, solemnity, and reverence are the same.

The Embodiment of Catholicism

In the semi-vacuum of learning and scholarship, literature, music, drama, and the arts during the Dark Ages, the oral and symbolic content of the Ancient Rite's ceremonial and texts became very influential. Enacted throughout Europe, it communicated the Christian world vision and values in a way that deeply resonated in minds and hearts. Thus, during the formative epoch of Western civilization, the "Mass of the Ages" functioned as the chief educational tool of the truths of the Catholic religion for the peoples of Europe.

Consequently, while there were multiple other factors leading to the birth of Christendom, the chief—not the only, but the chief—determining factor was religious motivation, and at the heart of this religious motivation was the experience of the religion of Catholicism through its central act of cult: the Mass. As the ritual occurring week after week and not infrequently, from the eleventh century onward, on a daily basis for the priesthood and nobility, contact with its texts and ceremonies enabled its truths to gradually change men's mentality and lifestyle. This was the institution that more than any other gradually, almost imperceptibly, with wavelike

[8] See Yitzhak Hen, *Culture and Religion in Merovingian Gaul: A.D. 481–751* (Leiden: Brill, 1995).

[9] "Canon" refers to a fixed and obligatory standard, as opposed to, in this instance, the use of changeable prayers.

constancy educated, elevated, and transformed the minds and hearts of Europe, configuring the soul of its culture and civilization.

But *why*? Why did this ritual of the "Ancient Rite" so deeply shape the culture of a civilization?

The answer lies in the fact that the Ancient Rite uncannily applies that key intuition of Catholicism—that the supernatural thrives when nature is allowed to unfold her capacities. The Church's priesthood encouraged countless artisans to adorn the Mass with all the force of language, art, architecture, music, tapestry, woodwork, and ironwork available. All this artistic genius carried out its task guided by the Catholic vision of God and man that had been shaped by the divinely revealed truths and the Greco-Roman insights into human nature.

Although the Ancient Rite was perfected over the span of centuries by countless craftsmen of language and art from so many diverse ethnic and linguistic backgrounds, nevertheless is a mysterious *unity* to its structure. This is due to the fact that all these artisans so identified with Christianity's central truths (dogmas) that their painstakingly careful touching and retouching of the holy of holies was able to achieve a masterpiece with organic unity. "It is not properly the beauty of an art-product which is manifested here, but rather the beauty of a living thing such as we admire in a blossoming tree which, no matter how irregular and haphazard the branches and twigs and leaves and flowers might be, yet maintains a dominant symmetry, because a life-principle, a soul, guides its growth."[10]

Thus, through this symbiotic bonding between the natural and the supernatural in the Ancient Rite, the truths of the Catholic Faith *resounded* in the lives of men. Carefully nuanced and theologically precise prayers, tender hymns, and symbol-rich ceremonial spoke eloquently to men's minds and hearts of the Gospel.

The most important dimension of the Ancient Rite was its *transparent* communication of the *truths* of *Catholicism*. In its language, symbols, and postures men found the Catholic Faith in *all* its integrity, with *all* its intellectual complexity, tremendous mystery, fearsome depth, defiant challenge to the world, tender solace, and power of regeneration. It was as clear and unchanging in its identity as the Catholic Faith itself and thus had the power to touch and transform the hearts of millions, who became, in great or small ways, creators and upholders of a Christian society. Through it, millions found a poignant way to awaken to the depths of their sinfulness, the greatness of the Savior's love, and their freedom-conditioned destiny of eternal happiness.

From Sacrifice to Sacrificial Love

The key truth that the Ancient Rite *thunders* is that the Mass is *Sacrifice*! In this emphasis it renews in man's soul his intuition that it is necessary for him, somehow, to express his sense of dependence on the Deity through the channel of a *sacrificial ritual*. As the history of civilizations illustrates, man has always felt this need.[11] The Ancient Rite, by expressing the nature of the Mass as the mystical and sacramental presence of the Sacrifice of Christ, prefigured and prophesied in ancient Israel, thus forcefully confirmed universal human intuitions and gave voice to existential needs

[10]Jungmann, *Mass of the Roman Rite*, vol. 1, p. 4.
[11]See Dawson, *Progress and Religion*, pp. 87–102.

Juan Carreño de Miranda, *Mass of St. John of Matha*, 1666.

deeply felt by the Romans, Celts, and Germanic pagans she sought to convert to the Gospel.[12]

Thus, men related to the Mass not as a type of religious lecture-service, but as a *sacrificial action*. By its texts and ceremonies the Ancient Rite *emphasized* the intrinsic connection between the Mass and the dramatic events of Good Friday on Calvary and between Christ's self-offering to the Eternal Father for man's salvation and the Christian's self-offering in union with Him during the Mass. It clearly presented the Mass as a mystical sacrifice occurring visibly through sacramental signs. It lucidly unfolded the nature of the Mass as the perpetual commemoration and recurring application of the merits acquired by the Savior's action on Calvary, mystically prefigured in the Last Supper when Christ had used the sacrificial terms "my body which is given for you" (Lk 22:19) and "my blood of the covenant, which is poured out for many for the forgiveness of sins" (Mt 26:28).[13]

The Ancient Rite by emphasizing the nature of the Mass as the mystic and sacramental prolongation of the sacrificial deed of the Crucified Christ poignantly touched the hearts and minds of men. For it enabled the deepest aspirations of the ancient pagans to become reality since the Holy Communion of the Sacrifice "does not only allow us to 'receive' the soul, the body, the blood and the divinity of Christ Jesus but it unites us in a sort of symbiosis to the cultic act of the well-beloved Son [of the Eternal Father] as it unfolds in the heavenly sanctuary: we are one with the acting person of Christ priest and victim. The *knowledge* outcomes into *co-action* in an order of reality where the frontiers of the earthly and the heavenly world are erased."[14]

Moreover, the Ancient Rite clearly articulated in its texts, symbolism, and ceremonials *why* it is a sacrifice, and *why* this Sacrifice of the Mass *matters*. Both in the unchanging parts of the rite and in those that varied (as, for instance, with the liturgical seasons or in commemorations of the saints), the Ancient Rite spelled out the

---

[12] See Christopher Dawson, *Enquiries into Religion and Culture* (Washington, D.C.: Catholic University of America Press, 2009), pp. 78–94.

[13] See Jungmann, *Mass of the Roman Rite*, vol. 1, pp. 179–95.

[14] Dom Gérard Calvet, *La Sainte Liturgie par un Moine Bénédictin* (Le Barroux: Editions Sainte-Madeleine, 1982), pp. 44–45. My translation.

key reasons for the necessity of the sacrifice: God's honor and man's salvation as its purpose; damnation as the reality from which it saves man; sin as the deadly danger because it impedes participation in the sacrifice and thus bars the way to salvation; spiritual warfare against the forces seeking man's ruin as life's serious business; eternal life as possible only through the Lord Jesus Christ and only through the Church founded by Him.

The Ancient Rite, by facing Catholics toward the east, gave a clear sense of direction to their existence. They were alert to the fact that they were facing toward history's watershed, the Sacrifice of Calvary—but also toward Paradise, and in the direction from which the Lord of history would one day return "at an hour you do not expect" (Mt 24:44). Thus, the Ancient Rite's texts and symbols immersed them in the ultimate meaning of time and eternity. They knew that *history* is *his story*. Time is not merely *kronos*, the juxtapositioned succession of moments, but is *kairos*, the divinely determined order of events intersecting *kronos* in function of man's salvation. And the climax of the divine interventions was the death and Resurrection of Christ in which they mystically participated through the Mass.

The Ancient Rite's emphasis on the Mass as *Sacrifice* was inextricably bonded to its implication—the *spirit of sacrifice*. This was the rock on which the new civilization that became known as Christendom was built. The Ancient Rite's call on man to *sacrifice* himself, modeling his daily existence on the Sacrifice of Christ on Calvary and drawing strength from it, became the truth that more than any other inspired the heroism and genius of the Christians of those centuries. It imbued zeal to missionaries; fortitude to martyrs; solace to hermits; inspiration to artists, musicians, and architects; motivation, strength, and peace to the multitudes—century after century, generation after generation, for almost two millennia.

Embedded Deep in the Existence of Catholics

"When Christ on the Cross cried out His *Consummatum est*, few were the men who noticed it, fewer still the men who perceived that this phrase announced a turning point for mankind, that this death opened into everlasting life gates through which, from that moment on, all the peoples of the earth would pass. Now, to meet the expectant longing of mankind, this great event is arrested and, through Christ's institution held fast for these coming generations so that they might be conscious witnesses of that event even in the latest centuries, and amongst the remotest nations, and might look up to it in holy rapture."[15]

The extent of the Ancient Rite's impact can be evaluated by putting together the evidence from the following four historical perspectives. Firstly, from its occurrence at innumerable major sociopolitical events in the West's history, thus pointing to the sway it exercised over men's minds and hearts. Secondly, from its effects on the humanities and fine arts. Thirdly, from its pervasive presence among all the social classes. And, fourthly, from the radically new worldview and ideals characteristic of the Western mind-set whose origins can be traced to their embodiment within the Ancient Rite's texts and ceremonial. The following chapters on chivalry, romanticism, music, art and architecture, and economics will allow at least a glimpse of this impact.

---

[15]Jungmann, *Mass of the Roman Rite*, vol. 1, p. 177.

Louis Duveau, *Une Messe en Mer* (A Mass at Sea), 1864. The scene is off the coast of Brittany in 1793, the year the French Revolutionaries threatened priests who would not take the oath of loyalty to the state with the death penalty. From then on, mountain, forest, and ocean became the havens for the Ancient Rite in Brittany, Maine, and the Vendée.

It is because it became embedded deep down in the life of the Christian peoples, colouring all the *via vitae* [roads of life] of the ordinary man and woman, marking its personal turning-points, marriage, sickness, death and the rest, running through it year by year with the feasts and fasts and the rhythm of the Sundays, that the eucharistic action became inextricably woven into the public history of the Western world.

The thought of it is inseparable from its great turning-points also. Pope Leo doing this in the morning before he went out to daunt Attila, on the day that saw the continuity of Europe saved; and another Leo doing this three and a half centuries later when he crowned Charlemagne Roman Emperor, on the day that saw that continuity fulfilled.

Or again Alfred, wandering, defeated by the Danes, staying his soul on this, while mediaeval England struggled to be born; and Charles I also, on that morning of his execution when mediaeval England came to its final end. Such things strike the mind with their suggestions of a certain timelessness about the eucharistic action and an independence of its setting, in keeping with the stability in an ever-changing world of the forms of the liturgy themselves.

At Constantinople they "do this" yet with the identical words and gestures that they used while the silver trumpets of the Basileus still called across the Bosphorus, in what seems to us now the strange fairy-tale land of the Byzantine Empire.

In this twentieth century Charles de Foucauld in his hermitage in the Sahara "did this" with the same rite as Cuthbert twelve centuries before in his hermitage on Lindisfarne in the Northern seas. This very morning I did this with a set of texts which has not changed by more than a few syllables since Augustine used those very words at Canterbury on the third Sunday of Easter in the summer after he landed. Yet "this" can still take hold of a man's life and work with it....

For century after century, spreading slowly to every continent and country and among every race on earth, this action has been done, in every conceivable human circumstance, for every conceivable human need from infancy and before it to extreme

World War II, the Pacific island of Saipan, June 1944, a U.S. Navy
chaplain offers the Holy Sacrifice of the Mass for Marines. Little mattered the difference in centuries: whether medieval French knights or
twentieth-century American Marines, Catholics revered in the Ancient
Rite the authentic expression of the mystical and sacramental enactment
of the Sacrifice of Christ, sole source of man's redemption.

old age and after it, from the pinnacles of earthly greatness to the refuge of fugitives
in the caves and dens of the earth.

Men have found no better thing than this to do for kings at their crowning and for
criminals going to the scaffold; for armies in triumph or for a bride and bridegroom in
a little country church; for the proclamation of a dogma or for a good crop of wheat;
for the wisdom of the Parliament of a mighty nation or for a sick old woman afraid
to die; for a schoolboy sitting an examination or for Columbus setting out to discover
America; for the famine of whole provinces or for the soul of a dead lover; in thankful-
ness because my father did not die of pneumonia; for a village headman much tempted
to return to fetich because the yams had failed; because the Turk was at the gates of
Vienna; for the repentance of Margaret; for the settlement of a strike; for a son for a
barren woman; for Captain so-and-so, wounded and prisoner of war; while the lions
roared in the nearby amphitheatre; on the beach at Dunkirk; while the hiss of scythes
in the thick June grass came faintly through the windows of the church; tremulously,
by an old monk on the fiftieth anniversary of his vows; furtively, by an exiled bishop
who had hewn timber all day in a prison camp near Murmansk; gorgeously, for the
canonisation of Saint Joan of Arc.

One could fill many pages with the reasons why men have done this, and not tell
a hundredth part of them. And best of all, week by week and month by month, on a
hundred thousand successive Sundays, faithfully, unfailingly, across all the parishes of
Christendom, the pastors have done this just to make the *plebs sancta Dei*—the holy
common people of God.[16]

---

[16] Gregory Dix, *The Shape of the Liturgy* (London-New York: Blooomsbury T&T Clark, 2005), p. 744.

Chapter 7

FATHERS OF CHIVALRY:
A NEW TYPE OF WARRIOR

Thomas Pettie, *The Vigil*, 19th c. Warriorhood kneeling before the Crucified Hero: a youth during the initiation ceremonies for knighthood. Illustration from "Romance and Legend of Chivalry" by A. R. Hope Moncrieff (color litho).

Vigil of Arms

The heavy oak doors banged shut behind him and the metal bars crashed into their grooves barring entrance to all: the Vigil of Arms for the induction to knighthood had begun.[1]

---

[1] For a description of the rite of initiation to knighthood, see Geoffroi de Charny, *A Knight's Own Book of Chivalry* (Philadelphia: University of Pennsylvania Press, 2005), pp. 91–93. The author, Geoffroi de Charny (ca. 1304–1356), one of the most respected knights of his age, wrote it as a guide for members of the Company of the Star, rival of the English Order of the Garter. This is the most authentic and complete manual on the daily life of knighthood in existence. Incidentally, de Charny is also the first identified Western European guardian of the Shroud of Turin.

He was now alone. Alone with God. The nocturnal silence would guard the intimacy of his prayer during these sacred hours.

Kneeling on the stone pavement of the Gothic church, he gazed on the silhouette of the immense crucifix behind the altar. The torches attached to the stone walls burned steadily, their light shimmering off the sword and glistening on the coat of chain mail and helmet placed on the raised step in front of him.

He closed his eyes. His grip tightened around the cross hilt of the sword.

The longed-for moment had finally come.

How the ten years had flown by since the morning he had left home as a nine-year-old in order to live at his feudal lord's castle. They had been happy years, for he had been treated like a son and a sibling. Alongside the other boys he had learned to ride, joust, use the sword and lance; he smiled as he recalled the day when he had graduated from page to squire at twelve years of age.

But now the vigil was actually happening. He remembered the explanation given him at the monastery the previous evening after he had made his confession of sins to the white-robed priest who had been his mentor during all these years, the man who was truly his spiritual father and his soul's deepest friend: "Every stage of the vigil will reveal to you the secrets of knighthood: a life of single-minded pursuit of Christlikeness as a warrior. To reach the goal you must keep the body in check, ever aware of your interior weakness as man, and ever on the alert for the Tempter—the fast for twenty-four hours before the Mass of initiation will remind you of this. Chivalry calls you constantly to purify yourself from sin: that is the symbolism of the ceremonial bath you will take before beginning the vigil. Yet amidst the many—aye, and bloody—interior battles a man must go through, his heart is strengthened by the thought of the end of the struggle and the repose of Paradise for the pure of heart—that is the symbol of the rest allowed you after the bath of purification."

He paused. From the other side of the cloister came the sound of chanting.

"Then," he continued, "you will don the ceremonial garments. Firstly, a long white tunic, symbol of chastity. Over it a red garment with long sleeves to show that you are ready to shed your blood for the honor of God, the defense of Holy Church, and for truth and justice. Finally, a black cape to remind you to persevere unflinchingly in the battle for virtue, even in the face of the ultimate fear, death.

"This done, they will lead you to the church where during the night you will go into watchful prayer, like Christ in Gethsemane. Those precious hours will help seal your conviction that prayer and grace must be the veteran companions of your journey. The sword you will hold during that vigil must ever stand not only for conquest, but above all, for self-conquest. Never sheathe that sword, my son, never, because as a knight of Christ you must engage in spiritual warfare until you cross the last frontier."

The wise eyes of the monk who was none other than the king's brother, once one of the country's most admired knights, had sensed something was worrying him. After a brief hesitation, he had reminded his spiritual father of the desire that had been growing within him in recent years, even as the accolade drew near: to give his life to God in the monastic priesthood.

He had been reassured: "Continue to protect this sublime aspiration for everything points to it as a call from God. Moreover, the Church needs—badly needs—warrior priests in our age. Your entry to knighthood will not impede your priestly vocation for it will require of you to walk along the same paths of chivalric love as a man must travel on the journey to sacred orders—radiant purity, spiritual warfare, constant daily prayer, and closeness to the sacraments in order to be a priest of God. In a year's time, after you are seen to live the life of a knight and yet remain firm in your decision, the great obstacle to your entry will be overcome. Your liege lord the king, who thinks so highly of you and would dearly like to have you in his service, will see God's providence in your determination and will cease to oppose your wishes. He will bless your departure for the higher chivalry—indeed, the highest: that of a life wholly dedicated to being gallant to God. Thus he has assured me. Go in peace my son. All will be well." And the monk raised his right hand in blessing over the young man's head.

Moonlight poured through the rose window and illuminated the crucifix.

He prayed with all his energy of mind and body for the strength to be faithful to the rigorous demands unto heroism to which he would commit himself the following morning: "Lord Jesus, first thou and thy holy Church and then—and only then—all else. My sword only for good, never for evil. May I defend the poor, orphans, and widows. May I ..." But gradually words came haltingly and then ceased as eyes, mind, and the very depths of his being left behind all thought of self and became immersed in the Crucified Hero.

The hours passed swiftly. Dawn's first rays pierced through the arched windows, and a nightingale could be heard in the gardens. Then the doors opened and his fellow squires arrived to escort him to his place for the ceremony. Family members, friends, and neighbors began filling the church. The king, queen, and retinue made their entrance. Close by stood the twelve noble knights who would act as his witnesses, among them his father and two uncles.

The Holy Sacrifice of the Mass began. The waves of Gregorian chant rose and descended throughout the Gothic church ... *Kyrie eleison, Christe eleison, Kyrie eleison ... Gloria in excelsis Deo*. Then, as the last echoes of the alleluia after the Gradual died away, carrying his sword and shield, he left his place, entered the sanctuary, genuflected, and handed them to the bishop who laid them upon the altar. Then he knelt, with his eyes and arms directed upward. The prelate sprinkled the sword with holy water before starting with grave, slow intonation the centuries-old prayers from the *Pontificale Romanum*:[2] "God, Guardian of all who put their hope in you, mercifully be attentive to our prayers and grant to this man, your servant, who with a sincere heart endeavors to gird himself for the first time with the sword of battle, that he may in all circumstances be protected by the helmet of your might; and just as you granted victory by the power of your strength to David and Judith against the

---

[2] A pontifical is a liturgical book containing the prayers, rites, and ceremonial protocol for bishops and abbots. The ritual, *Benedictio Novi Militis* (Blessing of the New Soldier) in the Pontifical of Guillaume Durandus (1292–1295), was based on blessings and prayers for knighthood, some of which are from the tenth century. However, the inspiration behind them goes back at least as far as the culture at the court of Charlemagne and Alcuin. "As visible assertions of both spiritual and temporal authority, then, these various ceremonies are expressive of the close reciprocation—entirely characteristic of medieval power structures—between ecclesiastical and secular power. As such they are embedded in broader soldierly assertions of combined sacred and secular might which ... first crystalized in the West in the Gallo-Frankish court culture of the eighth century." Andrew Kirkman, *The Cultural Life of the Early Polyphonic Mass: Medieval Context to Modern Revival* (Cambridge: Cambridge University Press, 2010), p. 115. From the fourteenth century this particular ritual of Guillaume Durandus remained largely unchanged and was adopted by the universal Church.

enemies of your people, so may he, defended by your aid, be victorious everywhere and advance the safety of Holy Church. Amen."[3]

Then came the blessing of the sword: "Hear our prayers, we beseech thee, O Lord, and deign, with the right hand of your Majesty, to bless this sword with which your servant desires to be girded, so that he may be the defender of churches, widows, orphans, and of all the servants of God against the ferocity of pagans, and may it inspire awe and dread among those seeking to ensnare him, assuring him fair completion of action and just defense."[4]

"Amen!" thundered all present.

Then he sprinkled the shield: "Lord God, Savior of the world, without whom the salvation of man is in vain, hearken to our humble prayer and pour forth the gift of your blessing upon this shield, shelter of the human body, so that he who places it at his side for his defense may have you as shield and safeguard against the enemies of soul and body. Thus fortified and protected on all sides he may bless the name of your glory in all his works. Amen."[5]

Then the bishop and the choir alternated in chanting: "Blessed be the Lord my God who trains my hands for battle, and my fingers to fight. My merciful One, and my refuge—my protector and my liberator. My protector in whom I have placed my hope—who subdues peoples under me. *Gloria Patri et Filio et Spiritui Sancto ...* Be to me, O Lord, a tower of strength in the face of my enemy. O Lord, hear my prayer—and let my cry come to you."

At that moment, the solitary voice of the prelate, his arms extended, began the solemn invocation:

> Let us pray: Holy Lord, Father Almighty, Eternal God, who alone, disposing and arranging all things in right order for the purpose of restraining the malice of the wicked and the protection of justice; who by a beneficial disposition has allowed the use of the sword among men; who willed to institute the militant order to protect your people; who did say, through Saint John the Baptist's words to the soldiers who came to see him, not to oppress anybody and to be content with one's wages: we humbly implore your mercy. We beseech you, that as you granted to the boy David the power to overcome Goliath, and to Judas Maccabeus the power to triumph over the nations that did not invoke your holy name, to grant this servant of yours who is about to take up your yoke and join the order of knighthood, the heavenly graces of strength, courage, and audacity to defend the Faith and justice; bestow upon him an increase in faith, hope, and charity; grant him equally fear and love, humility, perseverance, obedience, enduring patience; and order all within him so that with this sword, or any other, he may harm no one unjustly; that with it he may defend all upright and just causes; and as he is raised from a lesser degree to the new honor of soldierhood, may he leave behind the old man and his actions and put on the new

---

[3] See Adolph Franz, ed., *Die Kirchlichen Benediktionen im Mittelalter*, vol. 2 (Freiburg im Breisgau: M. Herder, 1909), p. 294. My translation from the original Latin.

[4] The *Benedictio Ensis* (Blessing of the Sword) according to the "Pontifical de Guillaume Durandus", quoted in Michel Andrieu, *Le pontifical romain au moyen-âge*, 4 vols., Studi e Testi, 86–89, vol. 2, *Le pontifical de la curie romaine au XIIIe siècle* (*The Pontifical of the Roman Curia in the 13th Century*) (Vatican City State: Biblioteca Apostolica Vaticana, 1940), p. 447. My translation from original Latin.

[5] See Franz, *Die Kirchlichen Benediktionen im Mittelalter*, vol. 2, pp. 296–97. My translation from the original Latin. For the original Latin texts of other blessings for knighthood, see Jean Flori, *L'essor de la chevalerie: XIe-XIIe siècles* (Genève, Switzerland: Librairie Droz, 1986).

man: so may he fear and worship you; avoid the company of traitors; show charity to his neighbor; obey his superior uprightly; and fulfill his duty thoroughly. Through Christ Our Lord. Amen.[6]

Then, the bishop took the sword which had lain unsheathed upon the altar and placed it in the right hand of the knight-to-be: "Accept this sword given to you with the blessing of God by which you will be able, through the power of the Holy Spirit, to resist and drive away all your enemies and any adversaries of the Holy Church of God."[7]

The chanting of the antiphon from Psalm 44 began: "[G]ird your sword on your thigh, o mighty one, in your splendor and majesty. In your majesty ride out victoriously for the cause of truth and meekness and righteousness; let your right hand teach you awesome deeds!"[8] The bishop girded him with the consecrated sword.[9] The new knight rose, joy filling his eyes, drew the sword from its scabbard and brandished it three times in the air, wiped it on his left arm as if it were already smeared with the blood of evildoers, and resheathed it. Then the new knight and the bishop exchanged the kiss of peace, before the bishop said: "Be a peaceful, energetic, loyal, and devoted soldier for God."[10] Then he gave him a light blow on the cheek saying: "Rouse yourself from the sleep of wickedness and be vigilant over the Faith of Christ and praiseworthy repute."[11]

Then he left the sanctuary, knelt before the King, and professed his vow of loyalty. The witnesses began to attire him. His two uncles helped put on the padded jacket, each of them lacing a sleeve. His father vested him with the coat of mail, a fabric of interlocking metal rings forming a strong, flexible, mesh armor. His cousins and friends attached breastplate, armlets, gauntlets, sword, and hauberk. Tied to his right sleeve he wore the blue scarf of Our Lady to whom he had consecrated his heart the year before. The king fastened the gold-gilded spurs to the heels of his boots.

The Holy Sacrifice of the Mass continued. Attentively he listened to the archbishop's sermon on the duties of knighthood. Kneeling he received Holy Communion. Finally, as all prepared to process from the church, in accord with the local custom, several of the knights led in a magnificent horse. After bowing toward the crucifix and the statue of Our Lady, he mounted, proudly held up his sword, and rode down the long aisle of the nave, through the open doors, forth into the sunlight.

---

[6] See Andrieu, *Le pontifical de la curie romaine au XIIIe siècle*, p. 448. My translation from the original Latin.
[7] See Franz, *Die Kirchlichen Benediktionen im Mittelalter*, vol. 2, p. 296. My translation from the original Latin.
[8] "Since this antiphon, the closing prayer that follows it, and the two prayers prescribed at the beginning were all present also in the [mid-tenth century] Romano-Germanic pontifical, it seems clear that the ritual [of William Durandus (1292–1295)] was already three centuries old." Kirkman, *Cultural Life of the Early Polyphonic Mass*, p. 113.
[9] In this pontifical, the girding with the sword constituted the actual accolade (dubbing), the central act in the ceremonies of the rite of passage for knighthood. The more famous form of accolade, a tapping of the sword on the neck or shoulder (*collée* or *paumée*), is not present in the Pontifical of Guillaume Durandus (1292–1295); see Andrieu, *Le pontifical de la curie romaine au XIIIe siècle*, pp. 447–50; 549–50. Through the centuries, the accolade varied: sometimes a blow with a naked fist on the neck or ear; other times a stroke with the flat part of the sword against the side of the neck; or else a tapping on the right or left shoulder or both. See Maurice Keen, *Chivalry* (New Haven, Conn.: Yale University Press, 1984), pp. 64–83.
[10] See Andrieu, *Le pontifical de la curie romaine au XIIIe siècle*, p. 449. My translation from the original Latin.
[11] Ibid.

Baptizing Men with Claws

The struggle to channel the passions of masculinity in a flawed human nature where dwell the breeding grounds of brute ferocity must ever be present in any civiliza-tion worthy of man. Wherever masculin-ity is identified with the will to power, wherever warfare is exalted as an ideal and allowed to dominate society, swiftly flow the rivers of blood and savagery, racism, class conflict, and even genocide. Recent history gives us enough instances: Nazism, fascism, Japanese militarism in the 1930s, and Soviet communism.

William Blake Richmond, *The Hun and the Crucifix*, 19th century. The beginnings of an interior revolution.

Much of the darkness of the Dark Ages was, as a preacher of the time remarked, because "men have claws and live with the wild beasts".[12] Neither warriorhood nor war knew the meaning of restraint among the Germanic tribes, Magyars, and Vikings; neither for that matter were the "civilized" Romans much better. It is to the undying glory of the Church during this era that she unleashed a mighty cultural struggle to forge a new type of soldier, forcing men to choose whether they would remain at the level of their animal instincts or would strive to rise to the heights of the just warrior. Never and nowhere has any other civilization witnessed the creation of such an idyllic model for the soldier class as Catholicism, through its priesthood, brought to birth: "the noble image of the just and upright warrior, haloed with virgin purity; whose aim is rather sacrifice than victory, blood offered than blood shed".[13]

It is the powerfully poignant saga of how priests, themselves often from warrior families and vowed to spiritual warfare on the battlefield of self-conquest for the sake of Christlikeness, created a new and original ethos, a culture for the ruling class in medieval Western Europe: *chivalry*. Some of their names surface in these pages. Many, however, will remain unknown to history as the hidden creators of prayers, symbolisms and rituals, statutes, texts of inspiration, and codes of conduct. Others influenced the institution as statesmen, spiritual fathers, and chaplains. One brought chivalry to the peaks of medieval idealism as the creator of the constitutions for the order of the Knights Templar, the prototype in many ways for the other military orders of knighthood.

We are all well aware that some medieval warriors remained at the level of brutes, a quality—as we look around at our own times—we realize they did not corner the market on. Aside from that, would any ideal be left standing if it were graded by its betrayers? What matters is that there were many who allowed the Church, through

---

[12] Quoted in Henri Daniel-Rops, *The Church in the Dark Ages* (London: J.M. Dent and Sons, 1959), p. 569.

[13] Henri Daniel-Rops, *Cathedral and Crusade: Studies of the Medieval Church, 1050–1350* (New York: Dutton, 1957), p. 280.

her supernatural life and worldview, to raise them to a higher level of manhood and to a military ideal unrivaled in splendor. The Church achieved this through her sacraments, prayer, rites, laws, discipline, and asceticism—yes, and also by condemnations and excommunications.

Hence, chivalry is no vague idealism; it is not merely a spirit of magnanimity or noble behavior but a precise ethos that is quintessentially Catholic, whose features show a clear resemblance to its mother, the Church. For without Catholicism, history would never have known chivalry. It is true that among the Germanic tribes there was a ceremony of military investiture by which a young man became a warrior. It involved a bath of purification and the conferring of the javelin, helmet, and shield by the youth's father. This warrior culture might well have matured into an elite group of Franks with a level of military prowess on a par with other high-quality forces such as the Samurai or the Janissaries. Likewise, by acquiring the culture of romantic love and courtesy originating in Arabic Spain, they might have carved out a niche in history as a somewhat exotic military class. However, with those features alone, what the world knows today as classic chivalry would not have existed. It was Catholicism that brought the new ethos to birth by raising the hearts and minds of men to the contemplation of the highest religious and ethical ideal for warriors, through a ritual and code accessed by a mystical and sacramental worldview. "Chivalry", said G. K. Chesterton, "might be called the baptism of Feudalism. It was an attempt to bring the justice and even the logic of the Catholic creed into a military system which already existed; to turn its discipline into initiation and its inequalities into a hierarchy."[14]

The social class of medieval knights was formed out of the horse soldiers who had acquired widespread military importance by the time of Charlemagne. This was largely due to the extensive use of the stirrup which had arrived to Europe with the Alans during the fifth- and sixth-century invasions. It gave riders more ability to maneuver in the saddle, thus allowing them to give stronger and more precise blows with sword and lance during battle, with the result that cavalry became more important than infantry. However, the costs of the horse soldier's suit of mail, sword, and shield, and sometimes his three horses and several attendants, were high. This made him dependent on kings or nobles who enabled him to finance everything by giving him a section of land (fief) in exchange for becoming a vassal. Vassalage involved doing military service at the soldier's own expense for a certain number of days per year (forty in France and Norman England). In this way the knight was inserted into the feudal system—indeed, the Anglo-Saxon word for knight, *cnith*, means "servant". The practice effectively created hereditary fiefdoms and a new social class of professional fighters who, when they went to war as a group with their lord, formed a *chevalerie*.[15]

From the tenth to the twelfth centuries, priests relentlessly strove, undaunted by countless failures, to create an effective Christianizing ideal for this social group.

---

[14] G. K. Chesterton, *A Short History of England*, chap. 6, quoted in Kevin L. Morris, ed., *The Truest Fairy Tale: An Anthology of the Religious Writings of G. K. Chesterton* (Cambridge: Lutterworth Press, 2007), pp. 172–73.

[15] See Richard W. Barber, *The Reign of Chivalry* (Woodbridge: Boydell Press, 2005), pp. 9–44; and Sidney Painter, *French Chivalry: Chivalric Ideals and Practices in Mediaeval France* (New York: Cornell University Press, 1957), pp. 28–65.

They tried to keep the social class of horse soldiers and the meritorious ranks of knighthood separate and distinct not only in theory but also in reality—just because you were a horse soldier didn't guarantee you automatic entrance to knighthood. In this way the Church sought to ensure that the accolade remained open to any foot soldier who merited it by providing an open class system facilitating upward social mobility. However, men being men, the equestrian military group rapidly acquired almost a monopoly for family members.[16]

Priests partly offset this serious flaw by imbuing the ceremony of admission to knighthood with a Christian mystique. In this way the Church obliged candidates, however low on merits, to at least stand in front of the ideal by putting them through a series of unforgettable rites charged with mystic splendor. Forever etched on their souls, these memories either inspired nobility or at least inhibited evil by provoking a healthy fear and guilt in the hour of temptation or sin. Of course the candidate still had to fulfill the military conditions for the accolade: good health, physical strength, and expertise in the skills of warfare. But thanks to the rite of passage created by the clergy, men became aware that something more than military prowess and bloodline was needed to merit the title of knight. As a medieval saying went: "He, it seems, alone is worthy who has these two things together, strength of body and goodness of soul."

Training Warriors to Wield and Sheathe the Sword

In her struggle to form a new ideal for soldiers, the Church first sought to break the barbarian mentality of ceaseless warfare. Stubbornly, from the fifth century the Church's leaders sought to tame the "wild West", to curb the savage private wars among the barbarians who recognized no law but that of the vendetta.

In the ninth century, as Charlemagne's empire disintegrated, although bishops formed in the mentality of Alcuin ardently desired imperial unity, they saw the inevitability of partition and realistically accepted the de facto situation of three kingdoms. Among the three sovereigns, Charlemagne's grandsons, they urged a brotherhood of kings, men "united by Christ's love". The 844 Synod of Yutz reminded the monarchs: "Take care to preserve charity amongst you.... Help each other by rendering good advice and

Hubert van Eyck, detail of St. George, on *The Knights of Christ*, from the left side of the Ghent Altarpiece, 1432 (oil on panel), St. Bavo Cathedral, Ghent, Belgium.

prompt aid. Instead of serving the discord which the Devil spreads among your peoples, serve peace, that peace which Christ, when He ascended into Heaven, left His

[16]See Keen, *Chivalry*, pp. 18–44.

disciples as the most precious of all gifts."[17] Not only did the Church speak, but she admirably promoted fraternal assemblies like those at Thionville (844), Meersen (847 and 851), Valenciennes (853), and Attigny (854) at which she managed to secure a series of laws common to all three kingdoms for the sake of the "common subjects" "under the common reign", with the implementation supervised by Church legates.

Constantly the Church sought to protect particularly the poor of Western Europe who lived in fear of Viking raids, Magyar intrusions, and even their own overlords, men ready to "fly at each other like dogs". Councils like that of Valence in 855 forbade the duel as a way of settling litigation—a most politically incorrect decision in the eyes of the military class. In warfare, bishops sought to prohibit the use of bows and crossbows between Christian armies; time and again Church councils, popes, and bishops thundered against murder. In the tenth century the Church had gained enough sociopolitical muscle to enable her to make a new assault on unjust warfare. What idealism she showed as she launched two institutions aimed at defending the defenseless during outbreaks of conflict: the Peace of God and the Truce of God.

The Peace of God was a popular peace movement led by the priesthood, notably the monks of Cluny, and heavily promoted by many episcopal gatherings from the Council of Le Puy in 975 to that of Narbonne in 1054. The goal was to keep war limited to the parties involved: warriors were told to keep their hands off commerce and culture and to avoid harming either the persons or possessions of the poor, peasants, widows, orphans, merchants, or unarmed clerics (a broader category of people than clergy), whether by stealing or destruction; nor was harm to be done to agricultural animals, olive trees, or wagons in the fields. To show that they were staunchly behind the movement, bishops backed up their words with the feared penalties of excommunication and interdict, as at the Council of Verdun in 1016. Interdict meant that no baptisms, marriages, funerals, or public Masses were permitted until the ruler genuflected before the Church and did penance for his crime. Some monarchs rallied to the ideal and sought to institute it in their realms, men like Henry II of Germany in 1021, and Louis VII of France in 1155.

A second institution, the Truce of God, first proposed by Pope John XV (988–996), built upon the Peace of God by forbidding war within defined time periods. A synod of 1017 ordered that all warfare stop "from the ninth hour of Saturday until the first hour of Monday". Another council ruled that a truce should reign from Wednesday evening to Monday morning, arguing that those days should be days of tranquility in honor of key events in Christ's life: Thursday because of his Ascension, Friday because of the Passion, Saturday on account of his burial, and Sunday in honor of the Resurrection. Penalties for infringements were severe: the Truce of God promulgated at Thérouanne, in 1063, imposed an exile of thirty years on violators. The institution spread through northern France, England, Belgium, up the Rhine, and into Italy and Spain.

A third valiant effort was made by the Leagues of Peace. In 1038, Aymon, Archbishop of Bourges, said that any Christian over fifteen years of age should stand as an enemy of peace-breakers and be willing to fight them. Hence, armed volunteer peace militias came into existence and spread through Western Europe, even though with little success and often becoming another source of conflicts.

---

[17] Quoted in Daniel-Rops, *The Church in the Dark Ages*, p. 440.

Nevertheless, in spite of many flaws and failures, these vigorous thrusts for peace improved the quality of life and had long-term effects. During the short-lived intervals in which peace reigned, the ordinary people breathed more easily, assured that they could go on with their daily existence without being under imminent threat from feuding overlords. The children of these centuries appreciated the Church's efforts and grew up close to the local abbeys and rural chapels whose walls they felt extended outward, surrounding their villages and countrysides like strong paternal arms; and so they came to love Catholicism as an integral part of their existence. Gradually, the Christian ethos of just warfare and the duty to toil for peace, although never entirely vanquishing the barbarian war addiction, restrained it, and instilled a new mentality in the West. "This striving after peace in a society that loved war, was a splendid dream, perhaps an example of midsummer madness, and certainly a paradox; but at least it expressed a justifiable Christian hope that would spread gradually throughout the world."[18] And spread throughout the world it did, as the Church, century after century, continued such "mad" efforts, never discouraged by the results. We cannot forget that the idea of world peace, and the institutions founded to promote it in the twentieth century—the League of Nations and the United Nations—were born in the lands of the former Christian civilization.

The Silhouette of the Christian Warrior Appears

As the Church, through both her doctrine and discipline, gradually eradicated the barbarian frenzy for warfare, she instilled the Christian meaning of warriorhood, clothing it with a mystique, embodying it in a sacred rite of initiation, and providing role models from among the saints.

By christening the rite of initiation, the priesthood gave a markedly Christian identity to the medieval warrior. This rite, which received its most splendid expression in the Roman Pontifical and in that of Guillaume Durandus, gradually evolved from the rite of the blessing of the sword which already existed in the Mainz Pontifical, composed around 950. But both the sword blessing and the act of girding as liturgical ceremonials first appeared in the

Wilfred Thompson, *Saint Martin and the Beggar*, 1918.

Church's rite of the coronation for monarchs. In turn, the act of girding with the sword was originally a nonreligious ceremony, as when Charlemagne girded Louis the Pious during his coronation as king of Aquitaine in 791 and Louis did likewise for Charles the Bald in 838.[19]

---

[18] Daniel-Rops, *Cathedral and Crusade*, p. 352.
[19] Keen, *Chivalry*, pp. 71–72.

Starting at the Council of Verdun-sur-Saone in 1016, ecclesiastics took another step by motivating the military class to make a solemn oath upon a copy of the Gospel, or on relics, to preserve peace. The medieval mind immediately recognized the grave implication of this action: any infringements would be sacrilegious, with consequences for one's eternal salvation. However, the clergy who authored this and all the other prayers, symbols, and blessings that gradually coalesced into a rite of initiation were not seeking merely to deter soldiers from evil. Above all, they wanted to inspire them with a vision and a standard intended to dignify warriorhood; one that would awaken them to the nobility of the military profession. The Church insisted that a soldier's actions in the pursuit of justice, and by means of justice, would be meritorious for the remission of sins and eternal salvation. Through the rite, the Church chiseled the cross upon the armor. Thus, she created the core of the ethos of chivalry in which a new standard was set against which knights could both measure themselves and be measured by the Church and society.

By the early twelfth century the Church had taken ownership of most of the rite of passage to knighthood, converting it well and truly from a secular to a sacred institution, as can be seen in the pontificals, the liturgical books containing the rites performed by bishops. A pontifical of the province of Reims, dating from the early eleventh century, states expressly that the bishop not only blesses the sword but also the banner, lance, shield, and the person of the future knight, and that even the sword is to be girded on by the bishop. This expansion of the priestly role is confirmed in the Pontifical of Guillaume Durandus, the core of whose rituals are either Roman or Carolingian, and which, with papal support, were universally used from the fourteenth century on.[20] In these pontificals, the Church sealed the institution's exclusively Christian character by stating that a man had to be "ordained" to the "order" of knighthood: the Church had introduced an ecclesiastical term to qualify knighthood as a distinct ecclesiastical class to which entry was possible only by consecration at the hands of the priesthood.

The Church made men "pay" for the honor by setting conditions for entry. The candidate had to promise to go to Mass daily or at least often, and to fast on Fridays. From as early as the tenth century the rituals kept emphasizing that the sword had to be used for good: to protect the poor, the widow, and the orphan; defend the Church; attack the evildoer; not murder a defenseless enemy; not give false judgment in a trial; never to give "evil advice" to a woman; and to help anyone in need. A prayer in the Pontifical of Bishop Guillaume Durandus (composed 1292–1295) sums up these requirements:

> Most Holy Lord, Almighty Father ... thou who hast permitted on earth the use of the sword to repress the malice of the wicked and defend justice; who for the protection of thy people hast thought fit to institute the order of chivalry ... cause thy servant here before thee, by disposing his heart to goodness, never to use this sword or another to injure anyone unjustly; but let him use it always to defend the just and the right.[21]

Another way in which the priesthood fashioned the mystique of chivalry was by offering role models for knights. Around 930, Odo, Abbot of Cluny, proposed one

---

[20] Marc Bloch, *Feudal Society*, vol. 2 (Chicago: University of Chicago Press, 1961), pp. 315–16.
[21] Ibid., p. 319.

such model in his biography of Saint Gerald of Aurillac.[22] Among the most popular were Saint Martin of Tours (316–397), Saint George (ca. 278–303), and Saint Maurice, an Egyptian officer of a Theban military unit, who, while fighting against rebellious Gauls, refused the emperor's order to sacrifice to the gods for the sake of obtaining military success, and was martyred around 287. Maurice became a patron saint of the Holy Roman emperors who possessed his supposed sword, lance, and spurs. The sword and spurs were among the emblems used at coronations of the Austro-Hungarian emperors up to that of Emperor Karl in 1916.

Rituals and blessings for all dimensions and moments of warfare reinforced the alertness to the supernatural among the military class, as, for instance, this prayer for an army from the Romano-German Pontifical of the tenth century:

> Provide, O Lord, the might of your mercy for our army. Grant us the aid we have implored of going forth under clear skies. Just as you arranged for the strength of Israel's security as she hastened to leave Egypt, so send an angel, a source of light, for your people going forth into battle, so that he may defend them by day and by night from all danger. May their journeying arrive without toil to its end, a provident outcome everywhere. May they travel without dread, live without monotony, moderate fragility without fear; may there be strength without terror, abundant supplies, and an upright will for warring. And when, under the leadership of your angel, the conqueror will stand forth, may he not attribute victory to his own strength but give thanks to the true victor, Christ, your Son, who by the humiliation of his passion on the cross triumphed over death and the prince of death. Amen.[23]

Chivalry's Christian meaning, rich in beauty, symbolism, and solemnity, seized the imagination of medieval man and ushered in significant changes in the code of warfare. But the effects went even deeper, for they created a new masculine ideal for the warrior. Throughout Western Europe, men agreed that knighthood was a rugged pathway on which the warrior should travel to masculine sanctity through just behavior in war and peace. Ramon Llull (ca. 1235–1315) in his *The Book of the Order of Chivalry*, while explaining the rituals of knightly initiation and the symbolism of the knightly trappings, enthusiastically put knighthood on a par with monastic consecration as the highest route to Christlikeness. After the dubbing, the youth who had conscientiously assented to the Church's requirements for initiation to chivalry rode away from the ceremony, his heart set on doing battle for the true and the good. Ever in his mind as the seasons of life went by were the words he had pronounced in church when he had consecrated himself to God. He was conscious that the horizons of knighthood were vast and luminous; that chivalry's moral standards were as daunting as they were lofty; that they called for far more than just a strong body: a heart intrepid, a spirit so towering that it disdained all that was mean, unjust, and impure. Wisdom was to mark his thoughts; love for truth and hatred for deceit, his words; fearlessness, his sword; self-conquest, his urges to lust, greed, and vanity; justice, the relations with his liege lord and servants; mercy, his combat with enemies; and tenderness, his contact with the poor, orphans, and widows.

---

[22] Odo, *The Life of St. Gerald* (Philadelphia: Penn State Press, 1954).

[23] See Cyrille Vogel and Reinhard Elze, eds., *Le pontifical romano-germanique du dixieme siecle* (The Romano-Germanic Pontifical of the Tenth Century), 2 vols., Studi e Testi, 226–27 (Vatican City State: Biblioteca Apostolica Vaticana, 1963), vol. 2, p. 380. My translation from the Latin.

When he followed a feudal noble to war it was no longer merely because he was bound by kinship or blind obedience, but for the sake of Christian-inspired bonds of fidelity that were mutually binding between him and the overlord. He considered himself to be not just a knight of a particular nation but a warrior of Christendom, and so he felt a brotherhood with all *chevaliers*. The overarching raison d'être for his life and action was the reality that he was a Christian who knelt before Jesus Christ, his Savior. Indeed, he reckoned his greatness to be dependent on the purity and single-mindedness of his Christian spirit: "The knight, in fact, no longer considered himself as a 'Christian soldier', but as a Christian who would serve God before all else, even in battle."[24]

The rough outline of the chivalric spirit can be seen in some of the medieval epic poems. The first and greatest of these *Chansons de Geste* (Songs of Heroic Deeds) was the legend the *Song of Roland*, written in the twelfth century, possibly by Théroulde, who may have been a Norman priest. It narrates—without much regard for historical facts—the grandeur of Roland, Charlemagne's nephew, who dies during the Battle of Roncesvalles in 778, supposedly at the head of twenty thousand Franks who are overwhelmed by four hundred thousand Saracens invading from Spain. Although the hero is in some ways a rather brutal figure, nevertheless, there is a notable Christian dimension to why Roland lived and died: offering his life and death to God as a self-sacrifice through the fulfillment of knightly duty for the benefit of others. Another such chivalrous personality was the Castilian warrior, El Cid, hero of *The Poem of the Cid*, the oldest preserved Castilian epic poem, set during the eleventh-century struggles with the Moors. The author was possibly a monk, Abbot Peter, who composed it sometime between 1195 and 1207.[25]

The Knight's Vision of Christ

Chivalry's vision of warriorhood penetrated the hearts of many of Europe's knights. Indeed it even roused some of them to lifelong heroism whereby they renounced all that men hold dear—marriage, family, independence, and fortune— to go and dwell in monastic fortresses, sallying forth to fight, and often die, amid desert sands in the Middle East for the defense of the Holy Land. For these knights, and for many others, a vital element of chivalry's ability to arouse self-sacrifice lay in its vision of Jesus Christ as the supreme hero and ideal warrior.

Burlison and Grylls, *The Vision of Sir Galahad*. The knight and horse are depicted after the painting by G. F. Watts. South nave of St. Saviour Church, Shotton Colliery, Durham, England.

---

[24] Daniel-Rops, *Cathedral and Crusade*, p. 284.
[25] Barber, *Reign of Chivalry*, pp. 45–94.

The literary and artistic origins of the chivalric Christ lie in the Dark Ages. As far back as the eighth century men had begun to depict in sermon, poem, and painting the image of Jesus Christ-Hero. In the stirring eighth-century Anglo-Saxon poem *The Dream of the Rood [Cross]*, the author (possibly Cynewulf, a priest of Lindisfarne, the abbey founded by Saint Aidan) portrayed Jesus Christ not as a victim who suffered passively but as a warrior, in full control of self and fate, who resolved to set out on the quest to save mankind. He, and not his enemies, chose the site of combat: "The young warrior stripped himself—he, God Almighty—strong and stout-minded; he mounted high gallows, bold before the throng, resolved to loose man's bonds."[26] This depiction of Christ as warrior became a typical literary figure during the medieval period. It can be seen in the fourteenth-century poem *The Vision of Piers Plowman*, where Christ is portrayed as a famous and redoubtable knight who rides to a tournament in disguise so that his enemies may not recognize him and decline to enter into contest. The Divine Knight, clad in armor, is portrayed with all the chivalric virtues; on the Cross of Calvary he jousts against his mortal enemy, Satan, in a conflict in which the stakes are nothing less than the fate of humanity. Another French medieval poem entitled "How God's Son Was Armed on the Cross" has the opening line characteristic of medieval chivalric romances, "Hear now, lords, about great chivalry." One written by the knight Geoffroi de la Tour Landry (ca. 1330–ca. 1404), is full of a soldier's poignant admiration for the Crucified Savior:

Byzantine mosaics, Archbishop's Palace, Ravenna. Painting of Christ as a warrior-emperor who dominates over a lion and a serpent, the symbols of power and evil, while holding in hand his weapons: the Cross and the Book of the Gospels, the latter displaying the words "I am the Way, the Truth, and the Life". The scene refers to Psalm 90:13: "You shall tread on the lion and the adder; the young lion and the serpent you will trample under foot."

> And thus for compassion and nobility the gentle knight fought and suffered five mortal wounds, as the sweet Jesus Christ did, who fought out of pity for us and all humanity. He had great compassion lest they fall into the shadows of Hell. Thus he alone suffered and fought the terribly hard and cruel battle on the tree of Holy Cross. His shirt of mail was broken and pierced in five places, namely his five grievous wounds received of his free will in his sweet body for pity of us and all humanity.[27]

This was the vision of Jesus Christ that resonated in the imaginations of medieval knights. By observing the God-Man from this angle, knights discovered a masculine

[26] See Michael James Swanton, *The Dream of the Rood* (Manchester: University of Manchester Press, 1970); also, J. A. W. Bennett, *Poetry of the Passion* (Oxford: Clarendon, 1982), p. 29.

[27] Quoted in Richard W. Kaeuper, *Holy Warriors: The Religious Ideology of Chivalry* (Philadelphia: University of Pennsylvania Press, 2009), p. 129.

heroism that made it possible for them to identify with him as warriors. Indeed, in the Divine Person who "for us men and for our salvation" (Nicene Creed) had stripped himself of the vestures of glory in order to be born in Bethlehem as a man "as we are, yet without sin" (Heb 4:15), they saw the peerless paragon of the hero. Heroism followed heroism in a life of generosity in which the God-Man unleashed his energies during long hours of prayer, endurance of temptations amid the desert, and fatiguing journeys along the roads of Israel. Surrounded by suspicious enemies and misunderstanding disciples, he took the road to Jerusalem knowing full well what awaited him. Rejecting all compromise, resolving in the darkness of Gethsemane to drink the bitter cup to the dregs, at the height of his manhood he seized the Cross as a knight would seize his sword and poured out his last drop of blood doing battle with the Prince of Darkness on the hill overlooking the world. *No deeper suffering! No greater heroism! No more glorious role model!*

Gazing on this image of the courageous Christ, men became aware that before riding to the theatre of war manhood demanded self-combat through struggle against sin—that in a fallen universe loyalty to Christ and eternal salvation implied unavoidable spiritual warfare, battling relentlessly and without giving an inch of ground against the triple enemy—the corruption of the world, the Prince of Darkness, and the gravitational pull toward egotism within the essentially good but warped human heart. They also came to view the risking of their own bodies in just warfare as their particular way of following Christ. A chronicler wrote of the courageous Louis IX that "as our Lord died for the love he bore His people, even so King Louis put his own body into adventure ... for the very same reason."[28]

Among the loftiest of chivalrous knights this was the inspiring vision. The official title of the Templars said it all: "Poor Fellow-Soldiers of Christ and of the Temple of Solomon". It was a spirit they had received from the Church through some of the men whose mission it was to teach, sanctify, and govern: the priests. Those priests who embodied the vision in their own lives were the most effective teachers. Among them, the one who brought chivalry to the peaks of idealism was the man who has been called "the conscience of the twelfth century": Bernard of Clairvaux (1090–1153).[29]

Idealist of Chivalry: Bernard of Clairvaux

The Man behind the Statutes of the Templars

Saint Bernard was born in 1090, the third in a family of seven children, six of whom were male. His parents were Tescelin, lord of Fontaines, and Aleth of Montbard, both from aristocratic families. His native land was Burgundy, a region in eastern France with fair hills whose slopes vaunt fine vineyards and from whose crests one can see far-off Alpine peaks. But it was also the soil on which the monastic capitals of two spiritual empires had arisen, both important for the course of Western civilization: Luxeuil founded around 587 by Columbanus, and Cluny by the reforming Benedictines in 910. The vigor of these priests whose ardor for Christ had led them to personal austerity and courageous efforts to reform the Church braced the air

[28] Daniel-Rops, *Cathedral and Crusade*, p. 372.
[29] Ibid., p. 98.

that Bernard inhaled as a child and youth.

Anyone who ever met Bernard never forgot him. Extraordinary purity of soul shone from his face; he had deep blue eyes, a broad forehead, fair hair, and an auburn beard; a natural dignity hung easily around the medium to tall, thin figure. From his youngest years he showed undaunted courage, impulsiveness, gentleness, sensitivity, and warm-heartedness combined with a certain reserve. Crowning these qualities was an ardor for God and the things of God that led him even as a teenager to seek solitude.

In his twenty-third year, this passionate youth resolved how he

Emile Signol, *St. Bernard Preaching the Second Crusade in Vézelay*, March 31, 1146 (1840). The voice that set Western Europe marching.

would live his life for God and went to knock at the door of Cîteaux, the abbey amid wild swamplands with a well-deserved reputation for severity. One can only imagine that day in 1113 when the astonished abbot, Stephen Harding, saw on his doorstep not only the third son of the lord of Fontaines but some thirty other outstanding young men from the wealthy and powerful elite of Burgundian society. Every one of Bernard's brothers, except Nivard, who was under the canonical age for admission, stood alongside their twenty-three-year-old leader. The knights exchanged the shining coats of mail or aristocratic clothing for the sober, knee-length, white tunic of wool, with its hood to shield the shaven head from rain and sun. Later, the fifteen-year-old Nivard, in spite of being the heir to both the family fortune and the title of lord of Fontaines, also resolved to travel heavenward through the narrow doorway of Cîteaux alongside his brothers.

Bernard, raised to the priesthood four years later, continued to be a magnet, drawing talented youth in their hundreds to the monasteries that one after the other he began founding. No one was safe from his spell: the school at Châlons-en-Champagne half-emptied, a group of knights on their way to a tournament stopped for a visit and remained for life, Englishmen crossed the Channel to enter; Henry, brother of the king of France, and Alexander, a canon of Cologne, donned the white robes—all came, whether singly or in clusters. By the year of his death, there were 700 monks at Clairvaux and 160 offshoot monasteries from Ireland to Hungary and from Scandinavia to Spain, all of which would grow exponentially over the years. By the seventeenth century there would be 10,000 Cistercian houses, 4,000 male and 6,000 female. Wherever he appeared, men fell under his enchantment before ever he uttered a word; his pale face "thin through austerity and fasting, gave him an otherworldly appearance, so impressive that the mere sight of the man convinces his listeners".[30] His eloquence, the result of a penetrating intellect, linguistic precision,

---

[30] From a letter written in 1149 by Abbot Wibald of Stavelot, Epistola 147, quoted in ibid., p. 97.

Georg Andreas Wasshuber, *Saint Bernard*, 1700. Based on a statue with a lifelike resemblance located at Clairvaux. Painting at Heiligenkreuz Abbey, Austria.

a classical education, prolonged practice, and ever appropriate gestures moved popes, kings, and crowds.

He was also an incisive writer on topics from art and architecture to politics, all of which he viewed in relation to the axis of his existence: Jesus Christ and the quest to unite men with him through the Church. His love for "Our Lady" was that of a knight, ardently devoted to the woman to whom he had vowed himself.[31] He lived the words he had written about her: "She never leaves your lips, she never departs from your heart ... never forget the example of her life. If you follow her, you cannot falter; if you pray to her, you cannot despair; if you think of her, you cannot err."[32] Transparent was his love for people, whether he was feeding the poor who came to Clairvaux or speaking with the king and nobles in Paris. Or, indeed, when he encountered injustice against the Jewish people. When a group of bigoted nobles and a wretched monk named Rudolph started to persecute them in Strasbourg, Mainz, Worms, Spire, and Cologne, Bernard, sick with fever, rose from his bed, rushed to the Rhineland, arrived in time to prevent the massacre, and had the monk confined to a monastery.

The white-robed monk became the conscience of both Church and state in the twelfth century. Indeed he became the uncrowned ruler of Western Europe, mediating between monarchs and nations, deciding the outcome of episcopal nominations and even a disputed papal election. When the honor of God was in danger, Bernard either took to the roads of Europe, preaching and counseling, or else wrote letters to kings and bishops. No one, no matter how powerful, was safe from Bernard's arrows and bull's-eye precision. To one of the leading French aristocrats, Thibault II, count of Champagne, went a sharp condemnation and a demand that he make reparation to the children of a man whom he had sent to trial by tournament, whose eyes he had gouged out, and whose goods he seized. The kings of France, Louis VI and Louis VII, also received guidance and censure, the former being called "a second Herod"! Nor were ecclesiastics immune. The man whom Abbot Peter of Cluny called the "candid and terrible friend" penned words that must have seared the soul of more than one prelate:

> Why do you get yourselves up like women, if you do not wish to be criticized like women? Be known for your works, not for your fur capes and embroideries! You think to shut my mouth by observing that a monk should not criticize a bishop? Would to heaven you might shut mine eyes also! But were I to remain silent, others would speak—the poor, the naked, and the starving. They would rise up and cry: "Your luxury devours our lives! Your vanity steals our necessities!"[33]

---

[31] For an integral presentation of Bernard's spirituality see Etienne Gilson, *The Mystical Theology of St. Bernard* (Kalamazoo, Mich.: Cistercian Publications, 1989).

[32] *Hom. 2 super Missus est*, 17 (PL 183:70–71), quoted in Benedict XVI, *Great Christian Thinkers: From the Early Church Through the Middle Ages* (Minneapolis, Minn.: Fortress Press, 2011), p. 216.

[33] Quoted in Daniel-Rops, *Cathedral and Crusade*, p. 104.

The powerful of Europe tried to dodge these arrows from the high plateau of Clairvaux, but, when pierced, they often changed their ways. For many of the elite were of the same mind as the masses about the white-robed monk—here was a superior man in intellect, heart, and selflessness. Everyone knew that the Burgundian aristocrat had turned his back on a life of ease to enter that infamous monastery amid the marshes—that at the start of his own foundation in Clairvaux he had lived on a diet of a stew of beech leaves, rough barley bread, nettle-leaves, and roots seasoned by salt and oil to make them digestible. In fact, as Bernard himself recognized, he had gone too far and had ruined his health: he remained an invalid for the rest of his life, with a stomach in such horrible condition that he frequently took liquids since he was unable to hold down solid food.

But was there ever so much accomplished by such frailty? The white-uniformed figure, fasting and praying, serene and inspiring serenity, journeyed for the sake of the Church from the hills of Burgundy to Sicily, Flanders, the Rhineland, even crossing the Alps on horseback during winter. Moreover, he was the most gracious, kind, and affectionate of men. Although Pope Eugene III, one of Bernard's own monks, received some strong reprimands from his pen and was told to clear out the "robbers' cave" of the Roman Curia, filled with men who "will sacrifice the people's salvation for the

gold of Spain", the same long letter, *De Consideratione*, also contained the tender words: "What matter that you have been raised to the Chair of Peter? Even should you walk on the wings of the wind, you could not cut yourself off from my affection; even though you wear the tiara, love recognizes a son."[34] Likewise, his praise for dedicated Christians such as the Irish bishop Malachy, whose friendship he treasured, was boundless.[35]

He was the idol of his age. The students of Paris cheered and cheered when he came to their city; in Milan the enthusiastic crowds almost crushed him to death; and in Metz they had to put him on a boat on the Moselle for safety. And yet he never lost something of that charming shyness of his youth. For Christ he asked everything; for himself nothing, refusing titles, bishoprics, and even the papal tiara. It is impossible not to be moved deeply at the sight of such a man who simply

St. Bernard of Clairvaux Venerates "Our Lady". Stained glass window in the parish church of Saint-Michel in Malaucène.

gave all to God. This was the priest in whom "contemporaries recognized beneath the Cistercian habit the invisible armor of a knight".[36] It was to him that his contemporaries assigned the writing of the statutes for the most influential of the military orders of chivalry: the Templars.

---

[34] Quoted in Henri Daniel-Rops, *Bernard of Clairvaux* (New York: Hawthorn, 1964), p. 71.
[35] See St. Bernard's *Life of St. Malachy of Armagh*.
[36] Daniel-Rops, *Cathedral and Crusade*, p. 110.

Background to the Templars: The Crusades

In 1093, a scion of the reforming movement of Cluny, Pope Urban II, convoked the Council of Clermont, where he delivered the momentous speech that launched the Crusades. Although there are differences between the five versions of the address recorded by people who were actually present, they all agree that Urban had three main points: firstly, the need for Europe's knights to put an end to violence among themselves, do penance for their sins, and promote the *Pax Dei* that the Church had been urging for over a century; secondly, there was the account of the horrifying atrocities committed against resident Christians and pilgrims after the Muslim conquest and occupation of Palestine around 1071; thirdly, the proposal of a military expedition in order to protect the persecuted, stressing, however, that no one should sign up for the crusade unless he had the highest of motives.

The history of Christians in the Middle East had been tumultuous for centuries. In 614 the Persians had invaded Palestine and had captured Jerusalem: churches and homes were set ablaze, indiscriminate massacres occurred, sixty thousand Christians perished, thirty-five thousand more were sold into slavery, and the city and countryside were devastated. The year 638 saw Islamic armies under Caliph Omar seize the Holy Land. In return for submitting to the conditions for tolerance laid down by Islamic law—payment of a special tax, no acceptance of any Muslim wishing to convert, no carrying of arms or riding on horseback—Christians were able to live peacefully under the new rulers. Until 1009. Then the caliph of Egypt, Al-Hakim, began an anti-Christian persecution: crosses were burned, many churches were pillaged or destroyed, Christians were forced to wear distinctive clothing, and freedom of movement was restricted. The dramatic climax of the harassment was the destruction of the Church of the Holy Sepulchre. Although Muslim tolerance for resident Christians returned after Al-Hakim's death in 1021, his successor only allowed the Byzantine Christians to begin rebuilding the Holy Sepulchre in 1036 when they agreed to pay a large sum of money. In addition, pilgrims were still not protected and continued to suffer robberies and beatings from bandits on their way to Jerusalem.

Furthermore, Islam, through the armies of the Seljuk Turks, was expanding at a pace that sent shivers down the spines of the Byzantines. Around 1071, the Seljuks seized control of most of the area of modern Turkey excluding the coastlands—they were now closing in on the Byzantine capital of Constantinople. The worried Emperor Alexios sent ambassadors to Pope Urban II asking for military help to defend the Christian East.

All this news combined to trigger passionate feelings in Europe where memories were still haunted by the eighth-century Islamic invasion which had penetrated as far north as Poitiers in central France. Such was the background as Urban spoke to the leaders of France in Clermont. Hence, the Crusades were legitimate in the original papal purpose: to protect the rights of harassed Christian residents and pilgrims, and to come to the aid of nations in the East suffering from Muslim military aggression. However, in the same breath one has to declare that the horrible and brutal atrocities that afterward some of the Crusaders committed are utterly to be condemned. In the midst of the confused mess of idealism and sordid politics that followed, many bishops and priests urged knights to fight for this just cause in a just manner. They succeeded with some; they certainly lost with others. Nevertheless, it must be said that although thugs sailed to the Holy Land, the vast majority of men on board the ships were there for chivalrous reasons. The fact that during the heat of war some of them wretchedly betrayed their ideal does not allow us to betray truth and deny their original intentions. Many made a deep sacrifice by leaving behind wife and children; frequently they sold off valuables and land to finance their expedition; and when it was all over they returned home, usually none the richer, to try once more to build up family and livelihood.

Indeed, there were men in their midst who lived such a high ideal of justice that their Islamic opponents highly respected them. Such was the case of Louis IX, the site of whose tomb (where lie some of his entrails) at Sidi-bou-Saïd, near Tunis, is venerated by Muslims. Of similar caliber was the king of Jerusalem, Baldwin III, for whom the Muslim population of Jerusalem spontaneously showed massive grief at the news of his death.

Foundation, Development, and Influence of the Templars

After the Crusaders had captured Jerusalem in 1099, the numbers of pilgrims travelling to the Holy Land increased. Once they managed to get inside the gates of Jerusalem they were safe, but between the port of Jaffa and the city walls they were likely to be robbed and sometimes even massacred. To protect them, seven knights led by Hugues de Payens and his relative Godfrey de Saint-Omer formed a brotherhood around 1119. King Baldwin II of Jerusalem gave them a residence on the site of the ancient Temple of Solomon, whence originated their group's name, which was popularly abbreviated to "Templars". In 1148 Hugh travelled to the Council of Troyes to get the Church's approval for his foundation

St. Bernard Giving the Templars Their Statutes, French School, 19th century.

and to recruit new members. Bernard de Clairvaux was present and was asked by the bishops to compose the Templar statutes.[37]

The man who knew only one passion—to imbue men and society with the spirit of Christ—instilled the Knights of the Temple, and the other military orders influenced by them, with the fire that burned within his own soul. He already understood chivalry, not only because he had been raised in one of the chivalric Burgundian families and was the nephew of André de Montbard, one of the co-founders of the Templars, but also because he lived the essence of its spirit as a priest and monk. Warriors respected Bernard de Clairvaux to such an extent that after the Second Crusade (a debacle partly because the incompetent leaders had not listened to Bernard's

---

[37]See Régine Pernoud, *The Templars: Knights of Christ* (San Francisco: Ignatius Press, 2009), pp. 11–19.

counsels), the prime minister of France, Abbot Suger, did not hesitate to ask him to become commander-in-chief of a new army.

As Abbot Suger did with Gothic architecture, Bernard did with chivalry. He coalesced all the elements that had been in the making for centuries and on the anvil of his own ardent Christian soul forged them into the ideal of the Christian knight consecrated to God in the very depths of his manhood. This was the ideal he inserted into the statutes of the Templars. Through these statutes and his book on Templar chivalry, *In Praise of the New Knighthood*, Bernard placed the final seal of the Christian spirit on the knight's armor. Chivalry with its virtues, notably supernatural love inspiriting heroic courage and chastity, resounded through the lives of so many of these warriors. Their own age certainly knew that. And so did writers of succeeding centuries who portrayed chivalric heroes in the mould of the Templar ideal.

For instance, in the literary cycle of the Holy Grail, the perfect knight was Sir Galahad, who exemplified the qualities of valor and purity characteristic of the Templars. Indeed, Galahad, who carried a Templar-like white shield bearing a vermilion cross, was the embodiment of purity, living a heroically noble existence like Jesus Christ and therefore on spiritual heights far above those of the other knights of King Arthur's Round Table. That is why he alone could find the Holy Grail (the chalice used by Christ on Holy Thursday). Such is the portrait painted in Sir Thomas Malory's *Le Morte d'Arthur*: "Then Sir Galahad ... began to break spears marvellously, that all men had wonder of him; for he there surmounted [vanquished] all other knights, for within a while he had defouled [unhorsed] many good knights of the Table Round save twain, that was Sir Launcelot and Sir Percivale."[38] Elsewhere, one of the characters who encounters Galahad states: "Galahad, the servant of Jesus Christ, whose coming I have abiden [awaited] so long ... for thou art a clean virgin above all knights, as the flower of the lily in whom virginity is signified, and thou art the rose which is the flower of all good virtues and in colour of fire. For the fire of the Holy Ghost is taken so in thee."[39] Alfred Lord Tennyson's *Idylls of the King* describes Galahad as: "One there was among us ... in white armour, Galahad. 'God make thee good as thou art beautiful,' said [King] Arthur, when he dubbed him knight; and none, in so young youth, was ever made a knight till Galahad."[40] In "Sir Galahad" Tennyson depicts the knight single-mindedly pursuing a lonely route, sacrificing so much that is precious in his resolve to reach the goal of his quest:

> My good blade carves the casques of men, / My tough lance thrusteth sure, / My strength is as the strength of ten, / Because my heart is pure ... / How sweet are looks that ladies bend / On whom their favours fall! / For them I battle till the end, / To save from shame and thrall: / But all my heart is drawn above, / My knees are bow'd in crypt and shrine: / I never felt the kiss of love, / Nor maiden's hand in mine. / More bounteous aspects on me beam, / Me mightier transports move and thrill; / So keep I fair through faith and prayer / A virgin heart in work and will ... / Then move the trees, the copses nod, / Wings flutter, voices hover clear: / "O just and faithful knight of God! / Ride

[38] Sir Thomas Malory, *Le Morte d'Arthur: King Arthur and of His Noble Knights of the Round Table*, vol. 2, bk. 13 (Boston, Mass.: Digireads.com Publishing, 2009), p. 383.

[39] Ibid., bk. 17, p. 441.

[40] Alfred Lord Tennyson, *Idylls of the King* (Mineola, N.Y.: Dover, 2004), p. 176.

Arthur Hughes, *The Knight Galahad on the Quest for the Holy Grail*, 1870.

on! the prize is near." / So pass I hostel, hall, and grange; / By bridge and ford, by park and pale, / All-arm'd I ride, whate'er betide, / Until I find the holy Grail.[41]

Bernard's statutes and his book *In Praise of the New Knighthood* left no doubt in anyone's mind about the level of idealism required to enter the Templars. Their uniform was to be the white habit of the Cistercians to which was added a red cross, symbol of the martyrdom the members were willing to undergo. In their rite of initiation, the superior told the candidate that he must not ask for admission to the Templar ranks for either "power or wealth, bodily ease, honor, or recognition" but only to "leave behind the sins of this world … to be at the service of Our Lord … to be poor and do penitence" for the sake of eternal salvation.[42]

The youth who entered the Templar knighthood turned his back on what youth in any age cherish. Through the vow of chastity he surrendered his body and heart exclusively to the love of Jesus Christ. By committing himself to poverty (symbolized by the image on the Templar seal of two knights on a horse), he owned nothing of any worth as an individual even if the order itself could—and did—become corporately wealthy. By obedience he gave free entrance to those who morally exercised authority in the stronghold of any man—his will. The Templars also took a vow of piety: to visit their fortresses was to see a monastic army barracks with a Cistercian-style chapel, refectory, and dormitory. Knights had their meals together in silence. They ate meat three times a week at most, and fasted not only on Fridays, the eve of feast days, and during Lent, but also in Advent from the Feast of Saint Martin of Tours to Christmas. They left behind them a medieval nobleman's favorite pastime, hunting, although with one exception—lions![43]

[41] Alfred Tennyson, "Sir Galahad", in *The Works of Alfred Lord Tennyson* (Ware, Hertfordshire: Wordsworth Editions, 1998), pp. 196–98.

[42] Quoted in Pernoud, *Templars: Knights of Christ*, p. 36.

[43] See ibid., pp. 19–44.

By this bonding to heroic Christian standards through lifelong consecration to God, warriors began to live an exceptionally disciplined lifestyle, one that would have astounded the ancient Romans, Greeks, and barbarians. They also became cosmopolitan, severing national allegiances in order to be at the service of Christendom, pledging themselves not only to the defense of the Holy Land but also to the care of any poor and defenseless Christian who came across their path. A contemporary chronicler, Jacques de Vitry, remarked that to see Templars was to see extraordinary men who were "in turn lions of war and lambs at the hearth; rough knights on the battlefield, pious monks in the chapel; formidable to the enemies of Christ, gentleness itself toward His friends".[44]

The Knights of the Temple were renowned as men both highly trained and *sans peur et sans reproche* (fearless and blameless). As the very models of chivalry they became the dream of European youth. Undeterred by the daunting lifestyle, idealistic young men began banging on the doors of Templar castles asking to join. Rapidly they grew in numbers to some fifteen thousand members at their zenith, of whom 10 percent were knights. Swiftly they built a network of monasteries, local headquarters known as preceptories, and over eight hundred castles crowned by the magnificent fortresses of Safed, Karak of the Desert, Castle Pilgrim, Tortosa, and Beaufort spanning the Middle East and Europe. They also developed their own fleet of ships and for some time owned the entire island of Cyprus.

In action, like all knights, they wore coats of mail and were armed with a heavy sword, lance, cutlass, and mace. First to charge in battle, they were the ones to whom fell the task of breaking the enemy lines. They vowed to hold their ground and never to retreat unless all the flags had fallen. One of their most important military feats was at the Battle of Montgisard in 1177, when 475 Templars in an outnumbered force led by the sixteen-year-old King Baldwin IV played the key role in defeating Saladin's army. In only two centuries the colossal number of twenty thousand Templars, both knights and sergeants, died in war. If defeated and captured, all bridges behind them had already been burned, for they had previously determined not to allow themselves to be ransomed. Time and again when imprisoned they contemptuously refused to apostatize in return for the Muslim offer of freedom.

No one denies that over time the Templars declined from their first fervor and that, like most organizations in similar conditions, they became somewhat fossilized by wealth and lack of renewal. Institutional pride bloated and rivalry with the Hospitallers damaged their mission. The massive numbers of casualties in war during the first 130 years probably led to lower standards in recruitment: always a time bomb in any institution. However, between this lessening of virtue and what they were accused of by their enemies—structural and widespread corruption—there is an abyss. And if failures of individual members are enough to justify the destruction of an institution, what institution, I ask you, can be left standing?

When the instigator of the Templars' suppression, Philip IV, became king of France in 1285, he entered into conflict with the papacy, partly, it must be said, because of unwise decisions by Pope Boniface VIII. The dramatic climax of their struggle occurred on September 7, 1303, in the little castle of Anagni, where Boniface had

[44]Quoted in Charles Moeller, "The Knights Templars", *The Catholic Encyclopedia*, vol. 14 (New York: Robert Appleton, 1912), p. 493.

taken refuge from the French king's forces. In that pleasant Italian town occurred the never-to-be-forgotten outrage when the defenseless Pope, wearing the tiara and liturgical vestments, was struck on the face by a royal partisan. During this conflict, the Templars, under direct papal allegiance and holding castles on French soil, were eyed uneasily by Philip IV. Moreover, the king was almost bankrupt—and the Templar headquarters in Paris was supposedly filled with treasure. At least, that was what many thought or wished to think. However, it is more likely that the Paris Temple only held 150,000 gold pieces in its vaults, a rather paltry sum for any national government.

When Philip assaulted the Order of the Temple, the successor of Pope Boniface, the aged Clement V, in spite of failing health, at a certain moment vigorously protested and insisted on independent investigations. At the end of all these inquiries only investigators in areas under the direct or indirect control of Philip found the Templars guilty. Everywhere else—England, Scotland, Ireland, Aragon, Castile, and Germany—handed in verdicts of "innocent". All to no avail. The French king's pressure was unrelenting and finally Clement V suppressed the order. But not before he had declared in a document known as the "Chinon Parchment", dated August 17–20, 1308, that he absolved the Templar leadership of the charges against them.[45] The Council of Vienne in December 1311 also concluded there was no evidence to justify a condemnation. To read the account of Philip's trial is to smell the stench of gutter justice, with legal proceedings pushed by greed, threats, lies, and torture. In Paris, on March 18, 1314, the elderly Grand Master of the Templars, Jacques de Molay, as he was about to be tied to the stake and burned alive, cried out with his last breath the innocence of the knights, and as the flames rose around the leader of those noble men, onlookers could see him facing the basilica of the Lady he venerated, his hands joined in prayer.

The influence of the Templars survived, for they became the model for new knighthoods as well as for the already existing orders that added a military purpose to their original mission.

An instance of the latter is the order of the Hospitallers (who continue today as the Sovereign Military Hospitaller Order of Saint John of Jerusalem, of Rhodes, and of Malta). Besides militarizing like the Templars, they also copied elements from their lifestyle such as praying the monastic Liturgy of the Hours. Their foundation arose out of a hospice, named in honor of Saint John the Baptist, founded around 1070 to care for sick pilgrims. At the time of the First Crusade (1095–1099) its head was one of those countless knights who lived chivalry to the hilt: Gerard. It is he whom the Knights Hospitaller regard as their founder. He and his dedicated companions lived a monastic lifestyle, probably modeled on the Rule of Saint Benedict; after the conquest of Jerusalem in 1099 they formed into a religious and military order.[46]

Sheer self-sacrifice is the only description that does justice to these Hospitallers. In Jerusalem, for instance, besides caring for the sick, they fed nearly two thousand poor people per day. Their mission statement was clear: a sick man was to be welcomed "like the master of the house". A story is told that after the Muslim leader

---

[45] Located in the Vatican Secret Archives; reference number Archivum Arcis Armarium D 218.
[46] See H. J. A. Sire, *The Knights of Malta* (New Haven, Conn.: Yale University Press, 1994).

Saladin had captured the city of Acre, he decided to visit the hospital of the order, disguised as a poor traveller, in order to verify the reputation of the knights. Once inside he was waited upon hand and foot but, to the dismay of the Hospitallers, he refused to eat. Finally, after much insisting, he told them he would eat nothing except some soup made from the foot of Morel, the magnificent warhorse of the Grand Master. Reluctantly and grieving, the conscientious leader nevertheless brought out his magnificent charger and prepared to kill him. But before he raised his sword, Saladin cried, "Halt!", revealed his identity, and departed, filled with admiration for the spirit of these Christian men.

An order closely connected to the Templars was the Order of Saint Lazarus, founded around 1100 in Jerusalem by crusaders suffering from leprosy who decided to give their lives caring for other lepers. They established the first hospital outside the walls of Jerusalem, and then founded other Lazar Houses throughout the Holy Land and Europe. By the end of the twelfth century they had also become a military order and had fought in battles such as the one at La Forbie in 1244, where all the Lazar Knights involved lost their lives.

The Order of the Holy Sepulchre traces its origins to Duke Godfrey de Bouillon, one of the principal leaders and most chivalrous knights of the First Crusade. The order received initial papal recognition from Paschal II around 1113. In 1122 Callixtus II issued the papal bull establishing them as a lay religious community with the mission of guarding the basilica of the Holy Sepulchre and the city of Jerusalem.

The Spanish and Portuguese military foundations—the Order of Aviz (1146), the Order of Alcántara (1156), the Order of Calatrava (1158), and the Order of Santiago (1164)—were modeled on the Templars and the Hospitallers. All of them, with the exception of the Order of Santiago, were connected to the Cistercians, the monastic order of Bernard of Clairvaux.

Chivalry's Finished Product: A King, a Hero, a Man—Louis IX

> Louis IX seemed a prince destined to reform Europe had it been capable of being reformed; to make France triumphant and civilized; and to be in every respect a model for mankind. His piety, which was that of a hermit, did not deprive him of any of the virtues of a king. A wise spending policy did not take away from generosity. He knew how to reconcile the deepest politics with the strictest justice and perhaps was the only sovereign who deserved this praise: in council he was wise and firm, in battle intrepid but not rash, and compassionate as if he had always been unfortunate. In a word, it is not in the power of man to carry virtue further.[47]

On June 4, 1249, the Thursday after the Feast of Pentecost, the sails of the ships carrying the crusader army could be seen approaching the Egyptian coast at Damietta. On the shores the Sultan's forces had gathered, their weapons glistening as they caught the sunlight. The following day, from the royal flagship, a man slightly built with clear blue eyes, "having the face of an angel",[48] fully armed, ignoring

---

[47]Voltaire, *Oeuvres de Voltaire: Essai sur les moeurs et l'esprit des nations*, vol. 17 (Paris, 1792), p. 270. My translation.

[48]The description of the thirty-four-year-old Louis by a contemporary, Salimbene; see Salimbene and Ferdinando Bernini, *Cronica* (Bari, Italy: Laterza, 1942), p. 317.

G. F. Watts, *Sir Galahad*, 1862 (oil on canvas). "[The Crusade] was led by a saintly hero, a veritable Sir Galahad, whose 'whole life was a prayer, his whole aim to do God's will'; a king whose high and noble character inspired universal trust and reverence; a leader whose courage and endurance rested on the sanctions of faith as well as on the obligations of knightly honor. The very loftiness and purity of his nature ..." (James Henry Breasted, *A History of Egypt from the Earliest Times to the Persian Conquest* [New York: Charles Scribner's Sons, 1909], pp. 231–32).

pleas from the papal legate and others that he should wait, jumped into the sea and, with the waters up to his armpits, began wading toward the shore. It was Louis IX, king of France, and he was determined to lead his soldiers into battle in person.

Louis IX, born in 1214, was king from 1226 until his crusader's death on the sands of Tunisia in 1270. Warrior second to none in courage, ruler of his country with self-less devotion, international statesman whose mediation was requested time and again as a man whose judgments were weighed before God and not men—he dominated the thirteenth century in the same way as Bernard of Clairvaux had dominated the twelfth. "A king, a hero, and a man";[49] in him we see fully embodied the virtues of chivalry that the Church had been sowing in the hearts of men for hundreds of years. He was a radiant figure, the very sight of whom restores our confidence that we fallen men can rise high above our wretched inclinations by opening ourselves to the power of supernatural grace.

We have a rather clear image of the king's personality from the documents of the canonization process, as well as from the account written by his friend de Joinville, a down-to-earth nobleman who was a sharp observer of human nature. Louis was not difficult to get to know. Frank and outgoing, he was a man who enjoyed conversation more than books, and was well able to make and take a joke; to all, both rich and poor, he showed respect but was never familiar. He was full of life and vitality—eleven children testify to that. Unlike many in his position, he was faithful to his queen, Margaret of Provence, in spite of the fact that he had little in common with the frivolous woman who caused him so much pain throughout the years. Nevertheless, no one could ever say that he had not lived up to the motto engraved on the inside of his wedding ring: *En cet annel, tout mon amour* (In this ring is all my love).

Nor did his love stop at the frontiers of his immediate family and friends. Like a powerful, steadily flowing river, his "orderly and virtuous compassion"[50] encircled

---

[49] The phrase is from Edward Gibbon, *The History of the Decline and Fall of the Roman Empire*, vol. 1 (London: J. Ogle Robinson, 1830), p. 1105.

[50] William of Saint-Pathus, a priest at the court of Louis IX, wrote a biography of the monarch, *Life and Miracles of St. Louis*.

the poor of France. That magnificent woman, his mother, Blanche de Castile, had taught him to travel in person to wherever his people suffered from bad harvests, epidemics, flooding, or any serious misfortune.[51] He did all that—and more. In 1246 he began campaigning to emancipate the serfs and led the way by liberating those in his own lands. Then, as a man who was never satisfied with half measures, he encouraged the aristocracy to follow his example, offering financial compensation whenever possible to those who hesitated for economic reasons.

He could turn up anywhere: in the fields of the countryside with the peasants, walking the streets of the cities to the delight of the townsfolk; and everywhere he saw pain there sprang up orphanages, hospices, and hospitals, often from his own purse. Personally he fed, clothed, visited, ransomed, and comforted the suffering. "Everywhere he listens in case anyone shouts to him, 'Help!'"[52] To a degree that became legendary he was hands-on, whether in the hospital at Compiègne where he looked after the worst cases, "oblivious of his defilement by pus oozing from lupus-sores"; or at his own table eating with "twenty poor folk whose filth and stench revolted the soldiers of his guard"; or heading directly toward a leper "whose distant rattle had attracted his attention and giving him a fraternal kiss".[53]

Men and women all over Europe envied Frenchmen during the reign of Louis because their country had become a land of high justice. In French taverns men spoke with respect of their king who, after attending the Holy Sacrifice of the Mass, went straight to the woods at Vincennes where, underneath an oak, he would hear the complaint of anyone, noble or serf. The wealthy of France were shocked when the powerful Baron de Coucy, for the mere "petty" crime of having hanged three boys who had poached on his land, was thrown into prison, forced to pay a massive fine, and sent on pilgrimage as expiation! Not even the king's brother, Charles of Anjou, was safe from the unbending sense of justice in Louis, as he found out to his cost.

Never did political correctness seem to be high on the list of the royal priorities. Guided only by justice, he could be as quick and adamant about saying no as yes, having made his own the guiding principle of his grandfather Philip Augustus: "No man can govern a country well if he is not able to refuse as boldly and bluntly as he is able to give". In 1260 the king angered many by abolishing knightly tournaments. He ordered judges to be scrupulously chosen and prohibited them from entering taverns or playing dice. To the capital as provost he sent Etienne Boileau, who made sure that "no evildoer, thief, or murderer dared to live in Paris.... Neither relationships nor lineage, neither gold nor silver were able to save him".[54] No wonder that the ordinary men and women loved their king and considered him to be a saint even during his lifetime.

Louis may have preferred conversation to books, but he was a friend of scholars. Under his reign Paris became Western Europe's apex of culture: his chaplain, Robert

[51] See Régine Pernoud, *Blanche of Castile* (New York: Coward, McCann and Geoghegan, 1975).

[52] "Il écoute partout si l'on crie, 'Au secours!'" Victor Hugo, *Eviradnus Ratbert: La Légende des Siècles* (Cambridge: Cambridge University Press, 1922), p. 3.

[53] Daniel-Rops, *Cathedral and Crusade*, p. 292. With regard to these anecdotes, the historian remarks they "are derived not from some 'Golden Legend', but from the most reliable histories". Ibid.

[54] Jean, Sire de Joinville, *Histoire de Saint Louis; Credo; et Lettre à Louis X* (Paris: Librairie de Firmin, 1874), p. 391. My translation.

de Sorbon, founded the famous college; students filled Mont Sainte-Geneviève; and that ethereal masterpiece of beauty, the Sainte-Chapelle, arose from the prayer of the man who went daily on his knees.

Although impetuous by temperament, he forged the self-restraint and thought-fulness characteristic of a wise statesman. He was wise but not street-smart, for it was justice not personal gain that guided him, and with virile fury the normally serene monarch silenced anyone who counseled Machiavellian tactics. His fellow European rulers were left open-mouthed at some of his policies. For instance, his dealings with England appeared to many at the time to go against the interests of France, yet Louis would have it no other way and in the end it was a "win-win" situation for both countries. No isolationism for this French king: when those around him counseled staying on the sideline while nations cut each others' throats, those blue eyes of his became the color of steel as he told them that to do so would be to "earn the hatred of God".[55] As international mediator and judge he ignored even the aspirations of his own brother Charles and his future son-in-law Thibaut. In the end, all of Western Europe benefited for he became a one-man European court of justice.

The grandeur of this monarch is explained by the form that his signature took in private correspondence: "Louis de Poissy". The preferred title of the wealthiest and most powerful king in Europe was that of the village of his baptism. For his union with God through sanctifying grace had meant everything to him from boyhood. This he owed largely to his mother, Blanche de Castile, a woman of many qualities who had acted as regent of France after the death of her husband until Louis came of age to be crowned. In a matter-of-fact manner she would sometimes remind her favorite son that, precisely because she loved him so deeply, she would prefer to see him dead at her feet rather than to hear he had committed a mortal sin.

This message was taken to heart, as de Joinville, Seneschal of Champagne, recalling a conversation he had held with Louis, narrated in his memoirs:

> On one occasion he called me ... "Which would you prefer—either to be a leper or to have committed a mortal sin?" And I, who never lied to him, answered that I would prefer to have committed thirty mortal sins than be a leper. After the friars had departed he called me to speak with him when he was alone, made me sit at his feet, and said: "Why did you say that yesterday?" I told him that I would answer in the same way again. "You spoke hastily like a fool," he said. "You should realize that there is no leprosy as hideous as being in mortal sin since the soul that is in mortal sin is like Satan—for that reason no leprosy can be so horrible. And it is important to recognize that when a man dies he is healed of the body's leprosy, but when a man who has committed a mortal sin dies, he cannot be certain that he had [lived] such repentance during his lifetime as to ensure God's forgiveness. That's why he must stand in great fear lest that leprosy of sin should last as long as God is in Paradise. So I implore you," he said, "as strongly as I can, for the love of God and for love of me, to resolve in your heart to prefer any evil that can happen to the body, whether it be leprosy or any other sickness, rather than allow mortal sins to enter into your soul."[56]

---

[55] Ibid., p. 377. My translation.

[56] Jehans de Joinville, *Livre des saintes paroles et des bons faiz nostre roy saint Looys*, chap. 4, quoted in Karl Bartsch, *La langue et la littérature françaises depuis le IXème siècle jusqu'au XIVème siècle* (Paris: Maisonneuve and C. Leclerc, 1887), p. 33. My translation.

From this bottom line his spirit soared to what showed all the signs of mystical heights of prayer. He certainly lived the Christian life with a generosity character-istic of mystics. Daily he recited the Liturgy of the Hours and read the Bible and the Fathers of the Church. He was enthusiastic about listening to quality sermons and took pleasure in reciting some of them to others. Every morning he attended the Holy Sacrifice of the Mass and gave orders that he was not to be interrupted unless for grave reasons. Six times a year he received Holy Communion, somewhat exceptional for that epoch. His personal prayers at nighttime were lengthy—to the annoyance of his bodyguards waiting outside the chapel—and indeed at times he simply lost track of time and place, finally rising from his knees asking, "Where am I?" Every Friday he went to confession. He fasted, wore a hair shirt underneath his garments, ate what was necessary and no more, and, in spite of his wife's complaints, insisted on dressing plainly. Spontaneously, often to the disconcertment of those concerned whether Christian, Jew, or Muslim, he spoke of the Catholic Faith as a man in love speaks of what most interests him.

He was the complete man, the vibrant Christian, the red-blooded warrior, the just ruler, the knight of uprightness and compassion, and esteemed even by his mil-itary enemies, the Muslims, who captured him during the crusade. For centuries, he fired the imagination of writers as they sought to depict the ideal knight, "fearless and faultless". Whatever weaknesses he had, such as his quick temper, he sought to control. Indeed, so great was his personal serenity that it rippled outward through the joyful, family-like atmosphere of the royal court into the cities and countryside of France, creating a land of true peace, *tranquillitas ordinis* (the harmony of order).

The most powerful monarch of Europe even toyed with the idea of setting aside his crown and joining either the Cistercians or the Franciscans, the two orders he most admired. Margaret, however, decisively put a stop to that idea, and Louis had to content himself with becoming a Franciscan tertiary. Nevertheless, his chivalrous spirit was molded by both Francis of Assisi and Bernard of Clairvaux: by Francis, the romantic troubadour who had learned that "the secret of recovering the natural pleasures lay in regarding them in the light of a supernatural pleasure",[57] for whom religion was a love affair, and who frequently called his followers either "troubadours of God" or "knights of the Round Table"; and by Bernard, who also incorporated romanticism into Christian prayer and brought warriorhood to the peaks of idealism.

Ever Relevant: "The Living Symbol of Force Subjected to the Spirit"

The Accolade portrays the spirit of medieval chivalry, the world vision at the heart of its idealism, that which makes it ever relevant.

Here all—utterly all—is mysteriously pure. This fragrance of purity, untainted by ambiguity or egotism, breathes from the overarching truths amid which every-one is living these moments. All are aware that for a few fleeting instants they are immersed in realities that transcend them. The ego is forgotten as mind and heart are enraptured. The young man being knighted is kneeling. He does not gaze on the beautiful lady before him. Nor does she regard him. The onlookers do not seem to

---

[57] G. K. Chesterton, *St. Francis of Assisi* (Mineola, N.Y.: Dover, 2012), p. 58.

be focused on either—a form of serene ecstasy, if you will, in which all are conscious that they are crossing the frontiers of time into eternity through the sacred words and gestures of the ritual of initiation to knighthood.

Edmund Blair Leighton (1853–1922), *The Accolade* (Knighting), 1901.

It is a moment when we catch a glimpse of the medieval spirit. Medieval man's mind was far-embracing, encompassing the natural and the supernatural. It was piercing because he was tirelessly curious about nature and God. It was precise and utterly rational as shown in the age's invention of the Scholastic method. Medieval man lived, so to speak, outside himself—in the open air amid field, stream, and mountain; under the sun, rain, and storms, never ceasing to marvel at the countless stars of the night sky. He stayed close to both his newborn infant and his dying parent. He raised his heart spontaneously in prayer. And so he knew that God was real, that life was flawed beauty, ever so lovely yet ever so fragile; and that immortality with unchanging happiness or despair was on the other side of the thin membrane of time. From the teenager to the old man, everyone present at the accolade was sensitive to the closeness of eternity. And they knew that, through the ceremony's sacramental ritual, supernatural light and strength of eternal depth pierced the soul of man.

For what else was knighthood but a warrior's initiation into an order designed to lead him toward a mystic relationship with God? What else but a code of conduct created to guide him on his quest for salvation? A quest that meant living in God's Presence, forging a Christlike nerve and sinew, whether in peacetime or in warfare. This was what made the chivalrous knight unique among the soldiers of history: the Church had baptized his sword, plunging it into the waters of Christian life, and drawing it forth again bathed in the Christlike virtues that revolutionized his warrior ideal. He heard from the Church the call to self-conquest before conquest, to "protect the weak, defenseless and helpless, and to fight for the general welfare of all"—unto heroism. This was the soul-subduing power without which horse soldiers would have remained merely an elitist military rank, like in so many other societies, men with free rein for their animal passions even if they uniformed them with etiquette. Here is the archetype of the soldier that has resonated in the hearts of Western men, never ceasing to fascinate unto emulation—an archetype that no other civilization has ever outdone; an ideal that the Church created in a struggle of centuries. This is the secret heart of chivalry, what makes it "the living symbol of force subjected to the Spirit",[58] a sure route along which masculinity is purified through the supernatural, prayer, and the cardinal virtues of wise judgment, mastery of the pleasure instinct, courage, and justice. This is why medieval chivalry has inspired Western civilization for a thousand years, alluring men as an ideal of masculinity, because it is something deep, strong, subtle, and mysterious.

[58] Daniel-Rops, *Cathedral and Crusade*, p. 112.

Even when the Catholic heartbeat of chivalry began to grow faint, the body with its trappings remained intact with its power to enchant the soul of man.[59] The chivalrous knight was still at least the platonic standard by which kings continued to judge the merits of individuals for entry to purely honorary orders of knighthood, such as the Order of the Garter (1348) and the Order of the Golden Fleece (1430), which were neither religious orders nor composed of soldiers. Even after the use of archery in battles such as Crécy (1346) and Agincourt (1415), along with the development of gunpowder and firearms, had rendered obsolete the military value of knights in warfare, there lingered in the Western mind the silhouette of the chivalrous knight. At the twilight hours of medieval Christendom, men could still be found who embodied its values, like Pierre Terrail de Bayard (1476–1524), the admiration of France, who died in battle at forty-eight, recognized as one of the great cavalry leaders of the century.

Within some of the leading religious orders the spirit of chivalry was highly influential in the original inspiration of the founder. Besides the Cistercians and the Franciscans, the Dominicans were founded by a priest who wanted his friars to be "champions of the faith". The sixteenth century saw the influence of chivalry embodied in the Basque knight Iñigo de Loyola (1491–1556), an influence that has resonated to every corner of the planet through the heroism of so many true Ignatians. Eighteenth-century European aristocrats sought to live up to the ghost of it with their leitmotif *noblesse oblige*; by it the nineteenth century established and measured its ideal of the gentleman. Modern times have seen fraternal associations surge from within the heartlands of Catholicism, vigorously reawakening the ideals of chivalry, such as the world's largest Catholic fraternal service organization, the Knights of Columbus, founded in the United States in 1882, and the Knights of Saint Columbanus in Ireland in 1915.

Literature has also kept alive the nostalgia: from Joinville's *Life of St. Louis* to the *Life of the Good Knight Bayard* written by an anonymous admirer, from Sir Thomas Malory's *Le Morte d'Arthur* and Chaucer's "The Knight's Tale" to Castiglione's *The Book of the Courtier* and Torquato Tasso's epic poem *Gerusalemme Liberata* (*Jerusalem Liberated*).[60] In early nineteenth-century England Sir Walter Scott revived the nostalgia with writings like *Ivanhoe*, opening men's eyes to an unknown medieval world.

One of those whose curiosity was sparked by Scott was Kenelm Henry Digby (1800–1880), the author of *The Broad Stone of Honour*.[61] Someone remarked that to read his book was to sense that the author "identifies himself as few have ever done with the good and great and heroic and holy in former times, and ever rejoices in passing out of himself into them". Indeed, Kenelm, raised a staunch Protestant, converted at twenty-five years of age to the Catholic Church largely because he had met her as he came to know chivalry during his studies at Cambridge University. Digby came to realize that the ethos of chivalry offered a way to help resolve a burning need of Charles Dickens' nineteenth-century, largely de-Christianized England with

[59] Barber, *Reign of Chivalry*, pp. 144–78.

[60] See the masterful translation and insightful notes in the English edition by Anthony Esolen, *Jerusalem Delivered* [*Gerusalemme Liberata*] (Baltimore: Johns Hopkins University Press, 2000).

[61] Kenelm Henry Digby (1797–1880), an Anglo-Irish writer, who in 1822 published *The Broad Stone of Honour*. For a few of the many treasures in *The Broad Stone of Honour*, see Kenelm Henry Digby, *Maxims of Christian Chivalry* (Montreal: Catholic Authors Press, 2003).

its lack of a vibrant Christian social ideal and a program of deep character formation for men. His work, *The Broad Stone of Honour*, certainly confirmed its author's intuition, for it influenced millions of youth, not only in England but worldwide, since among those who recognized the pedagogical value of its chivalric principles was Robert Baden-Powell, founder of the Scouting movement, who drew many of the Scout Laws from its pages.[62]

In our post-Western civilization we might well take another look at chivalry for several reasons.

The first is its clear portrait of masculine honor. In contrast to the blurred image of male maturity in our culture, chivalry displays a sharp profile with honor at the center, requiring a man to measure his manhood by his ability to stand his ground when pride or pleasure tempts him to dishonor his commitments. The chivalrous knight knew that there were pledges he had to keep in sickness and in health, for richer, for poorer—unto death. He knew that life was a battlefield; he prepared himself for the onslaught by self-conquest in peacetime; by going on his knees at dawn and in the twilight; and by confronting his failures, confessing them, and accepting the Church's penance without excuses. But many failed to live up to these standards on countless occasions, you say. Yes, you're right. But few ever denied the ideal. There lies the difference between then and now, a difference as great as between standing upon a rock and on a swamp. And let us not forget that many also did their damnedest to abide by the virtues of knighthood!

A second reason for attaching importance to chivalry at the beginning of the new millennium stems from the fact that the strength of the chivalric code of honor lay in its unbending defense of absolute right and wrong. Justice had to be done; evil had to be avoided *even if you were left standing on your own.* Nor was justice open to everyone's free interpretations based on "conscience"—something that in the twentieth century led to Gestapo officers thinking they were praiseworthy—but it was anchored in the unchanging precepts of the natural law interpreted by the guardian of that law, the Church. Chivalry's adherence to the natural law clashes in the modern world with the dominant legal philosophy under the dictatorship of relativism: positivism. Natural law is defined as the body of unchanging moral principles whose content is set by nature, thus forming the universally binding foundation for man's actions. Hence, any law of the state contradicting it is invalid. Positivism, however, states that laws are man-made, whether by legislature, judiciary, or political power, without any reference to nature but rather on the basis of political consensus. Practically, this implies that right and wrong are decided by the men—or man—with the power.

This was alien to the medieval knight. For he had learned from the Church to bend the knee only to authority, never to power, and only to authority because it was a faithful exercise of justice as determined by the Author of nature and the source of justice. Consequently, he saw any particular government as a mere holder of the scales of justice: if it tipped them toward evil, it served no purpose and should be replaced. In feudal times, the Church was as clear-minded about this as she had been in the age of the catacombs. The *Liber Feudorum*, a twelfth-century

---

[62] See Mark Girouard, *The Return to Camelot: Chivalry and the English Gentleman* (London: Yale University Press, 1981), pp. 56, 255–56.

Edmund Blair Leighton (1853–1921), *The Thanksgiving Service on the Field of Agincourt.*

collection of feudal customs that was widely recognized as governing the relations between lord and vassal, explicitly asserted that any vassal who refuses to side with his overlord in an unjust war may not be treated as a criminal. Popes, councils of bishops, and canon lawyers from Manegold of Lautenbach to Yves of Chartres, by defining concepts such as the unjust aggressor and the moral obligation to fight him, implicitly taught soldiers that chivalric honor must oppose injustice—even when it came from above.

This is the worldview that has made dictatorships always wary of convinced Catholics, realizing they could never quite depend on them. Down through the centuries Catholic chivalry split military officers into those who upheld its sense of justice and honor and those who adopted a mentality of soldiering for the sake of the state, giving blind obedience no matter what: "orders are orders, no matter who or where they come from".

It became evident in Nazi Germany. Some, like the regime's most decorated soldier, Colonel Hans von Luck, a tank commander, even years after the war had ended still offered no excuses and asked no forgiveness for serving the tyranny, considering it unimaginable to disobey. He and so many others had been raised with the Prussian military mentality of blind obedience to the state—for them defiance was simply out of the question.[63] By contrast, soldiers like the Catholic Colonel Claus von Stauffenberg, a descendant of knights in a seven-hundred-year-old aristocratic family, had been educated from boyhood to live by the principles of the natural law and chivalry. His university years brought him to fall in love with the concept of a "secret Germany", a nation to be created in the future inspired by Judaeo-Christian and chivalric

[63] Hans von Luck, *Panzer Commander: The Memoirs of Colonel Hans von Luck* (New York: Dell, 1991).

principles. As one of the leaders in the conspiracy to overthrow Hitler—codenamed "Operation Valkyrie"—he referred to the *Naturrecht* (natural law) as its justification. This was the source of his moral conviction, as he and his tiny band of conspirators stood almost alone, surrounded by a mentality of blind obedience to Hitler on account of the oath of loyalty to the dictator (*Reichswehreid*). For many German soldiers von Stauffenberg was a criminal since under German law he was committing high treason—to which he once defiantly retorted, "[I] am engaged in high treason with all the means available to me."[64] After the failure of the attempt, his last words, in the early morning of July 20, 1944, as he stood in front of the makeshift firing squad in a courtyard lit by the headlights of a truck, were "Long live our secret Germany!"[65]

Chivalry, therefore, armed the warrior to fight for peace. Peace, but not pacifism. The Catholic definition of peace, *tranquillitas ordinis* (the harmony of order), rejects pacifism as well as militarism since the former breeds war by allowing the unscrupulous and power-hungry to trample everyone on their way to the top. Hence, to educate youth in the spirit of chivalry is to build foundations for a just social order, guarantor of enduring peace. If—and here I confess that I am indulging in nostalgia tinged with bitterness—Europe were to have guarded this ethos, barbarism would have had less opportunity to raise its monstrous head in places like the Western Front from 1914 to 1918, with its poisoned gas, trench warfare, and millions of youth dead—all for the sake of *nothing*, all because of senseless, bloated individual and national egos! However, in a world of flawed men, where barbarism lies just below the surface in each of us in one form or another, we must not allow the soul to surrender to such emotions, for they would numb us into world-weary inactivity. We must realize that history is an unending battlefield; that institutions have to be renewed time and time again; that we must always be grateful for the partial victories gained—for the radiant spring that soon fades into autumn and winter.

Hence, we salute countless knights who sought to live the ideal. And we also raise our glasses to all those priests who created and developed chivalry. We salute you, and we thank God for you, not only for all the good that occurred because of you, but also for all the evil that never came to pass, for all the injustices prevented, for all the tears that never were—because of you, because you gave us a godlike ideal that made men "living symbols of force subjected to the Spirit"!

---

[64] Quoted in Peter Hoffman, *Stauffenberg: A Family History, 1905–1944* (Toronto: McGill-Queen's University Press, 1995), p. 242.

[65] Michael Baigent and Richard Leigh, *Secret Germany: Stauffenberg and the True Story of Operation Valkyrie* (New York: Skyhorse Publishing, 2008), p. 67.

Chapter 8

CLANDESTINE REVOLUTIONARIES
OF ROMANTICISM

> But what was the Romantic School in Germany? It was nothing else
> than the reawakening of the poetry [creativity] of the Middle Ages as it
> manifested itself in the poems, paintings and sculptures, in the art and life
> of those times. This poetry [creativity], however, had been developed
> out of Christianity; it was a passion-flower that had blossomed from the
> blood of Christ.

> —Heinrich Heine, *Die Romantische Schule*, 1833

Romanticism

Romanticism is usually associated
with the intellectual, literary, and
artistic movement of the late eighteenth and early nineteenth centuries which focused on the primacy
of the individual, intense emotion
as a source of intuition, and nature's
beauty as inspiration. It valued the
heroic; in painting, novel, poem,
and sculpture Romantics presented
heroes and heroines as models who
could nurture a new idealism. Turning their backs on the anti-intuitive
rationalism of the so-called "Age of
Enlightenment", the crass materi-
alism of the Industrial Revolution,
and the horrors of the French Revolution, Romantics faced toward
the medieval era, unintimidated by
the iron curtain built around the
epoch by two centuries of ideo-

Il Baciccio, *St. Francis Xavier Baptizes an Oriental Princess*, ca. 1704

logues. Romanticism, according to one of its leaders, Heinrich Heine (1797–1856),
was the "revival of the life and thought of the Middle Ages".[1] The name itself,
"Romanticism", sprang from the literary genre of the medieval prose and poetic narrative known as chivalric romance. As the founder of the German Romantic school,
a convert to Catholicism, Friedrich Schlegel, wrote, "I seek and find the romantic

---

[1] Quoted in W. L. Phelps, *The Beginnings of the English Romantic Movement* (Boston, 1893), p. 1.

among the older moderns, in Shakespeare, in Cervantes, in Italian poetry, in that age of chivalry, love, and fable from which the phenomenon and the word itself are derived."[2]

Frequently, romanticists give the impression that they knew little more about the Middle Ages than the "knight errant with castles, distressed damsels, and dragons".[3] But though it may well be true that they often lacked a comprehensive knowledge of medieval culture, their artistic genius intuited a mysterious world vision behind the age's cathedrals, poems, and prose. To a greater or lesser extent, members of the movement, like Baroness de Staël, recognized the Catholic ethos at its center: "[t]he word romantic has lately been introduced into Germany in order to designate that kind of poetry which is derived from the songs of the troubadours; that which owes its birth to the union of chivalry and Christianity".[4] They sensed that the medieval chivalric spirit formed an integral part of the utterly novel creativity of the Middle Ages, one that flowed from the fountainhead of medieval culture, the Catholic religion with the love of the crucified, heroic God-Man at its center; that it was, as Heine stated, "a passion-flower that had blossomed from the blood of Christ".[5]

And their hunch was right. Chivalric Romanticism took root, grew, and blossomed because of the climate of Catholicism; and its fragrance was felt throughout medieval society. The romanticist of the nineteenth century vaguely glimpsed what medieval man saw clearly: that the fact of Christmas night, by dramatically recasting man's understanding of God, had radically reconstructed not merely his "religion" but his entire outlook on *reality*, the cosmos, and man's raison d'être. It was an outlook that colored his world vision with love—to the point that he became hopelessly romantic. It transformed his idea of human love in all its personal and social dimensions. Catholicism, through a millennium-long struggle, had drawn out its implications for the rapport between the sexes by transforming masculine ideals through the institution of chivalry, and by achieving an unprecedented affirmation of the dignity of woman—all of which gave birth to the utterly original culture of romanticism: chivalric romanticism.

A Millennium-Long Struggle on Behalf of Women

The arrival of the Catholic Church uprooted the ancient world's view of woman and ushered in a radical program that, over the course of centuries, established the dignity of womanhood in Western culture.

---

[2] Friedrich Schlegel, *Dialogue on Poetry* (1800), quoted in Michael Ferber, *A Companion to European Romanticism* (Oxford: Blackwell Publishing, 2005), p. 2. Other leading figures of Romanticism who converted to Catholicism were Count Stolberg, Tieck, Novalis, Werner, de Staël, Carové, Schütz, and Müller.

[3] C. S. Lewis, *The Discarded Image: An Introduction to Medieval and Renaissance Literature* (Cambridge: Cambridge University Press, 1964), p. 9.

[4] Baroness Anne-Louise-Germaine de Staël, *Germany* (London: John Murray, 1813), p. 304.

[5] Heinrich Heine, *The Romantic School* (New York: Henry Holt, 1851), p. 6. However, the Romantics who were not Catholic often had only a shallow understanding of the medieval vision of reality and hence espoused a creativity uprooted from its roots in the orders of creation and redemption. See the insightful commentary in John Rao, *Black Legends and the Light of the World* (Forest Lake, Minn.: Remnant Press, 2012), pp. 751–54.

Catholicism proclaimed the revolutionary paradigm, so strange to the ears of the ancient world, that all persons share the same dignity and that woman is man's equal in nature and destiny: "There is neither Jew nor Greek, there is neither slave nor free, there is neither male nor female; for you are all one in Christ Jesus" (Gal 3:28). Unfolding the consequences of this axiom led to a four-hundred-year clash with the dominant culture of the Roman Empire followed by five hundred years of effort to create a new sociopolitical ethos in which feminine dignity would be respected.[6]

One of the first outrages against women that the Church fought against was female infanticide. Infanticide of both girls and boys was an age-old scourge. Indeed, it had become so common in ancient Greece that Polybius blamed it for the civilization's decline.[7] However, the infanticide of girls grew to such horrendous levels by the first century A.D. that in Italy, Roman North Africa, and the eastern Mediterranean area males outnumbered females by about 30 percent. Many families refused to raise a second girl. One pagan Roman soldier, Hilarion, wrote to his pregnant wife, Alis: "Know that I am still in Alexandria.... I ask and beg of you to take good care of our baby son, and as soon as I receive payment I will send it to you. If you are delivered of a child [before I come home], if it is a boy, keep it, if it is a girl discard it."[8] One after the other, Catholic leaders thundered against the crime—for instance, Athenagoras in his *Embassy for the Christians*, circa 176, and Pope Callistus in 222. As soon as the Church obtained some political clout after the Edict of Milan in 313, she swiftly rammed through legislation forbidding it. In 318 Constantine declared it to be a criminal offense, and in 374 Valentinian I repeated the ban.

However, since the creation of a Christian mentality among the masses was the labor of centuries, the fight against infanticide had to continue through the Dark Ages until the twelfth century. No small role in this struggle was played by the clergy. Besides condemning the crime, priests also acted with realism and compassion, telling the people that unwanted babies could be left at church or monastery doors. The foundlings were then brought to orphanages where devoted women and men educated them; and when they came of age their guardians sought employment for the young men and a dowry for the young women who wished to marry. Entire regiments of ardent souls came into existence in order to act as spiritual fathers and mothers to these children. Such was the Order of the Holy Ghost, founded in 1178 by Guy de Montpellier, which established about eight hundred orphanages, maternity-care centers, hospitals, and other institutions over the following century.[9] The Church also saved countless female lives by making abortion—a frequent cause of death for women—illegal and socially unacceptable.

"The dignity of marriage was restored by the Christians", wrote the historian Edward Gibbon, whom no one will suspect of being too Catholic-friendly.[10]

---

[6] See Patricia Ranft, *Women and Spiritual Equality in Christian Tradition* (New York: Palgrave Macmillan, 2000). The author shows how the accumulated evidence from Church texts and cultural indicators provides persuasive data for Catholicism's strong affirmation of feminine dignity throughout the centuries.

[7] See Polybius, *Histories*, 6.

[8] Quoted in Rodney Stark, *The Rise of Christianity: A Sociologist Reconsiders History* (Princeton, N.J.: Princeton University Press, 1996), pp. 97–98.

[9] Although the male branch of the order died out, it has been refounded in Gdansk, Poland, in 2003, by Fr. Wieslaw Wisniewski; see the Societas Spiritus Sancti (Towarzystwo Ducha Świętego) at http://gwidon.pl/.

[10] Edward Gibbon, *History of the Decline and Fall of the Roman Empire*, vol. 5 (London, 1821), p. 356.

Moreover, in an unprecedented way, the dignity of woman in marriage was promoted and protected as never before. Firstly, because priests led the way in campaigning against polygamy. Secondly, girls from Christian families were a lot less likely than those from pagan families to be married before thirteen years of age largely because, due to ecclesiastical law, the girl had to freely give her consent to any proposal, a decision that presupposed full awareness of the nature of marriage. Thirdly, the Christian conception of marriage as a sacramental expression of the heroic love of Christ for his Mystical Body, the Church, thereby implied a communion of hearts—a vision that was highly influential in eradicating, or at least controlling, the pagan and barbarian spirit of male chauvinism. Fourthly, the Church shocked pagan Romans by defining adultery as not only a wife's infidelity to her husband but also as a husband's betrayal of his wife. Throughout the first millennium priests fought constantly to defend women from being flung aside by adulterous husbands. Nor did they hesitate to oblige men who repented their adultery to undergo humiliating public penances. Indeed, priests sometimes put their very lives on the line defending women who had been betrayed.[11]

A subtle but powerful tool of the Church in its efforts to change the male chauvinist mentality was her practice, right from her earliest days, of elevating women as well as men to the highest ecclesial rank: canonized sainthood. Indeed, female heroines like Mary Magdalen, Agnes, Cecilia, Anastasia, Agatha, and Lucy were often venerated more highly than many male saints. As the American writer Flannery O'Connor remarked: "The Church would as soon canonize a woman as a man, and I suppose has done more than any other force in history to free women."[12]

Women of the ruling class in the Roman Empire recognized the revolutionary thrust of Christianity on behalf of female dignity, and this strengthened the decision of many of them to convert to the new religion in spite of the social stigma involved. Some of them soon exercised a notable influence within the Church, even acting as spiritual directors of some of the most important male Christians in the first centuries.[13] Catholicism also gave members of the female sex a new freedom to seek fulfillment outside of marriage when she declared virginal consecration equal in dignity to physical motherhood. In this way women acquired an autonomy unknown in any other culture as they formed their own self-governing communities and played a pivotal role in the development of Western culture.[14] How many millions of lives all over the world have been transformed by these nuns! How many hospitals, orphanages, schools, universities, and centers for the poor, the sick, and the dying

---

[11] Although it occurred centuries later, a well-documented instance occurred when Pope Nicholas I (ca. 800–867) refused to grant an annulment to Lothair II so that he might marry his mistress, Waldrada. The furious king marched on Rome with his army and for two days besieged Nicholas in St. Peter's Basilica, where the pontiff was without food. But the gutsy Pope did not bend, and Lothair withdrew in failure. And—even though it occurred outside of the medieval era—how can we forget that the Church of Rome was even prepared to risk losing the kingdom of England in 1527 rather than betray God's law and a woman, Catherine of Aragon?

[12] Letter of July 28, 1956, in Flannery O'Connor, *The Habit of Being: Letters of Flannery O'Connor* (New York: Farrar, Straus and Giroux, 1979), p. 168.

[13] See the chapter "Women Spiritual Directors of Church Fathers", in Patricia Ranft, *A Woman's Way: The Forgotten History of Women Spiritual Directors* (New York: Palgrave Macmillan, 2001), pp. 25–49.

[14] See Patricia Ranft, *Women and the Religious Life in Premodern Europe* (New York: Palgrave Macmillan, 1996).

arose from the heroine hearts of women like Scholastica, Clare of Assisi, Angela de Merici, Louise de Marillac, Catherine McAuley, and Teresa of Calcutta! And at the end of history we will learn how much supernatural power was unleashed by the prayer and penance of so many cloistered heroines.

The struggle for female dignity continued through the Dark Ages, and by the twelfth century it was evident in home, law, and politics that, amid the short-comings imposed by man's fallen nature, colossal progress had been made.[15] In the home, women ruled alongside their husbands over both family and property and retained control over what had belonged to them from before marriage. They were also free to take up professions and regularly practiced medicine, engaged in commerce, and became involved in politics. From the thirteenth-century survey ordered by King Louis IX we know that women were teachers and doctors, pharmacists and plasterers, dyers, copyists, salt merchants, hairdressers, millers— and crusaders![16]

Many were just as educated as men, thanks to the Church's convents.[17] A few were among the intellectual stars of medieval Europe: the abbess Hroswitha, a writer who influenced the development of both the German language and theatre; the abbess Herrad of Landsberg, who authored the twelfth-century encyclopedia *Hortus Deliciarum*; and the composer and polymath Hildegarde of Bingen.[18]

Politically, between the eleventh and thirteenth centuries, females like Blanche de Castille were even governing kingdoms as regents. Others like Héloïse, abbess of the Paraclete convent in France, governed large territories containing villages and parishes. There were even monastic estates where men and women lived in separate monasteries, both of which were ruled by a woman, such as at the abbey of Fontevrault. During the medieval era even the most powerful men were willing to be guided by a woman on account of the Catholic ethos whereby women just as much as men could be God's instruments in history.[19] When Pope Gregory XI decided to transfer the governmental center of the Church from the secure French city of Avignon back to the squalid and danger-infested Rome in 1376, it was all because of the ever-so-forthright urgings of the twenty-nine-year-old Catherine of Siena. And let us not forget how the male military leadership of France went into battle in 1429 under a seventeen-year-old female commandant-in-chief, Joan of Arc.[20] It was even widespread in medieval France and elsewhere for women to vote in elections: we know of a woman, Gaillardine de Frechou, who, during a ballot in her area of the Pyrenees, was the only one in the population to go against a certain proposal![21]

---

[15]See Régine Pernoud, *Women in the Days of the Cathedrals* (San Francisco: Ignatius Press, 1998). The author is a renowned historian with thirty years of experience as an archivist at the French National Archives and is the recipient of an award from the Académie Française.

[16]See Régine Pernoud, "Women without Souls", in *Those Terrible Middle Ages: Debunking the Myths* (San Francisco: Ignatius Press, 2000), pp. 97–115.

[17]See Patricia Ranft, *Women in Western Intellectual Culture, 600–1500* (New York: Palgrave Macmillan, 2008).

[18]See Katharina M. Wilson, *Medieval Women Writers* (Manchester: Manchester University Press, 1984).

[19]See Patricia Ranft, *A Woman's Way: The Forgotten History of Women Spiritual Directors* (New York: Palgrave Macmillan, 2001), pp. 67–107.

[20]Régine Pernoud and Marie-Véronique Clin, *Joan of Arc: Her Story* (New York: St. Martin's Press, 1999). An excellent English translation from the best-selling French edition containing meticulously researched information from contemporary documents.

[21]Pernoud, *Those Terrible Middle Ages*, p. 110.

Karl Friedrich Lessing, *The Thousand-Year-Old Oak* (detail), 1837. Lovers kneeling in prayer before an image of the Blessed Virgin Mary in the shelter of an ancient oak tree. "The Eternal Feminine leads us upward" (Goethe).

Throughout the Dark Ages, alongside her fight for the rights of women, the Church, ever so supernatural but ever so earthy, also got men, especially those among the ruling classes, into better shape for marriage. Particularly by urging knights to a genuine masculinity that required self-conquest, Catholicism gave man a pedagogy for acquiring inner strength for marriage whereby he would be readier to love—ardently and enduringly—woman, who was his equal in dignity.

Finally, there was the aura of supernatural awe with which the Church surrounded femininity through that quintessential dimension of Catholicism: reverence for the Blessed Virgin Mary. By teaching men to genuflect in her presence, the Church was implicitly training them to kneel before femininity. In the midst of dark centuries, ardent men sang ethereally beautiful hymns to the Queen of Heaven in Romanesque churches as the sun was setting. It was only a matter of time before poets, musicians, and artists followed in their footsteps, venerating not only the Woman par excellence but womanhood. That moment arrived—suddenly, explosively, triumphantly—in the twelfth century; Europe awoke—and gazed in wonder on men serenading women under their balconies on moonlit nights.

Birth of Chivalric Romantic Love

Love? An invention of the twelfth century![22]

Love is a great discovery of the medieval age, especially of twelfth-century France. Before that time it had not savored so fully of eternity and spirituality.[23]

Thus comes the thing called Romance, a purely Christian product.... The medieval Europe which asserted humility gained Romance; the civilization which gained Romance has gained the habitable globe.[24]

If it were not for the fact that the first remark above is from one of the founders of modern historiography with its insistence on the critical examination of manuscript

---

[22] "L'amour? Une invention du douzième siècle!" The French historian Charles Seignobos (1854–1942), quoted by Maurice Valency, *In Praise of Love* (New York: Macmillan, 1958), p. 1; and by Henri Daniel-Rops, *La Cathédrale et la Croisade* (Paris: Arthème Fayard, 1952), p. 364. Valency's book, a scholarly study of medieval love poetry, particularly in southern France and Italy, concludes that the tradition it created reached a peak in the spiritualized vision of love in Dante's *Vita Nuova*.

[23] "L'amour est une grande découverte du Moyen Age, et en particulier du XIIème siècle français" (Gustave Cohen, *La Grande Clarté du Moyen Age* [Paris, 1945], p. 85). Quoted along with the citation of Seignobos in Daniel-Rops, *La Cathédrale*, p. 364.

[24] G. K. Chesterton, *Heretics* (London: J. Lane, 1905), p. 70.

Edmund Blair Leighton, *The End of the Song*, 1902. The Irish Celtic princess Isolde and the Celtic knight of Cornwall, Tristan.

sources; the second a judgment from an illustrious Jewish historian of the medieval period; and the third from a philosopher and literary and art critic of towering genius, one might be tempted to dismiss the three remarks as crass hyperbole. Yet there is no mere rhetoric here; history will not budge on the essentials: romantic love, in which womanhood was idealized as never before, came to birth from the womb of Catholicism in the lands of twelfth-century Christendom.

This was no accident. Firstly, because Catholicism was the very climate and soil of romanticism. What religion could be more incurably romantic than one with its origins in a love-filled night when the God of Love, who had descended to the womb of a most beautiful Jewish maiden, was born to bring man eternal joy? Man's sense of his identity and value is now grounded on the fact that God has loved him unto death for no other reason than that he exists, a reality created in the divine image, who, because of sin, is in need of salvation. This gives a new tone to man's thought, a new insight to his imagination, a new daring to his will—and the awareness that love, not power, must seal all his relationships.

The second reason is because the Church, as we have just seen, had made the twelfth-century springtime possible by energetically sowing countless seeds for the dignity of womanhood during the long winter of the previous millennium. The medieval status of women would have bewildered the ancient Romans, Greeks, Chinese, and indeed all the ancient civilizations. Firstly, because they would have seen womanhood—and not merely individual women like Helen of Troy—placed on a pedestal. Secondly, they would have seen her held in awe, not for the sake of her body but for her complete self: her *femininity*, her feminine genius. Thirdly, they would have perceived an unprecedented atmosphere in which woman was wooed in song and poem by man, who stood underneath her window on summer evenings or wore her scarf on his sleeve as he rode to the tournament.

Under the old pagan order of Greece and Rome there had doubtlessly been countless instances of loving commitment unto death between husbands and wives. But woman was not regarded as man's equal (she had few legal rights) and was largely held to be in function of reproduction, with little in religion to stand in the way of her becoming a tool of men's passions. So, needless to say, men did not spend much time underneath balconies.

But with the arrival of Christianity the meaning of love between man and woman, like everything else, was deciphered by the purpose of human existence as revealed by Jesus Christ. Man was called to an eternal existence that would be no mere prolongation of his days on Earth, but a sheer ecstatic fulfillment of his entire being, body and soul: a new life in which all his powers to know and love would be utterly activated because they would be made divine. If life on Earth were lived gracefully in the radiance of the Savior's life, death, and Resurrection, human love need never fear decay and rupture; death would no longer have the final word, ending the bonds of love and aspirations to more and better. Such is the meaning behind the words placed by the Catholic writer Tolkien on the lips of the dying Aragorn as he bade farewell to a grieving Arwen: "Behold! We are not bound forever to the circles of the world, and beyond them is more than memory".[25]

From this alertness to life's eternal horizons came a new vision of marriage. Heightened was the sense of mutual responsibility of husband and wife to act as loyal companions to each other, and loving, vigilant guardians to their offspring, on life's dramatic journey toward the endless existence of immortal splendor willed by the Creator. For the male the paragon of his spousal grandeur was portrayed by the ultimate role model: Jesus Christ. He, the Perfect Man, acted as the perfect bridegroom in his relations with his bride, the Church, since he heroically "loved the Church and gave himself up for her" (Eph 5:25). The message was clear: farewell to all forms of domination—every man's spousal existence must be a lifelong thrust toward a Christlike sacrifice of self for the beloved.

In order to make this ideal visible and tangible, the Church's priests developed splendid ceremonies, rich in symbolism, around the institution of marriage, willingly incorporating even customs of non-Christian origin that helped to evoke its Christian meaning. The result was an aura of romanticism enveloping the nuptials.

The moment of engagement had its own ritual. The prospective bride and groom went to church where the priest inquired into their intentions; then he instructed the couple to join their right hands, his over hers, and asked each in their turn to repeat after him a solemn promise, pledging by the faith in their heart and by their baptism to take each other as spouse within a certain number of months. The priest proceeded to take the two ends of his stole and, placing them in the shape of a cross over the clasped hands of the couple, said, "I bear witness to your solemn proposal and I declare you betrothed. May what has been begun in you be brought to perfection for the honor of God and of Our Lady and of all the Saints. In the name of the Father and of the Son and of the Holy Spirit. Amen."[26] The groom laid down a "deposit", which if reneged upon would oblige him to pay a penalty equal to four times the betrothal amount. Then the couple kissed, went to their respective homes, and waited usually about forty days for the wedding.

On the day of the wedding, the bride and bridegroom presented themselves at the portal of the church where the ceremonies took place prior to entering for the nuptial Mass. They stood facing the church, a canopy held over them, the man standing on the right side with his fiancée on his left, symbolically recalling the account of woman's creation in Genesis where she is depicted as being formed out of a rib in the left side of Adam. The bride frequently wore blue, the traditional color of purity; on her head she sometimes wore a bridal veil, a custom introduced by knights returning from the Crusades; and occasionally a crown woven out of orange blossoms.

The priest, after firstly asking all present, and then the couple themselves, if they knew of any impediments to their reception of the sacrament, addressed the bridegroom saying: "N., wilt thou have this woman to be thy wedded wife, wilt thou love her and honor her, keep her and guard her, in health and in sickness, as a husband

---

[25]J. R. R. Tolkien, *The Lord of the Rings: The Return of the King*, Appendix A, p. 344.
[26]See Michael P. Foley, *Wedding Rites* (Grand Rapids, Mich.: Wm. B. Eerdmans, 2008), p. 12.

should a wife, and forsaking all others on account of her, keep thee only unto her, so long as ye both shall live?"[27] He questioned the bride in like manner, to which both answered by saying, "I will." Then the father gave the woman to her future husband. The ceremony continued with the pledging of the vows. "N., with my body I thee honor, and with this silver (or gold) I thee endow, and all that I have and will have I give and will give to thee in faithful fellowship and companionship. And I promise thee, here and before God, that I will carry thee in faith and loyalty, in health and in sickness, and in all the states that God might put thee; and that I will take care of thee, even as I do myself. And I will never abandon thee for another, so long as we both shall live."[28] Then the ring (which came into widespread use in Western Europe during the twelfth century), along with a bag of silver and gold, symbol of the man's ability to support his future wife and children, were handed to the priest, who placed them on the Bible and blessed them. He gave the ring to the bridegroom, who took the woman's right hand in his left, saying after the priest: "With this ring I thee wed, this gold and silver I thee give, and with my body I thee worship, and with all my worldly goods I thee endow, in the name of the Father, and of the Son, and of the Holy Ghost. Amen."[29] In saying, "In the name of the Father", the spouse put the ring upon the woman's thumb; "and of the Son", on the forefinger; "and of the Holy Ghost", on the middle finger; in saying "Amen" ["so be it"], on "that finger wherein beats the vein of the heart",[30] where he left it, symbol of undying loyalty and endless, ever youthful love.

At that point, the couple, with heads bowed, received the priestly blessing before entering the church, where they knelt before the altar and received another benediction. Then followed the Holy Sacrifice of the Mass. Before the couple went on their way, the priest blessed the first loaf of bread and wine they would share together. Nor did the Church's rites end there—in some places the priest incensed the marriage bed, sprinkling it with blessed water, while the spouses sat therein and prayed.[31] The following ninth-century benediction, written by Irish missionaries, was used by the priest for this moment:

> Let us pray, beloved brethren, to God, who deigned to spread the gifts of His blessing in order to increase the offspring of mankind: that he may watch over these His servants, N. and N., whom He hath chosen for the embrace of marriage. May He grant unto them gentle affection, similar minds, conduct bound in mutual love. If He should so wish, may they have children, whom He bestows as a gift. And thus may His blessing follow: that these His servants, N. and N., may zealously serve in the humility of one and the same heart Him whom they do not doubt to be their Creator. Amen.
>
> We pray, O holy Lord, almighty Father, everliving God, for Thy servants, N. and N., whom Thou hast bid to come to the grace of marriage, and who have longed for Thy blessing through our voice and prayers. Grant them, O Lord, the faithful fellowship of charity. May they put on the charity of Sarah, the wisdom of Rebecca, the love of

---

[27] Quoted in Emilie Amt, ed., *Women's Lives in Medieval Europe* (New York: Routledge, 1993), p. 84.

[28] A fourteenth-century rite from Cambrai, France, quoted in and translated by Foley, *Wedding Rites*, p. 63.

[29] Quoted in William Penketh, Sir Anthony Van Dyck, and Heinrich Goltzius, *River's Manual; Or, Pastoral Instructions Upon the Creed* (London, 1830), p. 262.

[30] Honorius of Autun, quoted in Henri Daniel-Rops, *Cathedral and Crusade: Studies of the Medieval Church, 1050–1350* (New York: Dutton, 1957), p. 287.

[31] See ibid.

Rachel, and the grace of Susannah. May Thy hand descend upon Thy servants, N. and N., as the dew of rain descends upon the face of the earth. May they quietly sense Thy Holy Spirit, and may they attain everlasting joy. Through our Lord Jesus Christ Thy Son, who liveth and reigneth with Thee in the unity of the Holy Spirit, God, forever and ever. Amen.[32]

Thus, under Catholicism love between man and woman now "savoured fully of eternity and spirituality".[33] Through Jesus Christ it had acquired a strength for romanticism that the world's religions and cultures never even suspected. A startling, unprecedented status for woman had been achieved; sometimes by ramming through new laws amid furious resistance; other times by hurling anathemas and interdicts in defense of womens' rights in the face of powerful rulers' violence; but most often it was done silently, anonymously, peacefully by clandestine revolutionaries, writing in quiet cloisters, thundering in the pulpit, and murmuring in the confession seat, whether as monks in austere abbeys, as bishops in Gothic cathedrals, or as pastors in tiny, rural hamlets. To many they seem rather paradoxical revolutionaries: romantics with their vow of chastity, lovers who promised lifelong celibacy. Yet, their vow, rather than causing love to be snuffed out, ignited a fire, a verve, and a vigor. For they had not embraced chastity due to lack of love but because of a greater love—for Christ and the salvation of souls. To reach ordination they had been willing to feel the soul-searing pain of renunciation of marriage and physical children—a heroic sacrifice that deepened and sensitized their hearts. The priests who led the way in Christianizing the West and creating the climate in which romantic love burgeoned were volcanoes of romanticism! The purer their love, the more intense it was; the more ascetic, the more ardent; and the more exclusively for Christ, the more inclusive it was of all people. For love that is vowed to Love in lifelong chastity is the very opposite of a destroying force: it liberates, elevates, and fulfills as Augustine, Benedict, Patrick, Columbanus, Columba, Boniface, Bernard, and countless others had discovered.

Clash: The Chivalric Romantic Ideal versus Troubadourism and Courtly Love

> Everyone has heard of courtly love, and everyone knows that it appears quite suddenly at the end of the eleventh century in Languedoc.[34]

Adding blazing color—and insidious danger—to these Catholic ideals of chivalric love and female dignity was a new and exotic culture that made its entrée in poem and song to the Christian West in the eleventh century.

The new cultural influence arrived from the milieu of the Islamic ruling class of the Caliphate of Córdoba in the southern Spanish province of Andalusia. There, in

---

[32] This blessing "has two pedigrees because it was written by Irish missionaries and used in Spain"; see Foley, *Wedding Rites*, p. 124.

[33] Cohen, *La Grande Clarté du Moyen Age*, p. 85. A modern-day chevalier who approached marriage with this sensibility was the statesman and "Father of European Unity" Alcide de Gasperi, who, in 1921, in a poignant letter proposing marriage to his future wife, Francesca Romani, wrote: "The personality of the living Christ draws me, captivates me and strengthens me as though I were a child. Come, I want you with me, to be drawn to that same attraction, as though to an abyss of light." Maria Romano Catti de Gasperi, *De Gasperi uomo solo* (Milan: Mondadori, 1964), n. 10, pp. 81–82. My translation.

[34] C. S. Lewis, *The Allegory of Love* (Oxford: Clarendon Press, 1936), p. 2.

Shield of Parade (detail), Flanders, 15th century. The battle-shield depicts a knight kneeling before a lady to whom he declares his love. Wearing a suit of plate armor, his helmet, pole-axe, and gauntlets lying at his feet, he is taking leave of the woman he loves, conscious of the dangers he is about to face in combat. These are symbolized by the ominous figure of Death, who emerges from behind, hands outstretched to bear him away. Above the knight's head the scroll——*Vous ou la mort* (You or Death)——proclaims that the knight would sooner lose life itself than the lady he loves.

the late tenth century, due largely to the Muslim military control of trade in the Mediterranean and to the advanced civilization inherited from Romanized Visigothic rulers, the wealthy lived in opulence. Visitors from Christian Europe were impressed by their lifestyle characterized by exquisite manners, complicated social rituals, and sensuousness—all of which presented a dizzying contrast to their own sternly rugged existence.[35]

Soon Italian merchants along with the last Norman kings of Sicily and Emperor Frederick adopted aspects of the Caliphate court's lifestyle in their surroundings. But it was in the cultural region of Occitania, largely coextensive with southern France, in the territory of the dukes of Aquitaine, that the new culture mesmerized the minds of the local elite. The ducal court had been won over through Moorish poets who had been brought back to Poitiers in the course of the Duchy's military and political entanglements in Spain 1030–1064. Under their influence, from the eleventh to the fourteenth centuries, Aquitaine became the land famous for its troubadours—composers and performers of lyric poetry in the local Occitan language, modeled to a significant degree (even if not exclusively) on that of Moorish Andalusia. Outstanding among them were men like Duke Guillaume IX (1071–1126), Bernart de Ventadorn, Giraut de Bornelh, Bertran de Born, and Arnaut de Mareuil.[36]

The new poetry was exotic and pleasure-loving; its delights were honor, wealth, beauty, joy, and, above all, love between the sexes. It allured the aristocracy to adopt a lifestyle of polished social manners, especially in courtship, and a love for exhibitionism in extravagant pageants. The spirit of the new romanticism spread into Christian Spain, Italy, and Greece. To northern Europe it travelled with the granddaughter of Duke Guillaume IX, the famous Eleanor (ca. 1122–1204), who, as queen first of France and then of England, popularized the troubadour culture at the royal courts.[37] Subsequently her daughters brought it to the palaces of Champagne, Blois, and Saxony. It helped to

[35] See Louis and Sir Charles Petrie Bertrand, *The History of Spain* (London: Collier, 1945), pp. 7–18.
[36] See Frederick Goldin, *Lyrics of the Troubadours and Trouvères* (Gloucester: Peter Smith, 1983).
[37] See Régine Pernoud, *Eleanor of Aquitaine* (New York: Coward, McCann and Geoghegan, 1968).

create the related movements of the *Minnesang* in Germany and *trovadorismo* in Portugal and Galicia. Swiftly, from the eleventh to the fourteenth centuries it penetrated all the courts of Western Europe.

However, from the start, the ethos of chivalry was on its guard against troubadour romanticism. The warm air and the pleasant valleys of southern France contrasted with the Alpine atmosphere of chivalry with its peaks of self-conquest and horizons of eternity that made men wary of pleasure. Although a truly Catholic mind can only rejoice at the ability of the troubadour lyrics to express the subtleties of human love, Catholic realism also recognizes that there is a fine line indeed between the God-given pleasures of the erotic and hedonism, a line that man ever so easily crosses to the ensuing wreckage of true love.

The lives and poetry of some of the troubadours blurred man's vision of the line. They were not so choosy, either in literature or real life, about distinguishing between love for a married and an unmarried woman. Their poetry and music, largely performed at the courts of the aristocracy or in the homes of the wealthy bourgeoisie who patronized them, helped spawn a shallow culture of flattery and pomp, necessarily reserved for the rich. The flash and frill of court trappings, pageants, tournaments, and festivals were of no great help to the thousands of poor peasants who could well have benefited from some of the massive amounts of money involved. Nor could the fanfare of trumpets at equestrian tournaments totally drown out the anguished weeping of wives and children, parents and friends, when knights were killed—pointlessly, for stupid bravado or as a way of gaining revenge—in the flower of manhood. Time and again the Church condemned the tourneys, notably in 1139 at the Second Lateran Council, but with only limited success since love of pleasure, once unleashed from wise judgment, is an almost uncontrollable beast.

The waves of this culture rose higher in the following centuries. The artificiality of troubadour-inspired etiquette in many fourteenth-century medieval courts helped to bloat the hypocritical manners and intrigues of many Renaissance palaces from the fifteenth to the seventeenth centuries that ultimately peaked in the monstrosity of eighteenth-century Versailles, where the elite played while France toiled. By then Catholic chivalry had been exiled to the frontiers of society while the new pseudo-chivalry tried to present itself as its lawful heir. It stripped off its Catholic character to such an extent that by the nineteenth century its descendant, the "gentleman", was by comparison a scrawny heir of the medieval knight. Nevertheless, we are still grateful for him: the afterglow reminds us of the splendor.

The decadence originally introduced by troubadourism provoked the criticisms of Cervantes and Shakespeare during the seventeenth century. Before them, some Catholics had attempted to harmonize the two cultures. Ramon Llull (ca. 1235–1315), a troubadour who had undergone a religious conversion, wrote a history and theory of knighthood entitled *The Book of the Order of Chivalry*, in which the best of troubadourism blended with chivalry. Other writers authored a new literature in which the tension between chivalry and troubadourism, high Christian ideals and pagan sensuality, conflict in powerful personalities like Tristan and Isolde, Abélard and Héloïse, Lancelot and Guinevere.[38] For instance, in the Lancelot-Grail cycle, mostly from the early thirteenth century, the story of the romance of Lancelot and

[38] See Régine Pernoud, *Héloïse et Abélard* (New York: Stein and Day, 1973).

Guinevere exudes the tension between the two conflicting standards of behavior. One experiences the contrast between Lancelot, the knight unfaithful to the integral ideal of chivalry, and his illegitimate son, Galahad, the perfect Christian warrior, as valiant as his father but, unlike him, pure—indeed purity embodied—and therefore capable of completing the quest for Christ's chalice.[39] Yet, Lancelot in the end converts, and at his conversion wept "as bitterly as if he had seen the object of his dearest love lying dead before him, and with the desperation of a man at his wit's end for grief".[40] This was the spirit present in much of this literature. Many troubadours upheld Catholic principles. In one way or another they recognized that the romanticism par excellence is the romanticism of the Crucified Hero, that Heaven is the goal of existence, and sin the greatest danger. One of them, Hugues de Berzé, both a crusading knight and a troubadour, in his act of repentance wrote that "laughter and song, jousting and adventuring and holding court", were fully acceptable in a man of honor, "so long as he keeps himself from sin".[41]

Triumph: A Sublime and Enduring Romanticism

Within chivalric romanticism medieval man had learned that love of the lady should impel him to fulfill more intensely the distinctively male triple role of procreator (spiritual and physical fatherhood), provider, and protector—all of which required him to practice a wide range of virtues, both theological and moral. Troubadourism, although regarded warily by chivalry, was allowed to contribute some of its expressiveness to the warrior ethos. The resulting fusion enhanced the chivalric mystique in two ways. Firstly, it taught the knight (and through him the other social classes) to look at his lady as the model and custodian of virtues native to feminine sensitivity, virtues that all too easily he tended to forget amid hunting, the encampments of war, and in the heat of battle. Secondly, it gave color, sparkle, and dash to the chivalric ethos. This was of no small importance. Troubadour courtly love empowered knights to articulate their sentiments in word, gesture, and symbol. To commit the body and its internal and external senses of touch, sight,

Edmund Blair Leighton (1853–1922), *God Speed!*, 1900. Before a knight departs for battle, his beloved assures him of her devotion by tying a scarf with her colors on his arm, a gesture deeply valued by warriors.

---

[39] See Norris J. Lacy, ed., *Lancelot-Grail: The Old French Arthurian Vulgate and Post-Vulgate in Translation*, 5 vols. (New York: Garland, 1992–1996); also, Sir Thomas Malory, *Le Morte d'Arthur*, first published in 1485 by William Caxton.

[40] Quoted in Anthony Esolen, *The Politically Incorrect Guide to Western Civilization* (Washington, D.C.: Regnery, 2008), p. 152.

[41] Hugh de Berzé, *La Bible au Seigneur de Berzé*, 127, quoted in Christopher Dawson, *Religion and the Rise of Western Culture* (London: Sheed and Ward, 1991), p. 187.

hearing, memory, and imagination to one's ideal is to mature and make steadfast inner certainties. In this instance, troubadour courtliness, by enabling vivid expression of the ideals of genuine masculinity, true femininity, and the authentic nature of male-female relationships, caused the explosion of a culture of romanticism that spread like wildfire in Europe. In poem, prose, song, and a thousand gestures of gallantry an entire civilization honored women publicly, surrounding the feminine ideal with an aureole of virtues, and venerating woman as she had never been venerated before in the history of the human race.

"Beauty in woman; the High Will's decree"[42], as one poet declared. Another exclaimed: "My lady looks so gentle and so pure / When yielding salutation by the way, / That the tongue trembles and has nought to say, / And the eyes, which fain would see, may not endure".[43] As Ulrich von Liechtenstein (1200–1275), both knight and poet, wrote in *Frauendienst* (Service of the Ladies):

> All virtue lies in woman and the health of the world. God has created nothing so good as a woman. No one can find a limit to the praise of women. He who can tell where the sunshine ends may proclaim also the end of their praise. Women are pure, and good, and fair; they impart worthiness; and make men worthy. Nothing is so like the angels as their beautiful form, and even the mind of an angel dwells in woman.[44]

The new romanticism, although most renowned for its cultivation of the male-female relationship, was an overarching vision of reality in high medieval society. Influential in the communication of this vision to the masses was a young Italian of Assisi, Francesco Bernardone. His radical conversion to Christ had refined his enthusiasm both for knightly chivalry and troubadour romanticism. By kneeling before Jesus Christ Crucified, his heart had been captured and transfigured by the most sublime romantic ideal, a transformation vividly symbolized by his stigmata. It led to new, vigorous, and delightful ways of expressing man's relationship with God, nature, and his fellow men. This was the romanticism of Francis as he raised his voice in the "Canticle of Brother Sun", but it was also his fiery dash and daring in crossing the battle lines in Egypt to propose conversion to the Catholic Faith to the Muslim sultan of Egypt Malik Al-Kamil.

Another who integrated both was Dante (1265–1321).[45] As Anthony Esolen points out, his immortal lines about "the now glorious lady of my mind, who was called Beatrice",[46] reveal the heart of a man whose existence had been changed by love for a woman whom he had only seen, never been close to, and yet through whom he had been enabled to glimpse something of divine beauty in human beauty, of divine love in human love: an ideal that would guide him through the dark woods of earthly life to the sunlit lands of eternity.[47]

---

[42] Guido Cavalcanti (ca. 1255–1300), the sonnet "He compares all things with his lady and finds them wanting", line 1, quoted in Dante Gabriel Rossetti, ed., *Selected Poems and Translations* (Abingdon, Oxford: Routledge, 2013), p. 132.

[43] Dante Alighieri, "My Lady Looks So Gentle", lines 1–4.

[44] Ulrich von Liechtenstein, *Frauendienst* (Service of Ladies), a self-styled autobiographical work completed in 1255, quoted in Kenelm Henry Digby, *The Broadstone of Honour* or *The True Sense and Practice of Chivalry: The Second Book, Tancredus* (London: privately published, 1828), p. 283.

[45] See Richard Lansing, ed., *The Dante Encyclopedia* (New York: Routledge, 2010), pp. 236–37.

[46] Dante, *The New Life*, chap. II; see Mark Musa, *Dante's Vita Nuova. New Edition: A Translation and an Essay* (Indianapolis: Indiana University Press, 1973), p. 3.

[47] Esolen, *Politically Incorrect Guide to Western Civilization*, pp. 149–50.

After I wrote this sonnet there came to me a miraculous vision in which I saw things that made me resolve to say no more about this blessed one until I would be capable of writing about her in a nobler way. To achieve this I am striving as hard as I can, and this she truly knows. Accordingly, if it be the pleasure of Him through whom all things live that my life continue for a few more years, I hope to write of her that which has never been written of any other woman. And then may it please the One who is the Lord of graciousness that my soul ascend to behold the glory of its lady, that is, of that blessed Beatrice, who in glory contemplates the countenance of the One *qui est per omnia secula benedictus* [who is throughout all ages blessed].[48]

El Greco, *St. Francis Receiving the Stigmata* (detail), 1585–1590. St. Francis is one of those who put troubadourism at the service of the chivalric romantic ideal supremely embodied by the Crucified Hero.

This spirit of chivalric romanticism continues to be influential into the twenty-first century, clashing however with the dominant secularized culture of post-Western civilization and its gender ideology.[49] This confrontation is between two utterly irreconcilable world visions: chivalry rooted in Catholicism with its radical realism grounded in the assent to the natural law and the Incarnation versus hedonism-stimulated individualism, a highway out of reality into a shadow world of agnosticism vulnerable to totalitarian relativism. The clash can be seen to some extent in the works of a modern non-Catholic novelist, John Steinbeck, who readily acknowledges his debt to the medieval chivalric ideal:

I think my sense of right and wrong, my feeling of *noblesse oblige*, and any thought I may have against the oppressor and for the oppressed came from this secret book [*Le Morte d'Arthur*].... It did not seem strange to me that Uther Pendragon wanted the wife of his vassal and took her by trickery. I was not frightened to find that there were evil knights, as well as noble ones. In my own town there were men who wore the clothes of virtue whom I knew to be bad.... If I could not choose my way at the crossroads of love and loyalty, neither could Lancelot. I could understand the darkness of Mordred because he was in me too; and there was some Galahad in me, but perhaps not enough. The Grail feeling was there, however, deep-planted, and perhaps always will be.[50]

Steinbeck's recognition of his debt to chivalry shows that, in spite of the destruction of Catholic civilization, poignant ruins still remind men of its ideals of womanhood, masculinity, and the relation between the sexes. In the coming centuries, Catholic creative minorities, as they once more guide their contemporaries to the

---

[48]Dante, *The New Life*, chap. 42; see Musa, *Dante's Vita Nuova*, p. 86. For an understanding of Dante and his romanticism see the insightful translation and notes in the following three-volume work: Anthony Esolen, ed. and trans., *The Divine Comedy* (New York: Random House, 2002–2007).

[49]See Gabriele Kuby, *The Global Sexual Revolution: Destruction of Freedom in the Name of Freedom* (Kettering, Ohio: Angelico Press, 2015); Rodolfo de Mattei, *Gender Diktat. Origini e Conseguenze di una Ideologia Totalitaria* (Chieti: Solfanelli, 2014).

[50]John Steinbeck, quoted on the back cover of Elizabeth J. Bryan, *Le Morte d'Arthur* (New York: Modern Library, 1999).

one true religion and the building of a new civilization, can point to these remnants as they explain their origins in the Catholic world vision with its eternal horizons of an infinite divine love revealed in Christ Crucified and Risen, and life as a dramatic battleground with resulting salvation or damnation. For chivalric romanticism expresses the heart of the Catholic ethos. That is why the incisive mind of a convert to Catholicism could state: "All who are adherents of romanticism (as I am) have it for their first and fixed and central principle that romance is more serious than realism. We say that romance is the grave and authoritative and responsible thing."[51] At the end of it all, the Catholic's view of life, reduced to its utter essentials, is "an image of love and war, as a quest with a prize ... an enlightening symbol and a legitimate simplification. St. George must kill the Dragon, or the Dragon will kill.... That seems to me a truer picture of the aim of life and the lot of man than any realistic novel."[52]

---

[51] G. K. Chesterton, "Romantic and Realistic Drama", *The Illustrated London News*, March 17, 1906.
[52] G. K. Chesterton, "The Attack on Romanticism", *The Illustrated London News*, April 18, 1931.

Chapter 9

MEN WITH MUSIC, ARTISTRY,
AND DRAMA IN THEIR SOULS

Art is under infinite indebtedness to religion but to none so much as the Catholic religion.

—The sculptor Antonio Canova (1757–1822),
addressing Napoleon

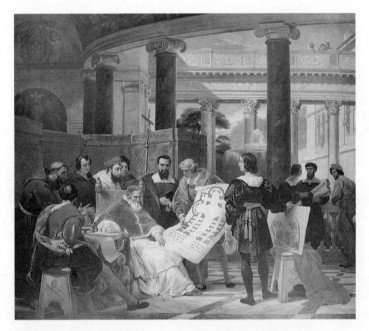

Emile Jean Horace Vernet, *Pope Julius II Ordering Bramante, Michelangelo and Raphael to Construct the Vatican and St. Peter's,* 1827. Pope Julius II surveying the proposals of Bramante for the construction of St. Peter's Basilica, plans that formed the basis of the design executed by Michelangelo (standing at Bramante's right, while Raphael stands at his left holding a painting).

"Total Art on the Grandest Scale": Gothic Architecture

Now this has been standing here for centuries. The premier work of man, perhaps in the whole Western world, and it's without a signature. A celebration to God's glory and to the dignity of man. All that's left, most artists seem to feel these days, is man. Naked, poor, forked radish. There aren't any celebrations. Ours, the scientists keep telling us, is a universe

Notre Dame de Chartres, nave and choir, organ
and windows.

which is disposable. You know, it might be just this one anonymous glory
of all things—this rich stone forest, this epic chant, this gaiety, this grand
choiring shout of affirmation—which we choose when all our cities are
dust, to stand intact, to mark where we have been, to testify to what we
had it in us to accomplish.

> —Orson Welles, in a soliloquy as he stood gazing at
> Chartres Cathedral in his last major film, *F for Fake*

The [Gothic cathedrals are the] greatest accomplishments of humanity in
the whole theatre of art. They are total art on the grandest scale, encompassing architecture at its highest pitch, and virtually every kind of artistic
activity from carpentry to painting.

> —Paul Johnson, *Art: A New History*

In the Gothic cathedral, "a diagram clothed in beauty",[1] the Christian is confirmed
in his conviction that reason is perfected and beauty is born when man has the
truths of Catholicism at the fountainhead of his creativity.

This was the frame of mind of medieval man. In both the "Father of Gothic
Architecture", Abbot Suger (pronounced "Soo-zhay"; 1081–1151), and the author
of the architectonic *Summa Theologiae*, Thomas Aquinas, we see Catholic minds in
love with reason expanding the frontiers of knowledge. This serene synthesis of the
Catholic Faith and rationality was alluded to by Abbot Suger's inscription upon
the great doors of the first Gothic masterpiece, the Basilica of St. Denis, near Paris:

---

[1] Louise Lefrançois Pillion, quoted in Henri Daniel-Rops, *Cathedral and Crusade: Studies of the Medieval
Church, 1050–1350* (New York: Dutton, 1957), p. 368.

"Whoever you are, if you seek to extol the glory of these doors, / Marvel not at gold and expense but at craftsmanship of work. / Bright is the noble work; / But, being nobly bright, the work should brighten the mind, / So that it may travel, through the light to the True Light where Christ is the True Door. / In what manner it is inherent to this world the golden door defines: / The dull mind rises to truth through the material / And, in seeing this light, is resurrected from its former submersion."[2]

The Gothic cathedral was designed to be one immense window for man onto the meaning of life and eternity:

> The cathedrals bear witness not to ambitions but to ideals; and to ideals that are still alive. They are more than alive, indeed they are immortal because they are ideals that no man has ever been able either to frustrate or to fulfill.... A Christian cathedral was more than an aspiration, it was a proclamation. It was not addressed only to the ultimate reality above us all; it was also addressed, in a very definite and a very detailed way, to us also; that is, to the ordinary, emotional and exasperated race of men. The spired minster [church] was not merely meant to strike the stars like an arrow; it was also meant to shake the earth like an explosion. If anyone wishes to know why the Gothic architecture was among all architectures unprecedentedly alive, luxuriant, exciting, complicated, and comic, the answer is in one word: because it was didactic. It had to be interesting as a schoolmaster has to be interesting. It had to be exciting as a demagogue has to be exciting. All architectures, presumably, must have taught; but this was the one that talked.[3]

Through Gothic architecture, man's existence—so labyrinthine to the mind outside the Catholic Faith—is now shown to be lit up by the light of Christ flooding its vast naves and mysterious nooks and crannies. Everywhere there was light because "God is light" (1 Jn 1:5). He whose first command had been "Let there be light" (Gen 1:3), "a light that with its power conquers chaos and darkness to give life"[4]—a light that came into the world embodied in Jesus Christ so as to enlighten man. Through Christ, history is seen to be no mere meaningless roundup of events: the cathedral's storied stained glass windows reveal a purpose-driven chronology; they unfold *his story*, the masterplan of God's great rescue of man from self-destruction for the sake of eternal happiness. The "piercing piety of Gothic",[5] its spires and soaring columns shooting upward, confirms man's soul in his aspirations to go higher, infinitely higher, to his heavenly destiny. All over the cathedral, light and height express the Catholic's ardent hope for a successful pilgrimage through life's battle-filled journey to the joyous ending of the undying splendor of eternity.

And everywhere, in Gothic glass or stone, man discovers that he is not alone—that he travels in the best of company, surrounded by the friendship of heroes, guided by angels, and with the maternal watchfulness of the Blessed Virgin Mary, "Star of the Morning". The light-filled haloes of these divine friends remind him that the men and women closest to God radiate truth and love because their minds and hearts have been enlightened by the divine life of sanctifying grace.

---

[2] Abbot Suger, quoted in Erwin Panofsky, *Abbot Suger on the Abbey Church of St. Denis and Its Treasures* (Princeton, N.J.: Princeton University Press, 1946), pp. 46–47.

[3] G. K. Chesterton, "The Riddle of Restoration", *Daily News*, May 27, 1911.

[4] Benedict XVI, Address of First Vespers on the Occasion of the 500th Anniversary of the Inauguration of the Sistine Chapel Ceiling, Sistine Chapel, October 31, 2012.

[5] G. K. Chesterton, *The Everlasting Man* (Mineola, N.Y.: Dover, 2007), p. 32.

The symbolism and ornamentation, statues and artwork, the very size and measurements of the cathedral, its towers, spires, windows, walls, and buttresses, teach him, as he kneels in prayer, that God is both majestic and intimate. Unlike the colossal pagan temples of ancient Greece, Rome, and Egypt where stark immensity only confirmed man in his sense of separation from the divine, Gothic was made to the measure of the God-Man: his divine awesomeness and his human approachability, his resurrected power and his crucified fragility.

Even the gargoyles, those grotesque, carved animals with their goggle-eyed faces, projecting from the eaves of the cathedrals, had a sublime message to offer:

> The sun ... gives life to all those earthly things that are full of ugliness and energy.... The ugly animals praise God as much as the beautiful.... Under the new inspiration they [medieval men] planned a gorgeous cathedral in the Gothic manner, with all the animals of the earth crawling all over it, and all the possible ugly things making up one common beauty, because they all appealed to God. The columns of the temple were carved like necks of giraffes; the dome was like an ugly tortoise; and the highest pinnacle was a monkey standing on his head with his tail pointing at the sun. And yet the whole was beautiful, because it was lifted up in one living and religious gesture as a man lifts his hands in prayer.... This was Gothic, this was romantic, this was Christian art.[6]

Medieval man wanted to Christify everything in the Gothic cathedral and all that happened therein; all was meant to be a total sensory experience of the truths of his religion; light, glass and stone, the waves of Gregorian and polyphonic chant, the sweet perfumes of oriental incense, the sight of soaring vaults, the rustle of silk chasubles, the touch of shining metal, and the shimmer of jewelled chalices. All these sensations, reflected Abbot Suger, raise man momentarily from the contingencies of his earth-bound existence to its eternal significance: "it seems to me that I see myself dwelling, as it were, in some strange region of the universe which neither exists entirely in the slime of the earth nor entirely in the purity of heaven; and that, by the grace of God, I can be transported from this inferior to that higher world in an anagogical manner [i.e., in a way that reminds me of eternal life]."[7]

The Gothic cathedral was everyman's cathedral. The Gothic churches were the churches of the people because the artistic, political, and ecclesiastical elites simply expressed in stone and glass a Catholic vision that they held in common with the man and woman of street and countryside. The Gothic cathedral was made to be the expression of everyman's convictions, sentiments, and aspirations. The priests, for instance, made sure to put the region's favorite saints in the niches. No wonder then that anyone, whether adult or child, noble or serf, who looked at the cathedral's spires from the distance of castle or wheat fields, felt pride in something deeply personal. All converged on the cathedral as the central institution of their lives where they lived some of the most joyous and poignant moments as individuals and as society.

They or their ancestors had willingly, indeed enthusiastically, helped build it, whether as craftsmen or by quarrying and carting the rock to the building site. The movement from quarry to site often resembled an offertory procession of men and women with hearts on fire to offer their best and greatest to God. Such is the message

[6] G. K. Chesterton, "On Gargoyles", quoted in Dale Ahlquist, Joseph Pearce, Aidan Mackey, eds., *In Defense of Sanity: The Best Essays of G. K. Chesterton* (San Francisco: Ignatius Press, 2011), p. 109.

[7] Abbot Suger, "On the Golden Crucifix", quoted in Panofsky, *Abbot Suger*, pp. 62–65.

of a letter from Aimon, Abbot of St. Pierre-sur-Dives, about the construction of the wonder child of Gothic, Notre Dame de Chartres:

> We saw powerful men, proud of their birth as of their wealth, and accustomed to a life of ease, harness themselves to a cart and haul a load of stone, lime, wood, or some other material. . . . Sometimes the load was so heavy that more than a thousand persons, men and women, were required to draw the cart. They worked so quietly that one heard not so much as a whisper. When they took a rest by the way one heard nothing but confession of faults and a humble prayer to God for remission of their sins. The priests exhorted them to be of one mind; hatreds were silenced, enmities vanished, debts were cancelled, and men's hearts returned to unity one with another. If anyone was so confirmed in wickedness that he would not forgive and listen to the priests, his offering was thrown from the cart as impure, and he himself driven with ignominy from the society of that holy people.[8]

The Man behind Gothic: Abbot Suger

For the gift of Gothic, many are the unknown Christian souls for whom we can raise a prayer of gratitude. Their names appear not in the records of history but only there where their hearts once lay, and their reward, we confidently hope, now resides. Yet, there is one man whom we well know and whom we cannot fail to mention, for he made such an incisive contribution that historians have given him the accolade of "Father of Gothic Architecture": Abbot Suger (1081–1151). This quiet figure of France's history was an able statesman under whose governance the ordinary man and woman felt confident that justice would be done. Even so, he is chiefly remembered as the genius who rebuilt the Basilica of St. Denis near Paris between 1137 and 1144 as the first major Gothic building with all of the style's characteristic features.

In what sense was Abbot Suger the Father of Gothic? He was certainly not the creative genius who drew forth from his own imagination the component architectural techniques. His role was rather that of the insightful author who brought together in one majestic edifice many of the technical innovations already present in primitive form in the Romanesque architecture of France, combining them with the Christian symbolism that was widespread in the twelfth century. Ideas drawn from his knowledge of the Gospel of Saint John, the writings of Pseudo-Dionysius, and also, possibly, those of his contemporary Hugh of St. Victor merged into a vision that carved, hewed, and shaped the wood, stone, and glass of the Basilica of St. Denis. With his own strongly Catholic identity he made Gothic happen. The finished masterpiece inflamed, and continues to inflame, the imaginations of men. Swiftly it gave birth to many other Gothic creations in France: Noyon, Sens, Laon, Notre Dame de Paris, Chartres, Reims and Amiens, Rouen, Bourges, Le Mans, Bayeux, Lisieux, and Coutances.

At the center of the Basilica of St. Denis was the high altar of the Holy Sacrifice, which Abbot Suger wanted to be dazzlingly bright, drenched in light, symbolizing the divine light and energy that stream from it to transform man the closer he approaches and the more he is united through it with the Crucified and Risen Christ.

---

[8] *PL* 181:1707, quoted in Daniel-Rops, *Cathedral and Crusade*, p. 355.

Jean-Baptiste Mauzaisse, *Louis VII (ca. 1120–1180), King of France, Taking the Banner in St. Denis in 1147*, (1840). Louis VII, the twenty-seven-year-old king of France, receives the pilgrim's staff and blessing from Pope Eugene III before he sets off on the Crusade. On the Pope's left is Abbot Suger, who became regent of France during the royal absence.

To achieve such brightness there and throughout the cathedral, Suger had to solve a problem: how to have large window spaces in spite of the fact that the walls needed to be solid and thick in order to support the high and broad roof. His solution was to bring together for the first time the features of the flying and close buttresses along with rib vaults resting on pointed (ogival) arches, all of which bear the weight of the ceiling at soaring heights, allowing the walls to devote themselves to window space.

Like other breakthroughs in Christian culture, the new architecture was not only the fruit of technical discoveries but also owed much to a baptized heart's experience of the effects of supernatural life. Seeing that Gothic owes so much to its Father, the priest Suger, we can allow ourselves to be curious about the personal story of this extraordinary individual. Much, of course, is hidden from us, but one thing we know for certain—since all the ruling class talked about it—is that at a certain moment his life underwent a dramatic change of direction: a second conversion to Christ. It was not a matter of renouncing an immoral lifestyle. By no means. Rather it was all about a quality leap of priestly intensity. For Suger, due to the attrition sustained during years of living at the summit of political power, had become more of a statesman than a man of God. As the king's prime minister, he was surrounded by "pride, pomp and circumstance",[9] such as the guard of sixty cavalry that accompanied him while

---

[9] William Shakespeare, *Othello*, Ignatius Critical Editions, ed. Joseph Pearce (San Francisco: Ignatius Press, 2014), act 3, scene 3, p. 95.

travelling. Providentially, Suger met "the conscience of the twelfth century":[10] Bernard of Clairvaux. The first conversations—rather cool in temperature, as one might expect—were followed intermittently by others that became increasingly cordial until finally, in 1127, the royal court saw the consequences of their friendship: the prime minister begin living as "the King's good servant but God's first".[11]

It showed in his building projects. As a contemporary remarked: "This man puts us all to shame; he builds, not as we do for ourselves, but for God."[12] Suger himself left on record that he had not begun building "with any desire for empty glory nor with any claim to the reward of human praise and transitory compensation".[13] "For God": there lies the entrance to the mystic secret of Gothic. To God, Creator and Savior, should be offered only the sublime, the magnificent and the exuberantly beautiful, especially in that supreme action, the Holy Sacrifice of the Mass. As the abbot explained:

> As for me, I confess that I took great pleasure in devoting all the costliest and most precious things I could find to the service of the administration of the Most Holy Eucharist. If, to fulfill an order from God manifested through the mouths of the Prophets, golden chalices, vases and cups were used to receive the blood of goats ... how much greater is our obligation to use, in order to receive the blood of Jesus Christ, in perpetual service and with the utmost devotion, vases of gold, gems, and everything that is considered most precious. Surely neither we nor our earthly goods can suffice such great mysteries. Even if, in a new creation, our substance were changed into that of Seraphim and Cherubim it would still be unworthy to serve the ineffable Host. We can however offer propitiation for our sins. Some, no doubt, would, in contradiction, tell us that all that is necessary is to bring to the cult a pure heart, a holy soul, and true intentions; we also think that these conditions are a prime necessity and have a very special importance. But we likewise affirm that the ornamentation of the sacred vessels used for the Holy Sacrifice should possess an outer magnificence which, so far as is possible, equals our inner purity. We must serve in every way and with the utmost circumspection our Redeemer, Him from whom we receive everything without exception.[14]

Abbot Suger, due in some measure to Bernard of Clairvaux, had opened his natural genius to supernatural energies. The result was an outpouring of Christian creativity—and the landscape of the West is forever grateful.

Before and After Gothic and Always

Before Abbot Suger there had already been a long line of priests and monks furthering the cause of architecture.

---

[10]Daniel-Rops, *Cathedral and Crusade*, p. 125.

[11]A version of St. Thomas More's last words before his execution on July 6, 1535. However, the phrasing was slightly different: "I die the King's good servant and God's first", according to the *Paris Newsletter* account of August 4, 1535, quoted in Gerard Wegemer and Stephen W. Smith, eds., *A Thomas More Source Book* (Washington D.C.: Catholic University of America Press, 2004), p. 357.

[12]Quoted in Daniel-Rops, *Cathedral and Crusade*, p. 138.

[13]Abbot Suger, quoted in Panofsky, *Abbot Suger*, pp. 40–41.

[14]Abbot Suger, "On the Use of Beautiful Objects in Worship", *On His Administration*, chaps. 25–26, quoted in Jean Leclerq, *The Love of Learning and the Desire for God* (New York: Fordham University Press, 1961), p. 250.

If we glance at the architectural landscape of Western Europe around the eighth century, we meet the dignified and sturdy Romanesque that by the year 1000 had created a "white mantle of churches"[15] covering the countryside. Throughout France, Spain, Lombardy, and Germany, this original style, with a harmony of elements from East and West, arranged itself differently from region to region. Solid and simple were these churches with their rough pillars, a central nave with twin aisles, a transverse nave (transept) crossing the main axis to form the shape of the cross, and towers.

Karl Friedrich Schinkel, *Gothic Cathedral with Imperial Palace* (detail), 1815.

There were flat roofs in some, but others had a stone vault either in barrel shape (semi-cylindrical) or groined (four convex enclosed spaces).

Until the twelfth century when the city cathedrals became the sites of architectural innovation, monks building their abbey churches were on the cutting edge. Motivated by the ardent desire to instill beauty into divine worship, the abbey of Cluny in Burgundy led the way under Abbots Hugh (1049–1109) and Peter the Venerable (1122–1156), who built their church with a vault ninety-eight feet high and a nave one hundred yards long. The Cluniacs greatly improved the techniques of vaulting, gave sculpture new life, and helped perfect stained glass windows. Cistercian abbeys at Fontenay, Frontfroide, and Pontigny expressed in their transparent simplicity the austere spirit of Saint Bernard. German abbeys like Hirschau and Maria-Laach were also pioneers in monastic architecture.

Beauty is the other side of the coin of truth, always and forever. Whatever the century, there is a constantly noticeable correlation between the beauty of the age's Christian architecture and the splendor of the age's soul that, when all is said and done, is determined by the souls of the creative minorities therein. For Christian genius always comes to birth in every age from Christified men in whom supernatural life has triumphed over the debilitating influence of a flawed nature. The degree of purity of the truths of the Faith in the Christian intellect and the intensity of self-dedication to God in the Christian heart overflow to express eternal truths in stone, metal, glass, and on canvas. The great Gothic cathedrals exemplify this par excellence: they sprung from the rich soil of a deeply Catholic Faith, pure in its orthodoxy, ardent in its prayer, and constant in its purification. But the other epochal styles are also insistent witnesses. Baroque in its youthful years was nourished on the stern but healthy, bone-building regimen of the decrees of Trent whose discipline enhanced Baroque's exuberance in expressing the Catholic passion for life, here and in eternity.

---

[15] Raoul Glaber (985–1047), *Historiarum libri quinque ab anno incarnationis DCCCC usque ad annum MXLIV*, vol. 3, chap. 4, edited and translated by John France, *The Five Books of the Histories* (Oxford: Oxford University Press, 1989), pp. 114–16.

Music That Rose into the Night: Gregorian Chant

Plainchant, a form of monophonic, unaccompanied sacred song, had been present in the Church since her early days, but it was from the fourth to the sixth centuries, during the turmoil of the Dark Ages, that it developed considerably:

> Among the promises of the light to come there is one particularly memorable one. This promise is expressed in the development of Christian singing, right in the very heart of the Barbarian epoch. Music has always been the consolation of those in sorrow and of periods of anarchy, and it is extremely moving to realize that the melodious voice of the Church rose into the night in the very darkest moment of the twilight age, as if she wanted thereby to strengthen men's souls to withstand the horrors surrounding them.[16]

The form of plainsong that became dominant in the Catholic Church is usually called Gregorian chant in honor of Pope St. Gregory the Great (540–604), during whose papacy different plainchant styles with their varying strands of psalmody, rhythm, and melody that had been developing for centuries came together, were standardized, and codified. The pontiff "impressed on the whole structure of ecclesiastical music the stamp of restrained dignity, naturalness, and simplicity which was the characteristic genius of this great Pope himself".[17] Gradually, over the following five centuries it spread throughout Western Europe. In 597, Benedictine monks brought it to England. In 754, Pope Stephen II, during his stay at the royal Abbey of St. Denis, north of Paris, brought it to the attention of the Frankish king, Pepin, and his son Charlemagne, when they attended several of the papal liturgies between Epiphany and Pentecost. Pepin was so impressed that he ordered the "Roman chant" to be sung throughout his kingdom. The monks disregarded the king's order, but gradually, under Charlemagne and Alcuin and their successors in the eighth and ninth centuries, the Roman chant assimilated the Gallican variety; and it is this amalgamated form that has come down to us today as "Gregorian chant".

The monks, more than any other group, perfected Gregorian chant. These men who rose in the silence of the night, cowled figures gliding through monastic cloisters to the house of God, with the intensity and focus of military on a mission, were dedicated to that most necessary of missions: men's salvation. Gravity marked their faces and deep emotions their hearts, and from their majestic souls rose Gregorian chant as the expression of lives dedicated to achieving the purpose of man's existence on earth: union with God. In that greatest, most sublime, and most necessary of projects, only perfection could be tolerated. That thrust for excellence had been called for by the "Father of Western Monasticism", Saint Benedict, who had stated that the monks should guide their singing efforts by the words of Psalm 137:1: "[B]efore the angels I sing your praise".

> What this expresses is the awareness that in communal prayer one is singing in the presence of the entire heavenly court, and is thereby measured according to the very highest standards: that one is praying and singing in such a way as to harmonize with the music of the noble spirits who were considered the originators of the harmony of the cosmos, the music of the spheres. From this perspective one can understand the

---

[16] Henri Daniel-Rops, *The Church in the Dark Ages* (London: J. M. Dent and Sons, 1959), p. 307.
[17] Ibid., p. 308.

Canute Listens to the Chanting Monks of Ely, ca. 1017. "On a certain day King Canute came to Ely in a boat, accompanied by his wife, the Queen Emma, and the chief nobles of his kingdom, hoping to keep there the solemn Festival of the Purification of the Virgin Mary [February 2], and when the boat came to the Portus Pusillus of the Monastery, the King raised his eyes aloft to the great church which close by stood up on the rocky eminence, and was aware of a sound of great sweetness, and listening intently heard the melody increase, and perceived it was the monks singing in the convent their psalms and chanting 'the hours', and, calling his people about him, he exhorted them also to sing with gladness, he himself with his own mouth expressing the joy of his heart" (Charles William Stubbs, *Bryhtnoth's Prayer and Other Poems* (London: T. Fisher Unwin, 1899), p. 7).

seriousness of a remark by Saint Bernard of Clairvaux on the poor singing of monks which, for him, was evidently very far from being a mishap of only minor importance. Using an expression from the Platonic tradition handed down by Augustine he describes the confusion resulting from a poorly executed chant as a falling into the "zone of dissimilarity"—the *regio dissimilitudinis*. Augustine had borrowed this phrase from Platonic philosophy in order to designate his own condition prior to conversion (cf. *Confessions*, VII, 10.16): man, who is created in God's likeness, falls in his god-forsakenness into the "zone of dissimilarity"—into a remoteness from God in which he no longer reflects him, and so has become dissimilar not only to God but to himself, to what being truly human is all about.

Bernard is certainly putting it strongly when he uses this phrase which indicates man's falling away from himself to describe bad singing by monks. But it shows how seriously he viewed the matter. It shows that the culture of singing is also the culture of being, and that the monks have to pray and sing in a manner that is to be measured by the standard of the grandeur of the word handed down to them, with its claim on true beauty. This intrinsic requirement of speaking with God and singing about him with words he himself has given is what gave rise to the great tradition of Western music. It was not a form of private "creativity", in which the individual leaves a memorial to himself and makes self-representation his essential criterion. Rather it is about vigilantly recognizing with the "ears of the heart" the inner laws of the music of creation, the archetype of music that the Creator built into his world and into men, and thus discovering music that is worthy of God, and at the same time truly worthy of man, music whose worthiness resounds in purity.[18]

To this day we wonder at the power to fascinate within Gregorian chant since its severe self-control—normally holding its range of pitch within a single octave plus one or two notes, allowing only a single melody, and forbidding instrumental accompaniment—would seem to inhibit expressiveness. And yet, it is the ascetic purity of sound that allows the sublime truths of the lyrics to pierce the soul so incisively—and that was the very reason for the birth of this music.

This yielding of sound to spirit radiated from the character of the men who had created plainchant. In order to achieve a lifetime of ardent love for God, they sought to

Carthusian Monks in Cowls and Habits Process to Matins at 2 a.m. Engraving by an unnamed artist, 1872.

harmonize the body with the Christian spirit by committing themselves to conquer their passions. Thus they became a new type of man unknown to the ancient world: one with the self-mastery of the ancient Roman senators and army officers, avoiding emotional excess and with rock-like moral strength and serenity; yet, alongside the *gravitas romana* (Roman seriousness) there was something new and revolutionary: the *caritas Christi* (love of Christ). The welding of both traits in the forge of monastic prayer and asceticism transformed these men and their monasteries into fortresses of Christian strength where Western Europeans of the Dark Ages went to be invigorated. Here there was strength, tenderness, and compassion in action as the black- or white-robed men fed the hungry and taught them agriculture, tended the sick and consoled the weary, educated the poor and also the rich, and threw open their doors to receive travellers with a generosity that became synonymous with hospitality. In these men Christlikeness was seen walking the roads of the Earth.

Gregorian chant was natural to these men. But to the modern sensibility, so used to a multilayered sound fabricated by various instruments and accentuated rhythms, Gregorian chant can appear to be too simple. In this sense Gregorian chant deceives since its simplicity is not on the near side of complexity but on the far side. Just as white light refracted in a prism reveals the color components, so does music passing through Gregorian chant reveal sounds in their distinctiveness and sentiments in their purity. It allures man to pray by provoking his most sublime sentiments through the union of nature's pristine sounds with divinity's texts

---

[18]Benedict XVI, "Apostolic Journey of His Holiness Benedict XVI to France on the Occasion of the 150th Anniversary of the Apparitions of the Blessed Virgin Mary at Lourdes (September 12–15, 2008), Meeting with Representatives from the World of Culture" (address, Collège des Bernardins, Paris, September 12, 2008).

about God and man's relationship to God. With its ethereal quality it pierces the heart, pointing no less heavenward than the interior of Gothic cathedrals, raising the soul in momentary ecstasies of adoration, gratitude, and repentance.

But the way it does so is *formidable*. Gregorian chant achieves all this by the call it makes on sound to be, not the master, but the servant of language, thereby guarding the right order of truth, love, and emotion. By limiting the range of sound and permitting only the voice without instrumental accompaniment, it jealously guards the soul's serenity, so necessary for raising intellect and will to Heaven. Yet it also arouses the most poignant emotions to sustain the heart's elevation. With the finesse and sensitivity of a true friend, it refuses to intrude roughly into the soul; it gently touches the heart through its sounds, not wishing to allow any emotion but the pure to come forth, careful always to avoid the flights of passion that can so quickly become the disturbers of interior order. For serenity is the ambience necessary for the soul's growth in knowledge of God and self—the indispensable gateway to arrive at prayer's summit: divine union.

That is why it has lasted fifteen hundred years, always fresh and vigorous "as though time had no power over it".[19] No wonder that through the ages the *Te Deum* has expressed man's joy in victory, sense of freedom from danger, and gratitude to God; that the *Dies Irae* has urged man to the awareness that time is a most precious gift that may not be wasted; and that the *Pange Lingua* has drawn out the wonder in his soul as he gazed on the Blessed Eucharist.

Some of the world's greatest composers and music experts have vied with each other to express admiration for Gregorian chant: Berlioz asserted that "nothing in music could be compared with the effect of the Gregorian *Dies Irae*";[20] Apel described the four Marian antiphons—the *Salve Regina*, *Alma Redemptoris Mater*, *Regina Caeli Laetare*, and *Ave Regina Caelorum*—as "among the most beautiful creations of the late Middle Ages";[21] Halévy viewed Gregorian chant as "the most beautiful religious melody that exists on earth".[22]

The monks also gave Western civilization the basics of musical notation. The Benedictine Guido d'Arezzo (ca. 995–1050) invented the contemporary Western notation (staff notation) that replaced neumatic notation. Staff notation accelerated progress by enabling performance of a melody by musicians who had never heard it before and by providing a graphic description of the precise pitch, intervals, and rhythm of the melody. To the two lines Guido found already existing he added a further two, which were considered to be enough for the range of the average Gregorian melody. Thanks to this Italian monk, we also have the helpful mnemonic "do-re-mi" ("ut-re-mi" as he called it); and he may also have been the inventor of the so-called Guidonian hand, a mnemonic system extensively used in the Middle Ages, relating the names of notes to parts of the human hand.

---

[19] François Auguste Gevaert (1828–1905), president of the Conservatoire de Bruxelles and author of *Les origines du chant liturgique de l'Eglise Latine* (Ghent, 1890), quoted in Stephen Thuis, *Gregorian Chant: A Barometer of Religious Fervor in the Church* (St. Meinrad, Ind.: Grail, 1952), p. 5.

[20] Quoted in ibid.

[21] Willi Apel, *Gregorian Chant* (Bloomington, Ind.: Indiana University Press. 1990), p. 404.

[22] Élie Halévy, quoted by Gerhard Gietmann in "Ecclesiastical Music", in *The Catholic Encyclopedia* (New York: Robert Appleton, 1911), p. 649. The same article quotes Mozart's statement "that he would gladly exchange all his music for the fame of having composed the Gregorian Preface".

In the ninth century, at the Abbey of St. Gall and elsewhere, Gregorian chant gave birth to the Church's polyphony which consisted in adding one or more simultaneous melodic voices. It was a remarkable novelty since both Romans and Greeks knew only monophonic music: the same sequence of notes performed by all instruments or voices. The tenth century treatises *Schola enchiriadis* and *Musica enchiriadis* are the oldest extant written instances that we possess of such polyphony. Peter the Venerable (ca. 1092–1156) introduced polyphonic for two and three voices to the influential Abbey of Cluny. In 1364, the priest Guillaume de Machaut composed the first polyphonic Mass: *La Messe de Nostre Dame*. Palestrina (1526–1594), a dedicated lay Catholic, proved to the Church that prayer had a powerful servant in a polyphony with excellent counterpoint and consonant harmony, as shown in his enchanting *Missa Papae Marcelli* (one of over ninety Masses that he composed), the *Stabat Mater*, and some six hundred motets. Scotland's greatest composer, the priest Robert Carver (ca. 1485–1570), a monk at the Augustinian Scone Abbey in Perthshire, composed at least five Masses and two motets, one of which, *O Bone Jesu* (O Good Jesus), is for nineteen voices.

Gregorian chant's influence has surged and waned through the ages. Through its melodies and texts it influenced the antiphonal chants and liturgical dramas of the Middle Ages. These gave birth to the cantata, which was perfected by Bach and used by Wagner in one of his religious works, *The Apostles Supper*. In the nineteenth century, Gregorian chant revived due to Dom Prosper Guéranger of Solesmes (1805–1875), one of the great leaders of the liturgical renewal, who sought to make church music a faithful and aesthetic interpreter of the liturgy, recognizing that it should unite harmoniously with the liturgy by evoking the sense of the sacred texts. In the twentieth century, its influence could be seen in the "Quatre motets sur des thèmes Grégoriens" by Maurice Duruflé (1902–1986). During the 1990s, recordings of chants at Solesmes, Santo Domingo de Silos, and Heiligenkreuz took top spots on music charts.

Besides the often anonymous role of priests in developing Gregorian and polyphonic music, some priests have also ranked among the leading composers; others have influenced music through their schools of spirituality; and a number have guided the history of music by being "soul-friends" of men of creative genius. The Venetian Antonio Lucio Vivaldi (1678–1741), ordained at twenty-five, was nicknamed "The Red Priest" because of his auburn hair. A virtuoso violinist and one of the greatest Baroque composers, he authored over forty operas, sacred choral works, and instrumental concertos, the most famous being *The Four Seasons*. To St. Philip Neri we owe the inspiration for a new type of music, the *oratorio*, since it was born in his Roman church, the Oratorio di San Girolamo. A story from the Bible or from the lives of the saints was selected and narrated by singers who expressed their sentiments in solos or in chorus, often in two moments separated by a sermon preached by St. Philip. This inspired the two-act form of early Italian oratorio. From this origin in a burning desire to unite men to God, the *oratorio* would give to mankind such masterpieces as Bach's *Passion according to St. Matthew*, George Friedrich Handel's *Messiah*, *The Childhood of Christ* by Hector Berlioz, the *Christus* by Franz Liszt, and compositions by Mendelssohn and Perosi.

Chapter 10

FOUNDERS OF FREE-MARKET ECONOMICS

"Those remarkable anticipators of modern economics, the Spanish school-men of the sixteenth century" (Friedrich Hayek, Lecture on receiving the Nobel Prize in Economics, December 11, 1974).

The Catholic Ideal behind Western Economic Progress

This bronze sculpture, outside the United Nations head-quarters in New York City, was presented to the UN as a gift from Spain by King Juan Carlos during an official visit in 1976. Francisco de Vitoria (1486–1546), besides initiating the School of Salamanca, birthplace of free-market economics, was also a "Father of International Law" along with Hugo Grotius. The white-robed Dominican, amid the cloisters, white-washed walls, coffered ceilings, and carved stone staircases of the University of Salamanca was a man whose "eloquence, simplicity, and great personal charm made his lecture-room ... a meeting place for all who were perplexed by the manifold legal and ethical problems that arose in the government of the far-flung Spanish Empire" (Marjorie Grice-Hutchinson, *The School of Salamanca, Readings in Spanish Monetary Theory, 1544–1605* [Oxford: Clarendon Press, 1952], p. 42).

Beijing, 2002: The speaker was a man in his late thirties, an intellectual of the state-controlled Chinese Academy of Social Sciences. Before addressing the visiting group of eighteen Americans in flawless English, he gave permission for his words to be recorded but asked that he not be identified by name:

> One of the things we were asked to look into was what accounted for the success, in fact the pre-eminence, of the West all over the world. We studied everything we could from the historical, political, economic, and cultural perspective. At first we thought it was because you had more powerful guns than we had. Then we thought it was because you had the best political system. Next we focused on your economic system. But in the past twenty years we have realized that the heart of your culture is your religion: Christianity. That is why the West is so powerful. The Christian moral foundation of social and cultural life was what made possible the emergence of capitalism and then the successful transition to democratic politics. We don't have any doubt about this.[1]

---

[1] David Aikman, *Jesus in Beijing: How Christianity Is Transforming China and Changing the Global Balance of Power* (Washington, D.C.: Regnery, 2003), p. 5. Aikman is the former Beijing bureau chief of *Time* magazine.

Although the Chinese intellectual's conclusion has been demonstrated by leading modern historians, it has not yet descended from the academic apex of intellectuals to the base of popular culture.[2] However, it was not "Christianity" (an
abstraction that has never existed anywhere) but the concrete institution of the
Catholic Church that gave birth to the ethos of the free enterprise system.

Max Weber's theory of the origins of the enterprise system in Protestant rather
than in Catholic societies is no longer acceptable to the vast majority of historians.
History points calmly to the existence of all the key features of modern free markets
in the cities of Catholic Western Europe from the twelfth century onward, long
before Luther came on the scene. The Italian city-states of Venice, Milan, Florence,
Genoa, and Amalfi all had successful market economies, and by the fourteenth century
had created an economic and financial empire stretching from England to India and
China. Even in the northern European centers of free enterprise usually associated
with Protestantism—London, Amsterdam, and elsewhere—the birth of open markets
occurred while the cities were still Catholic. Dutchmen, Flemings, and Englishmen
travelling in Italy had been impressed by the wealth and economic structures of its
city-states and had returned home determined to emulate them.[3]

Schumpeter, one of the most influential economists of the twentieth century, stated
that Weber had made a "fundamental methodological error" by constructing abstract
models of medieval and modern social systems, without paying enough attention
to historical facts, with the result that he had made it theoretically impossible for
capitalism to be born in the Catholic Middle Ages.[4] Weber's theory was characteristic of a certain worldview that had concluded that "the different components of
modernization were ... all part of a single package that somehow arrived with the
Reformation, Enlightenment, and Industrial Revolution".[5] However, attention to
history shows that "two of the basic institutions that became crucial to economic
modernization—individual freedom of choice with regard to social and property
relationships, and political rule limited by transparent and predictable law—were
created by a premodern institution, the medieval Church."[6] The "new" capitalist

[2] See Joseph A. Schumpeter, *History of Economic Analysis* (1954; repr., London: Allen and Unwin, 1986);
Rodney Stark, *The Victory of Reason: How Christianity Led to Freedom, Capitalism, and Western Success* (New
York: Random House, 2005); Fernand Braudel, *Civilization and Capitalism, 15th–18th Century*, 3 vols.
(New York: Harper and Row, 1979); Henri Pirenne, *Economic and Social History of Medieval Europe* (New
York: Mariner Books, 1956); John Gilchrist, *The Church and Economic Activity in the Middle Ages* (New York:
St. Martin's Press, 1969).

[3] The 1974 Nobel Prize winner in economics, Friedrich Hayek, wrote: "Long before Calvin, the Italian
and Dutch commercial towns had practised and later the Spanish schoolmen codified the rules which made
the modern market economy possible. See in this connection particularly H. M. Robertson, *Aspects of the Rise
of Economic Individualism* (Cambridge, 1933), a book which, if it had not remained unknown in Germany,
should have disposed once and for all of the Weberian myth of the Protestant source of capitalist ethics.
He shows that if any religious influences were at work, it was much more the Jesuits than the Calvinists who
assisted the rise of the 'capitalist spirit'." Friedrich A. Hayek, *Law, Legislation, and Liberty* (London: Routledge
and Kegan Paul, 1982), p. 203, n. 44.

[4] Schumpeter, *History of Economic Analysis*, n. 4, pp. 80–81. See another critique of Weber's ideas in H. M.
Robertson, *Aspects of the Rise of Economic Individualism: A Criticism of Max Weber and His School* (New York:
Kelley & Millman, 1959).

[5] Francis Fukuyama, *The Origins of Political Order: From Prehuman Times to the French Revolution* (New York:
Farrar, Straus and Giroux, 2011), p. 275.

[6] Ibid.

mentality had not suddenly erupted onto the stage of history; instead, it had existed as seeds in the furrows of the Dark Ages and, thanks to that era's creative and tena-cious cultivators, had put forth young shoots in the medieval centuries, and then blossomed from the Renaissance onward, due in no small measure, as we shall see, to the Scholastic thinkers of the School of Salamanca. To use Schumpeter's meta-phor, just as "the heliocentric system of astronomy was not simply a bomb thrown at the [medieval] scholastic fortress from outside—it originated in the fortress"[7], so likewise with free-market economics.

Before going any further, a definition of free-market economics is called for. Essentially it is the buying and selling of goods through free enterprise, by peaceful social cooperation, without any form of coercion from governmental intervention. When it gathers momentum, it becomes "an economic system wherein privately owned, relatively well-organized and stable firms pursue complex commercial activities within a relatively free (unregulated) market, taking a systematic, long-term approach to investing and reinvesting wealth (directly or indirectly) in pro-ductive activities involving a hired workforce, and guided by anticipated and actual returns."[8]

The features listed by this definition entail that it could not have been born in just any type of society: there had to be an appropriate sociocultural ecosystem that would nurture and protect it. This began forming during the Dark Ages, climaxed in medieval Christendom between the twelfth and fourteenth centuries, and continued to function, although with ever increasing difficulties, up to modern times. For three main reasons it empowered the birth of the free-market system and the science of economics. Firstly, Catholicism provided the worldview characterized by freedom that acted as the healthy womb empowering the free enterprise economy to be born alive in the West—and not stillborn as occurred in other civilizations. Secondly, the monastic estates had been the first incubators and prototypes of self-regulating socioeconomic institutions. Thirdly, a remarkable line of Catholic priests from the twelfth to the seventeenth centuries formulated the economic principles involved.

Freedom, a trait noticeable by its absence outside of Western civilization until modern times, triggered the new economics. Wherever dictators ruled, whether in the shape of caesars, sultans, czars, or oligarchies, without an institution in society to bridle their will to power, the second crucial element of the ecosystem was either absent or else unstable for lack of guarantees: private property. Take China for instance. One analyst, puzzling over the centuries-long static nature of Chinese society, in spite of its highly cultured elites, asserted: "Property is insecure. In this one phrase the whole history of Asia is contained".[9] Hyperbole certainly—but

---

[7] Schumpeter, *History of Economic Analysis*, p. 80. Schumpeter adds: "Nicolaus Cusanus (1401–64) was a cardinal. And Copernicus himself was a canon (though he did not actually take orders), a doctor of canon law, lived all his life in church circles, and Clement VII approved of his work and wished to see it published." Referring to Galileo, he remarks: "[I]t is clear that the case was quite exceptional; for the bulk of scientific work, that possibility [of condemnation] hardly existed at all. Moreover, Galileo's case was complicated by his impulsiveness and his unfortunate talent for personally antagonizing people who were in a position to make their resentment felt." Ibid., pp. 80–81.

[8] Stark, *Victory of Reason*, p. 56.

[9] Winwood Reade, *The Martyrdom of Man* (London: Watts, 1925), p. 108; quoted in Stark, *Victory of Reason*, p. 72.

with more than a grain of truth. The absence of liberty and guaranteed private ownership immediately sets off a chain reaction destroying the flow of energy throughout the economic ecosystem. It causes insecurity that bleeds the courage from the heart of entrepreneurship: fearful men work cautiously, satisfied merely to survive or to live without ambition. Hence production is dwarfed; money is hoarded rather than deposited in banks, thereby crippling the growth of banking; and investment and long-term projects are guillotined. The final outcome is devastating: state-controlled planned economies run by bureaucrats take over and continue to withhold oxygen from the spirit of initiative, thus aborting any embryonic free enterprise system.

This, however, did not occur in Western Europe. Instead it became a healthy womb because the Church functioned as placenta for the developing economic structure of the Dark Ages and the medieval period, connecting it to the uterine wall of the truths about human nature, notably man's dignity, and his God-willed eternal destiny to which all sociopolitical and economic systems must be subordinated. This is because Catholicism states that all sociopolitical and economic systems must be in function of God's purpose for man: eternal happiness. Since man must be free in order to live in the truth and thus conquer, with the aid of God's grace, his eternal fulfillment, the Church holds that all political systems must respect the individual's liberty. "The medieval Christian insisted that God gave man a charter. Modern feeling may not sympathize with its list of liberties, which included the liberty to be damned; but that has nothing to do with the fact that it was a gift of liberties and not of laws."[10] With this clear horizon the Catholic Church eliminated poisons that would have been fatal to capitalism, such as Byzantine-style despotism and an arbitrary understanding of law. The "Papal Revolution",[11] the dramatic struggle of the eleventh century that came to a climax with the confrontation between Pope Gregory VII and Emperor Henry IV amid the snows of Canossa, ensured there would be a practical separation of religious and civil authority in Europe and thus eliminated the possibility of an orientalized civilization with only one power holder, whether state or religion.

On these foundations Catholicism proceeded to mentor a legal system with rights for the common man and duties for rulers. The immigration of large barbarian populations into Western Europe and the collapse of Roman government had led to law becoming largely a matter of tribal customs between the fifth and the eighth centuries. Justice often implied vengeance, blood vendettas, or battles between champions; trials were frequently ordeals by fire and water. However, the Church had rescued the sense of legal order and justice in Roman legislation from the burning Forum, and through the centuries of darkness her priests zealously guarded it amid monastic libraries and in her own internal organization.

By the mid-twelfth century a Benedictine monk, Gratian, had assembled and reconciled some thirty-eight hundred texts regarding Church discipline, creating the first systematic and comprehensive body of law in medieval Europe. Gratian and

---

[10] G. K. Chesterton, *A Miscellany of Men* (Sioux Falls, N.Dak.: Nuvision, 1930 [2008]), p. 149.

[11] A term used by Harold J. Berman; see his *Law and Revolution: The Formation of the Western Legal Tradition* (Cambridge: Harvard University Press, 1983); also, Philippe Nemo, *Qu'est-ce l'Occident? (What Is the West?)* (Paris: Presses Universitaires de France, 2004).

other Church lawyers decided the validity of legal customs and procedures on the basis of their conformity to the natural law, with its universal principles regarding the rights and duties of the individual. Since the Church's laws dealt not only with internal ecclesiastical affairs but with many political, educational, and legal matters, her legislation affected every aspect of medieval society. Canon law thus became the fountainhead for many of the principles and methods in the legal systems of Western nations—elements such as a rational trial procedure, rules of evidence, and passing sentence only after evaluating a criminal's freedom of will in order to determine the degree of duress, error, fraud, and other extenuating factors.

Ultimately, what Catholicism gave to the Western world during the Dark Ages was therefore both a method of legislating according to the natural law and a *mentality*. As the non-Catholic philosopher Alfred North Whitehead expressed it: "It is important to notice that this legal impress upon medieval civilization was not in the form of a few wise precepts which should permeate conduct. It was the conception of a definite articulated system which defines the legality of the detailed structure of social organism, and of the detailed way in which it should function. There was nothing vague. It was not a question of admirable maxims, but of definite procedure to put things right and to keep them there."[12]

So, although ecclesiastics and monarchs failed on sundry occasions to live by these principles, the mind-set of society was able to hold them guilty and accountable, thereby forcing some to repent and putting others on a leash. Nowhere else did this occur. When, in Chinese or Islamic history, did an emperor publicly do penance for a massacre as Theodosius the Great was obliged to do in the presence of Bishop Ambrose of Milan at Christmas in 390? Where else was there an emperor kneeling in the snows outside the castle gates of a priest without an army? Or an archbishop standing over a tyrant-king as he signed guarantees of freedom in a *Magna Carta*? Saint Thomas Aquinas (1225–1274) justified not only restraining but getting rid of tyrants. This was to become deeply embedded in the Catholic mind-set and later surfaced in such men as Colonel Claus von Stauffenberg, one of the 1944 conspirators who plotted to oust Hitler:

> Authority acquired by violence is not a true authority and there is no obligation of obedience.... [When there is] domination obtained by violence and ruse, the subjects being unwilling or even forced to accept it, and there being no recourse open to a superior who might pronounce judgment upon the usurper: in this case he that kills the tyrant for the liberation of the country is to be praised and rewarded.[13]

Another implication of this Catholic mentality whereby the state exists in order to protect the individual's freedom is the guarantee offered to private ownership of property: the keystone of free-market economics. The University of Bologna professor Huguccio (Hugh of Pisa), in his *Summa* of 1188, went so far as to assert that private property was a sacrosanct right derived from the natural law. Albert the Great and Thomas Aquinas both argued for private property rights as an implication of Christ's teachings about human dignity and freedom. Schumpeter, commenting on the thought of such Catholic thinkers, stated that it was "remarkably individualist,

[12] Alfred North Whitehead, *Science and the Modern World* (New York: Macmillan, 1931), p. 17.
[13] St. Thomas Aquinas, *Scriptum Super Libros Sententiarum* II, dist. 44, q. II, a. 2.

utilitarian, and (in a sense) rationalist" and that "the individualist and utilitarian streak and the emphasis upon a rationally perceived Public Good runs through the whole sociology of St. Thomas".[14] Accordingly, continues Schumpeter, the medieval thinker favors private property as rational and justifiable on the grounds that people will take better care of and show greater initiative with regard to personal possessions; likewise social order and harmony will be better protected through the avoidance of quarreling that accompanies things held in common.

William of Ockham and other medieval theologians drew out the rather nauseating implication for many governments: private property can only be infringed upon for the sake of the public good and never at the sovereign's arbitrary discretion. This became commonly accepted Catholic teaching. Thus, the Church made a point that altered the mind-set of European man for centuries—never would he accept for long the rule of a state or a state-controlled economy that cast its shadow over hearth and altar—as the tearing down of the Berlin Wall on November 9, 1989, showed.

Nor was the medieval Catholic Church shy about calling on the warrior class to unsheathe the sword in support of these rights. This is exactly what happened on June 15, 1215, when every English bishop along with the Master of the Knights Templar and many of the nobility led by Stephen Langton, Archbishop of Canterbury, forced the despotic King John to sign the *Magna Carta*. That document—authored by Langton—struck a blow for subsidiarity and for free trade, marking the start of a constitutional regime in which Church and people had their rights legally protected. It told British monarchs that the Church had jurisdictional and property exemptions; that the cities and towns of England should have the scope to create their own laws on import duties and taxes; that merchants had rights for safe travel and immunity from "evil tolls"; and that twenty-five barons elected by the nobility would protect these rights (the beginning of the House of Lords).[15] Centuries later the *Magna Carta* crossed the Atlantic and became evident in American constitutional provisions like due process by law, a ban on cruel punishments, and the right of the people to keep and use arms.

François Théodore Devaulx, *The Signing of the Magna Carta*, 19th century. King John of England with the principal author of the *Magna Carta* on his right, the Archbishop of Canterbury, Stephen Langton.

Alongside the *Magna Carta* in importance in medieval England

[14]Schumpeter, *History of Economic Analysis*, p. 92.

[15]See A. E. Dick Howard, *Magna Carta: Text and Commentary* (1964; repr., Charlottesville: University of Virginia Press, 1997).

was the *Carta de Foresta* (Charter of the Forest) of 1217, which guaranteed enti-tlement of access to the forests, a vital need for the masses since the vast royal woodlands were not only the largest source of firewood and turf for cooking and heating but were also important for animal grazing. Thus, the authors proved loyal to the Catholic principle that although private property must be protected, it must never be a source of injustice for the poor. The Christian and Catholic roots of this document are evident in the lines that King Henry III penned to its introduction when he declared that it was "out of reverence for God and for the salvation of our soul and the souls of our ancestors and successors, for the exaltation of Holy Church and the reform of our realm"[16] that he had granted the liberties asserted in the charter.

Canon 22 of the Lateran Council, held in 1179, legislated to protect farmers and merchants from undue taxation, and ordered that only rulers introduce new tolls, thundering that "if anyone presumes to act against this decree and does not stop after warning, let him be deprived of Christian society until he makes satisfaction". By creating a cultural climate and legal safeguards favorable to private property rights, the Church made it possible for people to benefit personally from their work—a mighty incentive to produce more effectively. Such a stimulus leads not only to better products but to new ones; it favors reinvesting surplus; and putting money and time into the education of both employers and employees. Thus the Church motivated man to produce, a motivation noticeably absent in command-economies where either state ownership of the means of production or heavy socialist-style taxation breeds hoarding and sluggish minds.

Insisting on productivity came naturally to Catholicism. Year after year, in basilica or rustic chapel, her priests taught Romans and barbarians key texts of the Bible: that God the Creator had "created man in his own image" (see Gen 1:27); that he commanded man to "fill the earth and subdue it" (Gen 1:28); and that Christ in the Parable of the Talents called on everyone to use his intelligence and possessions to their utter limits for the sake of truth and goodness. This was how, under the power of supernatural life, man was meant to reach human fulfillment, becoming configured in an imperfect, blurred manner to the "new man" (Eph 4:24), patterned on Christ, that he was called to be flawlessly in Heaven.

The Church declared every genre of work valuable—including manual work in field and forge. Now that was revolutionary! Priests pointed to the model par excel-lence, the Eternal Son of God, whose mind had blueprinted the galaxies and given beauty to sky and ocean, yet whose brow became wet with perspiration while his hands carved, chiseled, and hammered wood in the workshop of Nazareth. Strange indeed was this idea to ancient Greece and Rome, to Byzantium and China! By ennobling manual work, Catholicism gave value not only to plowing, harvesting, felling trees, and logging firewood but also to their spin-offs: trade, commerce, accounting, and investing.

The sheer novelty, during the Middle Ages, of seeing these priests and monks, sometimes men of royal blood or of immense culture, doing manual work, cannot be overestimated—it marked a revolution in thought and action for civilization. Until

---

[16] The English translation of the *Carta de Foresta*, as issued in 1217, in Harry Rothwell, ed., *English Historical Documents*, vol. 3, 1189–1327 (London: Eyre and Spottiswoode, 1975), n. 24, pp. 337–40.

"Burgundian monks [Cistercians] cultivating the vineyard during the Middle Ages". A 19th century illustration from Louis Figuier, *Les merveilles de l'industrie* (Paris: Furne et Jouvet, 1873).

such men were seen tilling the soil and lifting huge stones for building purposes, manual work had been despised by "civilized" men. Even Aristotle disdained it as "philistine" and "unworthy of a free man"; proud Roman patricians of the empire could not even imagine dedicating their time to such plebeian tasks; and Chinese Mandarins grew their fingernails as long as possible to show that they had nothing to do with manual labor.[17]

The Catholic Church exiled that mentality from the West. During the Middle Ages, one could see men like Hugh of Lincoln, Archbishop of Lincoln, carrying stones for the construction of his cathedral; and Thomas à Becket, Archbishop of Canterbury, reaping the corn in the fields. In sermons priests reminded nobles and serfs that when they perspired in quarry, forge, or meadow, they were following in the footsteps of the Son of God, who had done the same in the workshop of Nazareth; and indeed, that they were thus cooperating with the Creator.

> The Graeco-Roman world did not have a creator God; according to its vision, the highest divinity could not, as it were, dirty his hands in the business of creating matter. The "making" of the world was the work of the Demiurge, a lower deity. The Christian God is different: He, the one, real, and only God, is also the Creator. God is working; he continues working in and on human history. In Christ he enters personally into the laborious work of history. "My Father is working still, and I am working." God himself is the Creator of the world, and creation is not yet finished. God works, *ergázetai*! Thus human work was now seen as a special form of human resemblance to God, as a way in which man could and might share in God's activity as creator of the world. Monasticism involves not only a culture of the word but also a culture of work without which the emergence of Europe, its ethos, and its influence on the world would be unthinkable. Naturally, this ethos had to include the idea that human work and the shaping of history is understood as sharing in the work of the Creator, and must be evaluated in those terms. Where such evaluation is lacking, where man arrogates to himself the status of god-like creator, his shaping of the world can quickly turn into destruction of the world.[18]

This ethos also led to the end of slavery among Europeans. An economy supported by slaves—the case of most major ancient civilizations—was inevitably a bungling system, geared to promote an economically lazy elite, abort new technology, and minimize productivity. By the twelfth century the Church had largely triumphed over the slave system in a manner incisively portrayed by G. K. Chesterton:

[17] Stark, *Victory of Reason*, p. 62.

[18] Benedict XVI, "Meeting with Representatives from the World of Culture" (address delivered at the Collège des Bernardins, Paris, September 12, 2008).

At the beginning of the Dark Ages the great pagan cosmopolitan society now grown Christian was as much a slave state as old South Carolina. By the fourteenth century it was almost as much a state of peasant proprietors as modern France.... This startling and silent transformation is perhaps the best measure of the pressure of popular life in the Middle Ages, of how fast it was making new things in its spiritual factory. Like everything else in the medieval revolution, from its cathedrals to its ballads, it was as anonymous as it was enormous. It is admitted that the conscious and active emancipators everywhere were the parish priests and the religious brotherhoods; but no name among them has survived and no man of them has reaped his reward in this world. Countless Clarksons and innumerable Wilberforces, without political machinery or public fame, worked at deathbeds and confessionals in all the villages of Europe; and the vast system of slavery vanished. It was probably the widest work ever done which was voluntary on both sides; and the Middle Ages was in this and other things the age of volunteers.... The Catholic type of Christianity was not merely an element, it was a climate; and in that climate the slave would not grow.[19]

First Incubators of Free Enterprise Principles

By the ninth century, the monasteries of Western Europe, particularly in Charlemagne's empire, had become important social and economic hubs. Some of the abbeys managed vast domains: Fulda in central Germany, for instance, owned fifteen thousand plough lands, and Lorsch had 911 estates in the Rhinelands. Their wealth came from the soil that preceding generations of monks had cultivated, often after draining swamps and clearing forests. As an American Protestant agriculturalist poignantly remarked: "Taking their lives in their hands, [the monks] flung themselves into the wild forests and abandoned wastes of Europe and the remoter East, and wrought a work which, so far as we can judge, could have been wrought in no other way; for it was done by men who gave up all that makes life dear and worth the living, for the sake of being good themselves and making others good."[20]

Henry Matthew Brock (1875–1960), *Labouring Monks*, illustration from H. D. M. Spence-Jones, *The Church of England: A History for the People*.

The monasteries were nurseries of creativity; here entrepreneurship had a pool of idealistic, intelligent, and energetic men, bonded to the ideal of the love of God

---

[19] G. K. Chesterton, *A Short History of England*, chap. 8, quoted in Kevin L. Morris, ed., *The Truest Fairy Tale: An Anthology of the Religious Writings of G. K. Chesterton* (Cambridge: Lutterworth Press, 2007), pp. 171–72.

[20] Henry H. Goodell, "The Influence of the Monks in Agriculture" (address delivered before the Massachusetts State Board of Agriculture, Lynnfield, Mass., August 23, 1901), in Calvin Stebbins, *Henry Hill Goodell: The Story of His Life, with Letters and a Few of His Addresses* (Cambridge: Riverside Press, 1911), p. 228.

and their fellow men since youth or even childhood. From such concentrations of talent sprung new techniques in irrigation, cattle breeding, horse raising, cheese making, the corn trade, and fish farming. As Montalembert in *The Monks of the West* reminded us, they brought salmon fisheries (and the pike, I might add) to Ireland, cheese making to Parma, the breeding, hatching, and rearing of fish to Burgundy, and the corn trade to Sweden. Celtic, Benedictine, and Cistercian monks cleared away forests and drained swamps to make farms from Lombardy to the Baltic. On the coast of Flanders, monks at the monastery of Les Dunes recovered some twenty-five thousand acres from marshes.[21] Loudon remarked that in France "the Norman clergy, and particularly the monks, were still greater improvers than the nobility; and the lands of the church, especially of the convents, were conspicuous for their superior cultivation."[22]

Monks ploughing the land with oxen. Engraving, Germany, 1872.

Agriculture allowed the monasteries to be self-sufficient, supplying their own modest requirements for food, drink, and cloth. But, inevitably, over time, such concentrations of highly intelligent, intensely focused, and hardworking men transformed many abbeys into small cities with forge, mill, pottery, tannery, saw mill, and numerous workshops at the center of large estates. The outcome was a surplus of goods and the gradual emergence of more features of the free enterprise system.

In the first place, specialization occurred. For instance the Carthusians in Dauphiné were the first medieval ironmasters, and the Cistercians in Fossanova raised quality horses. Others advanced the science of viniculture, and by their toil had the best vineyards amid the Rhinelands, Burgundy, and the Auvergne. Many practices in grape cultivation began with the medieval monks: pruning for quality, the study of the different varieties of grapes (varietals), and the science of terroir—namely, the attention to the complete set of local geographical circumstances (climate, soil type, topography) necessary for cultivation of quality grapevines. In Burgundy, the monks of Saint Bernard carefully studied the types of wine from the different vineyards and identified those areas that consistently produced vintages of similar body, color, and flavor—the concept of *cru*. It was only a matter of time before monasteries began producing some of the most appreciated wines and liqueurs in Europe since the monks put the same spirit into their production that they did into building Gothic churches, singing Gregorian chant, educating, and caring for the poor: a spirit alluded to by the initials "D. O. M." on the label of the liqueur *Bénédictine*— "*Deo Optimo Maximo*" (To God, Supremely Good, Supremely Great)—which, in Christianity, implies giving to one's fellow man the best and the greatest for God's sake.

---

[21] Jean Gimpel, *The Medieval Machine: The Industrial Revolution of the Middle Ages* (New York: Holt, Rinehart and Winston, 1976), p. 47.

[22] John C. Loudon, *An Encyclopedia of Agriculture* (London: Longman, 1825), p. 38.

Plan of a Medieval Monastery[23]

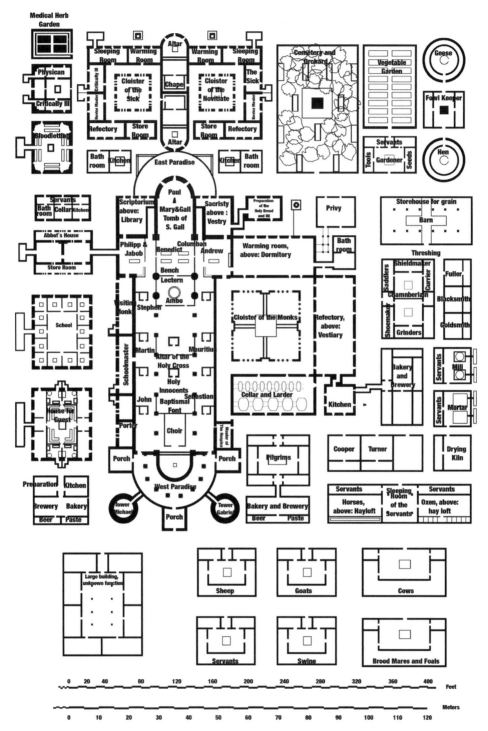

"Carolingian Culture at Reichenau and St. Gall: The Plan of St. Gall".

With specialization came trade. The networks for it were already in place: many monasteries had some fifty affiliates and the great Abbey of Cluny had hundreds. For practical reasons trade also led to the switch from bartering goods to buying and selling for cash, something that the monks of Lucca in Tuscany were doing as early as the ninth century. Monetary credit spun off this; already in the eleventh and twelfth centuries abbeys were lending at interest rates. Mortgaging was in by the thirteenth century.

All this led to monastic estates becoming highly successful businesses. Steady growth was favored by the abbeys having a membership of many of Europe's brightest young minds, thus ensuring privileged pools from which to elect abbots who had the requisite qualities not only to be paternal figures but also to be chief executives. Growth, trade, and monetary credit sharpened management techniques and improved accounting methods. There was also a diversification within the bounds of an agricultural economy. Undoubtedly, the monks did not create business companies exclusively dedicated either to manufacturing, trade, or finance. However, they certainly fashioned models for many of the systems on which a free enterprise economy runs. The monastic estate, in its mature form, was a prototype—modest certainly like most beginnings are—of a business working in an open-market society.

Another first-of-its-kind was the foundation by the Templars of an international financial services corporation with centers extending across Western Europe and the Mediterranean to the Middle East. The purpose behind this enterprise was the financial support of the order's fortresses in Palestine. In 1150 they began the first organized system to support the use of cheques, an innovation that was helpful to pilgrims travelling to Jerusalem who wanted to avoid robbery from the many brigands on the way. When the pilgrim entrusted his valuables to a local Templar center before departure, he received a letter of credit for the value of the deposit and then, with this in hand, he could ask for whatever funds he needed upon arrival at the Templar castles in Palestine.[24]

The monks were also technologists. They developed mining and foundries; built roads, bridges, churches, and monastic villages; and while achieving all this they brought machinery and mechanization to quite sophisticated levels. Although Europeans were not the first to have mechanical clocks—the Chinese had invented giant clocks during the Sung dynasty—clock-making thrived in Europe due to the enthusiastic encouragement of the Church. Monks, who were probably the European inventors, saw their value for organizing monastic schedules of work and prayer that included nocturnal chanting. We know that in 850 the archdeacon of Verona, Pacificus, built a water clock, and that in 996, in the German city of Magdeburg, the priest who would become Pope Sylvester II built another. The

---

[23] "The Plan of St. Gall is the earliest preserved and most extraordinary visualization of a building complex produced in the Middle Ages. Drawn and annotated on five pieces of parchment sewn together, the St. Gall Plan is 112 cm × 77.5 cm and includes the ground plans of some forty structures as well as gardens, fences, walls, a road, and an orchard. Three hundred and thirty-three inscriptions identify the buildings and their uses, including a church, a scriptorium, lodgings for visiting monks, a monastic dormitory, refectory, kitchen, bakery and brewery, guest house, the abbot's residence, an infirmary, along with numerous fields and industrial out-buildings." Carolingian culture at Reichenau & St. Gall, stgallplan.org/en/index_plan.html.

[24] See Régine Pernoud, *The Templars: Knights of Christ* (San Francisco: Ignatius Press, 2009), pp. 85–106.

Model of a monastery based on the plan drawn up for Gozbert, the Abbot of St. Gall (816–837 A.D.).

Abbot of St. Alban's Abbey in England, Richard of Wallingford (1292–1336), one of the initiators of Western trigonometry, also built a remarkably complex and large astronomical clock. This key invention would enable the precise coordination of production activities in factories during the eighteenth-century industrial revolution.[25]

There is one final, rather poignant, note to be made about the monastic capitalists. By the sixteenth century they had an enormous sociocultural influence throughout Western Europe. Their hard work in reclaiming marshes and clearing forests, as well as legacies of land received from grateful friends, had brought about large monastic estates, with some Cistercian houses, for instance, farming one hundred thousand acres. This led to the Church becoming Western Europe's largest landowner.

Much of this land they rented out to small farmers who cherished working with these plain-living men whom they affectionately regarded as the very best of landlords and the kindest of neighbors. Their care for tenants and workers, indeed for the entire local population, was notorious. To live near them was to benefit in a thousand ways. For instance, the people close to the abbeys of the Cistercians (who ate no meat) could obtain a constant supply of fresh carp and trout from their many ponds. The monasteries ensured unchanging reliable standards of living with a myriad of social assistance programs given by warm-hearted monks who educated the children of the local people, healed their sick, and were present at their bedsides at the hour of death to strengthen them and their families with the sacraments.

In England all this abruptly disappeared when Henry VIII destroyed these monasteries, leaving "bare ruin'd choirs, where late the sweet birds sang".[26] The destruction set in motion a cycle of poverty, sharp class divisions, and exploitation that accelerated during the Industrial Revolution of the eighteenth and nineteenth centuries, rippling down to our times. Someone who became aware of this was Benjamin Disraeli (1804–1881). At the height of the Industrial Revolution this great Jewish statesman and prime minister of England strove to alleviate the

---

[25] Alfred W. Crosby, *The Measure of Reality: Quantification in Western Europe, 1250–1600* (Cambridge: Cambridge University Press, 1997), pp. 19, 81–83, 137.

[26] Shakespeare, Sonnet 73.

Interior astronomical clock in the ambulatory of Chartres Cathedral, Eure-et-Loir, France.

sufferings of the masses of the working poor in the grimy, smoke-ridden cities. His efforts to understand the origins of the injustice led him to walk through the history of England, clearing his way through the fog of anti-Catholicism to discover an important cause: the ravaging of the medieval monasteries and the elimination of the monks. In his romantic novel, *Sybil*, set during the Industrial Revolution, one of the characters exclaims about the monasteries destroyed by Henry VIII: "If the world but only knew what they had lost! ... The monks were, in short, in every district a point of refuge for all who needed succour, counsel, and protection; a body of individuals having no cares of their own, with wisdom to guide the inexperienced, with wealth to relieve the suffering, and often with power to protect the oppressed."[27]

One of the most astonishing—and tragic—recent discoveries about medieval monks was that they had knowledge that might well have enabled them to launch the Industrial Revolution in the 1500s. A University of Bradford archeometallurgist, Gerry McDonnell, during the late 1990s discovered evidence near Rievaulx Abbey in Yorkshire, England, of technological know-how that historians up to then had linked to the eighteenth century. The monks had constructed a furnace with temperatures high enough to be able to extract iron from ore—and evidence indicates that they had the know-how to create a blast furnace for massive production of cast iron, probably the key factor in the Industrial Revolution. But it was not to be: Henry VIII, who began the alienation of the English from the "Ancient Faith" confiscated the monasteries of these high-tech priests, thereby clipping the wings of technological progress and its socioeconomic benefits for another 250 years.[28]

It is worth speculating on how different today's world might be if the Industrial Revolution had occurred under the spirit of Catholicism in the 1500s rather than in post-Catholic England of the eighteenth and nineteenth centuries.

Worldly Ascetics: The Priests Who Pioneered Modern Economics

Medieval and Renaissance Economic Thinkers

On December 11, 1974, Friedrich Hayek, during the official ceremonies in Stockholm, Sweden, in which he received the Nobel Prize in economics, shocked

---

[27] Benjamin Disraeli, *Sybil: Or the Two Nations* (1845; Oxford: Oxford University Press, 1998), pp. 61–62. See also Eamon Duffy, *The Stripping of the Altars: Traditional Religion in England, 1400–1580* (New Haven, Conn.: Yale University Press, 1992). The author documents the vibrant nature of English Catholicism before the assault launched by Henry VIII. In *The Voices of Morebath: Reformation and Rebellion in an English Village* (New Haven, Conn.: Yale University Press, 2003), Professor Duffy focuses on how one particular English village reacted to this destruction of its millennium-old culture.

[28] See Gerry McDonnell, "Monks and Miners: The Iron Industry of Bilsdale and Rievaulx Abbey", *Medieval Life*, no. 11, pp. 16–21; also, Thomas Woods, *How the Catholic Church Built Western Civilization* (Washington, D.C.: Regnery, 2005), pp. 36–38; David Derbyshire, "Henry 'Stamped Out Industrial Revolution'", *Telegraph* [U.K.], June 21, 2002; "Henry's Big Mistake", *Discover*, February 1999.

many with his lecture entitled "The Pretence of Knowledge".[29] He persuasively attacked the social engineering of politicians and intellectuals who seek to redesign society through coercive government, whether socialist or interventionist, especially through micro-managing the economy with the unworkable goal of thus assuring economic growth. Such a policy is "the destroyer of a civilization which no brain has designed but which has grown from the free efforts of millions of individuals".[30] While explaining a dimension of his position, Hayek cited two

The Monks: Men of Prayer. Detail from the fresco by Niccolò di Tommaso (Florence, 1346–1376) of Pope Celestinus V with Raimondo del Balzo and Isabella d'Eppe.

Spanish Thomists, the priests Luis de Molina (1535–1600) and Juan de Lugo (1583–1660), asserting that "the chief point was already seen by those remarkable anticipators of modern economics, the Spanish schoolmen of the sixteenth century".[31]

These "Spanish schoolmen" were philosophers and theologians who were mostly Thomist Scholastics, followers of the thought of Thomas Aquinas according to the Scholastic method, in that Renaissance intellectual tradition known as the "School of Salamanca".[32] For Hayek to assert that these men had invented the theoretical principles of a market economy was to contradict the widely held notion that Protestantism, especially the "Calvinist ethic" and the thought of Adam Smith (1723–1790), was its author.[33] However, the Nobel Prize winner's statement was no mere conjecture but a fact that has been historically documented.[34]

---

[29] Friedrich A. Hayek, "The Pretence of Knowledge", *American Economic Review* 79, no. 6 (December 1989): 3–7.

[30] Ibid., p. 7.

[31] Ibid., p. 4. Elsewhere, Hayek stated: "It would seem that H. M. Robertson … hardly exaggerates when he writes 'It would not be difficult to claim that the religion which favoured the spirit of capitalism was Jesuitry, not Calvinism'." Hayek, *Law, Legislation, and Liberty*, p. 179, n. 15; Hayek's reference is to Robertson, *Aspects on the Rise of Economic Individualism*, p. 164.

[32] "The scholastic method was essentially a rational investigation of every relevant problem in liberal arts, philosophy, theology, medicine, and law, examined from opposing points of view, in order to reach an intelligent, scientific solution that would be consistent with accepted authorities, known facts, human reason, and Christian faith." *New Catholic Encyclopedia*, vol. 12, p. 1145.

[33] "In its purest form this ethos regards it as the prime duty to pursue a self-chosen end as effectively as possible without paying attention to the role it plays in the complex network of human activities. It is the view which is now commonly but somewhat misleadingly described as the Calvinist ethic—misleading because it prevailed already in the mercantile towns of medieval Italy and was taught by the Spanish Jesuits at about the same time as Calvin". Hayek, *Law, Legislation, and Liberty*, p. 145.

[34] See Grice-Hutchinson, *School of Salamanca*; Schumpeter, *History of Economic Analysis*; Jesús Huerta de Soto, *The Theory of Dynamic Efficiency* (Oxfordshire: Routledge, 2009); Murray N. Rothbard, *Economic Controversies* (Auburn, Ala.: Ludwig von Mises Institute, 2011); Alves and Jose M. Moreira (Major Conservative and Libertarian Thinkers), *The Salamanca School* (New York: Continuum, 2009); Julius Kirshner, ed., *Business, Banking, and Economic Thought in Late Medieval and Early Modern Europe: Selected Studies of Raymond de Roover* (Chicago: University of Chicago Press, 1974); Jesús Huerta de Soto, *The Austrian School: Market Order and Entrepreneurial Creativity* (Northampton, Mass.: Edward Elgar Publishing, 2008); Murray N. Rothbard, *An Austrian Perspective on the History of Economic Thought*, vol. 1, *Economic Thought before Adam Smith* (Aldershot, U.K., and Brookfield, U.S.A.: Edward Elgar Publishing, 1995); vol. 2, *Classical Economics* (Aldershot, U.K., and Brookfield, U.S.A.: Edward Elgar Publishing, 1995); Alejandro Chafuen, *Faith and Liberty: The Economic Thought of the Late Scholastics* (Lanham, Md.: Lexington, 2003).

El Greco, *Saint Bernardino of Siena*, ca. 1603. Bernardino (1380–1444), leading economic thinker and idolized preacher of Italian piazzas, was a "worldly ascetic" whose life was fierily dedicated to God by the vows of poverty, chastity, and obedience, represented by the three knots on the rope belt dangling from his waist. The mitres laid at his feet symbolize the three offers from successive popes of the bishoprics of Siena, Ferrara, and Urbino, all of which he refused. When he sensed that his frail health was bringing him close to death, he travelled from town to town preaching nonstop for fifty consecutive days.

The founder of the School of Salamanca was Francisco de Vitoria (1486–1546). Blessed with Jewish ancestry, the young Spaniard began his preparation for the priesthood at thirteen years of age, studied in Paris, and then returned to Spain where he spent much of his life at the University of Salamanca. There he pioneered the application of the thought of Thomas Aquinas to the new social, political, and economic order of the sixteenth century created by the discovery of the Americas, Luther, the rise of humanism, and the wider distribution of an increasing amount of wealth. Remarkable thinkers such as Domingo de Soto (1494–1560), Luis de Molina (1535–1600), Francisco Suárez (1548–1617), Martín de Azpilcueta (1491–1586), and Tomás de Mercado (1525–1575) identified with his principles, and formed into a distinct intellectual tradition, within Thomism, that would span the sixteenth and seventeenth centuries. They were mostly Spanish and Portuguese priests, mainly Dominicans, Jesuits, and Carmelites. Besides researching, teaching, and writing, they also advised Emperor Charles V and other government leaders. Although a few of them worked in Italy at the Roman College, most were at the universities of Salamanca and Alcalá de Henares in Spain, at those of Coimbra and Évora in Portugal, or at centers in the Netherlands and Belgium. Since Portugal and Spain were the front-runners of commerce and trade in the fifteenth and sixteenth centuries—Spain still controlled the booming capitalist cities of the Netherlands and Belgium for most of the 1500s—many of these intellectuals were at the nerve center of the economic events shaping free-market economics.

Francisco de Vitoria and his fellow Thomists were on the cutting edge of innovation in socioeconomic philosophy and in the theory regarding the production, consumption, and transfer of wealth for two reasons. Firstly, the rationally sophisticated Scholastic method of investigation with its rigorous analysis of ideas, emphasis on precise distinctions, dialectical reasoning, and the use of debating was an excellent tool for making intellectual progress. Secondly, their unified, rationally ordered world vision, due to the bonding of the Catholic Faith with a realist metaphysics that was coherent with man's universal experience, provided clear principles about human nature, right and wrong, and the purposes of society, law, and government.[35]

---

[35] For an introduction to the Catholic theory of the relationship of faith and reason, see Antonio Livi, *Reasons for Believing* (Aurora, Col.: Davies Group, 2005). For an introduction to Scholasticism and specifically to St. Thomas' thought, see Edward Feser, *Scholastic Metaphysics: A Contemporary Introduction*

Due to their application of Thomistic anthropology and notion of natural law to the new problems of justice facing businessmen and government officials, these intellectuals pioneered new paths for understanding the operation of market processes. Indeed, their anthropological and legal principles regarding human rights, the morality of commerce, just pricing, the legitimacy of private property rights, taxation, and contracts are the theoretical foundations for free enterprise economics.

In the area of law, de Vitoria's genius has influenced many legal philosophers, and many have reckoned him to be a "Father of International Law" even though the size of his writings on the subject is relatively small in comparison to those of Hugo Grotius on whom the title is more frequently conferred and who was influenced by him.[36] Nevertheless, he merits the title, firstly, due to the genius of his insights and arguments regarding the principles of the discipline; secondly, because he created legal precedent in the area of human rights due to his legislation protecting Native Americans in the Spanish Empire; and thirdly, on account of his incisive contributions to the theory of the just war, freedom of the seas, and freedom of commerce, laid out in *De Indis Noviter Inventis* (About the Newly Discovered Indies) and *De Jure Belli* (About the Right of War).

De Vitoria, to the dismay of colonists who wanted the Indians of the newly discovered Americas as cheap slave labor, unfolded a rationale in support of the Church's principle of universal human dignity, rejecting the concept of "second-class" human beings, and any type of racial segregation. He and other members of the School explained why and how the state was bound by the natural law, both in regard to its own citizens and in international relations. In this way they demonstrated that there are universal standards for measuring political decisions and politicians, a view that sharply contrasted with the ghoulish paradigm laid out by their Italian contemporary, Machiavelli, who gave unbridled license to rulers. To De Vitoria and to his fellow priests in the School of Salamanca we can attribute a significant share of the groundwork that led to the formulation of the principles restricting government interventions in society.

Before unfolding the economic theories of the School of Salamanca, it is important to note that the independent academic discipline known as economics did not formally exist until the eighteenth century. Until then it was an appendix of ethics and law. Its late arrival is due to the fact that only around the fourteenth century was there a widespread increase in the production, consumption, and transfer of wealth: the subject matter of economics. Upward social mobility driven by riches, expansion of the affluent sector of the population, the growth of investment, moneylending, and interest rates all made it urgent for ethicists to dedicate more and more attention to wealth. Consequently, during the medieval period, although no thinker analyzed the mechanisms and practical aspects of the economic system, and neither Thomas Aquinas nor anyone else wrote a systematic economic treatise, the medieval Scholastics did contribute, on the basis

(Heusenstamm: Editiones Scholasticae, 2014); Edward Feser, *Aquinas: A Beginner's Guide* (Oxford: Oneworld, 2009); Etienne Gilson, *The Christian Philosophy of St. Thomas Aquinas* (Notre Dame, Ind.: University of Notre Dame Press, 1994).

[36] See J. B. Brown Scott, *The Spanish Origin of International Law: Francisco de Vitoria and His Law of Nations* (Oxford: Clarendon Press, 1934); Anthony Pagden, *Vitoria: Political Writings* (Cambridge: Cambridge University Press, 1991); Arthur Nussbaum, *A Concise History of the Law of Nations* (New York: Macmillan, 1947).

of their ethical and legal investigations, a number of brilliant insights that later thinkers, notably the School of Salamanca, unfolded and developed. By the sixteenth and seventeenth centuries, although no university had a faculty dedicated to "economics", the subject matter was intensely investigated and had started on its journey to academic independence.

By the end of the thirteenth century, theologians had come out in favor of the key features of free-market economics: the right to private property, the nature of a just price, the legitimacy of profit, free trade, credit, interest (distinguishing it from usury), and mortgage. Schumpeter credited these intellectuals with paving the road for the achievements of their Renaissance confrères: "In particular, no further explanation seems to be needed for the ease with which the economics of the doctors [the Scholastics of the fourteenth to the seventeenth centuries] absorbed all the phenomena of nascent capitalism and, in consequence, for the fact that it served so well as a basis of the analytic work of their successors, not excluding A. Smith".[37]

One of these early economic thinkers was Johannes Duns Scotus (ca. 1265–1308), who, according to Schumpeter, discovered the condition of competitive equilibrium, later known as the "law of cost". Schumpeter in his regard stated:

> Though he presumably thought of nothing beyond providing a more precise criterion of scholastic "commutative justice"—which was rightly rejected by the later scholastics—we must nevertheless credit him with having discovered the condition of competitive equilibrium which came to be known in the nineteenth century as the Law of Cost. This is not imputing too much: for if we identify the just price of a good with its competitive common value, as Duns Scotus certainly did, and if we further equate that just price to the cost of the good (taking account of risk, as he did not fail to observe), then we have *ipso facto*, at least by implication, stated the law of cost not only as a normative but also as an analytic proposition.[38]

Another influential medieval thinker was Jean Buridan (ca. 1300–1358), rector of the University of Paris, who unfolded the theory regarding money as a useful tool for economic development. His pupil Nicole Oresme (1325–1382), Bishop of Lisieux and confessor of King Charles V of France, wrote about inflation in *A Treatise on the Origin, Nature, Law, and Alterations of Money*, arguing against government intervention except in emergencies and only then with the approval by the community of money users. According to Jörg Guido Hülsmann, "Oresme pioneered the political economy of inflation; he set standards that would not be surpassed for many centuries, and which in certain respects have not been surpassed at all."[39] The principles of the "Founding Father of Monetary Economics" are still influential today in the Austrian School of Economics.[40]

Schumpeter declared the fifteenth-century Archbishop of Florence, Antonino (1389–1459), to be perhaps "the first man to whom it is possible to ascribe a

[37] Schumpeter, *History of Economic Analysis*, p. 94.
[38] Ibid., p. 93.
[39] Jörg Guido Hülsmann, "Nicholas Oresme and the First Monetary Treatise", Ludwig von Mises Institute, May 18, 2004, http://mises.org/library/nicholas-oresme-and-first-monetary-treatise.
[40] Ibid.

comprehensive vision of the economic process in all its major aspects".[41] Antonino examined economic activity itself (*industria*); unfolded the role of monetary capital in production and commerce; declared the importance of money-capital due to its role in launching business, thereby attacking Aristotle's theory of the "sterility of money"; recognized the social category of the *entrepreneur*; and, by applying the term *complacibilitas* ("desirability") to the valuation of goods, pointed out that their utility was not one of their intrinsic qualities but was the reflex of the wants and needs of potential buyers.[42]

Sketches of Personalities

Schumpeter, comparing the Scholastics to later economic thinkers, stated that they had a "more correct formulation of fundamentals and a wider view of practical problems" owing to their "detachment from the immediate practical issues of economic policy" and their "greater intellectual refinement".[43] These broad brushstrokes of his portrayal of the group are seen to be accurate when one gets closer to individual members like Father Juan de Mariana (1536–1623):

> The overall impression that Mariana offers is unique: an accomplished theologian, a perfect Latin scholar, a man with a deep knowledge of Greek and the oriental languages, a brilliant man of literature, a noteworthy economist, a politician with great foresight. That is the mind of the man. Add an irreproachable life, severe uprightness, a heart that does not know deceit, is incapable of flattery, and beats strongly at the very mention of freedom like those fierce republicans of Greece and Rome. A strong, fearless voice that speaks out against any kind of abuse, regardless of the powerful, without trembling when it speaks to kings. When you then ponder that all these qualities have converged in a man who lives in a small room at the house of the Jesuits of Toledo, you will have discovered a combination of virtues and circumstances that are rarely found in one person.[44]

But in fact Juan de Mariana was not so unique among these priest-intellectuals: many of the pioneering economists stood just as tall among the men of their centuries. They were all among the most brilliant and intellectually versatile men of their age, and all had vowed their bodies and souls to a selfless love of God and humanity within the Catholic priesthood. Most lived an austere lifestyle with no personal possessions, and any ambitions they had were directed toward the good of others. All the Dominicans, Jesuits, and Carmelites had Spartan living quarters; they fasted for about six months of the year; and they shied away from opportunities for personal power. Antonino of Florence only accepted the position of archbishop in his native city after the Pope threatened him with excommunication if he continued to refuse! Indeed, the historian Vasari has alleged that the one to "blame" for his appointment was the painter Fra Angelico, who proposed him to Pope Eugenius IV in order to escape being nominated himself! Even then, Antonino continued to wear the plain Dominican uniform as bishop of the leading capitalist city of his century.

---

[41] Schumpeter, *History of Economic Analysis*, p. 95.

[42] Ibid., pp. 97–104.

[43] Ibid., p. 136.

[44] See Jaime Balmes, "Mariana", in *Obras Completas*, vol. 12 (Madrid: BAC, 1949), pp. 78–79. My translation.

El Greco, *Don Diego de Covar-rubias y Leiva* (1512–1577), ca. 1600–1605. The bishop, a student of Father Francisco de Vitoria, became a powerful man of government in the Spanish Empire as president of the Council of Castile. He was a member of the School of Salamanca, an opponent of slavery, and a leading Renaissance economist.

What the Jewish intellectual, Murray Rothbard, called one of the great medieval economists, Bernardino of Siena, could be said of most of them: "the worldly ascetic".[45] This was not a bad epithet for men who were hard on themselves but desired to soften the lives of those around them. The selfless generosity that encompassed their lives from their late teens to their last heartbeat conferred transparent purity of intention to their economic theories. All they wanted to achieve with their lives was for the sake of souls and, along the way, the promotion of the public good and the prosperity of all, especially the poor. This was the driving force within the men who thoughtfully began to shape an economic philosophy favoring the free enterprise system.

Neither these Renaissance priest-economists nor their medieval predecessors were ivory-tower intellectuals living in isolated think tanks remote from the man in the street. For instance, the full-time occupation of Bernardino of Siena (1380–1444) was preaching, travelling the length and breadth of Italy, standing in churches and piazzas before the ordinary men and women, among whom he was as popular as a modern-day movie star. The same man who wrote about refined points of economics also spoke out against travelling businessmen who stayed away from home and family for long periods and were unfaithful to their wives. "San Bernardino of Siena", wrote Rothbard, "was a fascinating and paradoxical combination of brilliant, knowledgeable, and appreciative analyst of the capitalist market of his day, and an emaciated ascetic saint fulminating against worldly evils and business practices".[46] The famously forthright Juan de Mariana told the Spanish king that he should spend less on the royal family and cut back on awarding so many needless pensions, prizes, and commissions if he were serious about eliminating inflation and balancing the national budget. But he was not the only fearsome defender of economic sanity, social justice, and the rights of the common man. The soft-spoken genius Martín de Azpilcueta, a cousin of Saint Francis Xavier, once gave a lecture in front of Charles V in which he explained why rulers must govern for the sake of the well-being of the people. Another Scholastic was a powerful man of government—Bishop Diego de Covarrubias, president of the Council of Castile. Others, like Domingo de Soto (1494–1560), who became Emperor Charles V's personal confessor in 1548, were cherished guides of the souls of the men who

---

[45] Rothbard, *History of Economic Thought*, p. 81. See also Raymond de Roover, *San Bernardino of Siena and Sant'Antonino of Florence: The Two Great Economic Thinkers of the Middle Ages* (Boston, Mass.: Harvard Graduate School of Business Administration, 1967).

[46] Rothbard, *History of Economic Thought*, p. 83.

governed the Spanish Empire—under Charles V and Philip II the most powerful political reality in the Western hemisphere.

The very purpose of their writings on economic topics was to resolve questions of justice in business dealings for individual consciences, whether at the level of the empire rulers or local merchants. This required not only knowledge of ethics but also business acumen. It sent them out of their monasteries onto the streets, observing and questioning. Luis de Molina (1535–1600) could be seen in the marketplaces interviewing merchants and farmers as he did a detailed study of the Spanish wool trade. Leonardus Lessius (1554–1623) before he began writing about financial ethics went to the "Wall Street" of the epoch at Antwerp, where he acquired skills in financial and trading matters; to this day he is renowned for his subtle distinctions.

But there was another reason why these economists had such clear intuitions and a comprehensive grip on circumstances and motivations: their closeness to so many entrepreneurs who opened their hearts and minds to them because as priests they were "ambassadors of Christ" and "men of secrets". The thinkers of the School of Salamanca developed their monetary theory largely in response to the urgent needs of priests confronted with problems of conscience presented by merchants. Justice in pricing, for instance, was addressed by Father Antonio de Escobar's manual, *Theologiae Moralis*, published in 1652; it stated that the natural price was a prudential judgment that took into account "the scarcity or plenty of goods, buyers, sellers, and money, the manner of sale, the utility of the article in question, and the labour and expenses of merchants".[47] And just as these principles of future economic theories had been formed in reply to troubled consciences of ordinary men and women, so too upon formulation they trickled down from the University of Salamanca "think tank" through the confessionals of the Spanish empire (which included the flourishing capitalist city of Amsterdam) to the merchant class, helping to create an influential ethos in favor of the subjective theory of economic value, a key element of the free enterprise system. We can form some idea of the degree of influence of de Escobar and his fellow Jesuit theologians on ordinary life, even in France, by the fact that Pascal, who rejected their view of usury, felt it necessary to attack them in his *Provincial Letters* in 1656.

Men Alive with New Ideas

The number of pillars of modern economics erected by these Catholic thinkers of both medieval and Renaissance times is rather surprising.

Juan de Mariana's *On the Alteration of Money* argued that the king did not own his subjects' private property and could not demand taxes without their consent. Furthermore, he should not cause inflation by tampering with the market value of money except in exceptional circumstances such as war and siege; even then the ruler had the obligation of making satisfaction, once the emergency was over, to those who had financially suffered. Nor can one remedy the effects of inflation by setting maximum prices—one must control public spending and balance the budget. Both Mariana and Luis de Molina declared that there could be no double standards for the state and private individuals as regards right and wrong in economic matters. They branded

---

[47] As summarized by Grice-Hutchinson, *School of Salamanca*, pp. 74–75.

Pere Borrell del Caso, portrait of Father Jaime Balmes (1810–1848), formulator of the law of marginal utility. One of the leading Thomists of his century.

state monopolies as immoral, declaring that if a government gave monopoly rights to a certain group, it acted just as immorally as a private individual since it infringed on the consumer's right to purchase from the cheapest seller. For these priests, the right to the open market system was therefore an important value. One of them, Jerónimo Castillo de Bovadilla, pioneered the theory on the role of competition among entrepreneurs, affirming it to be an important way to drive down product market prices.

In the area of banking, the School of Salamanca split into two groups as regards fractional-reserve banking, the practice by which a bank invests part of a depositor's money—keeping a fraction in reserve—even though it seeks to ensure that the entire amount can be returned to the depositor on demand. Tomás de Mercado, Azpilcueta, and Saravia de la Calle belonged to the "Currency School" and were reticent about such banking investments, requiring that all of the depositor's money be held in deposit; de Molina and de Lugo were more open to the practice. Huerta de Soto has pointed out that these two groups became, in a way, the precursors of the two currents that arose three centuries later in Britain: the Banking and Currency Schools.[48]

These thinkers were also avant garde in the area of currency trading and foreign exchanges. Thomas de Vio (Cardinal Cajetan), who lived from 1468 to 1534, wrote an incisive explanation, *De Cambiis*, about the ethics of the foreign exchange market and is reckoned to be the founder of the expectations theory.[49] Azpilcueta also favored currency trading and even asserted that to shut down foreign-exchange markets "would be to plunge the realm into poverty".[50] When sixteenth-century Spain was hit by the influx of huge amounts of gold from the newly discovered Americas, a "price revolution" broke out. The problem was studied by Martín de Azpilcueta, who developed monetarist theory, being the first to integrally formulate the quantity theory of money and its effect on prices and the cost of living.[51] The Dominican, Domingo de Soto, resolved problems of exchange rates by applying the principles of supply and demand to them, thus becoming the originator of the principle of purchasing power parity (PPP), a standard for long-term equilibrium exchange rates based on relative price levels in two states.

[48] Jesús Huerta de Soto, "Juan de Mariana and the Spanish Scholastics", in Randall G. Holcombe, ed., *Fifteen Great Austrian Economists* (Auburn, Ala.: Ludwig von Mises Institute, 1999), chap. 1, p. 7. See also Jesús Huerta de Soto, "New Light on the Prehistory of the Theory of Banking and the School of Salamanca", *Review of Austrian Economics* 9, no. 2 (1996): 59–81. Dr. Jesús Huerta de Soto is the titular professor of political economy at the Complutense University in Madrid (founded by Cardinal Francisco Ximénez de Cisneros, 1436–1517).

[49] Rothbard, *History of Economic Thought*, p. 101.

[50] Quoted in ibid., p. 107.

[51] Martin de Azpilcueta, "Commentary on the Resolution of Money", in Stephen J. Grabill, ed., *Sourcebook in Late-Scholastic Monetary Theory* (Lanham, Md.: Lexington, 2007), pp. 18–107.

What De Soto was saying is that as the stock of money increases, the utility of each unit of money to the population declines and vice versa; in short, only the great stumbling block of failing to specify the concept of the marginal unit prevented him from arriving at the doctrine of the diminishing marginal utility of money. Azpilcueta ... applied the de Soto analysis of the influence of the supply of money on exchange rates, at the same time that he set forth a theory of supply and demand in determining the purchasing power of money within a country.[52]

Schumpeter summarized the monetary ideas of the Renaissance Scholastics in four points. Firstly, they generally held "a strictly metallist theory of money" vis-à-vis bartering. Secondly, they were also "practical metallists" condemning the debasement of coinage. Thirdly, some of them pioneered the quantity theory of money. "And, fourth, they dealt with a number of problems in coinage, foreign exchange, international gold and silver movements, bimetallism, and credit in a manner that would merit more attention and that compares favorably in some points with much later performance."[53]

Noteworthy also were the contributions of these priests to the theory of business profit. "The risk-effort theory of business profit", wrote Schumpeter, "is undoubtedly due to them. In particular, it may be mentioned that de Lugo—following a suggestion of St. Thomas—described business profits as 'a kind of wage' for a social service".[54] Some of the Scholastics, especially Martín de Azpilcueta, also argued that the time factor changed the value of money: the concept of time preference (now often called "delay discounting"). This concept was invented by a pupil of Thomas Aquinas, Giles Lessines, who, in 1285, wrote that "future goods are not valued as highly as the same goods available immediately, nor do they allow their owners to achieve the same utility. For this reason it must be considered that they have a more reduced value in accordance with justice."[55] In other words, we are talking about the discount or charge function: the higher one's evaluation of goods (such as money) in one's immediate possession, the higher the compensation one expects in the form of interest payments for lending them.

> Hence people with a low time preference will be willing to give up present goods in exchange for future goods valued only slightly higher, and they will perform exchanges in which they will hand over their present goods to people with a higher time preference, that is, people who value the present more intensely than they do. The very creativity and alertness inherent in entrepreneurship give rise to a process that tends to establish a market price for present goods with respect to future goods. From the viewpoint of the Austrian school, the interest rate is the market price of present goods in terms of future goods.[56]

Thus they developed the theory of interest, stating that the charging of interest was moral because money itself was not only a tool of commerce but a product in its own right; and consequently, that lending money merited a recompense through interest as compensation both for risks undertaken as well as for investment opportunities renounced.

[52] Rothbard, *Economic Controversies*, p. 144.
[53] Schumpeter, *History of Economic Analysis*, pp. 99–101.
[54] Ibid., p. 101.
[55] Quoted in Huerta de Soto, *Theory of Dynamic Efficiency*, p. 209.
[56] Huerta de Soto, *Austrian School*, p. 51.

Finally, these priest-economists helped to change attitudes toward business people. Bernardino of Siena (1380–1444) argued that society should be grateful to the entrepreneur for so many services he offers, especially the manufacturing of useful goods from raw materials and the transporting, storing, and distributing of products to make them more easily available for consumers. Such services are only possible because the capitalist does not shirk the hard work, risk, responsibility, and efficiency required. Consequently the man of enterprise merits to profit from his efforts. As the economist Rothbard pointed out, this was revolutionary talk, one of the first systematic defenses of the businessman who had been disdained by aristocrats and "religious" people since ancient Greece.

Installing the Engine of Free-Market Economics

These Renaissance priests developed a concept that is vital to the free-market system: the subjective theory of economic value, otherwise known as the utility theory.[57] This theory asserts that the value of a product or service should be determined not by an alleged intrinsic quality but rather according to the purchaser's personal valuation on the basis of the satisfaction of his needs and desires. This very personal appreciation fixes the price of the product for which it can be sold in the competitive market. Buyer and seller agree to trade on the presumption that any outcome is, in theory, a "win-win" situation for both of them.

Plato had prescribed an objective just cost, stating that a tradesman should name only one price for his product and if unable to obtain it should return home with his merchandise. Saint Augustine, however, had noted that the prices of products are based rather on the individual's subjective appreciation of the utility of things.[58] In the writings of Saint Albert the Great and Saint Thomas Aquinas, as indeed in Aristotle, we find both the objective and subjective theories of value. Nevertheless, Albert affirmed that the primary purpose of exchange is the satisfaction of human wants;[59] and Thomas affirmed that "this one standard which truly measures all things is demand. This includes all commutable [exchangeable] things inasmuch as everything has a reference to human need. Articles are not valued according to the dignity of their nature ... but they are priced according as man stands in

Matías Moreno González, *El Padre Juan de Mariano*, ca. 1878.

---

[57] For the subjective/utility theory of economic value, see Grice-Hutchinson, *School of Salamanca*, pp. 19–58; Emil Kauder, *A History of Marginal Utility Theory* (Princeton, N.J.: Princeton University Press, 1965); Woods, *Catholic Church Built Western Civilization*, pp. 163–65.

[58] Saint Augustine, *City of God* 11.16.

[59] See Saint Albert the Great, *Commentary on Aristotle's Nicomachean Ethics* 5.1.7e.

need of them for his own use."[60] Hence, the free interaction between buyers and sellers determines the calculation of the just price: an implicit approval of profit. This was then explicitly formulated by none other than the austere Franciscan Pierre de Jean Olivi (1248–1298). The Renaissance priests of the universities of Salamanca and Coimbra, who, as true Thomists, were "flexible of mind, attentive to new facts and doctrines, and [were] respectful of the honestly held opinions of the ordinary man",[61] went on to unfold its implications. One of them, Francisco de Vitoria (ca. 1492–1546), argued that the just price must not be fixed by the state but must be the result of a mutual agreement between producer and consumer according to supply and demand; governments must also protect free enterprise in international trade.

Diego de Covarrubias y Leyva (1512–1577), Bishop of Segovia, gave a clear definition of the principle of subjective valuation in his book *Variarum Resolutionum*: "The value of an article depends on the estimations of men, even if the estimation be foolish. Wheat is more expensive in the Indies than in Spain because [there] men esteem it more highly, though the nature of wheat is the same in both places."[62] Supporting that position Luis Saravia de la Calle, in his 1544 work, *Instrucción de mercaderes* (*Guidelines for Businessmen*), demonstrated that prices, rather than the labor of producers and traders, determine costs. The two seventeenth-century Jesuits Juan de Lugo and Juan de Salas both argued that the enormous variety of circumstances and subjective appreciations made it practically impossible to determine the just price of a product. Indeed, de Lugo summed up the situation by stating that "only God knows the just mathematical price" ("pretium iustum mathematicum licet soli Deo notum").[63]

Luis de Molina and Diego de Covarrubias developed a theory of prices that stated that since the usefulness of a product varies from person to person, just prices in a free-market economy would result from mutual agreement according to the laws of supply and demand. Cardinal Juan de Lugo in his *Disputationes de justitia et jure* stood against government regulation of prices and production levels. He declared that, practically speaking, the right price was the market price, as determined by buyers and sellers.

Conflicting with the subjective value is the theory of some objective or absolute value that belongs inherently to products or services and can be defined independently of people's needs and desires. This, it is argued, is what determines the just price of something. The most important version of the hypothesis states that a product's market price must be determined by the amount of labor and other production-related costs. Such was the starting point for many of the eighteenth- and nineteenth-century economists like Ricardo and Marx. Adam Smith's labor theory of value did not identify value with the amount of work needed to produce it, but nevertheless it continued to lean toward making "toil" the axis of economic theory.

In the opinion of Schumpeter, if Smith had built upon the Catholic philosophy of the subjective value of products that favored spontaneous pricing according to

---

[60] See Saint Thomas Aquinas, *Commentary on the Nicomachean Ethics*, bk., 5, lecture 9, chap. 5, no. 981.
[61] Grice-Hutchinson, *School of Salamanca*, p. 40.
[62] Diego de Covarrubias y Leyva, quoted in Patricia Donohue-White, Stephen J. Grabill, Christopher Westley, and Gloria Zúñiga, eds., *Human Nature and the Discipline of Economics: Personalist Anthropology and Economic Methodology* (Lanham Md.: Lexington, 2002), p. 3.
[63] Juan de Lugo, *Disputationes de iustitia et iure*, vol. 2 (Lyon, 1642), d. 26, s. 4, n. 40, p. 312.

supply and demand, "a considerable part of the economics of the later nineteenth century might have been developed from those bases more quickly and with less trouble than it actually cost to develop it, and that some of that subsequent work was therefore in the nature of a time—and labor-consuming—detour."[64] Rothbard asserted that Smith's idea of inherent value led to pseudo-scientific efforts seeking to measure and enforce prices by government interference—and that his emphasis on "costs determining prices" fostered the prejudice that prices are shoved up by businessmen or unions rather than by government inflation of the money supply.[65]

Kauder went so far as to state that Smith threw economics off course for a hundred years and that his ambiguity spawned enough confusion in nineteenth-century economic theory to leave the door ajar for the ideas of Karl Marx.[66] He argued that the economic principles in Adam Smith's *The Wealth of Nations* were influenced by his native Scotland's Calvinism, a religion that emphasizes the value of work to such an extent that it fails to clearly subordinate it in function of man's integral well-being, as Catholicism unequivocally teaches. The labor-value theory dominated in Protestant nations while the subjective-value position directed the thinking of Catholic economists in countries like France and Italy:

> Catholic countries, on the other hand, more deeply influenced by an Aristotelian and Thomist line of thought, felt no such attraction to a labor theory of value. Aristotle and Saint Thomas envisioned the purpose of economic activity to be the derivation of pleasure and happiness. Thus the goals of economics were profoundly *subjective*, insofar as pleasure and happiness were non-quantifiable states of being whose intensity could not be articulated with precision or in a manner that could be compared from one person to another. Subjective value theory follows from this premise as night follows day. "If pleasure in a moderate form is the purpose of economics," wrote Kauder, "then following the Aristotelian concept of the final cause, *all principles of economics including valuation must be derived from this goal*. In this pattern of Aristotelian and Thomistic thinking, valuation has the function of showing how much pleasure can be derived from economic goods."[67]

This logic of human fulfillment, so clearly unfolded within Catholicism, is in harmony with the instinctive thrust of man to look for personal contentment in all his decisions. In economics the subjective value theory merely recognizes that since the search for happiness is the energizer behind man's choices, accordingly the production and commerce of goods should seek to meet the needs and desires of the consumer who will thereby determine levels of supply and demand, and consequently pricing.

---

[64] Schumpeter, *History of Economic Analysis*, p. 97. See especially the entire chapter "The Scholastic Doctors and the Philosophers of Natural Law", pp. 73–114.

[65] The American economist Leland B. Yeager pointed out other defects in Adam Smith's work: "Adam Smith dropped earlier contributions about subjective value, entrepreneurship and emphasis on real-world markets and pricing and replaced it all with a labour theory of value and a dominant focus on the long run 'natural price' equilibrium, a world where entrepreneurship was assumed out of existence. He mixed up Calvinism with economics, as in supporting usury prohibition and distinguishing between productive and unproductive occupations. He lapsed from the laissez-faire of several eighteenth-century French and Italian economists, introducing many waffles and qualifications. His work was unsystematic and plagued by contradictions". Leland B. Yeager, "Book Review", *The Review of Austrian Economics* 9, no. 1 (1996): 183.

[66] See Kauder, *History of Marginal Utility Theory*, vol. 2, p. xi.

[67] Woods, *Catholic Church Built Western Civilization*, pp. 164–65; the enclosed quotation is from Kauder, *History of Marginal Utility Theory*, p. 9. Emphasis added by Woods.

As Thomas Woods rightly points out, there is no moral subjectivism implied, since the subjective theory of value restricts itself to identifying the most effective economic mechanisms, leaving the individual producer and consumer to apply the principles of the natural law to the concrete transaction.

Exile to Intellectual Siberia and Return

Schumpeter sums up the numerous contributions of the School of Salamanca by affirming that firstly they fully unfolded the economic sociology of their medieval predecessors such as Antonino of Florence and Bernardino of Siena; and secondly, that "it is they who come nearer than does any other group to having been the 'founders' of scientific economics ... the bases they laid for a serviceable and well-integrated body of analytic tools and propositions were sounder than was much subsequent work".[68] As Huerta de Soto has convincingly argued, they developed the key components of the theoretical foundations of the present-day Austrian School of Economics: the subjective theory of value; the dynamic nature of the market and competition; and the rebuff to any unjustified intervention by the state against entrepreneurial freedom, calling it a violation of natural law.[69] But their influence extends well beyond the Austrian School since some of their principles, notably the subjective theory of value, have become part of the commonly held norms of economics.

Nevertheless, in the seventeenth century the Anglo-Saxon world exiled these men of genius to intellectual Siberia by either largely ignoring or rejecting their ideas, or by a deafening silence about their authorship of so many economic notions. The reasons for the expulsion often cloaked the political and economic rivalry between Spain and England dating from Elizabethan times. Inextricably bound up with this enmity was a deeply felt anti-Catholicism directed particularly at priests and especially Jesuit priests on account of their special vow of obedience to a papacy that had excommunicated the English head-of-state and freed subjects from their duty of obedience. Swiftly, English propagandists, along with continental allies, conjured up the "black legend" about Spain that ran amok through the British Empire and the newly formed Anglo-Saxon American colonies, morally and intellectually disqualifying all things Spanish, and by implication all things Catholic.[70]

The School of Salamanca soon felt the heat of the assault since several of their leading members were Jesuits but particularly because their economics was bonded to their ideas of morality and law.[71] A notable instance was their opposition to the doctrine of the divine right of kings, championed by monarchs like James I of England, who banned Father Juan de Mariana's book, De rege (On Kingship), written at the suggestion of King Philip II of Spain and published in 1599 with

[68] Schumpeter, History of Economic Analysis, p. 97. See the entire chapter "The Scholastic Doctors and the Philosophers of Natural Law", pp. 73–114.

[69] Huerta de Soto, Theory of Dynamic Efficiency, pp. 204–28, especially p. 209.

[70] See Philip W. Powell, Tree of Hate: Propaganda and Prejudices Affecting United States Relations with the Hispanic World (Albuquerque: University of New Mexico Press, 2008). For a general background, see Henry Kamen, Empire: How Spain Became a World Power, 1492–1763 (New York: HarperCollins, 2003); Henry Kamen, The Spanish Inquisition: A Historical Revision (New Haven, Conn.: Yale University Press, 2014).

[71] See Rothbard, Austrian Perspective, pp. 97–134.

a dedication to Philip III. Mariana had written that the people have the right to reclaim political power if the ruler should abuse it; that they always retain the right to determine taxation, veto laws, and determine succession if the ruler has no heir; and, most importantly, he expanded classic scholastic doctrine justifying the murder of tyrants, stating among other things that any citizen can justly assassinate a tyrant by any means necessary.[72]

The resulting prejudice against the Spanish Scholastics left the field of economics open for the dominance of Adam Smith and his disciples in Great Britain, the United States of America, and to some extent in the largely Protestant areas of Germany and the Netherlands. However, in France, Italy, and Iberia the Renaissance Scholastics left a mighty and visible trail of influence among cutting-edge economists of succeeding centuries. Some of these were also priests, such as Ferdinando Galiani (1728–1787) and Etienne Bonnot de Condillac (1714–1780), who influenced the eighteenth-century French physiocrats with their dynamic theory of entrepreneurship and the implications of the purchasing power parity theory of exchange rates. Laissez-faire was their policy, opposing government interventionism unless it were for the protection of the common good. Another priest-economist, the Italian Giovanni Botero (ca. 1544–1617), author of *The Reason of State*, argued for more people-power in economic and political matters. He influenced the thought of the last of the early mercantilists, the Englishman Thomas Mun (1571–1641), and the Belgian thinker Justus Lipsius (1547–1606), and foreshadowed some theories of John Locke and Adam Smith. The Catalan priest, Jaime Balmes (1810–1848), the leading Thomist philosopher of early nineteenth-century Spain, in 1844 published an article entitled "The True Idea of Value: Thoughts on the Origin, Nature, and Variety of Prices", in which he fully formulated the law of marginal utility.

In modern times, Carl Menger (1840–1921), founder of the Austrian School of Economics, brought back the Spanish Scholastics from exile in the face of the still notable anti-Scholasticism in Anglo-Saxon intellectual circles. These had been prejudiced by Adam Smith's "treacherous platitude" ("The real price of everything, what everything really costs to the man who wants to acquire it, is the toil and trouble of acquiring it")[73] and by his ill-defined idea that quantity of labor "regulates" value, which had led them to oppose the Scholastic explanation of the subjective theory.[74] One of Menger's disciples, F. A. Hayek, recipient of the 1974 Nobel Prize for economics, authored *The Road to Serfdom*, in which he sounded the alarm about government control of economic planning, asserting it to be a sure highway to tyranny, whether right-wing or left-wing. His writings influenced President Ronald Reagan and many of the Eastern European leaders who, along with John Paul II, ousted communism in 1989.

In conclusion, the free enterprise system, conceived within Catholicism, began to appear during the Middle Ages, and by the sixteenth century was on its way to maturity. The intellectuals of the School of Salamanca then laid the foundations for

[72] See ibid., p. 117.

[73] From Adam Smith, *Wealth of Nations*, bk. 1, chap. 5, quoted in Schumpeter, *History of Economic Analysis*, p. 295.

[74] See Schumpeter, *History of Economic Analysis*, p. 295, where Schumpeter also states that although Smith never developed either a "toil" or a labor-quantity *theory* of value, his vague thought on these topics is at the root of Marx's labor-quantity theory of value; Huerta de Soto is of the same opinion, noting also that it has been used by Marx's socialist successors—see *Austrian School*, pp. 30, 35.

scientific economics. As Thomists they were realists and stated that the cause-and-effect relationships that constitute the free enterprise economy must be acknowledged as *facts* originating immediately or remotely from human action which is characterized by choice. For them, economics starts with the real actions of real men. Economic and moral evaluations must start with these facts—or lose all credibility. Consequently, their opposition to attempts by the state to manage the economy was based on the fact that such efforts are destined to failure because they defy the laws of human behavior.[75]

For these priests, the free enterprise economy is the most perfect system in an imperfect world for catering to man's material needs. They recognized that free-market economics respects that man is made in the image and likeness of the Creator in order to be a "sub-creator", penetrating the secrets of nature and using the goods of the Earth for the well-being of his family and fellow men. They held it to be congenially Catholic with its respect for private property and ability to provide man with opportunities to fulfill his aspirations: ensuring freedom to create something that is one's own; giving space to try out new ideas, to improve, to set out in search of progress; to organize and risk for the sake of growth; to invest and reinvest profit; and to have the joy of offering work and opportunity to others without being immobilized by state taxation and regulations.

---

[75] See the remarkably insightful work by an author who is both an economist and a historian: Thomas E. Woods Jr., *The Church and the Market* (Lanham: Lexington Books, 2015).

STANDING ON THE CAPITOLINE: GAZING TOWARD PAST AND FUTURE HORIZONS

All roads still lead to Rome and unless you place yourself there you will never be in the heart of the world or see it in its right perspective.

—George Santayana

"I wish it need not have happened in my time," said Frodo.

"So do I," said Gandalf, "and so do all who live to see such times. But that is not for them to decide. All we have to decide is what to do with the time that is given us."

—J.R.R. Tolkien, *The Lord of the Rings*

Horizons

To stand amid the ruins of ancient Rome, on the Capitoline Hill, at the top of the steep set of steps leading up to the Basilica of Santa Maria in Aracoeli, is to have an extraordinary vantage point from which to survey history with the gaze of memory and imagination. So felt Edward Gibbon, author of *The History of the Decline and Fall of the Roman Empire*, who, in his autobiography, vividly remembers how as a twenty-seven-year-old he had "first approached and entered the eternal City"[1] and, even at a distance of twenty-five years, could "neither forget nor express the strong emotions which agitated my mind".[2] He recalled that "after a sleepless night, I trod, with a lofty step, the ruins of the Forum",[3] and how at dusk, "on the fifteenth of

Caspar David Friedrich, *The Wanderer above the Sea of Fog*, 1818.

[1] Edward Gibbon, *The History of the Decline and Fall of the Roman Empire*, vol. 1 (London: R. Priestley, 1821), p. xx.

[2] Ibid., p. xix.

[3] Ibid.

October, 1764, as I sat musing amidst the ruins of the Capitol, while the barefooted friars were singing Vespers in the temple of Jupiter [Basilica of Santa Maria in Aracoeli], that the idea of writing the decline and fall of the City first started to my mind."[4] In 1909, on Easter Sunday, another prospective historian, the nineteen-year-old Christopher Dawson—five years later he would convert to Catholicism—walked up the same steps to the same church that graphically symbolizes in its classical columns, tombs, and cosmatesque floors covered with Christian symbols and art the Catholic Church's history as guardian of Greco-Roman culture. It was there that Dawson also decided to write history, but one that would reckon with the formative role of religion in culture. He recorded in his diary how he had made "a vow at Easter on the Ara Coeli" and acknowledged that he had since "had great light on the way it may be carried out. However unfit I may be, I believe it is God's will I should attempt it".[5]

Standing on that hill, amid monuments of two civilizations, one can also journey with the mind's eye beyond them and envision the remnants of other cultures that once existed around the Mediterranean and the Middle East: Greece, Crete, Egypt, Sumer, and Akkad. Roaming further, one imagines in the Far East the vestiges of the ancient civilizations of India, China, Japan, Korea, and Vietnam. Many thoughts can strike the mind on such an occasion, but one that is relevant to our present context is the awareness of the long, extensive time line of world history. When one positions the Catholic Church on this timescale, one realizes, as Toynbee remarked, that in comparison to the ancient civilizations of the Indus Valley and Mesopotamia, already in existence around 3000 B.C., the foundation of the Church is a rather recent happening.[6] This allows us to put Catholicism's two-thousand-year-old history in new retrospect. Instead of considering the Church as old, with the temptation to consider her youth and creative maturity as behind her, we face the fact that, for all we know, she may still be in her infancy.

One thing we do know for certain: the divinely constituted Church of Jesus Christ carries within her genes an eternal wisdom and energy that is capable of perennial rejuvenation. Neither persecution, nor inept or corrupt leadership, nor the catastrophes of history will ever succeed in devitalizing her. "Christianity", remarked Chesterton, "has had a series of revolutions and in each one of them Christianity has died. Christianity has died many times and risen again; for it had a God who knew the way out of the grave."[7] Her vitality, so manifest in the passage from catacombs to cathedrals in the first millennium, is fully capable of yet another herculean struggle to bring into existence another Christian civilization. Necessarily another civilization— let us leave aside any illusions—for the present-day "Western civilization", now the dominant global culture, is swiftly shattering every Christian symbol in its public domain, eliminating all Christian morality in its constitutions, educational programs, and medical directives and will soon have blown up the remnants of the Christian ethos that alone reinforces its foundations. The West has passed its own, seemingly irretrievable, tragic sentence upon itself.

---

[4] Ibid.

[5] Quoted in Christina Scott, *A Historian and His World: A Life of Christopher Dawson* (New Brunswick, N.J.: Transaction, 1992), p. 50.

[6] Arnold J. Toynbee, "Christianity and Civilization", in *Civilization on Trial* (London: Oxford University Press, 1953), pp. 238–39.

[7] G. K. Chesterton, *The Everlasting Man* (Mineola, N.Y.: Dover, 2007), p. 244.

The new Christian civilization may begin anywhere. Even, perhaps, once again in the West, in the Americas and Europe. For within this decaying society there are ardent men and women wholly convinced that Jesus Christ is Lord of all dimensions of existence; who are committed to being the creative minorities who will raise the phoenix of Christian social ideals from the ashes; who, even now, day after day, pray, study, speak, and act to build a Christ-centered culture of life and a social order of freedom built upon truth.

Yet, the deeply Catholic culture that will inspirit this new civilization may also begin to grow elsewhere: the Church is larger and greater than the West; her reality and her destiny are not bounded by the West's frontiers; for she is Catholic, universal, and her future may flourish signally among the vigorous Catholics of Africa or among the Chinese, Korean, Vietnamese and other Asian peoples who, in increasing numbers, are intrigued by Christianity. The post-Christian civilization of the West, now globally dominant, has providentially empowered the spread of the Catholic Faith to Africa and Asia along its global highways of the internet, other mass media, telecommunications, and in other material ways. The opportunity bears an uncanny resemblance to that offered two thousand years ago when the Roman Empire with its stone-paved roads and shipping routes provided Saints Peter and Paul and the other first Christians with the opportunity to establish the Church in city after city in Europe, North Africa, and the Middle East. The third-millennium apostles of Christ, the successors of Peter and Paul, Ambrose and Augustine, Benedict, Patrick and Columbanus, Boniface, Alcuin and Bernard, Francis Xavier and Matteo Ricci, can now travel on from the Tiber to the Yangtze and the Mekong, to the Nile and the Zambezi, by internet and in person.

In Order to Build the Future: Remember!

The task of building a Christian civilization is daunting, but we will be roused to action by recalling how it was built the first time: by the impetus of the convictions that Jesus Christ is Lord and mankind's only Savior, that in the Catholic Faith alone man finds the fullness of divinely revealed truth, that there can be no appeasement of the dictatorship of relativism, that neither syncretism nor false ecumenism is an option, that love of God and every man and woman impels Catholicism to be outward bound, proposing the "Ancient Truth"[8] intelligently and ardently to all, and that each one of us has a role to play.

For a civilization is built or destroyed not by nameless realities but by the cumulative force of the actions of individuals who, in the use of their creativity and freedom, under the power of sanctifying grace, bring about change. Before ever a social revolution ensues, an interior revolution occurs. It is in the soul where history is changed—in that secret sanctuary where all the political, legislative, military, and mass-media forces of a totalitarian regime are ultimately powerless. And it is this sanctuary that is the raison d'être of the priest: it is to the extent that he enters it with the divine truths, sanctifying it with the supernatural life, and guiding it to union with God within Christ's Mystical Body, that he becomes the irreplaceable builder of a truly Christian civilization.

---

[8] John Henry Newman, "The Intermediate State", in *Parochial and Plain Sermons* (San Francisco: Ignatius Press, 1997), p. 726.

In this most urgent and dramatic of missions—for what could be more urgent or dramatic than eternal salvation or damnation?—the priest will defy and be defied by the forces of a world hostile to Christ. "If the world hates you, know that it has hated me before it hated you. If you were of the world, the world would love its own; but because you are not of the world, but I chose you out of the world, therefore the world hates you" (Jn 15:18–19). So be it. In the heat of spiritual warfare his heart will be strengthened by the memory of the long line of heroic and creative priests who have preceded him, pointing the way. But there will be more than memory; there will be mystic presence.

> What shall sustain our faith (under God's grace) when we try to adhere to the Ancient Truth, and seem solitary? What shall nerve the "watchman on the walls of Jerusalem" against the scorn and jealousy of the world, the charge of singularity, of fancifulness, of extravagance, of rashness? What shall keep us calm and peaceful within when accused of "troubling Israel" and "prophesying evil"? What but the vision of all saints of all ages, whose steps we follow? What but the image of Christ mystical stamped upon our hearts and memories? The early times of purity and truth have not passed away! They are present still! We are not solitary, though we seem so. Few now alive may understand or sanction us; but those multitudes in the primitive time, who believed, and taught, and worshipped, as we do, still live unto God and, in their past deeds and their present voices, cry from the Altar. They animate us by their example; they cheer us by their company; they are on our right hand and our left, martyrs, confessors, and the like, high and low, who used the same creeds, and celebrated the same mysteries, and preached the same Gospel as we do.[9]

The priests whom we have recalled in these pages belong largely to the front ranks of heroism and genius; they are on the cover of Western civilization's narrative, and there is little fear that they will ever be forgotten. But there were so many others who were, and will remain, quiet unsung heroes, the ordinary yet so extraordinary priests who quietly worked and prayed and shepherded their people—and made an eternal difference to eternal souls. The quiet priests, those men of God who, through the centuries, as the hidden guardians of humanity, guided their people to the gates of Heaven on the pathways of the sacraments. They stood as sentinels on the ramparts of the city, watching over the destinies of men who, often insensitive to their peril, slept on. They were the ones who offered their own bodies to shield their flocks from the greatest danger the naive world so often ignores: sin, and the lord of sin, the Prince of Darkness; men who worked for the greatest liberation the world is in need of, eternal salvation; men who empowered the attainment of the greatest good, pure and undying joy in the Beatific Vision for the eternity of eternities. Priests, in "whose hearts are the roads to Zion. As they go through the Bitter valley they make it a place of springs",[10] springs from eternal sources that once irrigated the deserts of the West and brought to life a fertile and verdant culture.

If these priests had not existed or had not fulfilled their triple mission within Christianity from which surged this unexpected civilization, what type of world would we be living in today? If they had not guarded and developed the best of

---

[9] Ibid.
[10] Psalm 84:5–6, quoted in *The Liturgy of the Hours*, vol. 1 (London-Sydney-Dublin: Collins-Dwyer-Talbot, 1974), p. 325, using the Grail version of the Psalms.

Greco-Roman culture, for how many more centuries would intellectual barbarism have continued?

If they had not vigorously extracted the implications of human dignity and freedom from the Gospel, how else would Europe have had the *Magna Carta* and bills of rights? If priests like Gregory VII had not thundered against tyrants, would the West not have succumbed to despotism? If they had not stood up for the Christian truth about the dignity of womanhood, unleashing a cultural revolution that overthrew the thousand-year-old male chauvinism of Roman civilization, who would have done so? If they had not fought from the beginning to stop widespread female infanticide, who would have halted it? If slavery, so casual a part of the ancient world, had not been whittled away, unceasingly, year after year, by countless anonymous parish priests who preached—and lived—the Parable of the Good Samaritan, how many more centuries and how much bloodshed might it have taken to eliminate it?

If they had not poured out their lifeblood to educate millions?

If they had not fostered an economic system based on free enterprise?

If they had not brought to birth countless splendors of art, architecture, and music?

With gratitude to God, the source of all truth, goodness, and beauty, and with respect for the achievements of so many other men and women, it can be said of innumerable priests throughout two thousand years, on account of their ecclesial role and due to their leadership, heroism, and genius, what Leo XIII once asserted about the Church: "The Church, while directly and immediately aiming at the salvation of souls and the happiness which is to be attained in Heaven is yet, even in this life, the fountain of blessings so numerous and great, that they could not have been greater or more numerous had the original purpose of her foundation been the pursuit of happiness during the lifetime which is spent on earth."[11]

---

[11] Pope Leo XIII, Encyclical *Longinqua*, January 6, 1895, no. 4.

MAY THE LONG LINE NEVER BE BROKEN!

The great west doors of Notre Dame de Paris with our Lord Jesus Christ in
the center and the apostles flanking him on each side.

May the Long Line Never Be Broken!

Praise be to you, O Most Holy Trinity, for the long unbroken line of
true priests:

For those who wrote the divine truths on human hearts;

For the men who in history's hours of darkness kept the flame of faith
burning;

For the stalwarts who, century after century, never ceased to offer the
Sacrifice of the Mass at catacomb, cathedral, and battlefield;

For the men of infra-eternal vision who gave invincible hope to tired
spirits;

For the defenders of the honor of God and the dignity of man;

For the surgeons of the spirit who prevented the second death;

For the soldiers of Christ who fought against the Enemy—the
manipulative power behind the world's darkness—and the servants
of the Enemy, who unsheathed the sword of the spirit and barred
the way to Hell;

For the men who stood their ground when their numbers dwindled
and their days darkened;

For the many quiet and gracious sanctifiers who strengthened and took
the sting out of life's sorrows; whose blessing brought solace, whose
presence dried tears, whose words quenched the fires of revenge,
whose anointed touch healed soul-wounds;

For the ardent priests who purified this world;

For the noble regiments of missionary priests, cloistered priests, and
silent hermits;

For the channels of light, strength, freedom, and genius;

For the lineage of builders of the strong walls of Christian civilization;

For so many men of heroic heart—

And may the long line never be broken! AMEN!

SELECTED BIBLIOGRAPHY

Alcuin. *Opera Omnia*. In *Patrologia Latina*. Vol. 100. Paris: J.P. Migne, 1851.

Allott, Stephen, trans. *Alcuin of York: His Life and Letters*. York: William Sessions, 1974.

Andrieu, Michel. *Le pontifical romain au moyen-âge*. 4 vols., Studi e Testi, 86–89. Vol. 2, *Le pontifical de la curie romaine au XIIIe siècle* [*The Pontifical of the Roman Curia in the 13th Century*]. Vatican City State: Biblioteca Apostolica Vaticana, 1940.

Barber, Malcolm. *The New Knighthood: A History of the Order of the Temple*. Cambridge: Cambridge University Press, 1995.

———. *The Trial of the Templars*. Cambridge: Cambridge University Press, 2006.

Barber, Richard. *The Knight and Chivalry*. Revised edition. Rochester, N.Y.: Boydell Press, 2000.

Bardy, Gustave. *La Conversion au Christianisme durant les premiers siècles*. Paris: Aubier, 1949.

Belloc, Hilaire. *Europe and the Faith*. Charleston, S.C.: BiblioLife, LLC, 2011.

Berman, Harold J. *Law and Revolution: The Formation of the Western Legal Tradition*. Cambridge: Harvard University Press, 1983.

Bloch, Marc. *Feudal Society*. Vol. 2. Chicago: University of Chicago Press, 1961.

Braudel, Fernand. *Civilization and Capitalism: 15th–18th Century*. 3 vols. New York: Harper and Row, 1979.

Brown, Peter. *Augustine of Hippo: A Biography*. Berkeley: University of California Press, 2000.

———. *Triumph and Diversity, A.D. 200–1000*. 2nd ed. Hoboken, N.J.: Wiley-Blackwell, 2003.

Burns, C. Delisle. *The First Europe: A Study of the Establishment of Medieval Christendom A.D. 400–800*. London: G. Allen and Unwin, 1949.

Carroll, Warren H. *The Building of Christendom*. Front Royal, Va.: Christendom Press, 2004.

Charny, Geoffroi de. *A Knight's Own Book of Chivalry*. Philadelphia: University of Pennsylvania Press, 2005.

Chesterton, G.K. *The Catholic Church and Conversion*. New York: Macmillan Press, 1926.

Cohen, Gustave. *La Grande Clarté du Moyen Age*. Paris: Gallimard, 1945.

Coulanges, Fustel de. *Histoire des Institutions Politiques de l'Ancienne France*. Paris: Hachette, 1874.

Croce, W. "The History of the Parish". In *The Parish: From Theology to Practice*, edited by Hugh Rahner, pp. 9–25. Westminster: Newman Press, 1958.

Daniel-Rops, Henri. *Cathedral and Crusade: Studies of the Medieval Church, 1050–1350*. New York: Dutton, 1957.

———. *The Church of the Apostles and Martyrs*. Vol. 2. New York: Image Books, 1960.

———. *The Church in the Dark Ages*. London: J.M. Dent and Sons, 1959.

———, ed. *The Miracle of Ireland*. London: Clonmore-Burns and Oates, 1959.

Dante. *Divina Commedia*. Translated by Anthony Esolen. New York: The Modern Library, 2002.

———. *Inferno*. New York: Modern Library, 2002.

———. *Paradise*. Translated by Anthony Esolen. New York: Modern Library, 2004.

———. *Purgatorio*. Translated by Anthony Esolen. New York: Modern Library, 2003.

Dawson, Christopher. *Christianity and European Culture*. Washington, D.C.: Catholic University of America Press, 1998.

———. *The Dynamics of World History:* With an introduction by Dermot Quinn. 1958. Reprint, Wilmington: ISI Books, 2000.

———. *The Formation of Christendom*. San Francisco: Ignatius Press, 2008.

———. *The Making of Europe. An Introduction to the History of European Unity*. Washington, D.C.: Catholic University of America Press, 2002.

———. *Medieval Essays*. Garden City, N.Y.: Doubleday, 1959.

———. *Medieval Religion*. Washington, D.C.: Catholic University of America Press, 1935.

———. *Religion and the Rise of Western Culture*. New York: Doubleday, 1991.

Decarreaux, Jean. *Monks and Civilization: From the Barbarian Invasions to the Reign of Charlemagne*. New York: Doubleday, 1964.

Digby, Kenelm Henry. *The Broadstone of Honour*. London: F. C. and J. Rivington, 1846.

———. *Maxims of Christian Chivalry*. Montreal: Catholic Authors Press, 2003.

Dill, Samuel. *Roman Society in Gaul in the Merovingian Age*. New York: Barnes and Noble, 1970.

Duhem, Pierre. *Le système du monde: histoire des doctrines cosmologiques de Platon à Copernic* [*The system of the world: A history of cosmological doctrines from Plato to Copernicus*]. 10 vols. Paris: Herman, 1913–1959.

Duroselle, Jean-Baptiste. *L'Europe: Histoire de ses Peuples*. Paris: Hachette, 1998.

Einhard. *The Life of Charlemagne*. Translated by Samuel Epes Turner. New York: Harper and Brothers, 1880.

Esolen, Anthony. *The Politically Incorrect Guide to Western Civilization*. Washington, D.C.: Regnery, 2008.

Frale, Barbara. *The Templars: The Secret History Revealed*. Dunboyne: Maverick House Publishers, 2009.

Franz, Adolph, ed. *Die Kirchlichen Benediktionen im Mittelalter*. 2 vols. Freiburg im Breisgau: M. Herder, 1909.

Gaskoin, Charles J. B. *Alcuin: His Life and His Work*. London: C. J. Clay and Sons, 1904.

Gilchrist, John. *The Church and Economic Activity in the Middle Ages*. New York: St. Martin's Press, 1969.

Gilson, Etienne. *The Christian Philosophy of St. Augustine*. New York: Random House, 1960.

Gimpel, Jean. *The Medieval Machine: The Industrial Revolution of the Middle Ages*. New York: Holt, Rinehart and Winston, 1976.

Goldstein, Thomas. *Dawn of Modern Science: From the Ancient Greeks to the Renaissance*. 1980. New York: Da Capo Press, 1995.

Goodell, Henry H. "The Influence of the Monks in Agriculture". Address delivered before the Massachusetts State Board of Agriculture, Lynnfield, Mass., August 23, 1901. In Calvin Stebbins, *Henry Hill Goodell: The Story of His Life, with Letters and a Few of His Addresses*, pp. 228–253. Cambridge: Riverside Press, 1911.

Grant, A.J., ed. *Two Lives of Charlemagne by Einhard and the Monk of St. Gall*. Bk 1, n. 2. Boston, Mass.: Digireads.com Publishing, 2010.

Grant, Edward. *The Foundations of Modern Science in the Middle Ages: Their Religious, Institutional and Intellectual Contexts*. Cambridge Studies in the History of Science. Cambridge: Cambridge University Press, 1996.

Gregory of Tours. *History of the Franks*. Translated by O.M. Dalton. 2 vols. Oxford: University Press, 1927.

Guardini, Romano. *Letters from Lake Como: Explorations in Technology and the Human Race.* Grand Rapids, Mich.: Wm. B. Eerdmans, 1994.

Haskins, C. H. *The Renaissance of the Twelfth Century.* Cambridge: Harvard University Press, 1927.

———. *The Rise of Universities.* 1923. Cornell: Cornell University Press, 1957.

Heidemann, Steen. *The Catholic Priest, Image of Christ: Through Fifteen Centuries of Art.* Leominster: Gracewing, 2009.

Heilbron, J. L. *The Sun in the Church: Cathedrals as Solar Observatories.* Cambridge: Harvard University Press, 1999.

Jaki, Stanley L. "Medieval Creativity in Science and Technology". In *Patterns and Principles and Other Essays.* Wilmington, Del.: Intercollegiate Studies Institute, 1995.

———. *The Origin of Science and the Science of Its Origins.* Edinburgh: Scottish Academic Press, 1978.

———. *The Savior of Science.* Grand Rapids, Mich.: Wm. B. Eerdmans, 2000.

Johnson, Paul. *Art: A New History.* New York: HarperCollins, 2003.

Joinville, Jean de. *Histoire de Saint Louis* [*History of Saint Louis*]. Translated by James Hutton. London, 1870. Reprint, Cambridge: Cambridge University Press, 1992.

Keen, Maurice. *Chivalry.* New Haven, Conn.: Yale University Press, 1984.

Knowles, David. *The Evolution of Medieval Thought.* 2nd ed. London: Longman, 1989.

Labarge, Margaret Wade. *Saint Louis: The Life of Louis IX of France.* London: Eyre and Spottiswoode, 1968.

Lecky, W. E. H. *History of European Morals from Augustus to Charlemagne.* 2 vols. New York: D. Appleton, 1870.

Leclercq, Jean. *The Love of Learning and the Desire for God: A Study of Monastic Culture.* New York: Fordham University Press, 1982.

Lewis, C. S. *The Allegory of Love.* Oxford: Clarendon Press, 1936.

Lindberg, David C. *The Beginnings of Western Science.* 2nd ed. Chicago: University of Chicago Press, 2008.

Loudon, John C. *An Encyclopaedia of Agriculture.* London: Longman, 1825.

MacLeod, George. *We Shall Rebuild.* Glasgow: Iona Community, 1942.

McNeill, John T., and H. M. Gamer. *Medieval Handbooks of Penance: A Translation of the Principal Libri Poenitentiales and Selections from Related Documents.* New York: Columbia University Press, 1938.

Migne, Jacques-Paul. *Patrologiae cursus completus, series latina.* 222 vols. Paris, 1844–1864.

Montalembert, Charles Forbes, Comte de. *Les moines d'Occident depuis saint Benoît jusqu'à saint Bernard.* Vol. 2. Paris: Jacques Lecoffre, 1860.

———. *The Monks of the West from St. Benedict to St. Bernard.* Vol. 1. New York: P. J. Kenedy and Sons, 1912.

Morris, Kevin L., ed. *The Truest Fairy Tale: An Anthology of the Religious Writings of G. K. Chesterton.* Cambridge: Lutterworth Press, 2007.

Mould, D. P. *Ireland of the Saints.* London: B. T. Batsford, 1953.

———. *The Monasteries of Ireland.* London: B. T. Batsford, 1976.

Newman, John Henry. *The Idea of a University.* London: Longmans, Green, 1907.

———. *The Mission of the Isles of the North.* In *Historical Sketches.* Vol. 3. London: Longmans, Green, 1909.

Nicholson, Helen. *The Knights Hospitaller*. Woodbridge, UK: Boydell Press, 2001.

Niebuhr, H. Richard. *Christ and Culture*. New York: Harper and Row, 1951.

Page, Rolph Barlow. *The Letters of Alcuin*. Charleston, S.C.: Bibliolife, 2009.

Panofsky, Erwin. *Abbot Suger on the Abbey Church of St. Denis and Its Treasures*. Princeton, N.J.: Princeton University Press, 1946.

Papini, Giovanni. *Saint Augustine*. New York: Harcourt, Brace, 1939.

Paré, G., A. Brunet, and P. Tremblay. *La Renaissance du XIIème siècle. Les Écoles et l'Enseignement*. Paris: J. Vrin, 1933.

Pernoud, Régine. *Martin of Tours: Soldier, Bishop, and Saint*. San Francisco: Ignatius Press, 2006.

———. *The Templars: Knights of Christ*. San Francisco: Ignatius Press, 2009.

———. *Women in the Days of the Cathedrals*. San Francisco: Ignatius Press, 1998.

Phelan, Owen M. *The Formation of Christian Europe: The Carolingians, Baptism, and the Imperium Christianum*. Oxford: Oxford University Press, 2014.

Pirenne, Henri. *Economic and Social History of Medieval Europe*. New York: Mariner Books, 1956.

———. *A History of Europe from the End of the Roman World in the West to the Beginnings of the Western States*. 1936. New York: Doubleday Anchor, 1958.

Ranft, Patricia. *The Theology of Work: Peter Damian and the Medieval Religious Renewal Movement*. New York: Palgrave Macmillan, 2006.

———. *Women and Spiritual Equality in Christian Tradition*. New York: St. Martin's Press, 1998.

———. *Women in Western Intellectual Culture, 600–1500*. New York: Palgrave Macmillan, 2008.

Read, P. P. *The Templars: The Dramatic History of the Knights Templar, the Most Powerful Military Order of the Crusades*. Cambridge: Da Capo Press, 2001.

Riley-Smith, Jonathan. *The First Crusaders, 1095–1131*. Cambridge University Press, 1997.

———. *Hospitallers: The History of the Order of St. John*. London: Hambledon Press, 1999.

———. *The Knights of St. John in Jerusalem and Cyprus, c. 1050–1310*. London: Macmillan, 1967.

Ryan, J. *Irish Monasticism*. 1931. Dublin: Four Courts Press, 1992.

Salvian of Marseilles. *On the Government of God*. Translated by Eva Matthews Sanford. New York: Columbia University Press, 1930.

Schumpeter, Joseph A. *History of Economic Analysis*. New York: Oxford University Press, 1954. Reprint, London: Allen and Unwin, 1986.

Senior, John. *The Restoration of Christian Culture*. San Francisco: Ignatius Press, 1998.

Smith, Julia. "Einhard". In *Transactions of the Royal Historical Society*, p. 55. Cambridge, England, 2003.

Southern, R.W. *Scholastic Humanism and the Unification of Europe*. Vol. 1, *Foundations*. Hoboken, N.J.: Wiley-Blackwell, 1997.

———. *Scholastic Humanism and the Unification of Europe*. Vol. 2, *The Heroic Age*. Hoboken, N.J.: Wiley-Blackwell, 2001.

———. *Western Society and the Church in the Middle Ages*. New York: Penguin Books, 1970.

Sowards, J. Kelley, ed. *Makers of the Western Tradition: Portraits from History*. Vol. 1, 6th edition. New York: St. Martin's Press, 1994.

Stancliffe, Clare E. "Jonas's *Life of Columbanus and His Disciples*". In *Studies in Irish Hagiography: Saints and Scholars*, edited by John Carey, Máire Herbert, and Pádraig Ó Riain, pp. 189–220. Dublin: Four Courts Press, 2001.

Stark, Rodney. *Cities of God: The Real Story of How Christianity Became an Urban Movement and Conquered Rome*. New York: HarperOne, 2007.

———. *For the Glory of God: How Monotheism Led to Reformations, Science, Witch-Hunts, and the End of Slavery*. Princeton, N.J.: Princeton University Press, 2003.

———. *The Victory of Reason: How Christianity Led to Freedom, Capitalism, and Western Success*. New York: Random House, 2005.

Tasso, Torquato. *Jerusalem Delivered* [*Gerusalemme Liberata*]. Translated by Anthony Esolen. Baltimore: Johns Hopkins University Press, 2000.

Toynbee, A.J. "Christianity and Civilization". In *Civilization on Trial*. London: Oxford University Press, 1953.

———. *An Historian's Approach to Religion*. London: Oxford University Press, 1956.

Valency, Maurice. *In Praise of Love*. New York: Macmillan, 1958.

Vandenakker, J.P. *Small Christian Communities and the Parish*. Kansas City: Sheed and Ward, 1994.

Wallach, Luitpold. *Alcuin and Charlemagne: Studies in Carolingian History and Literature*. Ithaca, N.Y.: Cornell University Press, 1959.

Ward, Benedicta. *High King of Heaven*. Kalamazoo, Mich.: Cistercian Publications, 2008.

Watkin, David. *A History of Western Architecture*. 4th ed. London: Lawrence King Publishing, 2005.

Watkin, E.I. *Catholic Art and Culture*. London: Hollis and Carter, 1947.

Watkins, Oscar. *A History of Penance: Being a Study of the Authorities*. Vols. 1 and 2. London: Longmans, Green, 1920.

West, A.F. *Alcuin and the Rise of the Christian Schools*. New York: Charles Scribner's Sons, 1892.

Wilkins, David, ed. *Concilia Magnae Britanniae et Hiberniae, a synodo verolamiensi A.D. CCCC XLVI. ad londinensem A.D. M DCCXVII*. 4 vols. London: Gosling, 1737.

Willey, Petroc, Pierre de Cointet, and Barbara Morgan. *The Catechism of the Catholic Church and the Craft of Catechesis*. San Francisco: Ignatius Press, 2008.

Wilmot-Buxton, Ethel Mary. *Alcuin*. New York: P.J. Kenedy, 1922.

Woods, Thomas. *How the Catholic Church Built Western Civilization*. Washington, D.C.: Regnery, 2005.

ART CREDITS

xiii   Cathedral of Notre-Dame d'Amiens, France; central portal by night. Photo © Guillaume Piolle.

xiv   Ordination of the author, Father William Slattery, by Saint John Paul II, January 3, 1991, in St. Peter's Basilica, Rome. © L'Osservatore Romano Servizio Fotografico.

5   Cathedral of Notre Dame de Paris, main entrance. Photo courtesy of Jebulon.

9   *The Apostles.* These statues flank the main east door of Notre Dame Cathedral, Paris. Photo courtesy of Fr. Lawrence Lew.

13   Willem van de Velde the Younger, *The Gust*, ca. 1680.

15   Partial view of sculpture "Good Defeats Evil" on the grounds of the United Nations headquarters, New York. Created by Zurab Tsereteli. Courtesy of photographer Rick Bajornas and UN photos.

20   Etienne-Hippolyte Maindron, *Baptism of Clovis by Saint Remy*, 1865. Photo courtesy of Stéphane Mahot.

27   Sebastiano Ricci, *St. Cajetan Strengthens a Dying Man*, 1727. Photo courtesy of Pinacoteca di Brera, Milan, Italy.

39   Carle van Loo, *St. Augustine Preaching before Valerius, Bishop of Hippo*, 1755. Church of Notre-Dame-des-Victories, Paris, France/Bridgeman Images.

45   Philippe de Champaigne, *St. Augustine*, 1650. Photo courtesy of Los Angeles County Museum of Art.

62   *The Conversion of King Ethelbert* by Saint Augustine. Detail of a mosaic by Clayton & Bell in the chapel of Saint Gregory and Saint Augustine in Westminster Cathedral. Photo courtesy of © Fr. Lawrence Lew, O.P.

65   *St. Columba and His Brother Missionaries Land on the Isle of Iona.* Detail from a window in Holy Trinity Church in Stratford-upon-Avon. Photo courtesy of © Fr. Lawrence Lew, O.P.

70   Dorothy Burrows, *Saint Columba Arrives to Iona.* Heritage Image Partnership Ltd/Alamy Stock Photo.

72   Donald Gilbert of Sussex, wood carving in St. Columba's Cathedral, Oban. Photo courtesy of Ian McIntyre.

75   Window of Iona Abbey, Scotland. Photo courtesy of Michael Miller, Virginia Media Services.

76   Celtic cross at Monasterboice, Ireland, with a monastic round tower in the background. Photo courtesy of Nick Corble.

82   Domenico di Niccolo dei Cori, *The Confession*, ca. 15th century. Palazzo Pubblico, Siena, Italy/Bridgeman Images.

88   Edwin Longsden Long (1829–1891), *Confession*, 1862. Private Collection, photo © Bonhams, London, UK/Bridgeman Images.

91   Werner Henschel, *Statue of St. Boniface* (ca. 680–754), 1830, in Fulda, Germany. Photo courtesy of Frank Schulenburg.

94   *Alcuin at the Court of Charlemagne*. Engraved by an unnamed artist from a painting by Magaud, © Mary Evans Picture Library.

103   *Charlemagne and His Counsellors at Aix-la-Chapelle* (engraving). English School (nineteenth century), private collection, © Look and Learn, Bridgeman Images.

105   Jean Victor Schnetz, *Charlemagne and Alcuin*, 1830. The Art Archive/Alamy Stock Photo.

114   *Scholarly Monks*, engraving by Hermann Vogel, 1880–1883. Mary Evans Picture Library.

121   Eugen von Blaas (1843–1931), *Charlemagne and His Scholars*. Private Collection/The Stapleton Collection/Bridgeman Images.

126   Vilhelm Bissen, *Bishop Absalon Hvide*, 1901. Photo courtesy of Stephen J. Kennedy.

130   Harry Mileham (1873–1957), *Alfred Translates "Pastoral Care" ("Liber Regulae Pastoralis")* by Pope Gregory the Great, 1909. Private Collection/Bridgeman Images.

147   World War II, the Pacific island of Saipan, June 1944, a U.S. Navy chaplain offers the Holy Sacrifice of the Mass for Marines. Photo by Sgt. Steele. Courtesy of U.S. Marines, National Archives Catalog.

148   Thomas Pettie, *The Vigil*, 19th c. Warriorhood kneeling before the Crucified Hero: a youth during the initiation ceremonies for knighthood. Illustration from "Romance and Legend of Chivalry" by A. R. Hope Moncrieff (color litho), © Tate, London 2016.

153   William Blake Richmond, *The Hun and the Crucifix*, 19th century. Laing Art Gallery, Newcastle-upon-Tyne, U.K./© Tyne and Wear Archives and Museums/Bridgeman Images.

160   Burlison and Grylls, *The Vision of Sir Galahad*. The knight and horse are depicted after the painting by G. F. Watts. South nave of St. Saviour Church, Shotton Colliery, Durham, England. Photo courtesy of Dave Webster.

161   Byzantine mosaics, Archbishop's Palace, Ravenna. Photo courtesy of John A. Donaghy.

163   Emile Signol, *St. Bernard Preaching the Second Crusade in Vézelay*, March 31, 1146 (1840). Château de Versailles, France/Bridgeman Images.

164   Georg Andreas Wasshuber, *Saint Bernard*, 1700. Based on a statue with a lifelike resemblance located at Clairvaux. Painting at Heiligenkreuz Abbey, Austria. Photo courtesy of © www.stift-heiligenkreuz.at.

165   *St. Bernard of Clairvaux Venerates "Our Lady"*. Stained glass window in the parish church of Saint-Michel in Malaucène. © Photographer: Reinhardhauke.

167   *St. Bernard Giving the Templars Their Statutes*, French School, 19th century. Bibliotheque des Arts Decoratifs, Paris, France. Archives Charmet/Bridgeman Images.

173   G. F. Watts, *Sir Galahad*, 1862 (oil on canvas). Fogg Art Museum, Harvard Art Museums, USA: Bequest of Grenville L. Winthrop: Bridgeman Images.

182   Il Baciccio, *St. Francis Xavier Baptizes an Oriental Princess*, ca. 1704. Photo by A. Jemolo.

187   Karl Friedrich Lessing, *The Thousand-Year-Old Oak* (detail), 1837. Photo courtesy of Heidemarie Niemann, Mainz.

192   *Shield of Parade* (detail), Flanders, 15th century. Photo courtesy of Rex Harris.

196   El Greco, *St. Francis Receiving the Stigmata* (detail), 1585–1590. Courtesy of Walters Art Museum.

198   Emile Jean Horace Vernet, *Pope Julius II Ordering Bramante, Michelangelo and Raphael to Construct the Vatican and St. Peters*, 1827. Louvre, Paris, France/De Agostini Picture Library/G. Dagli Orti/Bridgeman Images.

199   Notre Dame de Chartres, nave and choir, organ and windows. © Photographer: Mmensler.

203   Jean-Baptiste Mauzaisse, *Louis VII (ca. 1120–1180), King of France, Taking the Banner in St. Denis in 1147*, (1840). Château de Versailles, France/Bridgeman Images.

207   *Canute Listens to the Chanting Monks of Ely*, ca. 1017. © Mary Evans Picture Library.

208   *Carthusian Monks in Cowls and Habits Process to Matins at 2 a.m.* Engraving by an unnamed artist, 1872. © Illustrated London News Ltd./Mary Evans.

211   This bronze sculpture, outside the United Nations headquarters in New York City, was presented to the UN as a gift from Spain by King Juan Carlos during an official visit in 1976. Courtesy of UN Photo/Mark Garten.

216   François Théodore Devaulx, *The Signing of the Magna Carta*, 19th century. Photo courtesy of Geraldine Wilson, http://travellinghistorian.com/.

218   "Burgundian monks [Cistercians] cultivating the vineyard during the Middle Ages". A 19th century illustration from Louis Figuier, *Les merveilles de l'industrie* (1873). Photo courtesy of El Bibliomata.

219   Henry Matthew Brock (1875–1960), *Labouring Monks*, illustration from H. D. M. Spence-Jones, Private Collection/The Stapleton Collection/Bridgeman Images.

220   Monks ploughing the land with oxen. Engraving, Germany, 1872. © Mary Evans Picture Library.

221   Diagram of the medieval monastery plan of St. Gall, Switzerland. Courtesy of © UCLA's Center for Medieval and Renaissance Studies. http://www.stgallplan.org/en/index_plan.html.

223   Model of the Historical Association of the Canton of St. Gall, 1877, located in the Historical Museum of the City of St. Gall. Model of a monastery based

on the plan drawn up for Gozbert, the Abbot of St. Gall (A.D. 816–837). Courtesy of Carolingian Culture at Reichenau and St. Gall: The Plan of St. Gall, http://www.stgallplan.org/en/index_plan.html.

224   Interior astronomical clock in the ambulatory of Chartres Cathedral, Eure-et-Loir, France. Photographer: Selbymay.

225   *The Monks: Men of Prayer*. Detail from the fresco by Niccolò di Tommaso (Florence, 1346–1376) of Pope Celestinus V with Raimondo del Balzo and Isabella d'Eppe. Courtesy of © photographer Carlo Raso.

232   Pere Borrell del Caso, portrait of Father Jaime Balmes (1810–1848). © Mary Evans/Thaliastock.

247   The great west doors of Notre Dame de Paris with our Lord Jesus Christ in the center and the apostles flanking him on each side. Photo courtesy of © Fr. Lawrence Lew.

INDEX

Page numbers in italics indicate illustrations.

abortion, 184

academics. *See* education

The Accolade (Leighton), 176–77, *177*

Adam of Bremen, 131–32

Adams, John, 3

Adelard (saint), 116

Admonitio Generalis (Charlemagne), 122

Adomnán of Iona, 69, 74

adultery, 81, 185

Aeneas Bearing His Father Anchises from Burning Troy (van Loo), *17*

Agincourt, Battle of (1415), 178

Agobard of Lyons, 128

agriculture, monastic advances in, 4, 73, 219–20

Aidan of Lindisfarne (saint), 70, 77, 107, 123

Aimon (abbot), 202

Alaric (king of Visigoths), 16, 17, 22

Albert the Great, 215, 234

Alcántara, Order of, 172

Alcuin and Charlemagne (Wilson), *107*

Alcuin of York (saint)
  as architect of Charlemagne's empire, xvi, 48, 100–101, 106–7
  asceticism of, 108
  background of, 107–8
  Catholicism as experienced by, 109–10
  character of, 107, 108–9
  Christian culture under, 52, 65, 70, 93, 131
  cultural preservation efforts of, 118
  death of, 125
  educational initiatives under, 25, 90, 105, 114–16, 119–20, 122
  epitaph for, 125–26
  "In Dormiturio", 109
  intellectual influence of, 116, 117–19
  literacy movement under, 73
  moral reform efforts of, 110–12
  on pagan conversions to Christianity, 112–13
  portraits of, *94*, *105*, *107*
  restoration of Roman Empire and, 20

Alfred the Great (king of Wessex), 130

Alfred Translates "Pastoral Care" (Mileham), *130*

Altus Prosator (Columba of Iona), 55

Ambrose (saint)
  application of Christianity to social order, 101
  background of, 32
  baptism of Augustine by, 37
  death of, 35
  as Father of Western Culture, xvi, 18, 31
  on papal authority, 51
  portraits of, *32*, *35*
  role in state affairs, 34–35
  social justice promotion by, 33

St. Ambrose Bars Emperor Theodosius the Great from Entering Milan Cathedral (van Dyck), *32*

Ampère, M. J-J., 122

Ancient Rite, 139–47
  alterations to, 141
  components of, 140n4
  in creation of culture of Christendom, xvi, 142, 145
  as embodiment of Catholicism, 142–43
  formation of, 139, 140–41
  historical perspectives on extent of impact, 145–47, *147*
  as sacrificial ritual, 143–45

Angilbert, 106, 110

Anianus of Orléans, 22

Anselm of Canterbury, 43

Ansgar (saint), 20

Antonino of Florence, 228–29, 237

Apel, Willi, 209

The Apostles Supper (Wagner), 210

Aquinas. *See* Thomas Aquinas

architecture. *See also* Gothic architecture
  Baroque, 205
  in Carolingian Empire, 120
  monastic, 205
  Romanesque, 120, 202, 205

Arendt, Hannah, 43–44

Aristotle, 218, 229, 234, 236

Arnarson, Ingólfur, 20, 71

Arno of Salzburg, 104, 106, 110, 116

art, in Carolingian Empire, 120

Aspects of the Rise of Economic Individualism (Robertson), 212n3

astronomy, Catholic development of, 4

At the Monastery Gate (Waldmüller), *30*

Attila the Hun, 49, 50, 146

Augustine of Canterbury (saint), 70

Augustine of Hippo (saint)
  application of Christianity to social order, 101, 133
  background of, 35–36
  baptism into Catholic Church, 37
  City of God, 44, 48, 51, 53, 101–2

Augustine of Hippo (saint) (*continued*)
    Confessions, 37, 38, 43
    conversion efforts of, 20, 41, 54–55
    death of, 49
    as Father of Western Culture, xvi, 18, 31
    humanity of, 38
    on papal authority, 51
    portraits of, *36*, *39*, *45*
    priesthood as influence on, 39–42
    Rule of St. Augustine, 42
    sociopolitical order envisioned by, 44–49
    theological and philosophical contributions
        of, 42–44
    On the Trinity, 42
    works authored by, 37–38
    on zone of dissimilarity, 207
St. Augustine (Champaigne), *45*
*St. Augustine Preaching before Valerius, Bishop of
    Hippo* (van Loo), *39*
Augustine with Monica (Scheffer), *36*
Austrian School of Economics, 228, 237, 238
Avitus of Vienne, 18, 20
Aviz, Order of, 172
Aymon, 156
Azpilcueta, Martín de, 226, 230, 232, 233

Bach, Johann Sebastian, 210
Baden-Powell, Robert, 179
Baldwin II (king of Jerusalem), 167
Baldwin III (king of Jerusalem), 167
Baldwin IV, 170
Balmes, Jaime, *232*, 238
banking practices, 232
baptism, 18, 20, 22, 80, 84
Baptism of Clovis by Saint Remy (Maindron), *20*
Baronius, Caesar, 18*n*10
Baroque architecture, 205
battles. *See specific name of battle*
Baudelaire, Charles, 46
Bayard, Pierre Terrail de, 178
Bede (saint), 60, 88–89, 107–8
Being and Time (Heidegger), 43
Bellesini, Stefano, 29
Belloc, Hilaire, 134
St. Benedict (Fra Angelico), *57*
Benedict XVI (pope), 8, 44, 56, 90, 119
Benedict (saint). *See also* Benedictine monks
    background of, 56–57
    monastic communities founded by, 57–58
    portraits of, *57*, *59*
    Rule of St. Benedict, 57–58, 61
    scientific mentality of, 62–63
    on singing by monks, 206
    solitary life led by, 57, *58*

*Saint Benedict Instructing the People in Sacred
    Doctrine* (Bazzi), *59*
Benedictine monks, 58–63
    agricultural practices of, 220
    ascetic framework for formation of,
        58–59
    conversion efforts of, 20, 54
    cultural preservation efforts of, 60–61
    Gregorian chant used by, 206
    missionary efforts of, 55, 63
    monastic communities founded by, 162
    spread of influence, 63, 90
    Western mind-set influenced by, xvi,
        60–63
Berlioz, Hector, 209, 210
Berman, Harold, 4
Saint Bernard (Wasshuber), *164*
Bernard of Clairvaux (saint)
    accomplishments of, 165
    background of, 162
    character of, 163–64
    conversion efforts of, 204
    De Consideratione, 165
    Knights Templar statutes authored by, 165,
        167, 167–68, 169
    Louis IX as influenced by, 176
    monasteries founded by, 163
    political power of, 164
    In Praise of the New Knighthood, 168, 169
    on singing by monks, 207
*St. Bernard Preaching the Second Crusade in
    Vézelay* (Signol), *163*
Bernard of Vienne, 128
Bernardino of Siena, 230, 234, 237
Saint Bernardino of Siena (El Greco), *226*
Bernardone, Francesco (Francis of Assisi), 176,
        195
Berzé, Hugues de, 194
Bible. *See* New Testament; Old Testament
Bishop Absalon Hvide (Bissen), *126*
*Bishop Ambrose of Milan Absolves Emperor
    Theodosius* (Subleyras), *35*
bishops
    in Dark Ages, 21–23
    missionary efforts of, 24
    role in state affairs, 34
    sanctuary laws defended by, 30
    social importance of, 40
Blanche de Castile, 174, 175, 186
Blessing of the New Soldier, 150*n*2, 152*n*9
The Blessing of the Wheat in the Artois (Breton),
    128
Boileau, Etienne, 174
Bonaventure (saint), 43
Boniface VIII (pope), 170–71

Boniface (saint)
  background of, 92
  character of, 91–92
  Christian revolution triggered by, 69
  conversion efforts of, 20, 70
  death of, 93
  formation of Western civilization in
      Germany, xvi, 91, 92–93
  papal-Frankish alliance negotiated by, 96,
      97
  portrait of, *91*
The Book of the Order of Chivalry (Llull), 159,
  193
Borromeo, Charles, 29
Botero, Giovanni, 238
Bouillon, Godfrey de, 172
Braudel, Fernand, 4
Brendan of Clonfert, 123
Brigid of Kildare, 123
The Broad Stone of Honour (Digby), 178, 179
Buridan, Jean, 228
Burke, Edmund, 27
business profit theories, 233

Caesarius of Arles, 80
St. Cajetan Strengthens a Dying Man (Ricci),
  27
Calatrava, Order of, 172
calligraphy, 118
Callistus (pope), 184
Callixtus II (pope), 172
Calvinism, 225, 225n33, 236, 236n65
canon law, 4, 215
Canova, Antonio, 198
cantatas, 210
Canute Listens to the Chanting Monks of Ely
  (unknown), *207*
capitalism, 211, 212–13
Carloman (king of Franks), 92, 96, 97
Carlyle, Thomas, 6
Carmelites, 226, 229
Carolingian Empire. *See also* Charlemagne
  art and architecture in, 120
  Christianity in, 100, 101, 129–30, 142
  cultural renaissance in, 129–31
  decline of, 126–27
  education in, 25, 115–16, 119–25, 129
  episcopate of, 104
  intellectual culture in, 118–19
  monastery development in, 65
  women in, 123, 124
*Carthusian Monks in Cowls and Habits Process to
  Matins at 2 a.m* (unknown), *208*
Carver, Robert, 210
Castillo de Bovadilla, Jerónimo, 232

cathedrals. *See also specific cathedrals*
  as centers of religious life, 23–24, 201–2
  Gothic, 199–202
  schools established by, 107–8, 114–15, 117,
      119, 125, 131
Catherine of Siena (saint), 186
Catholic Church. *See also* bishops; confession;
    Mass; monks and monasteries; papacy;
    parishes; priests
  Ancient Rite as embodiment of, 142–43
  baptism into, 18, 20, 22, 80, 84
  chivalry as creation of, 153–54
  free-market economics and, 4, 212, 213,
      238–39
  ideal behind Western economic progress,
      211–19
  independence of, 128–29
  legal system influenced by, 4, 48–49, 214–15
  milestones in building new civilization
      (A.D. 200–1300), 9–11
  natural law compatibility with, 55
  on racism, 132
  role in state affairs, 34–35, 48, 102–4,
      128–29
  in Roman Empire, 15, 15n1
  sanctuary-asylum laws for, 30
  science and, 61–63
  on timeline of world history, 242
  in Western civilization formation, 3–5,
      133–35
  women in, 183–87
Cathulf, 95, 99
Caussin, Nicholas, 88
Celtic crosses, 76, *76*
Celtic monks and monasteries, 69–90
  achievements of, 70–71
  agricultural practices of, 73, 220
  Christian vision of life held by, 74–76
  in cultural renaissance, 116–17
  educational institutions of, 73
  historical accounts of, 71–72
  influence of, 89–90
  Irish method of confession by, xvi, xviii,
      81–88
  justice in, 73–74
  map of, *64*
  on martyrdom classifications, 77, 77n43
  missionary efforts of, 74
  place-names in honor of, 69
  plight of church and society upon arrival of,
      78–81
  priests as viewed by, 77–78, 85
  qualities of, 65, 72–73
  travels and influence of, 66, 79
  warrior spirit of, 76, 76n41

Charlemagne (Roman emperor)
  Admonitio Generalis, 122
  character of, 97–98
  Christian culture under, 9, 65, 70, 93,
    129–31
  De Litteris Colendis, 120–21, 122
  death of, 126
  educational initiatives under, 25, 90, 105,
    114–17, 120–23
  ideals behind empire of, 100–102
  influences on, 98–99
  intervention in church affairs, 103–4
  legislation by, 99, 100, 113
  literacy movement under, 73
  liturgy and, 120
  map of empire, *95*
  on paganism, 112, 113
  Palace Academy of, 104–6, 115
  portraits of, *97, 100, 103, 105, 107, 121*
  restoration of Roman Empire and, 20
  as warrior-king, 99
Charlemagne (Dürer), *97*
Charlemagne and Alcuin (Schnetz), *105*
Charlemagne and His Scholars (von Blaas), *121*
Charles II the Bald (king of France), 128, 157
Charles of Anjou, 174
Charny, Geoffroi de, 148*n*1
Charter of the Forest (1217), 217
Chesterton, G.K., 13, 133, 137, 154, 218–19,
  242
Childebert II (king of Franks), 54
The Childhood of Christ (Berlioz), 210
Chinon Parchment (1308), 171
chivalry
  Catholicism in creation of, 153–54
  in epic poems, 160
  as ideal of Western manhood, xvi, 131, 159,
    177–78, 179
  knights and, 149, 150, 153, 158, 160, 168
  literary examples of, 178–79
  in modern times, 177–81
  natural law and, 179–80, 196
  religious orders influenced by, 178
  romanticism and, 183, 187–91, 196–97
  troubadourism vs., 193–95
  warriors and, 131, 153–54, 160
Christ. *See* Jesus Christ
Christianity. *See also* conversion to
    Christianity; culture of Christendom; Jesus
    Christ; *specific denominations*
  application to social order, 101, 133
  in Carolingian Empire, 100, 101, 129–30,
    142
  Celtic explanations of, 74–76
  in Dark Ages, 13, 18

  in Middle East, 166
  persecution of believers, 101, 166
  as revolutionary force, xvi, 45, 69, 131–32
Christus (Liszt), 210
El Cid, 160
Cistercians
  agricultural practices of, 4, 220
  architecture of, 205
  chivalry as influence on, 178
  growth of, 163
  labor of, *218*
  military foundations associated with, 172
City of God (Augustine of Hippo), 44, 48, 51,
  53, 101–2
Clare of Assisi, 5, 186
Claussen, M.A., 124
Claver, Peter, 87
Clement V (pope), 171
Clement VII (pope), 213*n*7
Clermont, Council of, 166
clock-making, 222–23, *224*
Clovis (king of Franks), 16, 18, *20*, 22, 96
Cluny Abbey, 20, 156, 162, 205, 210, 222
Colombière, Claude de la, 88
Columba of Iona (saint)
  Altus Prosator, 55
  attire worn by, *65*
  character of, 69
  conversion efforts of, 70
  hymn composed by, 55
  monasteries founded by, 69
  Picts and, 70, *72*
  prayer of, 74–75
Saint Columba Arrives to Iona (Burrows), *70*
Columbanus (saint)
  character of, 65, 67
  Christian revolution triggered by, xvi, 69
  conversion efforts of, 20, 64–65
  En Silvis Caesa, 68
  monasteries founded by, 54, 65, 67, 68, 162
  on penance, 84
  plight of church and society upon arrival of,
    78–81
  travels and influence of, *66*, 90
commutative justice, 228
competitive equilibrium, 228
The Concept of Love in Augustine (Arendt), 44
Concordat of Worms (1122), 129
Condillac, Etienne Bonnot de, 238
confession
  ancient methods of, 80–81
  Irish method of, xvi, xviii, 81–88
  Mediterranean system of, 84
Confession (Long), *88*
The Confession (Niccolo dei Cori), *82*

Confessions (Augustine of Hippo), 37, 38, 43
convents, education in, 123, 124, 186
The Conversion of King Ethelbert (Clayton & Bell), *62*
conversion to Christianity. *See also* missionaries
  Alcuin of York on, 112–13
  Augustine on, 41
  Benedictine monks in, 20, 54
  Europe and, 18–20, *19*, 54–55
  pagans and, 112–13
converters of culture, 44
Copernicus, 213*n*7
Coronation of Charlemagne (Kaulbach), *100*
cost, law of, 228
Coucy, Baron de, 174
Councils of the Church
  Clermont, 166
  Dvin, Second Council of, 83
  Lateran II, 193
  Lateran III, 217
  Lateran IV, 83, 87
  Le Puy, 156
  Narbonne, 156
  Neocæsarea, 24
  Orléans, 30
  Toledo, 86
  Trent, 87, 141
  Valence, 156
  Verdun, 156, 158
  Vienne, 171
court chaplains, 87–88
courtly love, 191–95, *192*
Covarrubias, Diego de, 230, 235
Crécy, Battle of (1346), 178
cross-vigil, 76
Crusades, 131, 166–68, 171, 172
culture of Christendom, 129–35
  Ancient Rite in creation of, xvi, 142, 145
  birth and development of, 9, 65, 93, 142
  in education, 131
  in formation of Western civilization, 133–35
  individualism and, 132–33
  lifestyle changes resulting from, 131–32
  priesthood in creation of, 139
  racism and, 132
  sociopolitical framework for, 142
  spirit of sacrifice in, 145
  spread of, 130
  synthesis of Roman and Teutonic culture in, 52, 70, 129–30
culture of Islam, 191–92
Currency School, 232
curriculum, educational, 119, 122
Cuthbert the Deacon, 89

Cynewulf, *The Dream of the Rood*, 161
Cyril (saint), 20

Damien of Molokai, 6
Daniel-Rops, Henri, xix, 69, 90
Dante, 195–96
d'Arezzo, Guido, 209
Dark Ages, 15–31
  barbarian kingdoms during, 17, 101
  birth of new civilization following, 3–4
  bishops and priests during, 21–23
  Christianity during, 13, 18
  conversion of Europe during, 18–20, *19*
  decline of Roman Empire as beginning of, 15–16, *16*
  economic development in, 213, 214
  end of, 137
  monasteries during, 59
  natural law in, 48
  parishes during, 23–31
  racism in, 132
  spirit of reform in, 69
  use of term, 9, 18*n*10
Dawson, Christopher, xix, xx, 32, 90, 134, 242
De Consideratione (Bernard of Clairvaux), 165
De Litteris Colendis (Charlemagne), 120–21, 122
de Soto, Domingo, 226, 230–31, 232–33
de Soto, Huerta, 232, 237, 238*n*74
delay discounting, 233
Desiderius (saint), 22, 23
Dhuoda, 124
Dicuil, 71, 117
Digby, Kenelm Henry, 178–79
Disraeli, Benjamin, 223–24
Dominicans, 20, 42, 178, 226, 229
Don Diego de Covarrubias y Leiva (El Greco), *230*
The Dream of the Rood (Cynewulf), 161
Drogo of Metz, 127
du Dézert, Georges Desdevises, 6
Duhem, Pierre, 4, 61
Duns Scotus, Johannes, 228
Durandus, Guillaume, Pontifical of, 150*n*2, 152*n*9, 157, 158
Duruflé, Maurice, 210
Dvin, Second Council of, 83

Eangtha, 124
Ebbo of Reims, 125, 128
Ecgbert, 107
economics, 211–39. *See also* free-market economics
  as academic discipline, 227, 228
  banking practices and, 232

economics (continued)
  Benedictine influences on, 61
  business profit theories and, 233
  capitalism and, 211, 212–13
  Catholic ideal behind Western progress in,
    211–19
  entrepreneurship in, 214, 219, 229, 232,
    234, 238
  foreign exchange markets and, 232
  inflation and, 228, 230, 231
  interest and, 233
  laissez-faire policies, 238
  medieval and Renaissance thinkers, 224–32
  pricing theories in, 231, 235–36
  Scholasticism and, 213, 225, 227–28, 238
The Ecstasy of St. Gregory the Great (Rubens),
  52
Edgeworth, Henry Essex, 88
Edict of Milan (313), 184
education
  in Carolingian Empire, 25, 115–16, 119–25,
    129
  in convents, 123, 124, 186
  curriculum for, 119, 122
  monastic, 57, 73, 90, 122
  in parishes, 25, 124–25
  public, 105
  reform movements in, 122
  universal, 120–25
  in universities, 4, 119
  of women, 123, 124–25
Egyptian monastic ideals, 72
Einhard, 97, 98, 103, 106, 107
El Cid, 160
Eleanor of Aquitaine, 192
Eligius, 23
Embassy for the Christians (Athenagoras), 184
En Silvis Caesa (Columbanus), 68
The End of the Song (Leighton), 188
Enlightenment, 87, 182, 212
entrepreneurship, 214, 219, 229, 232, 234, 238
epic poems, chivalric spirit in, 160
Eriugena, Johannes Scotus, 117
Escobar, Antonio de, 231
Esolen, Anthony, 195
Ethelbert (king of Kent), 20, 30, 54–55, 133
Eugene III (pope), 165
expectations theory, 232
Exupéry of Toulouse, 22

Faber, Frederick W., 139
famines, 27–28, 29
Fardulf, 106
farming, monastic advances in, 4, 73, 219–20
Faustus of Riez, 76

Felix of Nantes (saint), 22, 23
feudalism, 130, 154, 155
Finnian of Clonard (saint), 82
First Crusade, 171, 172
Forbes, Charles (Comte de Montalembert), 4,
  69, 220
foreign exchange markets, 232, 233
The Four Seasons (Vivaldi), 210
Fourth Lateran Council, 83, 87
fractional-reserve banking, 232
Francis of Assisi (Francesco Bernardone; saint),
  176, 195
St. Francis Receiving the Stigmata (El Greco), 196
St. Francis Xavier Baptizes an Oriental Princess (Il
  Baciccio), 182
Franciscans, 141, 178
Franks
  Christian factions of, 18, 22, 52
  invasion of Roman Empire by, 16
  missionary efforts supported by, 92
  papal alliance with, 96, 97
Frauendienst (von Liechtenstein), 195
Frechou, Gaillardine de, 186
free-market economics, 212–24
  barriers to, 214
  Catholicism in formation of, 4, 212, 213,
    238–39
  defined, 213
  emergence of, 219–20, 222–24
  features of, 228
  monasteries and, 219–20, 222–23
  objective theory of value in, 235
  pricing theories in, 235–36
  productivity in, 217
  property rights in, 213–14, 215–17
  sociocultural ecosystem for emergence of,
    213–14
  specialization in, 220, 222
  subjective/utility theory of value in, 234–35,
    236–37
  theological support for, 228
  theoretical foundations for, 227, 231, 237
  trade networks in, 222
  value of occupational diversity in, 217–18
French Revolution, 35, 88, 133
Fukuyama, Francis, 22, 129, 134
Fulrad, 96, 97, 99
fundamental methodological errors, 212

Galahad (legendary knight), 160, 168–69, 169,
  173, 194
Galiani, Ferdinando, 238
Galileo Galilei, 213n7
gargoyles, 201
Garter, Order of the, 148n1, 178

Gaskoin, Charles J.B., 122
Gasperi, Alcide de, 191n33
gender considerations. *See* men; women
Genseric (king of Vandals), 16, 49, 51
Geoffroi de la Tour Landry, 161
George (saint), 159
Gerard, 171
Gerbert of Aurillac. *See* Sylvester II
Germain of Auxerre, 22
Gesta Danorum (Saxo Grammaticus), 60–61
Gibbon, Edward, 134, 184–85, 241–42
Gilchrist, John, 4
Gildas the Wise, 60
Gimpel, Jean, 4
God Speed! (Leighton), 194
God's Javelin (Peiffer), 21
Golden Fleece, Order of the, 178
Goldstein, Thomas, 4
Good Defeats Evil (Tsereteli), 15
Goodell, Henry H., 4
Gospels
    John
        8:10–11, 82
        12:35, 57
        15:18–19, 244
    Luke
        1:68–79, 87
        22:19, 139, 144
    Matthew
        16:25, 60
        24:35, 17
        24:44, 145
        26:28, 144
        28:19, 89
Gothic architecture, 198–205
    modern sentiments regarding, 198–99
    ornamentation and symbolism in, 201
    precursors to, 205
    Suger (abbot) and, xvii, 117, 199–200, 201,
        202–4
    synthesis of faith and rationality in, 199–200
Gothic Cathedral with Imperial Palace (Schinkel),
    205
Gothic Church on a Rock by the Sea (Schinkel), 1
Goths, 15, 16, 20, 22, 44
Gratian (Roman emperor), 83, 214–15
Great Famine (1845–1850), 27–28, 29
Great St. Bernard Pass, 3, 26
Gregorian chant, 71n32, 120, 125, 150, 206–10
Gregory I the Great (pope)
    Ancient Rite during reign of, 139, 140
    background of, 52
    on Benedict (saint), 57
    character of, 53
    conversion efforts of, 54–55, 56

on death, 16
    as Father of Western Culture, xvi, 18, 31
    Pastoral Rule, 53
    portraits of, 52, 54
    priesthood as influence on, 53
    scientific mentality of, 62–63
St. Gregory the Great (Goya), 54
Gregory II (pope), 92, 96
Gregory IV (pope), 103
Gregory VII (pope), 128–29, 214, 245
Gregory XI (pope), 186
Grotius, Hugo, 227
Guéranger, Prosper, 210
Guidelines for Businessmen (Saravia de la Calle),
    235
Guidonian hand, 209
Guillaume IX (duke of Aquitaine), 192
Gundrada, 110
The Gust (van de Velde), 13

Halévy, Élie, 209
Handel, George Friedrich, *Messiah*, 210
Harding, Stephen, 163
Haskins, C.H., 4
Hayek, Friedrich, 211, 212n3, 224–25, 225n31,
    238
Heidegger, Martin, 43
Heilbron, J.L., 4
Heine, Heinrich, 182, 183
Heiric of Auxerre, 117
Héloïse (abbess), 186
Henry III (king of England), 217
Henry VIII (king of England), 223, 224
Henry II (king of Germany), 5, 156
Henry IV (king of Germany), 129, 214
Hermenegild, 20
Herrad of Landsberg, 5, 186
Hexameron (Ambrose), 33
Hildegarde of Bingen, 5, 186
Hincmar of Reims, 104, 128
Holy Ghost, Order of the, 184
Holy Sepulchre, Order of, 172
Hortus Deliciarum (Herrad of Landsberg), 5,
    186
Hospitallers, 171–72
"How God's Son Was Armed on the Cross"
    (poem), 161
Hroswitha of Gandersheim, 5, 124, 186
Hugeberc, 124
Hugh (abbot), 205
Hugh of Lincoln, 218
Hugh of Pisa, 215
Hülsmann, Jörg Guido, 228
Hume, David, 60
The Hun and the Crucifix (Richmond), 153

Huns, 49, 50
Husserl, Edmund, 43

"I See His Blood upon the Rose" (Plunkett),
    74
Idylls of the King (Tennyson), 168
Ignatius of Loyola (saint), 178
"In Dormiturio" (Alcuin of York), 109
In Praise of the New Knighthood (Bernard of
    Clairvaux), 168, 169
individualism, 87, 132–33
Industrial Revolution, 182, 212, 223, 224
infanticide, 184, 245
inflation, 228, 230, 231
Innocent III (pope), 141
interracial marriage, 132
investiture, 128–29
Iona Abbey (Scotland), 75
Ireland. *See also* Celtic monks and monasteries
    confession methods in, xvi, xviii, 81–88
    famine in, 27–28, 29
    parish priests in, 27–29, 28n20
    Young Irelanders movement, 28
iron-grey martyrdom, 77
Isidore of Seville (saint), 22, 60
Islam and Muslims
    Crusades against, 131, 166–68, 171, 172
    cultural characteristics of, 191–92
    expansion of, 94, 166
Ita, 123
Ivanhoe (Scott), 178

Jaki, Stanley, 4, 61
Jerome (saint), 17, 40–41, 142
St. Jerome in the Scriptorium (Parral), *118*
Jesuits, 212n3, 225n31, 226, 229, 237
Jesus Christ
    chivalric, 161–62
    knightly vision of, 160–62
    literary and artistic portrayals of, 161, *161*
    manual labor performed by, 218
    monastic ideals inspired by, 58–59
    priests of, 8, 32
    revelation of God's providence through, 17
    as role model for husbands, 189
Jews, persecution of, 164
Joan of Arc (saint), 186
John II (pope), 43
John XV (pope), 156
John (king of England), 216
John Chrysostom (saint), 80, 101
John Paul II (pope), 238
Johnson, Paul, 199
Joinville, Jehans de, 173, 175, 178
Jonas, 65

The Journey of the Mind to God (Bonaventure),
    43
*Pope Julius II Ordering Bramante, Michelangelo
    and Raphael to Construct the Vatican and St.
    Peter's* (Vernet), *198*
Jungmann, Joseph, 141
justice
    commutative, 228
    in monasteries, 73–74
    in parishes, 29–30
    tribal customs of, 214
Justinian (Byzantine emperor), 16

Kauder, Emil, 236
*The Knight Galahad on the Quest for the Holy
    Grail* (Hughes), *169*
knights, 148–62
    artistic portrayals of, 176–77, *177*
    attire of, 152
    Blessing of the New Soldier, 150n2, 152n9
    chivalry and, 149, 150, 153, 158, 160, 168
    Christianizing ideal for, 154–55, 159–60,
        177
    in feudal system, 154
    Jesus Christ as viewed by, 160–62
    military orders of, 153
    requirements of, 158
    role models for, 158–59
    Vigil of Arms for induction of, 148–52
The Knights of Christ (van Eyck), *155*
Knights of Columbus, 178
Knights of Saint Columbanus, 178
Knights Templar
    Bernard of Clairvaux as author of statutes
        for, 165, *167*, 167–68, 169
    chivalry and, 168
    financial services corporation established
        by, 222
    foundation, development, and influence of,
        167–72
    growth of, 170
    literary portrayals of, 168–69
    official title of, 162
    as prototype for military orders of
        knighthood, 153
    requirements for entry, 169
    suppression of, 170–71

La Forbie, Battle of (1244), 172
labor theory of value, 235, 236, 236n65
Labouring Monks (Brock), *219*
laissez-faire economic policies, 238
Lancelot (legendary knight), 193–94
Langton, Stephen, 216
The Last Chapter (Penrose), *89*

Lateran Councils
  II, 193
  III, 217
  IV, 83, 87
law. *See* legal system; natural law
Le Puy, Council of, 156
League of Nations, 157
Leagues of Peace, 156
Leander of Seville, 20
Lecky, W. E. H., 4
legal system
  canon law as template for, 4, 215
  Catholic influences on, 4, 48–49, 214–15
  of Celtic monasteries, 73–74
  natural law and, 215
Léger (saint), 22–23
Leo I the Great (pope)
  background of, 49–51
  character of, 50
  on confidentiality of confessions, 83
  as Father of Western Culture, xvi, 18, 31
  on judgment, 7
  on papal authority, 51–52
  political power of, 50–51
  portrait of, *31*
Pope Saint Leo the Great (Herrera el Mozo), *31*
Leo III (pope), 100, 113
*Pope Leo X with Cardinals Giulio de Medici and
  Luigi de Rossi* (Sanzio), *4*
Leo XIII (pope), 245
Lessines, Giles, 233
Lessius, Leonardus, 231
Lindberg, David, 4
Lipsius, Justus, 238
Liszt, Franz, 210
literacy movements, 73
Llull, Ramon, 159, 193
Locke, John, 238
Lombards, 20, 54, 96
The Lord of the Rings (Tolkien), xv–xvi, 189,
  241
Loudon, John C., 4
Louis I the Pious (king of Aquitaine), 157
Louis VI (king of France), 164
Louis VII (king of France), 156, 164
Louis VII (Mauzaisse), *203*
Louis IX (king of France; saint)
  background of, 173
  Catholicism of, 176
  character of, 172, 173–74
  Christian nation built by, 5
  as crusader, 173
  death of, 162, 167
  intellectual culture under, 174–75
Louis XVIII (king of France), 88

love
  chivalric romantic, 187–91
  courtly, 191–95, *192*
  sacramental, 47, 185
  sacrificial, 143–45
Lugo, Juan de, 225, 232, 233, 235
Lullus of Mainz (saint), 104, 106
Luxeuil Abbey, 67, 89–90, 123, 162

Macaulay, Thomas Babington, 1
Machaut, Guillaume de, 210
Machiavelli, Niccolò, 227
Magna Carta (1215), 216, 245
Magyars, 126, 153
Mainz Pontifical, 157
Malory, Thomas, *Le Morte d'Arthur*, 168, 178
Mariana, Juan de, 229, 230, 231–32, 237–38
  On the Alteration of Money, 231
Marillac, Louise de (saint), 186
marriage
  dignity of women in, 184–85
  interracial, 132
  romanticism in, 189–91
  sacramental love in, 47, 185
Martel, Charles, 92, 96
Martin of Tours (saint), 24, 71, 159
Saint Martin and the Beggar (Thompson), *157*
martyrs and martyrdom, 77, 77*n*43, 93, 97, 159
Marx, Karl, 236
Mary (mother of God), 187, 200
Mass. *See also* Ancient Rite
  Gregorian chant at, 71*n*32, 125
  order of penitents at, 81, 82
  polyphonic compositions for, 210
  Tridentine, 139, 141
  uniformity in performance of, 120
The Mass: A Study of the Roman Liturgy
  (Fortescue), *141*
A Mass at Sea (Duveau), *146*
The Mass of Saint Giles (Master of Saint Giles),
  139
Mass of St. John of Matha (Carreño de
  Miranda), *144*
Maurice (saint), 159
McAuley, Catherine, 186
McDonnell, Gerry, 224
McNamara, JoAnn, 124
The Meeting between Leo the Great and Attila
  (Sanzio), *50*
men. *See also* knights; marriage; monks and
  monasteries
  chauvinism of, 185, 245
  chivalry as ideal for, xvi, 131, 159, 177–78,
    179
  role of, 194

Mendelssohn, Felix, 210
Menger, Carl, 238
Mercado, Tomás de, 226, 232
Merici, Angela de, 186
Messiah (Handel), 210
Methodius (saint), 20
Middle Ages
    capitalism in, 212
    Catholic Church during, 4, 128–29
    government in, 94
    monastic orders of, 42
    occupational diversity in, 217–18
    science in, 61, 63
    use of term, 9
missionaries. *See also* conversion to Christianity
    in barbarian nations, 52, 56, 96
    bishops as, 24
    cultural renaissance spread by, 130
    monks as, 20, 55, 63, 74, 89
    papal initiatives for, 54, 55
    on racism, 132
    training for, 70
Molay, Jacques de, 171
Molina, Luis de, 225, 226, 231–32, 235
monetarist theory, 232
monks and monasteries. *See also specific orders*
    agricultural advances of, 4, 73, 219–20
    architecture of, 205
    building plans for, *221*, 222*n*23, *223*
    cultural preservation efforts of, 60–61,
        118
    in Dark Ages, 59
    destruction of, 223, 224
    educational institutions of, 57, 73, 90,
        122
    Egyptian ideals of, 72
    free-market economics and, 219–20,
        222–23
    Gregorian chant and, 206–8
    justice in, 73–74
    labor of, 218, *220*
    missionary efforts of, 20, 55, 63, 74, 89
    sociocultural influence of, 223
    technological sophistication of, 4, 222–23,
        224
    trade networks of, 222
The Monks: Men of Prayer (Tommaso), *225*
The Monks of the West (Montalembert), 220
Montalembert, Comte de (Charles Forbes),
    4, 69, 220
Montgisard, Battle of (1177), 170
Montjou, Bernard de, 26
Montpellier, Guy de, 184
Le Morte d'Arthur (Malory), 168, 178
Mun, Thomas, 238

music, 206–10
    cantatas, 210
    Gregorian chant, 71*n*32, 120, 125, 150,
        206–10
    oratorios, 210
    plainchant, 206, 208
    polyphony, 201, 210
Muslims. *See* Islam and Muslims

Narbonne, Council of, 156
natural law
    chivalry and, 179–80, 196
    compatibility with Catholicism, 55
    defined, 179
    legal system and, 215
    School of Salamanca on, 227
    state subjugation to, 35, 47, 48
Neocæsarea, Council of, 24
Neri, Philip (saint), 210
New Testament. *See also* Gospels
    1 Corinthians
        3:1–2, 113
        7:9, 47
        12:26, 85
    2 Corinthians 5:14, 78
    Ephesians
        4:24, 217
        5:25, 47, 189
    Galatians
        2:20, 75–76
        3:28, 184
    Hebrews
        4:15, 162
        13:7–8, 91
        13:14, 25, 45
    1 John 1:5, 200
    1 Peter 2:11, 24
    Philippians 1:21–23, 75
    Revelation 3:5, 8
    Romans
        8:28, 18
        12:2, 24
        12:5, 85
        13:13–14, 37
        14:7–8, 32
Newman, John Henry, 4, 43
Nicholas I (pope), 128, 185*n*11
Notre-Dame Cathedral (Amiens), *xv*
Notre-Dame Cathedral (Chartres), *199*, 202
Notre-Dame Cathedral (Paris), *5, 9, 247*
nuns, 123, 124, 185–86

objective theory of economic value, 235
O'Connor, Flannery, 185
Odo (abbot), 158–59

Odo (architect), 106
Odoacer (king of Italy), 16, 56
Old Testament
Deuteronomy 6:5, 46
Genesis
1:3, 200
1:27–28, 217
Psalms
44, 152
63:3, 78
137:1, 206
Olivi, Pierre de Jean, 235
On the Alteration of Money (Mariana), 231
On the Trinity (Augustine of Hippo), 42
oratorios, 210
Order of. *See specific name of orders*
Oresme, Nicole, 228
Orléans, Council of, 30
orphanages, 184
Ostrogoths, 16
Ouen (saint), 23

Pacificus, 222
El Padre Juan de Mariano (González), *234*
Palace Academy, 104–6, 115
Palestrina, 210
papacy. *See also specific names of popes*
alliance with Frankish monarchy, 96, 97
civil rulers crowned by, 96–97, 100
political power of, 50–52, 103
Papal Revolution, 214
parishes, 23–31
defined, 23
education in, 25, 124–25
justice in, 29–30
linguistic considerations, 24–25
origins of, 24
priests in, 26–29, 28n20
social role of, 25–26, 31
Parkman, Francis, 7
Pascal, Blaise, 231
Paschal II (pope), 172
Paschasius Radbertus, 125, 128
Passion according to St. Matthew (Bach), 210
Pastoral Rule (Gregory I), 53
Paul (saint), 32, 47, 75–76
Paul Orosius, 18
Paul the Deacon, 53, 105–6
Paulinus of Aquileia (saint), 104, 105, 110, 113
Paulinus of Nola, 18, 22
Payens, Hugues de, 167
Peace of God movement, 156
Penal Laws, 27
penance, 80–84, 86
penitents, order of, 81, 82

The People and the House of God in Augustine's Doctrine of the Church (Benedict XVI), 44
Pepin (king of Franks), 52, 92, 96–97, 99, 206
Perosi, Lorenzo, 210
persecution
of Christians, 101, 166
of Jews, 164
of priests, 27
Abbot Peter, *The Poem of the Cid*, 160
Peter of Cluny, 164
Peter of Pisa, 105
Peter the Venerable, 205, 210
Petrus Hibernicus, 117, 117n67
phenomenology, 43
Philip II Augustus (king of France), 174
Philip IV (king of France), 170–71
Philosophical Investigations (Wittgenstein), 43
physics, philosophical pillars of, 4
Pirenne, Henri, 4
Pius V (pope), 141
Pius VI (pope), 103
Pius X (pope), 33n3
Pius XI (pope), 6, 65n16, 79, 90
plainchant, 206, 208
Plan of St. Gall, *221*, 222n23
Plato, 234
Plunkett, Joseph, 74
The Poem of the Cid (Abbot Peter), 160
polyphony, 201, 210
Pontifical of Guillaume Durandus, 150n2, 152n9, 157, 158
popes. *See* papacy; *specific names of popes*
positivism, 49, 179
PPP (purchasing power parity), 232–33, 238
pricing theories, 231, 235–36
priests
ascetic framework for formation of, 58–59
Celtic reverence for, 77–78, 85
in construction of Western civilization, xviii, 5–9, 243–45
as court chaplains, 87–88
in culture of Christendom, 139
in Dark Ages, 21, 23
on infanticide, 184, 245
in Irish method of confession, 82–84, 85–87
mission of, xviii, 8, 40
moral reform efforts targeted at, 111
musical contributions of, 210
in parishes, 26–29, 28n20
persecution of, 27
prayer for, 247–48
sanctuary laws defended by, 30
as warriors, 149–50, 153

property rights
    in free-market economics, 213–14, 215–17
    renouncement by church officials, 41
    for women, 186
public education, 105
purchasing power parity (PPP), 232–33, 238

quantity theory of money, 232, 233
Quigley, Hugh, 28
Quodvultdeus, 22

Rabanus Maurus, 116, 127
racism, 132
Rado, 106
Reagan, Ronald, 238
Reccared I (king of Visigoths), 20, 54
red martyrdom, 77
Rémy of Reims, 18, 22
Richard of Wallingford, 223
Riché, Pierre, 124
Rigobert of Reims, 23
risk-effort theory of business profit, 233
The Road to Serfdom (Hayek), 238
Robertson, H.M., 212n3, 225n31
Roman Catholic Church. See Catholic
    Church
Roman Empire, 15–16, 15n1, 16, 20, 44–45
The Roman Monk (Cabanel), 56
Roman Pontifical, 150, 157
Romanesque architecture, 120, 202, 205
Romano-Frankish missal, 120
Romano–German Pontifical, 152n8, 159
Romantic Landscape with Monastery (Lessing),
    137
romantic love, 187–91
romanticism
    chivalry and, 183, 187–91, 196–97
    courtly love and, 191–95, 192
    features of, 182–83
    idealism of womanhood and, xvi, 195
    in marriage, 189–91
    in prayer, 176
    spread of, 195
Romulus Augustus (Roman emperor), 16, 56,
    100
Roncesvalles, Battle of (778), 160
Rothbard, Murray, 230, 234
Royal Road (Smaragdus of Saint-Mihiel), 106
Rule of St. Augustine, 42
Rule of St. Benedict, 57–58, 61
Russell, Bertrand, 43

sacramental love, 47, 185
sacrificial love, 143–45
Saint Bernards to the Rescue (Emms), 25

St. Denis Basilica, 96, 117, 199–200, 202
Saint Lazarus, Order of, 172
Saint-Michel Church, 165
Saint-Omer, Godfrey de, 167
saints. See specific names of saints
Saladin, 170, 172
Salamanca, School of, 4, 213, 225–28, 231,
    232, 237–39
Salas, Juan de, 235
Salvianus, 18
Santayana, George, 241
Santiago, Order of, 172
Saracens, 126, 160
Saravia de la Calle, Luis, 232, 235
Saxo Grammaticus, Gesta Danorum, 60–61
Schlegel, Friedrich, 182–83
Scholarly Monks (Vogel), 114
Scholastica (saint), 5, 186
Scholasticism
    economics and, 213, 225, 227–28, 238
    features of, 225n32, 229
    monetary ideas of, 233
    rationality of, 4, 177
school. See education
School of Salamanca, 4, 213, 225–28, 231, 232,
    237–39
Schuman, Robert, 90
Schumpeter, Joseph, 4, 212, 213, 215–16,
    228–29, 233, 235–37, 238n74
science, 61–63
Science and the Modern World (Whitehead),
    62–63
Scott, Walter, 178
Scouting movement, 179
Scripture. See New Testament; Old Testament
Second Crusade, 167–68
Second Lateran Council, 193
Sen, Amartya, 27
Sigismund (king of Burgundy), 18, 20
The Signing of the Magna Carta (Devaulx), 216
sin, defined, 42
Sir Galahad (Watts), 173
"Sir Galahad" (Tennyson), 168–69
Siri, Giuseppe, 7
slavery, 49, 166, 218–19, 245
Smaragdus of Saint-Mihiel, Royal Road, 106
Smith, Adam, 225, 235–36, 236n65, 238,
    238n74
social assistance programs, 4, 223
Song of Roland (Théroulde), 160
Sorbon, Robert de, 174–75
Southern, R.W., 4
specialization, 220, 222
St. See specific entries at saint
Staël, Baroness de, 183

staff notation, 209
Statue of St. Boniface (Henschel), *91*
Steinbeck, John, 196
Stephen II (pope), 96, 206
Stephen IV (pope), 103
Stevenson, Robert Louis, 6
Stone of Destiny, 70
Strabo, 76n41
Suárez, Francisco, 226
subjective/utility theory of value, 234–35,
    236–37
Subleyras, Pierre, 35, *35*
Suger (abbot), xvii, 117, 125, 199–200, 201,
    202–4
Summa Theologiae (Thomas Aquinas), 199
Sybil (Disraeli), 224
Sylvester II (pope), 116, 125, 222
Synod of Mâcon, 25n17
Synod of Yutz, 155–56

Tariq ibn Ziyad, 94
technology, monastic, 4, 222–23, 224
Templars. *See* Knights Templar
Tennyson, Alfred, 168–69
Teresa of Calcutta (saint), 186
Teutonic culture, 52, 70, 93, 129, 135
The Thanksgiving Service on the Field of Agincourt
    (Leighton), *180*
Theodolinda, 5, 54
Theodosius the Great (Roman emperor),
    34–35, 215
Theodulf of Orléans, 104, 105, 110, 111, 116,
    123
Theologiae Moralis (Escobar), 231
Thibault II (count of Champagne), 164
Third Lateran Council, 217
Thomas à Becket (saint), 22, 218
Thomas Aquinas (saint)
    educators of, 117, 117n67
    influence of Augustine on, 42
    on property rights, 215
    Scholastic method and, 225
    Summa Theologiae, 199
    synthesis of faith and rationality in works of,
        199–200
    on tyrants, 215
    on value theories, 234–35, 236
Thorgilsson, Ari, 71
The Thousand-Year-Old Oak (Lessing), *187*
Toledo, Council of, 86
Tolkien, J.R.R., *The Lord of the Rings*, xv–xvi,
    61, 189, 241
Tours, Battle of (732), 96
Toynbee, Arnold J., 61, 63, 242
trade networks, 222

*A Treatise on the Origin, Nature, Law, and
    Alterations of Money* (Oresme), 228
Trent, Council of, 87, 141
Tridentine Mass, 141
troubadours, 176, 183, 192–95
Truce of God, 156
Twain, Mark, 29

United Nations, 157
universal education, 120–25
universities, Catholic origin of, 4, 118–19
Urban II (pope), 166
utility/subjective theory of value, 234–35,
    236–37

Valence, Council of, 156
value, theories of, 234–37
Vandals, 16, 22, 49, 51
Variarum Resolutionum (Covarrubias y Leyva),
    235
Vasari, Giorgio, 229
vassalage, 154
Vedast of Arras, 22
Verdun, Council of, 156, 158
Vienne, Council of, 171
The Vigil (Pettie), *148*
Vigil of Arms, 148–52
Vikings, 20, 71, 126–27, 131–32, 153
Vio, Thomas de, 232
Virgin Mary, 187, 200
Visigoths, 15, 16, 20, 22, 55, 80, 86
The Vision of Piers Plowman (Langland), 161
The Vision of Sir Galahad (Burlison & Grylls),
    160
Vitoria, Francisco de, 49, *211*, 226, 227, 235
Vitry, Jacques de, 170
Vivaldi, Antonio Lucio, 210
von Liechtenstein, Ulrich, 195
von Luck, Hans, 180
von Stauffenberg, Claus, 180–81, 215

Wagner, Richard, 210
Wala of Corbie, 116, 128
The Wanderer above the Sea of Fog (Friedrich),
    241
warriors. *See also* knights
    Celtic monks as, 76, 76n41
    chivalry and, 131, 153–54, 160
    Christian, 157–60
    initiation rites for, 157–58
    Jesus Christ depicted as, *161*, 161–62
    kings as, 99
    priests as, 149–50, 153
    training of, 155–57
The Wealth of Nations (Smith), 236

Weber, Max, 212, 212n3
Welles, Orson, 198–99
Wemple, Suzanne, 124
Wenceslaus of Bohemia, 5
West, A. F., 4
Western civilization. *See also* architecture;
    economics; education; legal system; music
  agricultural advancements in, 4, 73, 219–20
  Catholic Church in formation of, 3–5,
      133–35
  church and state relationship in, 34–35, 48,
      102–4, 128–29
  individualism in, 87, 132–33
  Industrial Revolution in, 182, 212, 223,
      224
  marriage in, 132, 184–85, 189–91
  milestones in building of, 10–11
  priests in construction of, xviii, 5–9, 243–45
  property rights in, 186, 213–14, 215–17
  science in, 61–63
  technological advancement in, 4, 222–23,
      224
  women in formation of, 5
white martyrdom, 77
Whitehead, Alfred North, 52, 62–63, 215
William of Ockham, 216
Willibrord of Utrecht (saint), 70

Wilson, Woodrow, 94
Wittgenstein, Ludwig, 43
women. *See also* marriage
  canonization of, 185
  in Carolingian Empire, 123, 124
  in Catholic Church, 183–87
  contributions to formation of Western
      civilization, 5
  dignity in marriage, 184–85
  education of, 123, 124–25
  infanticide of girls, 184, 245
  in intellectual culture, 123–24
  legal rights of, 48–49, 186
  as nuns, 123, 124, 185–86
  occupations of, 186
  political power of, 186
  priests in pursuit of social dignity for, 8
  property rights for, 186
  romanticism and idealism of, xvi, 195
Woods, Thomas, 237

Yeager, Leland B., 236n65
Young Irelanders movement, 28

Zachary I (pope), 96
zone of dissimilarity, 207
Zosimus (pope), 24